HISTOR
ENLIGHTENMENT

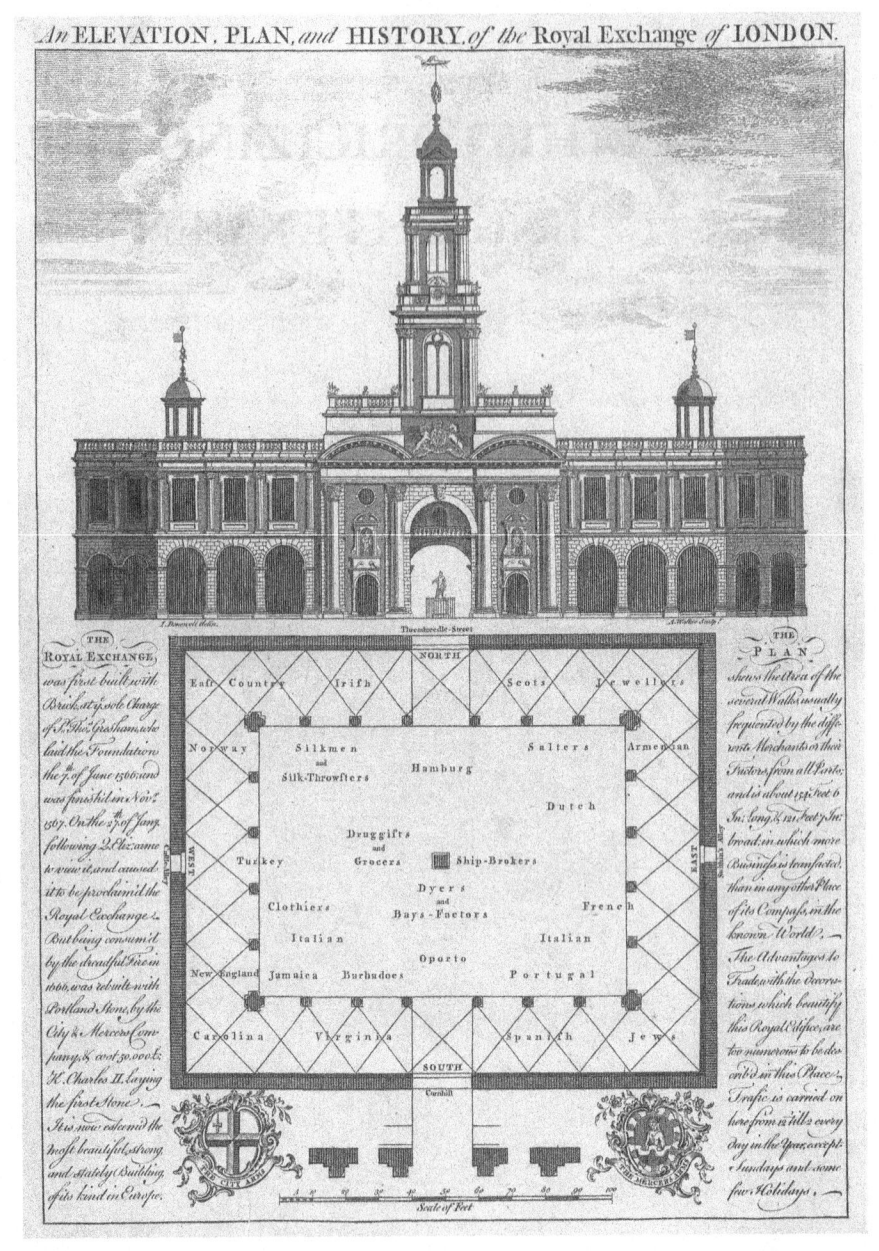

Frontispiece. Anthony Walker (1726–1765), *An Elevation, Plan, and History of the Royal Exchange of London*. Engraving. Yale Center for British Art, Paul Mellon Collection. B1977.14.18046. Left: brief "History" of Royal Exchange. Right: "Plan" diagrams inner courtyard (compare cover), showing "several Walks, usually frequented by the different Merchants or their Factors, from all Parts." "Walks" mix local and foreign, kinds of product and production, collapse spatial difference and temporal development, thereby capturing emergence of modern, virtual "stock market" of commodity exchange out of face-to-face trading in actual livestock of traditional marketplace like Smithfield (see cover of volume 1). Joseph Addison's account reflects this imagined superimposition of virtual on actual exchange: see ch. 4 in the present volume, n.38, and *Historicizing the Enlightenment*, vol. 1, ch. 3, n.23.

HISTORICIZING THE ENLIGHTENMENT

Volume 2

Literature, the Arts, and the Aesthetic in Britain

MICHAEL MCKEON

BUCKNELL
UNIVERSITY PRESS

Lewisburg, Pennsylvania

Library of Congress Cataloging-in-Publication Data
Names: McKeon, Michael, 1943– author.
Title: Historicizing the Enlightenment / Michael McKeon.
Description: Lewisburg, Pennsylvania : Bucknell University Press, [2023] |
  Includes bibliographical references and index. | Contents: V. 1. Politics, Religion,
  Economy, and Society in Britain—v. 2. Literature, the Arts, and the Aesthetic.
Identifiers: LCCN 2022054831 | ISBN 9781684484713 (v. 1 ; paperback) |
  ISBN 9781684484720 (v. 1 ; hardcover) | ISBN 9781684484737 (v. 1 ; epub) |
  ISBN 9781684484744 (v. 1 ; pdf) | ISBN 9781684484768 (v. 2 ; hardcover) |
  ISBN 9781684484751 (v. 2 ; paperback) | ISBN 9781684484775 (v. 2 ; epub) |
  ISBN 9781684484782 (v. 2 ; web pdf)
Subjects: LCSH: Great Britain—Intellectual life—18th century. | Enlightenment—
  Great Britain. | Great Britain—Civilization—18th century.
Classification: LCC DA485 .M35 2023 | DDC 941.07—dc23/eng/20230203
LC record available at https://lccn.loc.gov/2022054831

A British Cataloging-in-Publication record for this book is available from the British Library.

Copyright © 2023 by Michael McKeon

All rights reserved

No part of this book may be reproduced or utilized in any form or by any means, electronic or mechanical, or by any information storage and retrieval system, without written permission from the publisher. Please contact Bucknell University Press, Hildreth-Mirza Hall, Bucknell University, Lewisburg, PA 17837-2005. The only exception to this prohibition is "fair use" as defined by U.S. copyright law.

Credit lines for previously published material are listed in the Source Notes section.

References to internet websites (URLs) were accurate at the time of writing. Neither the author nor Bucknell University Press is responsible for URLs that may have expired or changed since the manuscript was prepared.

♾ The paper used in this publication meets the requirements of the American National Standard for Information Sciences—Permanence of Paper for Printed Library Materials, ANSI Z39.48-1992.

bucknelluniversitypress.org

Distributed worldwide by Rutgers University Press

Contents

Introduction — 1
   (Neo)classic and Romantic — 3
   The Radical Break — 5
   Imitation and Expression, the Mirror and the Lamp — 7
   "Revolution" — 9
   Preromanticism — 12
   Modernism: Structuralism and Poststructuralism — 15
   "Rules" and the Genre System — 15
   The Novel Tradition — 18

1   The Sciences as a Model for the Arts: A Synchronic Inquiry — 20
   Ancients and Moderns, Arts and Sciences — 20
   Experience and Experiment — 22
   Controlling for Time, Place, and Persons: The Two Unities — 25
   Controlling for Time, Place, and Persons: The Dramatic Aesthetic — 28
   The New Principle of Pleasure — 30
   The Judgment of Aesthetic Value — 35
   The Aesthetic Imagination and the Origins of the Social Sciences — 39
   Controlling for Time, Place, and Persons: The Narrative Claim to Historicity — 46
   Novelistic Plots as Experimental Hypotheses — 49
   Controlling for Time, Place, and Persons: The Novel Aesthetic, or Realism — 54

2   From Ancient Mimesis to Modern Realism: A Diachronic Inquiry — 61
   Aristotelian Mimesis — 61
   Verisimilitude: Italian Theory — 62
   Verisimilitude: French Theory — 63
   Probability: English Theory — 67
   Realism — 70
   The Rise of Fictionality? — 77

3   The Historicity of Literary Conventions: Family Romance — 80
   The History of a Convention? — 80
   Literary Convention as Social Convention — 82
   Family Romance as Ideology — 84
   True Nobility in the Service of Patrilineal Nobility — 86

True Nobility as Female — 87
True Nobility as Puritan — 89
Novelistic Parody of Patrilineal Nobility — 90
Discovery Within — 94
Conclusion — 100

4 The Historicity of Literary Genres: Pastoral Poetry — 103
What Is Pastoral? — 103
Pastoral and Periodization — 107
Capitalism Began in the Countryside — 110
From Forms to Fetters? — 116
Pastoral Poetry: Changing Places — 117
Retreat — 120
Locational Pastoral — 121
Taking the Measure of the City — 125
Renaissance Pastoral Parodied — 130
Explicit Critique of the Pastoral Tradition — 133
Object as Subject: Laboring Pastoral — 135
Women's Pastoral — 138
Pastoral Internalized: Micro-pastoral — 141
Pastoral Externalized: Macro-pastoral — 144
The North-South Axis — 145
The East-West Axis — 148

5 Political Poetry: Comparative Historicizing, 1650–1700, 1930–1980 — 154
The Modern Problem of Political Poetry — 154
Politics as Form — 165
Tradition: The Tacit Distinction of Politics and Poetry — 171
State Poetry: The Enlightenment Emergence of "Political Poetry" — 176
A Model: Religious Poetry and "Religious Poetry" — 183

6 *Paradise Lost* as Parody: Period, Genre, and Conjectural Interpretation — 187
Parody — 187
Mock Epic — 188
Christian Typology — 190
Christian Accommodation — 192
Domestication — 194
Heroic Poetry — 199
Secret History — 203
Obviating Accommodation, Forgoing Domestication, Precluding Allegory — 209
The Novel — 213

Acknowledgments — 219
Notes — 221
Source Notes — 251
Index — 253

HISTORICIZING THE ENLIGHTENMENT

Introduction

To "historicize" is to enclose what we think we know in a frame that totally transforms its meaning. To historicize the Enlightenment requires that we try to imagine what it was like to live through the first emergence of concepts and practices that are now commonplace.

"Enlightenment" is a cognitive state or action. "The Enlightenment" situates this state or action in a particular historical period. My concern in this study is with the period of the English—after 1707, the British and Scottish—Enlightenment, which by loose convention comprises the century and a half from 1650 to 1800.

Historicizing the Enlightenment consists of two volumes: *Politics, Religion, Economy, and Society* (volume 1) and *Literature, the Arts, and the Aesthetic* (volume 2). Although united in their focus on the British Enlightenment, the two volumes differ not only in subject matter but also in how those subjects need to be historicized. The introduction to the first volume provides a basis for reading its chapters as more or less direct responses to a consistent strain of criticism that's been made of the Enlightenment over the course of the past century. The following several paragraphs provide a brief summary of that argument.

The Enlightenment commitment to principles of analysis, division, reduction, abstraction, objectification, quantification, and universalization has been acutely criticized both in itself and as bearing responsibility for some of the most destructive developments of modern life. This criticism has a European relevance insofar as it takes the Enlightenment period to be broadly inclusive and Enlightenment thought to be broadly coherent. What's wrong with this criticism is conceptual. Understood in its own terms, Enlightenment thought dissolved the presumed integrity of traditional cognitive wholes by applying rational and empirical standards to their analysis. Tradition tacitly understood a given whole to be a self-evident totality that goes without saying, and its parts were seen as the means to that greater end rather than as ends in themselves that bore their own autonomous being and purpose. The premise of Enlightenment division was that this assumption obscured or denied the integrity of the parts themselves, which were knowable and epistemologically self-sufficient wholes in their own right.

My argument in volume 1 schematizes this understanding by means of a set of terms that will recur in the present volume as well. In traditional thought, categories were *tacit* wholes in the sense that their parts were distinguishable but not separable. Enlightenment thought partialized these wholes by an *explicit* analysis that separated their parts from each other. Conceptual *distinction*, once subjected to analytic *separation*, yielded parts that, newly autonomous wholes, were susceptible in turn to further *conflation*. Self-consciously initiated, these conflations couldn't be taken for granted as what goes without saying but were subject to debate and ongoing reconsideration. Only when parts are detached from each other sufficiently to be conceived as such can they be entered into active relation. And because the nature of the relationship between parts contributes to their meaning, their separation alters and sharpens their semantic and substantive force. The fruit of Enlightenment thought is therefore not only the detachment and separation of the parts that constitute traditional wholes, but also the innovative conflations that are consequent on those separations. Modern separation is not a finite and static operation but the necessary precondition for the distinctively modern categories of thought that result from conflation.

Enlightenment separation creates the conditions for a new sort of power, the knowing self-constitution of knowledge. Once separated, conceptual parts become subject to actively willed reconception and resituation in relation to other parts, whether in reciprocal mutuality or competitive conflict, but in either case as parts of a whole that is new by virtue of its ostensive, self-conscious fabrication. This may enable the resolution of old problems that had not been amenable to solution, but also the conceptualization of new problems that couldn't have risen to awareness under the aegis of tradition. I use the term "conflation" advisedly to suggest convergence rather than blending, which might suggest the illusory revival of a whole consisting of distinct but inseparable parts. The result of Enlightenment conflation is instead a dialectical category, a self-standing whole that's both divisible into its component parts and subsumable into a greater whole of which it constitutes one part. My aim in volume 1 of *Historicizing the Enlightenment* is to show that the broad historical trajectory from tradition to Enlightenment is defined in conceptual terms by the schematic movement from tacit difference to explicit separation, and then, sometimes quite punctually, to conflation.

The critique of Enlightenment thought has been defective because it fails to understand the grounds and nature of this process. And because Enlightenment thought is also a period discourse, the failure of its critique can be seen not only in conceptual terms but also in historiographical terms. The argument of volume 1 is that the critique of the historical period of the Enlightenment has abstracted it from its past, present, and future—from its history.

The past: the modern charge that the Enlightenment had a direct and harmful influence on its future ignores the Enlightenment's past—that is, the Enlightenment's own explicit and self-conscious reaction against the traditional domination of unexamined authority. When we criticize the innovations of the Enlightenment, we do so as human agents who are capable of both action and passion—who can both act in pursuit of our choices and suffer effects not of our choosing. However, our conception of Enlightenment agents is too often by this standard partial: we ascribe to them the former but not the latter capacity, and if we suffer the consequences of their actions we tend not to ask what they may have suffered and whether their actions may be understood as a consequence of that suffering.

The present: the modern critique ignores, and projects into its own wiser futurity, the Enlightenment's counterbalancing reflection on and response to its own analytic principles. Enlightenment division wasn't a static dogma but a dynamic and dialectical movement. Propelled by its initial momentum, Enlightenment thought extended its reactive analysis of the past to its own present through self-analysis and self-criticism, setting in motion the self-conscious reflexivity that is a hallmark of modernity. In this process the Enlightenment also generated those modern impulses that complicate, mitigate, or overcome negative aspects of the divisions that it had initiated.

The future: On the one hand, a common modern devaluation of the Enlightenment achievement is unhistorical because measured against modern achievement and incongruous with what might be expected when Enlightenment innovation was first underway. On the other hand, from a modern perspective, what can look like the failure of the Enlightenment must be distinguished from the failure of its modern posterity—of its future—to sustain Enlightenment principles. Belated and distorted versions of Enlightenment principles have too often been read back into the Enlightenment.

The first volume of *Historicizing the Enlightenment* counters what has taken shape as a critique of European Enlightenment; however, its evidence and argument are attuned specifically to the British context. The focus on Britain in the present volume is even fuller—so much so that although it concerns the same period as the first volume, the critique it counters can seem at times only obliquely related to the idea of the Enlightenment and instead internal to British cultural discourse about itself over the past two centuries. There's a real basis for this perception. However, I aim to show how the concerns of this internal discourse cut across and overlap with those of the Enlightenment critique, and as intellectual histories the two volumes are in frequent dialogue with each other.

These differences in focus also dictate a different, and more straightforward, historicization. The misconception of eighteenth-century British literature, the arts, and the aesthetic has amounted to an erasure of their innovative character and its displacement to a later period, principally the Romantic. That is, the eighteenth-century critique of tradition has been misread as the culmination of tradition itself.[1] Two cultural movements have been primarily instrumental in popularizing this misreading: Romanticism and modernism (that is, structuralism and poststructuralism). Whatever the differences between these movements, the following discussion will document their common effect in this regard.

(Neo)classic and Romantic

The most familiar view of eighteenth-century literature as a period that revived the aesthetic attitudes of classical and especially Roman antiquity has often had recourse to the prefix "neo-," which acknowledges an element of distance in the perspective from which the revival was undertaken. This would reflect the difference between the relatively complaisant reception of "the new learning" in the early Renaissance and the more complex response reflected in the seventeenth-century Quarrel of the Ancients and Moderns. Both contemporary and modern uses of the epithet "Augustan" assume a close relationship in the recourse of Restoration and early eighteenth-century literature to Roman forms. But although this usage implicitly includes the importance of Horatian, Juvenalian, and Menippean satire, it tends not to acknowledge how commonly the target of English irony and parody has been the Roman forms themselves. Of course, parody bespeaks both imitation and criticism. Nonetheless, in the periodization of (neo)classic Augustanism and Romanticism this element of distance tends to be ignored. Walter Jackson Bate's highly influential text on this topic is a case in point. On the one hand, by linking the two periods with the through line of "sensationalism" and "associationism," Bate precludes the simple opposition between "classic" and "Romantic" that would be enabled by treating Augustan classicism as a naive and uncritical devotion to the past.[2] On the other, Bate institutes that opposition by finding in English Augustanism a naive and wholesale dedication to the "rules" laid down by ancient, and in particular Augustan, theory and practice.

The idea of the rules is most closely associated for us with Aristotle's dramatic unities of time and place, which French dramatists honored but English dramatists tended to reject. Bate treats the English as only slightly less dogmatic than the French. For Dryden, Addison, Burke, and Johnson, playwrights assumed in the audience a judgment of probability, analogous to the standard that was emerging in natural philosophy, that entailed an expectation that representations would approximate the actual rather than reproduce it with literal fidelity or certainty. Probability was based on an empirical assessment of likelihood. Bate instead equates this innovative and active standard of probability with an a priori, "universal and ideal" criterion and "broad governing rule of decorum" (14, 15, 16). The English looked back to Aristotle's principle of probability in ordering the sequence of events in a tragic plot. Bate transforms this formal principle into the ontological rule that what should be imitated is "the fundamental order and decorum of the universal" (19). Preferring Thomas Rymer and Charles Gildon to Dryden as guides to Restoration literary-critical thought, Bate characterizes the aesthetic rules as part "of an infallible and universal rule of order" in accord with "the essence of mathematical thought" and "Newton's mathematical discoveries" (27, 34, 35).

Historicizing the Enlightenment offers evidence that across a range of subjects, contemporaries analyzed traditional categories of thought into their separate parts, enabling a conflation of particulars into innovative categories of the general whose coherence was tested and adjusted by the ongoing dialectical comparison of the particular and the general. Bate unaccountably reduces this new affirmation of self-conscious method to its opposite—to a campaign to methodize and justify the rules themselves in order to facilitate their dogmatic application "with almost mathematical precision" (26). By this reduction, the empirical separation out from the general or constant of all that was variable—"either personal or else local and fashionable"—becomes in Bate an end in itself rather than part of a coherent experimental method (12). Bracketing its specific aim to divest the language of natural philosophy of ambiguous reference, Bate encourages us to see the Royal Society's concern to limit the technical use of metaphor through the narrow (and unsubstantiated) lens of its "effect on poetic theory and practice" and broad language use (38). Yet because it's based in sensation, empiricism has for Bate's eighteenth century both an anti-imaginative and an anti-rational bias. For "insight into the objectively general, empiricism substitutes the mere term 'generalization,' with its connotation of a subjective act of mind" (93). Bate's reference to the subjective might seem to adumbrate a continuity between classic and Romantic. But this is illusory, because he blocks that continuity by consistently denying in neoclassicism the role of the imagination in the fundamental work of representation even though it's clearly crucial to the eighteenth-century interpretation of Aristotelian imitation. Bate's erasure of the imagination from the eighteenth-century aesthetic, and of particularity from its dialectic with generality, is a familiar falsification of neoclassicism that Romanticism had given lasting authority and that Bate therefore believes he need do no more than summarize. Thomas Quayle had perpetuated the banal dogma two decades earlier: "In its insistence on generalized or abstract forms, eighteenth-century poetry, or at least the 'neo-classical' portion of it, reflected its inability to achieve that intensity of imaginative conception which is the supreme need of all art."[3] Two decades later Harold Bloom falsified the complexity and nuance of Samuel Johnson's judgment by selecting the phrase "the dangerous prevalence of the imagination" as representative of it.[4]

The Radical Break

Bate's moderation of the discontinuity between the two periods isn't typical. For Romantics, a radical break in the nature and quality of English poetry was grounded in a radical break in literary theory. George Sherburn reminds us that what debased poetry from Dryden to Pope, Romantics believed, was its slavish submission to the neoclassical rules. "The criterion of art later most deplored by Romantic critics was the rules." But Sherburn's critical detachment is unsteady. "Although many of the dogmas imported from the Continent were never completely accepted in England, the common-sense aspect of neo-classicism easily domesticated itself. To follow the distinguished methods of the best ancients, that is, to follow 'the rules' deduced by common sense from ancient procedure, seemed obviously practical. . . . [Yet] few were the critics of the period 1650–1750 who did not pay excessive attention to these rules."[5]

The notion of a radical break was advanced most punctually and trenchantly by the Romantics themselves. In 1807 Robert Southey wrote, "The time which elapsed from the days of Dryden to those of Pope, is the dark age of English poetry. . . . Thomson recalled the nation to the study of nature, which, since Milton, had been utterly neglected. . . . Meantime the growing taste for Shakespeare gradually brought our old writers into notice. [This] was forwarded more effectually by the publication of [Thomas Percy's] Reliques of Ancient [English] Poetry [1765], the greatest literary epocha of the present reign."[6] Southey renewed this argument three decades later: "The age from Dryden to Pope is the worst age of

English poetry.... It was the pinchbeck age of poetry." The art "was debased, and it continued to be so long as Pope continued lord of the ascendant.... If Pope shut the door, Cowper opened it.... Thomson brought with him, from his own beautiful country, a deep perception and true love of the beauties of nature, for which the English poets, from Dryden to Pope, seem to have had neither eye, nor ear, nor heart."[7]

In the first two decades of the nineteenth century, William Hazlitt gave an account of the neoclassical rules, broadly expanded from the dramatic unities, from which he claims poetry was instantaneously liberated by the Romantic poets. Hazlitt asserts that this poetic revolution developed its powerfully radical aesthetic under the influence of the French Revolution, with which it was contemporary. The speed and breadth of the change in Hazlitt's account reflect the modern transformation in the meaning of "revolution," from a return to first principles to total innovation:

> Our poetical literature had, towards the close of the last century, degenerated into the most trite, insipid, and mechanical of all things, in the hands of the followers of Pope and the old French school of poetry. It wanted something to stir it up, and it found that some thing in the principles and events of the French revolution. From the impulse it thus received, it rose at once from the most servile imitation and tamest common-place, to the utmost pitch of singularity and paradox.... All the common-place figures of poetry, tropes, allegories, personifications, with the whole heathen mythology, were instantly discarded; a classical allusion was considered as a piece of antiquated foppery; capital letters were no more allowed in print, than letters-patent of nobility were permitted in real life; kings and queens were dethroned from their rank and station in legitimate tragedy or epic poetry, as they were decapitated elsewhere; rhyme was looked upon as a relic of the feudal system, and regular metre was abolished along with regular government. Authority and fashion, elegance or arrangement, were hooted out of countenance, as pedantry and prejudice. Every one did that which was good in his own eyes. The object was to reduce all things to an absolute level.[8]

Hazlitt's risible overstatement might seem to moderate the extremity of these broad claims, but this is belied by his discovery of an absolute level, at once poetic and social, in Wordsworth: "His popular, inartificial style gets rid (at a blow) of all the trappings of verse, of all the high places of poetry.... The distinctions of rank, birth, wealth, power . . . are not to be found here."[9] Given the explicit campaign against social hierarchy in both the form and content of eighteenth-century literature, Hazlitt's hyperbole is absurd; yet Meyer Abrams thinks he makes "a very plausible case." Abrams would have it both ways. He knows that "eighteenth-century critics and poets had carried far the work of breaking down the social distinctions built into a poetic developed for an aristocratic audience." Nonetheless, he contends that Wordsworth had "achieved revolution against the *ancien régime*," that he "had not only leveled, he had transvalued Renaissance and neoclassic aesthetics, by deliberately seeking out the ignominious, the delinquent, and the social outcast as subjects for serious or tragic consideration."[10]

Wordsworth's confidence in the experimental and innovative aims of his own poetry—marked by his insistence that each of the poems in *Lyrical Ballads* "has a worthy *purpose*"—could dull his sensitivity to what was experimental and innovative in the poetry of his predecessors. A well-known case in point is his curt dismissal, as "poetic diction," of selected lines in Gray's "Sonnet on the Death of Mr. Richard West" without discerning the "purpose" that motivates their diction. Gray's pastoral elegy transpires in the most conventional of tropes. The speaker's grief is stifled by his awareness that nature doesn't sympathize with him. At the same time, the poem conveys a deeper awareness that the obstacle to feeling is not that nature is oblivious but that the conventionality of the trope itself blocks the speaker's 's emotional expression. (As Johnson says of Milton's "Lycidas," it is "easy, vulgar, and therefore disgusting.") Wordsworth sees that in terms of form, only five lines in the sonnet are prosaic and devoid of "poetic diction." But he doesn't see that in terms of content, these are also the only lines in which the speaker owns his grief rather than seeking it in nature. In other words, the purpose of the poem is given as a reciprocal relation of form and content. Poetic language that's borrowed from convention and emotions that require external confirmation affirm, by negating, the value of unmediated self-expression.[11]

Imitation and Expression, the Mirror and the Lamp

There may be a lesson here, especially in the indirection of formal reflexivity, for those Romantic critics who are convinced of Romanticism's difference without attending as closely and carefully as they might to the poetry from which they would distinguish it. But the Romantic reduction of eighteenth-century poetry was grounded in a less subtle sort of misreading than Wordsworth's inattention to Gray's purpose. We owe to Abrams the most memorable terms for differentiating between neoclassicism and Romanticism, a difference in literary theory that is said to define a transitional moment in literary history, a "change from imitation to expression, and from the mirror to the fountain, the lamp, and related analogues." The mirror and the lamp are "two common and antithetic metaphors of mind, one comparing the mind to a reflector of external objects, the other to a radiant projector which makes a contribution to the object it perceives."[12] In what he calls the Age of Johnson, Abrams finds "standards for art running the gamut." Nonetheless, these variations "took place mainly within a single aesthetic orientation: . . . All these forms and qualities are conceived to be inherent in the constitution of the external world, and the work of art continues to be regarded as a kind of reflector" (41–42). But this isn't true. Both the mirror and the lamp, and the reflective and expressive assumptions they stand for, are actively in play for the entire eighteenth century. The comparison would be different if it were between Romantic and "Renaissance aesthetics" (which as we've seen Abrams is willing to run together with the "neoclassic"), because then the difference between the two periods would be significant both chronologically and substantively. But

Abrams's focus is on the eighteenth century, a determinate and continuous interval in which aesthetic thought is in constant debate, and key critics and philosophers are at every stage self-consciously and experimentally concerned to inquire into the relationship between imitation and expression, perception and imagination, the general and the particular, the external and the internal, object and subject, society and individual, the conscious and the unconscious, effect and affect, utility and pleasure, copy and parody—and more broadly, between the actual and the virtual, positive and negative liberty, tradition and innovation.[13]

The partiality of this view is most striking in the way that not only the Romantics but also Romanticists like Bate and Abrams misconstrue the cardinal category "imitation." In the *Poetics*, Aristotle describes a crucially double perspective—the pleasing re-presentation of what is painful when present—that was central to the theory of the dramatic aesthetic and narrative realism that eighteenth-century authors had developed. The double structure of literary imitation is formally binding; however, the distance between the imitation and what's imitated becomes subject to alteration and adjustment as it enters the parodic continuum from imitation to criticism. This is the realm of literary experimentation that profoundly preoccupies eighteenth-century "Augustanism," and as a mode of formal innovation its subtlety flies under the radar of Romanticism, which misrecognizes neoclassical imitation as a flat and static reflectionism devoid of the sublime imagination needed for a transcendence of the given—and devoid of the Enlightenment skepticism that recognizes mirror-like reflection to be illusory.

What neoclassical imitation posits is not a transcendence of the given but a self-conscious recognition of it, a simultaneous reference to the empirical actuality of the object and to its imagined virtuality. The Romantic reduction of imitation became the mainstream modern view. In the modern view, art that takes a position on the political or moral character of its object is termed "didactic," a negative judgment that runs counter to its "aesthetic" value. From this perspective it might seem persuasive to view the explicit pedagogy of didacticism as the traditionality that the enlightened modernity of the aesthetic replaces. However, it's more plausible to see the didactic and the aesthetic as new names for former parts of a traditional whole that tacitly conceived all knowledge, however particular its province, according to moral standards. In the realm of poetry this coextension finds loose expression in Horace's advice that poets excel in both *dulce et utile*, delight and instruction. Enlightenment scrutiny separated out these parts and conflated them, with a newly explicit understanding of their complementarity, in the innovative category of the aesthetic. But in the coming years, the idea of the aesthetic would be drained of its dialectical energy, and the pejorative term "didactic" would come to tarnish art that was judged too committed to taking on its object in the process of representing it.[14]

One effect of this devolution, which is especially frustrating given the period field of its application, was the idea of the "persona" as deployed several decades ago by scholars of Augustan literature.[15] Derived from the ancient practice of literally masked speech in theatrical orality so as to acknowledge the figurative impersonality of ironic discourse, the doctrine of the persona soon served the gratuitously apologetic purpose of depersonalizing satiric criticism. It reified impersonation as artistic technique: not really what the author is "saying" but an instrument he's momentarily "using" to artistic ends that may be segregated from the personality and personhood of the author himself. Paradoxically this critical strategy was sometimes justified in the name of rhetorical "art"—as though rhetoric is a set of verbal techniques divorced from the political and moral purposes they subserve. True, naive and mindless attacks on the immorality of Swift and Pope required correctives. But the idea of the persona went much further, providing wholesale support for the notion that to be aesthetic, literary imitation had to eschew the "didactic."

Neoclassical imitation is manifestly a formal inquiry into the conditions of historical difference, which fine-tunes the ratio between continuity and discontinuity, between the preservation and the supersession of the past, with an experimental inventiveness that invites a range of prefixes—"counter-," "mock-," "anti-," "neo-"—to capture degrees of formal difference. Again, the imitative distance taken from the object imitated is not formally binding, not given but chosen—a self-conscious choice that expresses the author's decision about how and how far to depart from the image of the object, and that therefore (in Abrams's terms) "makes a contribution to the object it perceives." In other words, once the specious metaphor of direct mirroring is set aside, a close analysis of what's entailed in literary imitation allows us to see that imitation and expression are not opposed but reciprocal. By the same token, English neoclassicism is not a simple renewal of classical standards but an oblique modernization, a process that submerges the ancient past in a radically empirical and skeptical solution that leaves nothing unchanged. Romantic critics tend to recognize that the mock forms that are central to Augustan literature need to be accounted for in their estimate of eighteenth-century poetry. But they don't know how to because they see imitation as nothing but the diametrical opposite of expression.

"Revolution"

"Poetry is the spontaneous overflow of powerful feelings." Abrams quotes Wordsworth's famous analogy, drawing attention to the brilliance of its concision by pointing out the factors it leaves out: "the conditions of the given world, the requirements of the audience, and the control by conscious purpose and art as important determinants of a poem." These omissions, he observes, are the "extreme consequences latent in the central analogue to which Wordsworth gave impetus in England," and they "did not appear in that country until three decades later, in such critics as Keble, Carlyle, and John Stuart Mill" (48). We might take this to suggest that Abrams aims to rescue Wordsworth's poetic theory from this simplifying reduction, but instead he endorses its extremity as his own. He began *The Mirror and the Lamp*, "inevitably," using "convenient simplifications" to generalize about Romanticism as a world-historical innovation. But now, four chapters in, "by shifting the focus and selecting the examples, we can readily show that Romantic aesthetics was no less an instance of continuity than of revolution in intellectual history" (70). So the mirror and the lamp, with which Abrams began, was no less an extreme analogue than the spontaneous overflow of powerful feelings. The difference is that whereas Wordsworth's analogue isn't really extreme because it appears in a larger argument that acknowledges those other factors, Abrams bases his entire argument on the convenient simplification of the mirror and the lamp. The title of Wordsworth's argument is descriptive: "Preface" to *Lyrical Ballads*. The title of Abrams's is a patently disingenuous, if convenient, simplification, the ideology of a historical watershed—a "revolution"—that falsifies an intellectual process that actually transpired over the previous century and a half. Literary historians like Abrams have constructed this watershed ideology to some extent, as we've seen in Hazlitt, out of the self-images of the Romantic movement itself. But in assembling passages where Romantic poets associate their ambitions with the energies of the French Revolution, Abrams involves himself in that association with an enthusiasm that's hard to distinguish from "the spirit of the age" he purports to document (in "English Romanticism," 44–75).

By the nineteenth century this modern meaning of revolution as innovation was losing its plainly ideological thrust and becoming an unmarked replacement for the traditional construal of revolution as renovation. The traditional and accurate sense of the word was also ideological, and the seventeenth-century experience was making this unavoidably explicit. Like the Protestant Reformers, the enemies of Stuart absolutism justified their rebellion against the king as a return to the norm of tradition—immemorial law and the ancient constitution—as did those who celebrated the Restoration of the Stuart line in 1660 and even the deposal of James II in 1688. But with the lapsing of Charles's personal rule at the end of the 1630s, the assertion of parliamentary privilege against royal prerogative entered an unprecedented political trajectory that wasn't easily assimilated to the myth of the common-law mind.

Looking back on the "century of revolution," Romantic critics were at best inattentive to what it taught about the complexity of political, and poetic, revolution. Premised on the interlocked assumptions that Augustan poetry was derivative rather than innovative and inferior to Romantic poetry, Romanticists read the seventeenth-century crisis as an unequivocal cultural disaster. Informed alternative readings, more thoughtfully attuned to an Enlightenment perspective, were available. In the 1680s, George Savile, Marquess of Halifax, looked back on the civil wars and reflected: "The liberty of the late times gave men so much light, and diffused it so universally amongst the people, that they are not now to be dealt with, as they might have been in an age of less inquiry."[16] Romanticists might see these sentiments—about what many have called the "English Revolution"—as at least compatible with their more fulsome enthusiasm for the "apocalyptic longings" of the Romantic poets and the French Revolution. Instead, they repudiate the "revolutionary longings" of the previous century. According to Harold Bloom, "It was a brutal and anarchic collapse of a settled society into a chaos of rebellion and sectarianism," in response to which Enlightenment poets "set themselves against every innovation, every mark of dissent, every extreme position in ethics, politics, metaphysics, or art" (xxi). David Duff concurs: "The civilizing mission of neoclassical criticism, with its love of regularity and order, can be interpreted as a reaction to the chaos of fanaticism of the 1640s and 1650s" and as "an attempt to keep at bay traumatic cultural memories."[17] Opinions like these disclose a reactionary politics at the heart of the Romanticist embrace of the "revolutionary."

Duff's subject here is the neoclassical attitude toward genre, which he treats as a synecdoche for neoclassical criticism and then specifies as "the neoclassical genre-system," which he finds to be a rigid macro-rule composed of strict micro-rules. The "neoclassical paradigm" entails "a finite number of genres each of which has its own 'laws' or 'rules,' adherence to which is necessary for a successful performance of that genre." The rules state what is "permissible." They're derived from the practice of specified authors "whose achievements are regarded as an ideal standard against which subsequent performances in that genre are measured." "All literature is an 'imitation' of nature, each genre representing its own portion of nature. . . . The genres are hierarchically ranked, a genre's status representing the social class of the characters represented, the seriousness of the subject matter, and the scale and complexity of the form" (31–32). Finally, the idea of genre is "a fantasy of simultaneity," a static form that for neoclassical critics has no historicity or history (145).

Duff derives this paradigm principally from authors whom other romanticists also prefer to cite when documenting neoclassical dogmatism—Rymer, Gildon, and Dennis—and from others whose stated purpose is not to reflect on genre but to provide cut-and-dried rules for how to write poetry. Absent from these sources are Dryden and Pope, whom the Romantics labeled "the French school"—"pejoratively," Duff allows even as he uses that label himself (21, 95). True, neoclassical authors like Dryden composed and discussed "hybrid, parodic genres"; but these "had no place in the neoclassical genre-system," let alone the kind of historicity of which even the traditional genres are innocent (44). Needless to say, Dryden's inquiry into the history of satire, *Discourse concerning the Original and Progress of Satire* (1693), makes no showing in the neoclassical "uses of genre" Duff documents. This is because the texts he consults are those that restrict the treatment of genre to the most dogmatic and prescriptive purposes imaginable. However, there's no such restriction at work in his treatment of the Romantic uses of genre, and the self-fulfilling result of this radical disparity in Duff's principle of selection is dichotomous difference.

Compared with classicism, English neoclassicism only intensified "the prescriptive character of genre criticism," and "the analogy with mathematics, pervasive in literary criticism of this period," indicates a "desire to establish *criticism* as a *science*" (34, 35). There's no mention in Duff's book of Dryden's *Essay of Dramatic Poesy* (1668), a critical landmark notable both for repudiating the French dogma of the unities and for a subtly formulated and vastly consequential comparison between poetry and natural philosophy (that has nothing to do with

12 Introduction

mathematics). Duff postpones for decades the English rejection of the unities, passing over Addison and Johnson (and in the process their speculations on the relation between poetry and science), and he reserves for a later, German-inspired moment the transit from a deductive and objective rhetorical focus to an inductive and subjective aesthetics—"a new science of psychological causes and effects"—even though the transit is evident in Addison's papers comparing the "pleasures" of the "imagination" and the "understanding" (43, 47).

So, following in Abrams's footsteps, Duff fashions an overarching "shift from mimetic to expressive criteria" (49). And like Abrams he would establish a critical distance between himself as a Romanticist critic and the Romantics themselves, although he takes a different approach to this end. With disarming candor Duff observes that "what often proved irresistible" was the "temptation for Romantic writers to think of neoclassical poetics," "with its hierarchical genre-system and armoury of generic rules," "as an *ancien régime* to their 'revolutionary poetical system' [Byron's ironic phrase] . . . [,] a repressive critical ideology from which modern literature had emancipated itself." But within the space of a sentence the appearance of detachment disappears: "The reorientation of critical attitudes [was] sufficiently radical and far-reaching to make terms like 'revolution' and 'paradigm shift' appropriate" (30–31). Again: "Like all self-serving polemics, however, Romantic constructions of neoclassicism distort a more complicated reality." Duff's citations make clear that these constructions were simply erroneous. Yet he documents the "more complicated reality" not by correcting those errors but by broadly remarking that neoclassical and romantic thought weren't discontinuous (40). And although this is not his argument about Romanticism, in the end Duff's book exemplifies the kind of historical revision that was required to justify the skepticism about genre as a literary-critical category that permeates modern thought (to which I'll return).

Preromanticism

A major contribution to what I've called a watershed ideology is the notion that the "Romantic revolution" was foreshadowed by midcentury poets, Collins and Gray in particular, who had wistfully summoned up the great English poets of the past and wondered if that glorious lineage, now arrested, might flourish once more. Modern critics, focusing on Spenser, Shakespeare, and Milton (but omitting Dryden, whom Gray had included in the line), find in the midcentury poets an inspired anticipation of the Romantics—and with more or less indirection, the Romantics themselves ponder the retrospection of Collins and Gray as prophesying their own revival of that native poetic line. Abrams furthered this narrative (e.g., in "English Romanticism," 52–53), and Harold Bloom made it central to his story of how Romanticism rose to eminence.[18] In this way, the feelings of a group of poets writing at a certain moment have been made to define the historical framework of English poetry. So, in 1863 William Rushton wrote with satisfied finality: "All the critics are now agreed that English poetry, during the middle of the 18th century—say from 1740 to 1760–80—is exceedingly wearisome, except what was written by Gray, Thomson, and Goldsmith; and that the first poet who did much to bring back genuine feeling and a natural style was William Cowper."[19]

"Some years back," George Sherburn wrote in 1967, "the academic discussion of eighteenth-century literature eddied about the 'romanticism' of the second half of the century. To the present writer it seems that such discussion has tended to describe the eighteenth century as seen distorted through the spectacles of the nineteenth" (971n4). Northrop Frye agreed. Noting a prevailing uncertainty about how to name the literature of the later eighteenth century, Frye proposed the "Age of Sensibility," which he distinguished from the "Augustan age" and the "Romantic movement" that framed it as being preoccupied by literary process rather than, as they were, by the finished result or product. Frye offered this period term as a mediation of the gulf between what were too commonly seen as "a reptilian Classicism, all cold and dry reason," and "a mammalian Romanticism, all warm and wet feeling," bridging that gap without reducing one of the framing periods to the terms of the other. "As for the term 'pre-romantic,'" he added, "that, as a term for the age itself, has the peculiar demerit of committing us to anachronism before we start, and imposing a false teleology on everything we study."[20] Others also have doubted the value of the term.[21]

Undeterred, Marshall Brown titled his book *Preromanticism* and prefaced it with a straightforward rationale: "It does not designate a preliminary state of romanticism or a predisposition." Rather, "I call the period preromantic precisely because it was *not yet* romantic. . . . The term 'preromanticism' has always been attacked for its teleology, but that is the very reason I welcome it. The great authors were striving ahead for something new. . . . A telos is a goal in the distance; it is not yet there when a teleological process is under way." It seems to me that Brown's account of why he welcomes "teleology"—because it describes a process toward a goal—is tautological. The problem with "preromanticism" is not that the seemingly unnameable "something new" it points toward hasn't arrived yet. The problem is that "preromanticism" names it: the Romantic. A second problem is that by naming that goal "the Romantic," Brown prejudges as having a Romantic character a body of eighteenth-century texts while the process of establishing its character is, as Brown would say, still under way. Brown thereby contributes to the simple model of a Romantic revolution simply by chipping off a body of earlier literature and calling it Romantic.[22]

The resonance of revolution that Romantics and Romanticists value has been associated, by Dror Wahrman, not with the French but with the American Revolution. By "the making of the modern self," Wahrman refers to "a very particular understanding of personal identity, one that presupposes an essential core of selfhood characterized by psychological depth, or interiority, which is the bedrock of unique, expressive individual identity."[23] This understanding replaced the *"ancien régime* of identity" around 1780, he writes, as a consequence of the British experience of the American Revolution, and it was symptomatic, Wahrman believes, of a broad cultural revolution that was in effect the making of modernity as such. The eighteenth-century ancien régime entailed "a consistent and wide-ranging set of assumptions that defined the meaning, significance, and limits of identity up to the last two decades of the century" (xiii). At this moment there was a "sharp and distinctive transformation," marked by the sudden emergence of the self (xiv).

The problem with this formulation lies as much in Wahrman's terminology as it does in the substance of his account. This can be seen in the ambivalence of the notion that the assumptions of the former period are both "consistent and wide-ranging." The eighteenth century wasn't an ancien régime on matters of identity and the self, and Wahrman's discrimination between the two is crucial to his argument. He must acknowledge that Locke inaugurated the idea of personal identity early in the Enlightenment, so he exports the distinctively modern specificity of psychological depth and interiority that were entailed in Locke's and Hume's category to that of the self, and then locates the beginning of the self's modern dominion toward the end of the Enlightenment. But both Enlightenment philosophers deployed the already available language of the self in their efforts to define the emergent category of personal identity.[24] And over the course of the eighteenth century, "personal identity" and "the person" were debated with the energy characteristically expended on Enlightenment categories once they've emerged into public discourse and become subject to explicit analysis. I think Wahrman is right in discerning a change toward the end of the eighteenth century. Broadly speaking, experimental innovation moderated and the central ideas became more conventional. The conceptual ferment of the Enlightenment was slowing down, and some of the emergent categories, like the aesthetic, were losing their dialectical plasticity in critical discourse. However, this is a moment not of sharp transformation but of a consolidation of what had come before, a historiography very far from Wahrman's counterintuitive model of epistemic break.

Wahrman's justification for his account is puzzling given how much it runs counter not only to the logic of the account itself but also to the evidence. Like Abrams, he selects his evidence and discounts manifest signs of difference that precede 1780, and like Abrams he argues by metaphors that lay claim to a clarity that becomes blurred when put to the test of less figurative descriptions. Wahrman's persistence in so untenable a direction may be partially explained (if that's the right word) by his observation of the "echoes in it of Foucault's insistence on the need to escape from a universalized unitary fixed self and on a fundamental rupture in the Western episteme in the late eighteenth century"—as though the only way to escape transhistorical idealism is through an idealizing historical rupture (xvii).

And what about Romanticism? Surprisingly late in the book Wahrman remarks that "many of the developments routinely associated with literary Romanticism are precisely those I have identified for the new regime of identity" (290). With a diffidence bordering on dismissal, Wahrman alludes to the "conventional critical wisdom that has identified time and again the Romantic 'conceptual shift'" (291). I think Wahrman's hesitancy betrays a recognition that this elephant in the room, "the Romantic revolution," is a well-established thesis that does the work of his own and renders it superfluous. My own skepticism about the thesis of a Romantic conceptual shift is very different from Wahrman's. I don't think it actually happened, whereas for Wahrman a great epistemic break is an article of belief. I think his diffidence subserves this belief. But it thereby locates an angle from which to doubt the Romantic revolution that differs from my own but arrives at a similar conclusion.

Modernism: Structuralism and Poststructuralism

Here and elsewhere in this study I've remarked on the baneful influence Michel Foucault's brand of structuralism has had on eighteenth-century studies. Scholars and critics whose achievements are evident in writings that are free of this influence have fallen into a deep sleep under the spell of the Foucauldian historiography of epistemic rupture, separating continuity from discontinuity with a finality that eschews conflation and in a multitude of ways deprives the Enlightenment of its due. The results and effects of Foucault's influence on Enlightenment studies are well known, and rather than rehearse them here I'll limit my notice of Foucault to what I've said here, which opens the final section of this introduction to the second volume of *Historicizing the Enlightenment*.

"Rules" and the Genre System

Fredric Jameson points out that genre criticism has been "thoroughly discredited by modern literary theory and practice."[25] Rene Wellek writes, "The theory of genres has not been at the center of literary study and reflection in this century. Clearly this is due to the fact that in the practice of almost all writers of our time genre distinctions matter little."[26] "Perhaps the most striking feature of modern literature," according to Philippe Sollers, "is the appearance of a new monolithic, comprehensive mode of writing, in which the distinctions among genres, which have been completely abandoned, give way to what are admittedly 'books,' but books for which, we might say, no method of reading has yet been worked out."[27] This familiar principle of postmodernism has a provenance. The early modern disenchantment with the system of literary genres culminated, in its first manifestation, with the Romantic movement. The modern disenchantment with genre is coextensive with the modern valorization of free innovation as such. In the history of thinking about genre, this process reflects the difference between the traditional assumption that the system of genres has a hermeneutic function and the modern view of it as a deductive taxonomy. In tacit usage, genres were traditionally seen as models for making formal choices within a larger realm of formal determinacy, models not for the solution but for the initial articulation of problems of form. The determinacy of a genre required an attention to the way the idea it evoked had been formally achieved in a broad range of past literary practice. However, this experience of genre as an enabling condition of discursive practice was overbalanced by the modern stereotype of tradition as sponsoring the view that genre is a grid imposed, on writer and reader alike, from without. The result was the "genre system," a master compendium of "rules" in the sense of the term that became codified by the Romantics and was representative of a broader historical trend that involved the Romantic movement but extended well beyond it. In modern thought, resistance to the genre system, like resistance to the rule of economic protectionism, became a fundamental expression of negative liberty.[28]

In literary production, modern critics have flown the anti-generic banner of negative liberty most conspicuously, if paradoxically, in the form of the new genre "the novel." This is because, in the celebrated analysis of Mikhail Bakhtin, "the novel parodies other genres (precisely in their role as genres); it exposes the conventionality of their forms and their language; it squeezes out some genres and incorporates others into its own peculiar structure, re-formulating and re-accentuating them. . . . In an era when the novel reigns supreme, almost all the remaining genres are to a greater or lesser extent 'novelized.'"[29] This perspective might be taken to confirm that the novel lacks generic identity because it parasitically takes its form from the traditional genres it parodies. But this is only to describe a heightened form of the subtly imitative historicity characteristic of all works modeled on a given genre. The difference lies in the self-consciousness of the novel's engagement in this process, which might be seen as the novel's special function: the role of enacting for modern culture the meaning of freedom as a detachment from what exists over against it. The modern shift in the idea of genre—from an enabling hermeneutic to a constraining taxonomy—is coextensive with the emergence of the novel because the novel explicitly articulates a problem that is tacit, hence nonproblematic, in traditional genre theory. The novel crystallizes genreness, self-consciously incorporating, as part of its form, the problem of its own categorial status. The illusion that the novel lacks generic identity lies not in its parasitic "nature" but in its reflexive tendency to reflect on its nature—which of course alters its nature in the process.

The novel might be said to emerge at the eighteenth-century moment when contemporaries disabused themselves of the notion that its literary legitimacy requires a naive claim to provide an exact reflection of the world. Instead, the novel coalesces as the great modern genre with the recognition of its singular capacity of "double reflection"—its capacity to conflate the reflection of the external world with reflexivity, the self-conscious reflection on the internal formal process by which that external reflection is accomplished. So, the form of the novel consists of its awareness of its own formality, which bears the distinctive hallmark of Enlightenment thought: tacit knowledge made explicit.

Freud frames his famous essay of that name with the recognition that the uncanny bears a relation to aesthetics—"not merely the theory of beauty but the theory of the qualities of feeling." His essay may "have satisfied *psycho-analytic* interest in the problem of the uncanny"; "what remains probably calls for an *aesthetic* inquiry."[30] The present study may shed light on what that inquiry entails.

Freud proposes that "the uncanny is something which is secretly familiar, which has undergone repression and then returned from it. . . . An uncanny experience occurs either when infantile complexes which have been repressed are once more revived by some impression, or when primitive beliefs which have been surmounted seem once more to be confirmed" (245, 249). To exemplify the uncanny effect, Freud draws our attention to the difference between traditional forms, like fairy tales, on the one hand, and *"literature"* or "imaginative productions," on the other (249). The difference is that literary narrative involves an interaction between everyday experience and what lies beyond it. "As soon as the writer pretends to move in the world of common reality," "he can select his world of representation so that it either coincides with the realities we are familiar with or departs from them in what particulars he pleases" (250, 249). This departure produces the uncanny effect, and the narratives Freud cites to exemplify it locate the emergence of the uncanny—as one scholar puts it, its "invention"—in the period of the Enlightenment.[31]

Freud's uncanny has the character of Enlightenment thought: knowledge, traditionally tacit, is made explicit. States of mind once indivisible are separated out and thereby become subject to conflation, along with an awareness of their former "familiarity." In the Enlightenment this basic cognitive process has a temporal structure—what was, now is—that given the period's historical self-consciousness is deepened by historicity: what has passed, now returns with a difference. "We—or our primitive forefathers—once believed that these possibilities were realities, and were convinced that they actually happened. Nowadays we no longer believe in them, we have surmounted these modes of thought; but we do not feel quite sure of our new beliefs, and the old ones still exist within us ready to seize upon any confirmation" (247). This "historical uncanny" comes to a head toward the end of the Enlightenment in the gothic movement.

The literary concepts that emerged in the Enlightenment, realism and the aesthetic, named this movement of the mind and evince the double structure that was first theorized in Aristotelian imitation but formalized in the self-conscious reflexivity or double reflection that's peculiar to literature. Grounded in the skeptical analysis of what traditionally was taken for granted, these concepts enact an epistemology that affirms empirical reality as the basis for imagined worlds, a kind of knowledge aptly described by Coleridge as the willing suspension of disbelief. On an institutional level, the secret familiarity of imagined actuality is evident in the realm of virtual reality that, in its coexistence with the actual, has transformed the modern world.

Novelistic realism, an eighteenth-century achievement, is seldom credited to the Enlightenment. F. R. Leavis represents a broad trend in denying to the eighteenth-century novel the prestige of this accomplishment: "Jane Austen, in fact, is the inaugurator of the great tradition of the English novel—and by 'great tradition' I mean the tradition to which what is great in English fiction belongs."[32] The text in which this reflexive awareness was first made explicit is Henry Fielding's *Joseph Andrews* (1742). But Clifford Siskin, under a Foucauldian influence, extends Leavis's claim by conjoining Austen with Wordsworth and assimilating her to the model of the Romantic break, misreading Fielding's internal reflexivity as no more than external reflection and his innovative parody of traditional genres as a pious imitation of them.[33]

However, the heavy lifting needed to deny to the eighteenth century its innovation of the novel form was done not by Romanticists but by modernists, first structuralists and then poststructuralists. The most opportunistic strike was made by enthusiastic followers of the Russian formalist Viktor Shklovsky, whose meticulous reading of Sterne's technique of "baring the device" (the reflexive display of form on the level of content) is perennially cited to proclaim that *Tristram Shandy* (1760–1767), although composed in the Enlightenment, was somehow a modernist text *manqué*.[34] In a recent refinement of this argument, Jens Martin Gurr construes *Tristram Shandy* as a radical critique of Enlightenment principles on the authority of Horkheimer and Adorno's crypto-modernist attack on Enlightenment thought.[35] But the historical revisionism sponsored by modernism appropriated as its own the innovations not only of the eighteenth- but also of the nineteenth-century novel. For Shklovsky, the internal reference of novelistic reflexivity coexists with the novel's external reference to the world. Later critics, notably Roland Barthes and Gerard Genette, think differently.

Linguistic theory had been transformed by Ferdinand de Saussure's famous differentiation between the paradigmatic or synchronic and the syntagmatic or diachronic axes of language. Structuralist literary critics treat this achievement as justifying the opposition of "narration" or "telling" to "imitation" or "showing." In this view, narration is the way words mediate or "signify" other words; imitation is how words "refer" to something beyond words and language—and because reference has no narratological (that is, structural) purpose, it has no role in literary analysis. Moreover, this dichotomy between telling and showing at the micro-level of language is taken by structuralists to imply that at the macro-level of history, the understanding of literary forms is best attained when they are unconditionally separated from their historical instances. The theoretical opposition between the internal and the external, problematic in itself, is doubly so in practice, and it has had an adverse effect on the study of both language and history.

The Novel Tradition

So, both structuralist theory and Romanticist theory are grounded in a spurious invalidation of imitation as naive reference, and both have enabled a spurious interpretation of the history of the novel. Although not explicitly theorized in these terms, "verisimilitude" was the word most often used by critics to refer to the double perspective of Aristotelian imitation and the double reflection of the eighteenth-century novel. Over the course of the nineteenth century, the term "realism" was increasingly applied to this technique, although its theorization was achieved only in the twentieth by critics such as György Lukács. Modernist theory, whose word for intrinsic "structure" was "form," debunked realism, most commonly by ignoring its formal reflexivity and attributing to it the illusion that it provided a transparent window onto reality.[36]

But modernist theory was confounded by the paradox of the novel tradition. The wholesale valorization of novelty in which modernism participated buttressed its ideology of intrinsic form and enforced a conviction that what was authentically modern must be intrinsically unprecedented, a conviction that impedes, even more than the historiography of progress, the ability to think historically. To have coherence, all historical things must display both the continuity of an integral entity and, within that continuity, the discontinuity that confirms its existence over time and space, its capacity to change without changing into something else. Therefore, to have a historical existence, the novel must possess a discernible continuity, a tradition. But the only tradition compatible with modernity must be characterized by the wholesale discontinuity of intrinsic innovation. Consequently, the history of the novel sanctioned by structuralism and poststructuralism is intelligible only as a series of discontinuous stages—typically realism, modernism, postmodernism, postcolonialism—each of which is claimed to be a radical innovation on the form of its predecessor, even though none go beyond the radical innovation of the first stage, realism. This may be embraced as the death of genre, even of history. But the fate of a posterity that appropriates eighteenth-century innovation is to repeat it unknowingly as though it were new.

1 The Sciences as a Model for the Arts

A SYNCHRONIC INQUIRY

Although inquiry into the nature of beauty is as old as Plato, it's become a commonplace that the idea of the aesthetic, and its narrative equivalent realism, emerged during the Enlightenment and is therefore a modern phenomenon. What distinguishes the idea of *the aesthetic* from more general thought about beauty, art, taste, and the like—often loosely called *aesthetics*—is its reference to a particular kind of experience. The guiding principle of the aesthetic is epistemological. The aesthetic coheres as a body of knowledge when its status as a mode of knowledge becomes the central focus of inquiry—an inquiry not, as traditionally, into the nature of the beautiful object but into the way we know it. According to empirical epistemology, all knowledge comes to us through experience. Because the senses are the gateway of experience, to ask how we know art is to ask what is singular about our perception of, our somatic response to, and our subjective attitude toward aspects of experience that we deem aesthetic.[1]

Yet if the idea of the aesthetic was thus formulated as a subcategory of empirical epistemology, customary modern usage instead tends to construe aesthetic experience in opposition to broadly empirical and specifically "scientific" knowledge; and this oppositional tendency also is rooted in Enlightenment developments. For the well-known Renaissance efforts to conceive the arts as a distinctive sort of activity bore substantial fruit only in the late seventeenth-century Quarrel between the Ancients and the Moderns, which posited the division between the humanistic arts and the empiricist sciences that was to become a defining feature of modern culture.[2] This is only a seeming contradiction: the effort to define the integrity and autonomy of aesthetic response and aesthetic judgment—of the epistemology and psychology of the art experience—took place not in opposition to but in explicit emulation of a normative model of empirical and scientific cognition. It was by imitating the emergent method and value system of the natural sciences that the arts learned their own distinctive, aesthetic mode of being. Although other national cultures made important contributions to this story, I have confined myself for the most part to English sources.

Ancients and Moderns, Arts and Sciences

We begin with a basic example of the process characteristic of Enlightenment thought, the partialization of a former tacit whole: the division of knowledge into the arts and the sciences. The late seventeenth-century Quarrel of the Ancients and the Moderns marks the final stage in a momentous diachronic division of two historical periods, a division whose origins lie in the earliest decades of the Renaissance. Why did the Quarrel also occasion an equally momentous first stage in a synchronic separation out of two fundamentally different modes of knowledge and practice? Ancients versus Moderns entailed arts versus sciences because the more closely Moderns examined the grounds for claiming the superiority of either period over the other, the clearer it became that any claim to superiority turned on which kind of knowledge was under consideration. On the one hand, by the first years of the seventeenth century, enough evidence had accumulated to show that in matters of what we call science and contemporaries called "natural" or "the new philosophy," Aristotle in particular had gotten much of it wrong. On the other, the excellence of Homer and Aeschylus, Virgil and Horace persisted over time in a way that seemed impervious to the sort of standard by which Aristotle confidently could be criticized.

This was a standard of empirical demonstrability that dictated an inductive method of inquiry that, in the words of Francis Bacon, "derives axioms from the senses and particulars, rising by a gradual and unbroken ascent, . . . opening and laying out . . . a road for the human understanding direct from the sense, by a course of experiment orderly conducted and well built up."[3] By the later decades of the seventeenth century, the Baconian method was being adapted across a range of endeavors. What about the arts? It's difficult to know what contemporaries thought on this issue because the separation of the arts and the sciences was in process at this time, and those terms could be used both to discriminate between modes of knowledge and, more traditionally, to describe, like *scientia*, the general category of knowledge as such. In his own usage, Bacon approached a consistent discrimination between "the sciences" and "the arts," but only because he tended to divide the two not in modern terms but as the difference between theoretical and practical knowledge. So when Bacon describes the "gradual and unbroken ascent" of inductive progress, he associates it with the "arts" rather than the "sciences": "What is founded on nature grows and increases; while what is founded on opinion varies but increases not." Today "the sciences stand where they did [two thousand years ago] and remain almost in the same condition; receiving no noticeable increase, but on the contrary, thriving most under their first founder, and then declining. Whereas in the mechanical arts, which are founded on nature and the light of experience, we see the contrary happen, for these (as long as they are popular) are continually thriving and growing" (*New Organon*, I, aph. 74 [277]).

When, in his essay *Of Dramatic Poesy* (1668), John Dryden inquired into the nature of drama fifty years after Bacon wrote, terminological usage was still uncertain, but the oppositional relationship that Bacon had established between two different modes of acquiring knowledge was beginning to resemble what soon would be called the difference between the sciences and the arts. And the clarity of the difference owed in part to the fact that the two claimed a special relationship with the same entity, the realm of nature. Dryden has one of his speakers, Lisideius, define a play as a *"just and lively image of human nature."* In response to this, another speaker, Crites, begins his announced defense of the Ancients with a spirited panegyric to the new philosophy over against the mediocrity of modern, especially English, "poesy": "Is it not evident in these last hundred years (when the study of philosophy has been the business of all the virtuosi in Christendom) that almost a new nature has been revealed to us? That more errors of the school have been detected, more useful experiments in philosophy have been made, more noble secrets in optics, medicine, anatomy, astronomy discovered, than in all those credulous and doting ages from Aristotle to us? so true it is, that nothing spreads more fast than science, when rightly and generally cultivated."[4] In defense of modern poetry, Eugenius replies that "your instance in philosophy makes for me: for if natural causes be more known now than in the time of Aristotle, because more studied, it follows that poesy and other arts may, with the same pains, arrive still nearer to perfection." (Dryden, 1:32). But before it could be argued that poetry, because it too aims at nature, can follow the path of the new philosophy, commentators had to better understand what that path might be and how well equipped poetry was to pursue it. Bernard de Fontenelle was perhaps the first to offer clear guidance by clarifying the difference between the two modes of knowledge:

> If the moderns are to be able to improve continually on the ancients, the fields in which they are working must be of a kind which allows progress. Eloquence and poetry require only a certain number of rather narrow ideas as compared with other arts, and they depend for their effect primarily upon the liveliness of the imagination. Now mankind could easily amass in a few centuries a small number of ideas, and liveliness of imagination has no need of a long sequence of experiments nor of many rules before it reaches the furthest perfection of which it is capable. But science, medicine, mathematics, are composed of numberless ideas and depend upon precision of thought which improves with extreme slowness, and is always improving.[5]

By observing how scientific knowledge improves over time, Fontenelle and his contemporaries formulated a diachronic principle of progress so persuasive that it has forestalled the conception of a synchronic idea of progress derived by observing the qualitative accumulation and ramification of knowledge at a single moment or within a single product of understanding.

Experience and Experiment

Fontenelle's notion of a kind of knowledge that "allows progress" because it slowly "improves" over time requires "a long sequence of experiments," the logic of whose ordering is determined by a "precision of thought" that successively derives "rules" from each experiment to determine what the next one should be. This explicit language of careful deliberation and self-conscious analysis encapsulates the Enlightenment perspective, which is distilled in the procedure of scientific method that Fontenelle and his contemporaries already were laboring to formulate. Bacon had laid the groundwork by describing in highly figurative language how the comparison of a multitude of samples will eliminate variables and disclose over time what is constant in all of them: "In the process of exclusion are laid the foundation of true Induction, which however is not completed until it arrives at an Affirmative, . . . solid and true and well defined, . . . naked and standing by itself, . . . disenthralled and freed from all impediments." Bacon also had announced that the cornerstone of this method, and of the new philosophy itself, would be quantification: "Inquiries into nature have the best result, when they begin with physics and end in mathematics" (*New Organon*, II, aphs. 19, 16, 24, 8).

In 1694 William Wotton wrote that the

> *Mathematical and Physical Sciences* . . . are Things which have no Dependence upon the Opinions of Men for their Truth; they will admit of fixed and undisputed *Mediums* of Comparison and Judgment: So that, though it may be always debated, who have been the best Orators, or who the best Poets; yet it cannot always be a Matter of Controversie, who have been the greatest *Geometers, Arithmeticians, Astronomers, Musicians, Anatomists, Chymists, Botanists*, or the like. . . .
>
> The Thing contended for on both Sides is, the *Knowledge of Nature*. . . . In order to this, it will be necessary, (1.) To find out all the several Affections and Properties of Quantity, abstractedly considered; . . . (2.) To collect great Numbers of Observations, and to make a vast Variety of Experiments upon all sorts of Natural Bodies. . . .
>
> The most verbose Mathematicians rarely ever said any thing for saying Sake, theirs being Subjects in which Figures of Rhetorick could have no sort of Place, but they made every Conclusion depend upon such a Chain of Premises already proved, that if one link were broke, the whole Chain fell in Pieces.[6]

Wotton's account exemplifies how the comparison of the Ancients and the Moderns seems to dictate a comparison between (in our terms) the arts and the sciences. If we would judge that, and how far, the Moderns excel the Ancients, we must isolate and describe a special mode of knowledge whose standards of comparison are "fixed" because its criteria of judgment are those of quantity, number, logical sequence, and abstraction. Experiment is the means by which these standards with great labor may be isolated and distinguished from those that pertain to other modes of knowledge, in which the qualitative judgment of "opinion" and "rhetoric," on the contrary, plays an important role.

The Royal Society of London was the founding institution of the new philosophy. In 1667, only four years after it was officially established, its historian, Thomas Sprat, gave an exploratory account of experimental method as it was then being formulated. The members of the society, Sprat wrote,

> have endeavour'd, to separate the Knowledge of *Nature*, from the Colours of *Rhetorick*, the Devices of *Fancy*, or the delightful Deceit of *Fables*. . . . They

have tried to put it into a Condition of perpetual Increasing; by settling an inviolable Correspondence between the Hand and the Brain. They have studied, to make it not only an Enterprise of one Season, or of some lucky Opportunity; but a Business of Time; a steady, a lasting, a popular, an uninterrupted Work.... Those, to whom the Conduct of the *Experiment* is committed, ... after they have perform'd the *Trial*, ... bring all the *History* of its *Process* back again to the Test. Then comes in the second great Work of the *Assembly*; which is to *judge* and *resolve* upon the Matter of *Fact*. In this part of their Imployment, they us'd to take an exact View of the Repetition of the whole Course of the *Experiment*; here they observ'd all the *Chances*, and the *Regularities* of the Proceeding; what *Nature* does willingly, what constrain'd; what with its own Power, what by the succours of Art.[7]

And the Royal Society's master experimentalist, Robert Hooke, described that procedure from the perspective of the practicing technician:

In the making of all kind of Observations or Experiments there ought to be a huge deal of Circumspection, to take notice of every the least perceivable Circumstance that seems to be significant either in the promoting or hindering, or any ways influencing the Effect. And to this end, ... it were very desirable that both Observations and Experiments should be divers times repeated, and that at several Seasons and with several Circumstances, both of the Mind and of Persons, Time, Place, Instruments and Materials.... [These are the] ways by which Nature may be trac'd, by which we may be able to find out the material Efficient and Instrumental Causes of divers Effects, not too far removed beyond the reach of our Senses.[8]

Judging by the testimony of Sprat, Hooke, and Wotton, experiment is only a methodical exploitation of experience through techniques of detachment and abstraction. According to John Locke's vastly influential empirical epistemology, experience is gained through sense impressions and is the sole source of knowledge. But if we would know nature well, we must distance it from what inevitably clouds its perception and description, which is to say from the local, punctual, and merely sensible experience of its knowing. The Lockean proposition that understanding requires the separation of the subject from the object of knowledge found its most rigorous application in the development of experimental method. "Experience" is the product of the senses as they are deeply embedded in the spatial and temporal contingencies of social practice; "experiment" names the protracted and wide-ranging effort to disembed experience, to detach what is generalizable—nature as such—from the diversity of concrete practices. Our normal knowledge of nature is conditioned by our experience. Experiment seeks (in Bacon's words) to "disenthrall and free" nature from those conditions by treating them as variables that can be controlled for by methods of quantification. Variable conditions can be recognized for what they are, and their effects can be neutralized, by a process of distantiation that involves multiplying and averaging the number of observations, observers, experiments, and experimenters so as to isolate that quantity of "nature" that can be seen to persist, invariably, across a range of artificial variations. The persistence of nature is evident in its susceptibility to quantitative measures that show it to be the same under varying conditions; variations are qualitative in the sense that experience adds to natural entities an element of irreducible difference that renders them unassimilable to, and incomparable by, a single standard of measurement.

But if my argument is that the first response of the arts to the new philosophy was emulative, the critique of "rhetoric," "eloquence," and the language arts by Sprat, Wotton, and others must raise serious problems. Although it's clear (e.g., in Dryden) that poetry and the other arts also aim to know nature, these early formulations of scientific method seem almost to be saying that nature is what remains once it has been detached from art. And from the most obvious perspective, the ambition to make the arts "scientific" is by definition futile—namely, the perspective from which art and nature are antithetical to each other. If scientific experiment aims to disclose what is constant in "nature" by separating it from the artificial experience in which it's embedded, science must be the very negation of art. The problem is not as intractable as it might seem, since the new philosophers are using the term "art" in a broader sense than this, to refer not simply to the language arts of "rhetoric," "fancy," and "fables" but to what we might call "culture": all those "artificial" factors that complicate and confuse our engagement with "the matter of fact" in itself. However, we can't ignore that what the new philosophers mean by "art" certainly does include the linguistic figures of "rhetoric" and "eloquence," which were also the bread and butter of poetic language. The best-known passage in Sprat's *History of the Royal Society* is his amusingly anti-rhetorical rhetoric urging his readers "to return back to the primitive Purity and Shortness, when Men deliver'd so many Things, almost in an equal Number of Words . . . bringing all Things as near the mathematical Plainness as they can" (113). Sprat's tongue-in-cheek longing for the prelapsarian transparency of Edenic language draws the line at utopianism because language is clearly indispensable to all human progress. For that matter, what is experiment itself but an artificial shaping of experience? (a point well taken by early opponents of experimentalism like Thomas Hobbes). But if the critique of the language arts could not be made absolutely, the new philosophers and their allies undertook with seriousness the ambition to reform language in the direction of simplicity and utility, to "improve" language on analogy with the way scientific technology had lately improved the visual sense through the invention of the telescope and the microscope. The question was, At what point do artificial methods stop serving the purpose of knowing nature and begin to frustrate that knowledge?

Controlling for Time, Place, and Persons: The Two Unities

During the Restoration period, the major legacy of the Quarrel of the Ancients and the Moderns to the arts was an optimistic dedication to exploring how the method of natural philosophy might be extended to them as well. It's not hard to see why drama was the first of the verbal modes on which was focused the ambition to elevate the arts to the status of a quasi-scientific knowledge. For one thing, the theater was still the most important of the verbal arts. Even more significant for our purposes, unlike printed literature, plays combine language with physical, material performance, and this makes their relationship to the naturalness of sensible experience a good deal more immediate than literature's can be. But as we've seen, proximity to the senses was not understood to be an unqualified good. The development of experimental method in science depended on two basic insights: first, that the knowledge of nature must proceed through sense experience; second, that the knowledge of nature must be distanced from the multiple and variable circumstances of time, place, and person under which it is impressed upon the senses. The earliest attempts to practice scientific method in the arts tended to honor the first insight a good deal more than the second. And in dramatic theory, one means of emulating the success of science seemed ready to hand in the neoclassical doctrine of the three unities. The unprecedented accomplishments of natural philosophy during the past century had gone far toward overturning the authority of Aristotle on physics, biology, and astronomy. What should be the modern attitude toward Aristotelian poetics? On the one hand, freedom from ancient dogmatism would seem to dictate freedom from the doctrine of the unities. On the other, the substance of that doctrine seemed to support, as the scientific Aristotle did not, a rigorously empirical approach to the dramatic representation of nature that was fully compatible with the nascent principles of natural philosophy. And when Moderns read it closely, Aristotle's *Poetics* was found to be far more circumspect on the unities than it had been thought to be.[9] In fact, even his deductive dogmatism in the sciences turned out to be a function less of what Aristotle wrote than of how he was received by posterity.

Dryden's *Of Dramatic Poesy*, to which I now briefly return, does full justice to this complexity through a dialogue about the knowledge of nature—its degree, kind, and probability—that's proper to dramatic representation. Crites, we recall, begins by broaching the Quarrel, as well as the superiority of modern science in having revealed in the past century "almost a new nature." In English plays, however, nature is "torn and ill represented": English drama is inferior to both ancient and modern French drama because it fails to observe the two unities of time and place. In Crites's view this makes English drama "unnatural," and it will continue to be so unless the amount of time and the extent of space undertaken to perform a given play are, quantitatively speaking, "as near as can be" to the duration and the locale that are represented within that play (1:26, 27, 28). In other words, if the dramatic representation is to be credible to its spectators, their theatrical experience must be as close as possible to that of the characters: representation aspires toward spatiotemporal presence. (Aristotle's third unity, that of action, was uncontroversial because most commentators agreed that it was important and that Aristotle clearly had affirmed it.) Lisideius soon enters the debate on the side of maintaining the two unities, and he reinforces the superiority of the ancient to the modern drama by aligning that contrast with the superiority of modern French to modern English drama. In the process, however, he invokes another Aristotelian teaching on which the French are once again more correct than the English—the teaching that extreme or improbable actions like violent death should be described in words, not represented onstage—that takes the debate to another level (see Aristotle, *Poetics*, 1460a). Time and place now become symptoms of a more fundamental problem of credibility, that of dramatic representation as such, which even the naive literalism of the unities could not hope to satisfy. "For what is more ridiculous," says Lisideius, "than to represent an army with a drum and five men behind it, all which the hero of the other side is to drive in before him; or to see a duel fought, and one slain with two or three thrusts of the foils, which we know are so blunted that we might give a man an hour to kill another in good earnest with them [?]" (Dryden, 1:51).

In replying to Lisideius, Neander acutely addresses this more general level of the argument: "For why may not our imagination as well suffer itself to be deluded with the probability of it as with any other thing in the play? For my part, I can with as great ease persuade myself that the blows which are struck are given in good earnest, as I can that they who strike them are kings or princes, or those persons which they represent" (1:62). In this capacity of the imagination to persuade us that representations are "in good earnest" lies the germ of the theory of the aesthetic. And when the debate turns from the unities to the choice between blank and rhymed verse, Neander similarly observes that by the strictest standard of the natural, both kinds of verse—in fact, verse itself—must be judged distortions rather than enhancements of nature. No more than the scientist's, the playwright's aim is not the immediacy of presence but a certain degree of detachment, not the futile avoidance of artful instruments of imitation but the use of those that are appropriate to and facilitate the dramatic knowledge of nature. And so Neander affirms the use of verse as a "tool," a "rule and line by which [the playwright's judgment] keeps his building compact and even" (1:91).

But if science and the dramatic arts seemed to share a methodological dependence on epistemological distance, the degree of distance they take on sense impressions is clearly very different. Moreover, the conjunction of the two proved highly controversial once it was concretized as a comparison between two performance spaces, the theater and the laboratory. Some contemporaries described the Royal Society's experiments as though they were popular entertainments akin to juggling acts, magic shows, and displays of prestidigitation.[10] The comparison was most acute and suggestive when it was self-consciously thematized in a number of plays, notably Ben Jonson's *The Alchemist* (1610), Dryden and William Davenant's revision of Shakespeare's *The Tempest* (1667), George Villiers, Duke of Buckingham's *The Rehearsal* (1671), and Thomas Shadwell's *The Virtuoso* (1676). Although both the theater and the laboratory suffered by this comparison, the broadest impulse of these satirical and often reflexive plays was to use the ancient practice of dramatic representation to hold an unflattering light to an innovative practice that appeared to imitate the apparatus of dramatic art even as it sought to eschew all associations with artistic framing. Brought to the stage, not only the laboratory but also the entire technology of experimentalism became a reflexive mirror of theatrical technology and its arts of illusion. So for a while, natural philosophy's quest for nature was metonymically incorporated within a dramatic practice that itself was learning to emulate the epistemology of experiment.[11] By the eighteenth century, the theater and the laboratory had become reciprocal performance arts. "By disciplining, and ultimately helping to legitimate, experimental philosophy, the eighteenth-century stage helped to naturalize an epistemology based on self-evident, decontextualized facts that might speak for themselves. In this, the stage and the lab jointly fostered an Enlightenment culture of spectacle that transformed the conditions necessary for the production and dissemination of scientific knowledge."[12]

Controlling for Time, Place, and Persons: The Dramatic Aesthetic

Dryden's essay never returns to the comparison between the emergent arts and science raised early on by the Quarrel of the Ancients and the Moderns. Forty years later, however, Joseph Addison used faculty psychology to bring the arts and the sciences into a common framework that defined their relationship to each other according to their respective proximity to and distance from the realm of the senses. For reasons of space I'll focus my attention on Addison's framework, which provides a general model for the way some of the most eminent minds of the following decades undertook the question that had been raised by the Quarrel: What is the epistemological status of the arts in comparison with that of the sciences? By the end of the eighteenth century, the challenge had been met and the modern view of the arts as a distinctively "aesthetic" way of knowing had been established.[13]

In Addison's usage, the degree and kind of pleasure afforded by a mental faculty is an index of the knowledge it provides. "The Pleasures of the Imagination," he writes, "taken in their full Extent, are not so gross as those of Sense, nor so refined as those of the Understanding." That is, the imagination mediates between the senses and the understanding, and its character can be assessed by its relation to them. With respect to the senses, a "Man of a Polite Imagination . . . often feels a greater Satisfaction in the Prospect of Fields and Meadows, than another does in the Possession. . . . A Man should make" the imagination "the Sphere of his innocent Pleasures" and find there "such a Satisfaction as a wise Man would not blush to take." Indeed, a "Beautiful Prospect delights the Soul, as much as a Demonstration [by the understanding]." With respect to the understanding, nonetheless, the more fully refined and abstracted pleasures of the understanding are "more preferable" than those of the imagination "because they are founded on some new Knowledge or Improvement in the Mind of Man," words that recall the norms of demonstrable truth and incremental progress emphasized by Bacon and his followers. Still, for these very reasons, the pleasures of the imagination, because they're more embedded in the realm of the senses, are less distant, "more obvious, and more easie to be acquired" than those of the understanding, and "do not require such a Bent of Thought as is necessary to our more serious Employments," which demand "too violent a Labour of the Brain."[14] Addison may expect that these comparisons and contrasts of the two mental faculties will be confirmed by what we readers know of their respective products. The understanding achieves a great distance from, and a great refinement of, the senses, and this gives a sensible opacity to its products, which are concepts, symbols, and numbers. The products of the imagination, because they are less distanced and refined than these, are more accessible and more legible because they take the representational form of images or imaginative enactments.

What follows in Addison's analysis of the pleasures of the imagination has a striking coherence. He has established that the ultimate superiority of the understanding to the imagination as a mode of knowledge is correlated with its distance from the senses, which is reflected in the extreme abstraction of its products from what is legible by, or intelligible to, the senses. Addison now proceeds to use that same basic principle of comparative distance and abstraction to distinguish between the relative degrees of pleasure achieved by the several pathways of the imagination that are available to us. First, he distinguishes between the "Primary" pleasures of the imagination, which proceed from objects that are actually present to us, and the "Secondary" pleasures, which proceed from the ideas of objects that are not present but represented to us by the several different media of representation. Presence entails less distance and abstraction from the senses than does representation. So, on analogy with the previous operation, the primary pleasures of the imagination are to the secondary pleasures as the imagination itself is to the understanding. Nonetheless, the primary pleasures play a crucial role in producing pleasure greater than their own because the "Secondary Pleasure of the Imagination proceeds from that Action of the Mind, which compares the Ideas arising from the Original [i.e., present] Objects, with the ideas we receive from the Statue, Picture, [verbal] Description, or Sound that represents them." Emphasizing the significance of the pleasure entailed in this act of comparison, Addison conjectures on why this should be in terms that suggest he has in mind the experimental model: "The distinguishing one thing from another, and the right discerning betwixt our Ideas, depends wholly upon our comparing them together, and observing the Congruity or Disagreement that appears among the several Works of Nature."[15]

Addison now uses the same criteria of distance and abstraction to assess the pleasure derived from each of the representational media (except for sound or music, which seem to him problematic as representations of ideas). "*Statuary* . . . shews us something *likest* the Object that is represented" (*Spectator* 1712). Painting lacks the third dimension but at least "bears a real Resemblance to its Original" (*Spectator* 1712). But "*Description* runs yet further from the thing it represents than Painting," and for this reason produces greater pleasure than the other media when mentally juxtaposed to the object (*Spectator* 1712). This is so far true that when Addison addresses the question of how pity and fear are raised by tragedy, he explicitly and consistently speaks of reading rather than watching drama because the literate experience is yet more distanced from the sensible object than is the experience of its performance.

The New Principle of Pleasure

The pleasures of imaginative reading are thus three times "refined" or abstracted: the imagination from sight, the representational from the visual imagination, and literate description from the other media of representation. Stimulating the imagination through reading therefore comes closer to attaining the understanding's distance from the senses than do the other media of representation. But the pleasures of the imagination also involve an element that is absent from the pleasures of the understanding. This is the pleasure afforded by comparing the image of the object produced by the senses and the image of the object produced through the distance of representation. A self-conscious reflexivity, this is, again, "a new Principle of Pleasure, which is nothing else but the Action of the Mind, which *compares* the Ideas that arise from Words, with the Ideas that arise from the Objects themselves."[16] Addison's "new principle" grows out of the peculiarly literate and presumably printed mode of representation whose relative detachment offers an opportunity to advance from a singular view of the world produced by the ideas of it that derive from our sense perceptions, to the ideas of it that derive from the virtuality of descriptive language, and to a comparative view of their simultaneity. This new principle exemplifies the cognitive process that is most fundamental to the Enlightenment turn from tacit to explicit knowledge, a process we've seen in other cases but scarcely with such clarity. Aesthetic knowledge and pleasure are a function of the distance of our virtual perspective from our actual sense perceptions, and it entails their explicitly reflexive comparison. The products of the understanding, because they are far more distant from the senses than the products of the imagination, lack the resemblance required for this comparability; but of course they provide their own technological knowledge and pleasure.

Addison's analysis allows him to restate Neander's defense of drama in a more positive register. Not only is a close approximation to actual time and place unneeded to maintain the belief of the dramatic spectator, it's detrimental to the kind of knowledge that's appropriate to drama. Immediate sense experience is as likely as not to lead to passions corrupted by "Vice," "Folly," and the "Criminal," but the emotions that are raised by the imagination are very different from the passions that are embedded in immediately sensible experience.[17] The imaginative mediation of sense experience possesses its own system of refinement that filters out the brute materiality of the senses and purifies their emotional heft. Like Dryden, Addison demonstrates this with the example of drama; and like the understanding, the dramatic imagination refines experience by controlling for time and place.

Dryden had used the so-called Aristotelian unities to pose the question of dramatic credibility: How can we believe in what we see when we know it is not actual but virtual or representational? In order to pose the same question, Addison turns to the Aristotelian locus classicus: If pity and fear are the emotions proper to tragedy, he asks, why is it that "such Passions as are very unpleasant at all other times, are very agreeable when excited by proper Descriptions" (*Poetics*, 1448b)? His answer is that dramatic representation provides us with both a physical and a psychological distance from the temporal and spatial actuality that prevails in more immediate sense experience:

> When we look on such hideous Objects, we are not a little pleased to think we are in no Danger of them. We consider them at the same time, as Dreadful and Harmless; so that the more frightful Appearance they make, the greater is the Pleasure we receive from the Sense of our own Safety.... It is for the same Reason that we are delighted with the reflecting upon Dangers that are past, or in looking on a Precipice at a distance, which would fill us with a different kind of Horror, if we saw it hanging over our Heads.... This is, however, such a kind of Pleasure as we are not capable of receiving, when we see a Person actually lying under the Tortures that we meet with in a Description; because, in this Case, the Object presses too close upon our Senses, and bears so hard upon us, that it does not give us time or leisure to reflect on our selves.[18]

Natural philosophy controls for time and place through the technology of the laboratory and experimental repetition, and it thereby generalizes from the sensible experience of nature to its universal character. The experience of drama—and especially of drama that is read—controls for time (like "reflecting upon Dangers that are past") and place (like "looking on a Precipice at a distance") through the multiple techniques of representation, refining the passions of brute experience into emotions that are universally pleasurable. The distance the understanding takes on the world enables a belief that is justified because it is grounded in empirical knowledge. The lesser distance taken by the imagination on staged or read events enables the mixed sort of belief that is peculiar to reflexivity, a state of mind that is both earnest and reserved, one that allows us to consider "hideous Objects" as both "Dreadful and Harmless."

By juxtaposing the imagination and the understanding, Addison goes far toward meeting the challenge to the arts posed by the Quarrel of the Ancients and the Moderns and its incipient separation out of the arts and the sciences. The challenge is met by theorizing the imagination as an aesthetic and therefore an empirical faculty, based in sense experience but abstracted from it in a fashion and to a degree different from the abstraction peculiar to the understanding. The modern aesthetic was also the answer to Aristotle's question. The imagination's relative proximity to the senses gives it a representational force that the understanding lacks. It disembeds and refines the evidence of the senses less fully than does the understanding, producing not concepts or numbers but virtual images of sensible actuality, whose connection to the normal experience of nature remains mimetically recognizable to the senses. The result is the pleasure of reflexivity. The pleasures of the understanding are experienced at the end of the refinement process, when virtual knowledge of the natural constant, isolated in its instrumental integrity, can be used to intervene within, and to exploit, the operations of nature itself. However, the pleasures of the imagination are experienced in tandem with the refinement process, and they consist in the reflexive comparison between the immediately sensible presence of nature and its mediated, semi-abstracted re-presentation. The aesthetic imagination is a double consciousness. It overwrites actuality with virtuality, action with enactment, identity with identification, combining in one experience two seemingly incompatible points of view whose conflation depends on their prior separation. In Coleridge's famous phrase, the aesthetic entails "that willing suspension of disbelief for the moment, which constitutes poetic faith."[19] Because its suspension has been consciously willed, notional belief coexists with disbelief, an imaginative and aesthetic coexistence of (to cite Addison's example) the dreadful and the harmless. And in contrast to the common French theorization of the aesthetic, the British aesthetic depends not on the technological illusions of theatrical production but on the powers of the imagination.[20]

Early in his career (as we saw), Fontenelle captured well the emergent difference between the arts and the sciences. Years later, and on the theory of the aesthetic, Fontenelle showed himself to be an uncommon Frenchman:

> It is certain, that, in the theatre, the representation has almost the effect of reality; yet it has not altogether that effect. However we may be hurried away by the spectacle; whatever dominion the senses and imagination may usurp over the reason, there still lurks at the bottom a certain idea of falsehood in the whole of what we see. This idea, though weak and disguised, suffices to diminish the pain which we suffer from the misfortunes of those whom we love, and to reduce that affliction to such a pitch as converts it into a pleasure. We weep for the misfortune of a hero, to whom we are attached. In the same instant we comfort ourselves, by reflecting, that it is nothing but a fiction: And it is precisely that mixture of sentiments, which composes an agreeable sorrow, and tears that delight us.[21]

Fontenelle's speculation accords well with Addison's, although it lacks the framework of faculty psychology that gives Addison's account of aesthetic affect its explanatory resonance. When we try to imagine objects that have a real existence but are too distant from our sensible experience to afford access, Addison writes, we have only limited success because we venture into territory that is properly that of the understanding. There are no writers "who more gratifie and enlarge the Imagination, than the Authors of the new Philosophy, whether we consider their Theories of the Earth or Heavens, the Discoveries they have made by Glasses, or any other of their Contemplations on Nature." And yet such imaginative "Speculation" on the plurality of worlds, although "founded on no less than the Evidence of a Demonstration," meets its limit where the dimensions of time and space expand or contract beyond the empirical. "The Understanding, indeed, opens up an infinite Space on every side of us, but the Imagination, after a few faint Efforts, is immediately at a stand. . . . Our Reason can pursue a Particle of Matter through an infinite variety of Divisions, but the Fancy soon loses sight of it."[22] This is to say that the operations of the imagination are analogous to, but less powerful than, those of the understanding. In coming decades, the category "the sublime" will be elaborated to account more precisely for this kind of speculation at the limits or threshold (*sub-limine*) of the imagination, and with such success that by the end of the century the epistemology of the sublime will have come to stand, loosely but effectually, for that of the imagination as such. In the process, the crucial connection of the imagination to sensible experience, "not too far removed beyond the reach of our Senses," will have been largely forgotten, and the emergent epistemology of the aesthetic will have lost its constitutive equilibrium between immanence and transcendence. This imbalance is not yet evident in the work of the most important English formulator of the theory of the sublime, Edmund Burke.

We are so accustomed to reading Burke's influential early treatise through the lens of post-romantic theories of sublime infinitude and inexpressibility that we are in some danger of ignoring the nature of the debate into which it entered. This was to a great extent Addison's debate. Burke begins the *Philosophical Enquiry* (1757) with the empirical and experimentalist aim to perform "a diligent examination of our passions in our own breasts" and with a skepticism learned from Locke and Hume: "He [Burke] found that he could not reduce his notions to any fixed or consistent principles; and he had remarked, that others lay under the same difficulties." Nonetheless, from the passions he will move to the body that excites those passions, thence to the properties of objects that influence the body, and finally to the laws of nature that determine this influence.[23] Insisting that "Longinus's" categories of the sublime and the beautiful must be separated out from one another, Burke finds that this separation also discloses their basic similarity, if not their conflation. This similarity consists in the fact that both are relative passions that arise not in the immediate presence of bodily sensation but at a certain temporal and spatial remove from it. Thus, our feeling for the beautiful arises as the passion of love for an object rather than as the passion of sensual lust, but of love mixed "with an idea at the same time of having irretrievably lost" that object (pt. 1, sec. 18, 51). This temporal distance from the loved object is also a spatial detachment from it similar to the relatively disinterested pleasure that Addison finds in the "prospect" rather than the "possession" of a landscape. Thus Burke distinguishes love as "that satisfaction that arises to the mind upon contemplating any thing beautiful, of whatsoever nature it may be, from desire or lust; which is an energy of the mind, that hurries us on to the possession of certain objects, that do not affect us as they are beautiful, but by means altogether different" (pt. 3, sec. 1, 91).

As with the beautiful, so, more famously, with the sublime. In terms of the temporal dimension, the passion of the sublime becomes available to us in a relationship with painful sensation, but only in the "ceasing or diminution," the "removal or moderation" of pain, as the present moment is increasingly distanced from a painful past (pt. 1, sec. 4, 35). To describe the spatial register of the sublime in general terms, Burke echoes Addison: "When danger or pain press too nearly [elsewhere "too close"], they are incapable of giving any delight, and are simply terrible; but at certain distances, and with certain modifications, they may be, and they are delightful" (pt. 1, sec. 8, 14, 40, 46). Burke also has recourse to the Aristotelian example of the terror produced by the dramatic experience of tragedy, although for him the distance necessary for the delight of the sublime to be felt is minimal compared with Addison's analysis:

> I am convinced we have a degree of delight, and that no small one, in the real misfortunes and pains of others; . . . [and] I imagine we shall be much mistaken if we attribute any considerable part of our satisfaction in tragedy to a consideration that tragedy is a deceit, and its representations no realities. The nearer it approaches the reality, and the further it removes us from all ideas of fiction, the more perfect is its power. But be its power of what kind it will, it never approaches to what it represents. Chuse a day on which to represent the most sublime and affecting tragedy we have; . . . let it be reported that a state criminal of high rank is on the point of being executed in the adjoining square; in a moment the emptiness of the theatre would demonstrate the comparative weakness of the imitative arts. (pt. 1, sec. 14, 15, 45, 47)

In other words, the only sort of sensible experience that precludes the delight of sublimity is that which directly impinges on one's own body, making one not a spectator at all but a suffering agent.

I will continue this brief survey of texts, in which the prototypical argument of aesthetic detachment from the senses emerges in the debate over the pseudo-Aristotelian unities, with Samuel Johnson, whose repudiation of "the rules" in his "Preface" to *The Plays of William Shakespeare* (1765) is perhaps its most celebrated instance:

> The necessity of observing the unities of time and place arises from the supposed necessity of making the drama credible. . . . [But] it is false, that any representation is mistaken for reality; that any dramatic fable in its materiality was ever credible, or, for a single moment, was ever credited. . . . Delusion, if delusion be admitted, has no certain limitation. . . . The truth is, that the spectators are always in their senses, and know, from the first act to the last, that the stage is only a stage, and that the players are only players. . . . It will be asked, how the drama moves, if it is not credited. It is credited with all the credit due to a drama. It is credited, whenever it moves, as a just picture of a real original. . . . If there be any fallacy, it is not that we fancy the players, but that we fancy ourselves unhappy for a moment. . . . The delight of tragedy proceeds from our consciousness of fiction; if we thought murders and treasons real, they would please no more. Imitations produce pain or pleasure, not because they are mistaken for realities, but because they bring realities to mind.[24]

Johnson's commonsense critique does not do justice, perhaps, to the reflexive or doubled state of mind that other commentators have emphasized. To affirm that the spectators are "always in their senses" lacks the necessary precision if the real question is the degree to which they are in their senses. But Johnson shows his customary acuity by extending the empirical criterion from the by-now-familiar question of aesthetic response to the difficult problem of aesthetic judgment, and he does this by invoking and turning to his own ends the division between the arts and the sciences.

The Judgment of Aesthetic Value

A subcategory of empirical knowledge, the aesthetic refines sense experience in a way that is operationally analogous to, but substantively different from, the work of scientific experiment. In scientific experiment, refinement is a product not only of the laboratory arts of instrumentation but also of multiple repetitions, under varying circumstances, of the laboratory experiment itself. In what might be called "aesthetic experiment," however, the representational arts are sufficient in themselves to winnow out the contingencies of merely sensible experience so as to leave the more essential elements to which we respond with aesthetic pleasure. To put this another way, the efficacy of scientific experiment requires a multiplicity of "witnesses"; the efficacy of aesthetic experiment can be registered within a single person. Can we generalize from a body of aesthetic experiments so as to demonstrate the abstract uniformity of aesthetic pleasure not only for any given person but also across a number of different people? Is this where the analogy between aesthetic and scientific experiment ceases to be instructive—that is, at the border that separates one from many instances, quality from quantity?

The search for a uniform measure of aesthetic judgment tempted and defeated a multitude of commentators over the course of the eighteenth century. If no one found exactly what was being sought, Johnson approached the problem in a distinctive fashion by explicitly attempting to apply the experimental method of controlling for variables. Hume's essay "Of the Standard of Taste" (1757) anticipates Johnson in its brief remarks on "the durable admiration, which attends those works, that have survived all the caprices of mode and fashion, all the mistakes of ignorance and envy. The same HOMER, who pleased at ATHENS and ROME two thousand years ago, is still admired at PARIS and LONDON. All the changes of climate, government, religion, and language, have not been able to obscure his glory. Authority or prejudice may give a temporary vogue to a bad poet or orator; but his reputation will never be durable or general."[25] As we might expect, Hume's discussion is broadly informed by the speculative comparison of evaluative standards in "science" and "sentiment." Johnson's "Preface" to *The Plays of William Shakespeare*, from which I have already quoted, begins with the Quarrel of the Ancients and the Moderns and moves quickly to the same comparison between science and the arts.

"To works," Johnson writes, "of which the excellence is not absolute and definite, but gradual and comparative; to works not raised upon principles demonstrative and scientifick, but appealing wholly to observation and experience, no other test can be applied than length of duration and continuance of esteem. What mankind have long possessed they have often examined and compared, and if they persist to value the possession, it is because frequent comparisons have confirmed opinion in its favour." Johnson seeks what might be called the closest equivalent, for works of art, to the standard of judgment available for works of science, and he discovers it in the quantifiability of which both empirical and aesthetic experience is susceptible. But the comparison of qualitatively different objects cannot in itself yield a standard of aesthetic value because differences in quality are by definition incomparable. What is needed is a mechanism of quantification, a standard by which qualitatively different works can be rendered comparable, and Johnson finds this standard in the test of time. Shakespeare "has long outlived his century, the term commonly fixed as the test of literary merit [see Horace, *Epistles*, II, i, 39]. Whatever advantages he might once derive from personal allusions, local customs, or temporary opinions, have for many years been lost.... The effects of favour and competition are at an end; the tradition of his friendships and his enmities has perished; his works support no opinion with arguments, nor supply any faction with invectives; they can neither indulge vanity nor gratify malignity, but are read without any other reason than the desire of pleasure, and are therefore praised only as pleasure is obtained" (59–61).

As Hooke's experimentalism abstracts the constants of nature from the variables of mind, persons, time, place, instruments, and materials, so Johnson's test of time abstracts the constants of pleasure from the variables of personal allusions, local customs, temporary opinions, favor, competition, friendship, enmity, vanity, and malignity. In Johnson's analysis, the test of time enables judgments of aesthetic value because it entails a generalizing abstraction from the variables that constituted the experiential context in which Shakespeare's plays were first written, viewed, and read. The test of time is like a scientific experiment that controls for variables and isolates what is constant—abstract pleasure—not by means of a laboratory apparatus but by a temporal version of experimental repetition, the winnowing effect of the winds of time. It accommodates the quantitative standards of scientific experiment to literary judgment. Two points are worth making. First, Enlightenment empiricists themselves advocated a method comparable to Johnson's that used reading to extend the authority of the actual experiment to virtual conditions. Contemporaries spoke of "thought experiments"; historians of science have used the term "virtual witnessing."[26] Second, Johnson's test of time extends to the diachronic dimension the principle of distance or abstraction from the senses that he, with Addison, Burke, and others, describes as the synchronic achievement of the imagination. And in this sense, the history of art, like the history of science, might be said to possess an intrinsic developmental mechanism by which quantitative and qualitative standards of value are commensurable.

Johnson concludes these introductory reflections with the famous statement that in the present context reminds us that the means by which the positive judgment of Shakespeare's aesthetic value is made are the same as those by which his plays make their aesthetic claim on our imaginations: "Nothing can please many, and please long, but just representations of general nature" (61). Lest this pronouncement seem (as it too often has) to celebrate transcendence of particularity alone as the aesthetic norm, Johnson soon after complements it with the praise that "the dialogue of this authour is often so evidently determined by the incident which produces it, and is pursued with so much ease and simplicity, that it seems scarcely to claim the merit of fiction, but to have been gleaned by diligent selection out of common conversation, and common occurrences" (63). Like the inductive method, the aesthetic method entails a dialectical reciprocity between the particular and the general according to which neither can prevail in the absence of the other. By the same token, Johnson's famous principle of "general nature" isn't an a priori dogma (as it too often has been taken to be) but the experimental outcome of an ongoing observation of particulars

The eighteenth-century theorization of the aesthetic is continuous with and laid the ground for William Wordsworth's defining act of romantic poetic theory. *Lyrical Ballads* (1800, 1802) was published, he writes, "as an experiment, which, I hoped, might be of some use to ascertain, how far, by fitting to metrical arrangement a selection of the real language of men in a state of vivid sensation, that sort of pleasure and that quantity of pleasure may be imparted, which a Poet may rationally endeavour to impart." For "all men feel an habitual gratitude . . . for the objects which have long continued to please them: we not only wish to be pleased, but to be pleased in that particular way in which we have been accustomed to be pleased." Like Johnson, Wordsworth writes with the conviction that literature and science have a shared project and purpose. The poet "converses with general nature with affections akin to those, which, through labour and length of time, the Man of Science has raised up in himself, by conversing with those particular parts of nature which are the objects of his studies."

Lyrical Ballads is an "experiment" whose aim is to produce "pleasure" as a determinate entity known as to quality but also as to "quantity" by the criterion of its duration. Like Addison, Wordsworth affirms that the "knowledge both of the Poet and the Man of science is pleasure," and like Addison he begins his poetic experiment at the empirical level of sense impressions: "I have wished to keep the Reader in the company of flesh and blood . . . [and] I have at all times endeavoured to look steadily at my subject." Wordsworth has chosen as his subject "incidents and situations from common life" represented "in a selection of language really used by men" in "humble [the 1800 edition reads 'Low'] and rustic life." This is to speak of low, sensible things, "because, in that condition, the essential passions of the heart find a better soil," and "the manners of rural life germinate from those elementary feelings." Moreover, the life of rural commoners is likely to afford a common language "because, from their rank in society and the sameness and narrow circle of their intercourse, being less under the influence of social vanity, they convey their feelings and notions in simple and unelaborated expressions."[27]

Wordsworth describes the emergent capacity of aesthetic detachment in terms that are familiar to us from his predecessors; and if he risks being accused of a "triviality and meanness, both of thought and language," he also believes in the abstract universality of this language, which, "arising out of repeated experience and regular feelings, is a more permanent, and a far more philosophical language, than that which is frequently substituted for it by Poets." In other words, Wordsworth's poetry has the character of experimentalism. It generalizes from the evidence of actual use by a multitude of particular people whose language is itself a virtual generalization—and therefore "more philosophical"—from repeated experiences.[28]

Wordsworth is concerned to ensure aesthetic distance as a feature not only of the represented object but also of the reader's affective response and the poet's state of mind. If the poet describes common incidents in "a selection of language really used by men," he must also "throw over them a certain colouring of imagination." Hooke describes an experimental perspective "not too far removed beyond the reach of our Senses," and according to Aristotle, this removal, achieved through the imaginative coloring of imitation, is the key to poetic pleasure. By the same token, Wordsworth's poet must have pursued a principle for selecting his language on which he can "depend for removing what would otherwise be painful or disgusting" and which "will entirely separate the composition from the vulgarity and meanness of ordinary life." Wordsworth's account of the mentality required of the poet recalls the words of his friend Samuel Coleridge—"the willing suspension of disbelief for the moment, which constitutes poetic faith"—that we usually associate with the mentality of the reader. The poet must have the "ability of conjuring up in himself passions which are indeed far from being the same as those produced by real events, yet . . . do more nearly resemble the passions produced by real events, than anything which, from the motions of their own minds merely, other men are accustomed to feel in themselves." Indeed, "it will be the wish of the Poet to bring his feelings near to those of the persons whose feelings he describes, nay, for short spaces of time, perhaps, to let himself slip into an entire delusion, and even confound and identify his own feelings with theirs." This is not the delusion of immediate identity and presence naively sought by the doctrine of the two unities. Rather, it's a detachment of the sort described by Addison and Burke, a self-consciously virtual re-presentation, a spatial and temporal extension—"near to," "for short spaces of time"—from the dimension of the actual. For poetry "takes its origin from emotion recollected in tranquillity: the emotion is contemplated till, by a species of reaction, the tranquillity gradually disappears, and an emotion, kindred to that which was before the subject of contemplation, is gradually produced, and does itself actually exist in the mind."

In fact, Wordsworth's famous defense of verse and meter is similarly couched in terms of the detachment they allow readers from too immediate an experience of the real (in Addison's words, when "the Object presses too close upon our Senses"), and it reminds us of Dryden's defense of rhyme on the same grounds. Distance, so far from impairing aesthetic response, is essential to its pleasure. For "from the tendency of metre to divest language, in a certain degree, of its reality, . . .

there can be little doubt but that more pathetic situations and sentiments, that is, those which have a greater proportion of pain connected with them, may be endured in metrical composition, especially in rhyme, than in prose" (I, 123, 137, 138, 138–139, 145, 147, 149).

The Aesthetic Imagination and the Origins of the Social Sciences

My principal aim in this chapter has been to provide evidence for the thesis that the idea of the aesthetic emerged in often explicit emulation of the emergent idea of scientific method. An argument of influence would seem to imply an inequality of maturity and coherence between two bodies of thought; but I want to propose an approximate coemergence that gives form to the same pre-existing concept. My proposal invites a more particular—one might say experimental— investigation of the empirical grounds on which its generalization is based and by which it may in turn be further refined.[29] On this basis I'll add that in the later decades of the eighteenth century, the aesthetic attitude had become familiar and persuasive enough to offer, in turn, a model for the emergence of modes of knowledge whose object, like that of the aesthetic, was not natural but cultural or social. The first book of Hume's *Treatise of Human Nature* (1739) is a remarkable but singular instance of this proto-disciplinary relationship in that its analysis of what Hume variously calls "moral philosophy" and "the science of man" and we might call "epistemology" begins with the experimentalist paradigm of natural philosophy but concludes by absorbing that paradigm itself within the aesthetic paradigm of the reflexive imagination.[30] More commonly the aesthetic model is turned to account for emergent bodies of thought other than moral philosophy without also subsuming natural philosophy itself under the aegis of the aesthetic. The following remarks about political theory, and in modern parlance "social psychology," aim to be no more than suggestive.

It may be the self-conscious experimentalism of his *Philosophical Enquiry* that leads Burke to draw the line between broadly empirical and aesthetic experience so close to the realm of the sensible. Whatever the case, the result is that the production of aesthetic response in Burke requires less imaginative detachment from sensible experience than it does in Addison: the time and place of the public execution are actual in a way that the virtuality of theatrical representation by definition precludes. Over thirty years later and in his most celebrated piece of writing, *Reflections on the Revolution in France* (1790), Burke took a crucial next step: empirical knowledge and aesthetic knowledge are not just related but overlapping. The actuality of public execution, and of political rule itself, owes its authority and efficacy to the distancing and refining powers of the imagination. And in the shadow of the Revolution, the quantifications of "sophisters, economists, and calculators" are not the solution to the problem of representation but the problem itself. The fall of the French monarchy is a "real tragedy" because, as we behold it, "our minds . . . are purified by terror and pity." But it also forces us to see that the theatrical pleasure of catharsis that's aroused by such a fall is only a heightened instance of the aesthetic pleasure we take in the institution of monarchal rule itself. By demystifying monarchy, the French Revolution has destroyed our ability—what Coleridge would soon call "that willing suspension of disbelief"—to experience political life as something more than a brutal struggle for power in a Hobbesian state of nature, the unrelieved realm of the senses:

> All the pleasing illusions which made power gentle and obedience liberal, which harmonized the different shades of life, and which, by a bland assimilation, incorporated into politics the sentiments which beautify and soften private society, are to be dissolved by this new conquering empire of light and reason. All the decent drapery of life is to be rudely torn off. All the superadded ideas furnished from the wardrobe of a moral imagination, which the heart owns and the understanding ratifies as necessary to cover the defects of our naked shivering nature, and to raise it to dignity in our own estimation, are to be exploded as a ridiculous, absurd, and antiquated fashion. . . . To make us love our country, our country ought to be lovely.[31]

The abstraction "aristocracy" is preferable to the "metaphysical" doctrine of "the rights of men" because our historical detachment from it ensures our epistemological detachment from it, which in turn paradoxically ensures our belief in aristocracy. This is not the sort of belief that is, like the rights of man, invested in a priori essences, but an imaginative and aesthetic belief that arises, like our judgment of Shakespeare, from the historical experience of duration. "Instead of casting away all our old prejudices, we cherish them to a considerable degree . . . because they are prejudices; and the longer they have lasted and the more generally they have prevailed, the more we cherish them" (69, 98–99). And so we cherish monarchy not because of its essential value but because it gives us pleasure to do so, and in our affective response to it lies the ground of its social utility: not the immediate coherence of sociocultural embeddedness but the mediated pleasure of self-conscious reenactment. Burke's skepticism lies at the heart of the modern strain of conservative political philosophy that developed toward the end of the eighteenth century. William Godwin, as skeptical as Burke about the political justice of representative democracy, nonetheless has a few good words to say about it in rejecting Burke's plea for "salutary prejudices," which he identifies, in pre-Coleridgean terms, as aesthetic in their appeal: "But at the same time that he tells us, we should cherish the mistake as mistake, and the prejudice as prejudice, he is himself lifting the veil, and destroying his own system. . . . The moment they begin to write books, to persuade us that we ought to be willing to be deceived, it may well be suspected that their system is on the decline."[32]

Burke was not the only writer to exploit his own early argument that aesthetic experience might be had in the absence of conventionally artistic activities like watching plays and reading novels. Two years after the *Philosophical Enquiry* appeared, Adam Smith published his *Theory of Moral Sentiments* (1759), in which Burke's insights were extended to the proposition that all sociable experience is aesthetic experience. In the process of making this argument, Smith clarified the difference between sense impressions that have a purely physical presence and those that undergo refinement through imaginative representation. He writes,

> Passions which take their origin from the body excite either no sympathy at all, or such a degree of it, as is altogether disproportioned to the violence of what is felt by the sufferer. It is quite otherwise with those passions which take their origin from the imagination. . . . The person who has lost his whole fortune, if he is in health, feels nothing in his body. What he suffers is from the imagination only, . . . and we sympathize with him more strongly upon this account, because our imaginations can more readily mould themselves upon his imagination, than our bodies can mould themselves upon his body.

Smith's most common touchstone for communicating the workings of sympathy is the affect of spectators at a tragic performance: "In some of the Greek tragedies there is an attempt to excite compassion, by the representation of the agonies of bodily pain. . . . In all these cases, however, it is not the pain which interests us, but some other circumstances." The distance of tragic spectators from those they view in the virtuality of dramatic representation is crucial to their feelings about them; and for the Humean Smith this is more than a simple analogy for the way we feel in the actual presence of people: "As we have no immediate experience of what other men feel," he writes, "we can form no idea of the manner in which they are affected, but by conceiving what we ourselves should feel in the like situation. Though our brother is upon the rack, as long as we ourselves are at our ease, our senses will never inform us of what he suffers. They never did, and never can, carry us beyond our own person, and it is by the imagination only that we can form any conception of what are his sensations." For this reason Smith favors a theatrical vocabulary according to which we are all either "spectators" of the passions of others or what I have called "suffering agents" and he calls "persons principally concerned."[33]

In the theory of moral sentiments, imagination is the means by which we simultaneously distance ourselves from our own sense impressions and decrease the distance between our own and others' sense impressions. Empirical knowledge presupposes a detachment of the knowing subject from the object of knowledge. The function of imaginative sympathy is, by acknowledging and exploiting it, to defeat this detachment through a willing suspension of disbelief. The virtual reality of "society" itself is produced by imaginative acts of sympathy, which refine the actual particularity of others into the virtual particularity of others-as-ourselves, who thereby become susceptible to collective generalization. As when we are moved by seeing or reading a play, so when we encounter other people, we experience a revival of the social coherence and solidarity of traditional cultures, but at the level of imaginative identification, not of physical presence. And equally, as when we are moved by seeing or reading a play, so when we encounter other people, we are like the "virtual witnesses" to a scientific experiment who confirm its probability without actually being present at the event.[34] At this fundamental level, sympathy is therefore an inescapable faculty of "man" the social animal. It entails the reciprocal efforts of the spectator and the person principally concerned to modulate their emotions—respectively, to raise and to "lower" the "violence" of their pitch—so as to approach each other, "for the harmony of society," halfway. But the reciprocity of sympathetic identification makes us all by turns both spectators and persons principally concerned, and Smith's treatise is a theory of not only social but also psychological harmony because it posits that all ethical subjects internalize this social dialectic by suspending their disbelief in order to look upon themselves as simultaneously spectator and person principally concerned. We know ourselves only as we sympathetically internalize the social other. Addressing the problem Hume raised regarding the special sort of thought experiment that involves experimenting in one's own thoughts, Smith writes that "we can never survey our own sentiments and motives, we can never form any judgments concerning them; unless we remove ourselves, as it were, from our own natural station, and endeavour to view them as at a certain distance from us." Imagine a man raised in the absence of all society. "Bring him into society, and he is immediately provided with the mirror which he wanted before. It is placed in the countenance and behaviour of those he lives with" (22, 83, 110).

In this way Smith suggests that the aesthetic attitude is the basis not only for that species of identification we experience when we view plays and read novels, but also for social and psychological knowledge. And in this extension, the mediatory function of the imagination, which in aesthetic theory operates between the senses and the understanding, has a different valence. As an analytic category, Smith's imagination has been detached from its strict function in faculty psychology and become a free-floating principle of sympathy that names, both in society and in psychology, that image-making power that accommodates to each other high and low, outside and inside in all dimensions of human life. In other words, although Smith's dominant concern in the *Theory* is with social interaction, methodologically speaking he begins with individual psychology and its aesthetic powers of imagination, which provides a template for developing a theory of social sympathy. Consequently, he feels free to leave the categories of sense and understanding relatively undifferentiated from each other because their importance to him is not as putatively separate faculties but as they model manifestly separate selves.

In the modern world, aesthetic value is commonly understood to be antithetical to the quantifying standard not only of empirical materialism but specifically of commodity exchange on the market. The preceding argument suggests that aesthetic value and exchange value, both inspired by the power and success of empirical epistemology, instead may be versions of each other. Although Smith's *The Wealth of Nations* (1776) does not exploit aesthetic epistemology in the mode of *The Theory of Moral Sentiments*, a brief consideration of its method will suggest some of its broader ties both to that mode of knowledge and to that earlier work. "Every faculty in one man," Smith writes in *The Theory of Moral Sentiments*, "is the measure by which he judges of the like faculty in another." As the spectators "are constantly considering what they themselves would feel, if they actually were the sufferers, so [the person principally concerned] is constantly led to imagine in what manner he would be affected if he was only one of the spectators of his own situation. As their sympathy makes them look at it, in some measure, with his eyes, so his sympathy makes him look at it, in some measure, with theirs" (19, 22). The equivalent of sympathy in the economic system—that is, the mechanism of "measure" that renders qualitative difference into quantitative comparability—is the capacity of the market to turn objects of consumption and use into objects of circulation and exchange, or commodities. The "real measure" of exchange value, "the real price of all commodities," is the "quantity of labour we exchange for what is supposed at the time to contain the value of an equal quantity.... But though labour be the real measure of the exchangeable value of all commodities, it is not that by which their value is commonly estimated," a result that is achieved "not by any accurate measure, but by the higgling and bargaining of the market, according to that sort of rough equality which, though not exact, is sufficient for carrying on the business of common life."[35]

Unlike Johnson's test of time, commodity exchange works in a basically synchronic rather than a diachronic dimension; but like the test of time, it deracinates the object or experience from its particular and local uses so as to isolate it in the purity of its sharability: in the case of the commodity, its monetary value; in the case of the art work, its abstract pleasure. The idea of sharability is of course also central to *The Theory of Moral Sentiments*. In Smith's social psychology, the mediating capacity of sympathy to overcome emotional difference is analogous to the capacity of the market, in Smith's political economy, to overcome material differences between articles of consumption. True, "the imagination," the term Smith uses to name the mechanism that actualizes sharability in social psychology, plays no such role in his political economy. Like his contemporaries, however, Smith recognized the notional quality of the concept of "the market" as over the course of two centuries it had come to denote not only the actual marketplace but also the virtual realm of economic exchange, a recognition that can be seen in the most famous, quasi-secularizing claim of his most famous treatise: "Every individual is continually exerting himself to find out the most advantageous employment for whatever capital he can command.... He intends only his own gain, and he is in this, as in many other cases, led by an invisible hand to promote an end which was no part of his intention" (bk. 4, ch. 2, pp. 454, 456). Theatrical presentation and the market are imaginative places that we willingly suspend our disbelief to enter in order to obtain actual pleasure and profit.[36]

With empirical experimentalism, commodity exchange was one of the great Enlightenment methods of reconciling differences between actual particulars by a virtual and general measure. The conceptual structure of aesthetic response and judgment shares a number of features with these methods. All three reflect the basic innovation of Enlightenment thought: the explicit differentiation and separation of actual particulars, enabling their conflation within a more general virtual category. The Enlightenment innovation required an ongoing dialectic of reciprocity between actual particularity and virtual generality in order to address problems of partiality, inequality, and exclusivity that were endemic to traditional thought. As we've seen, contemporaries were aware of the similarities between these three methods, most commonly, perhaps, insofar as they were becoming conscious of the role played by the imagination, whether or not aesthetic, in the interstices of common life. Defoe and Swift, ideological antagonists in other respects, had similar misgivings about financial credit and nonlanded property as possessing no more than "imaginary" value, which might suggest that the virtuality of value in exchange lost track of and homogenized the actual needs and uses of things once they were exchanged for other things.[37] However, no one made the connection between the market and the aesthetic with the proleptic perspicuity of Alexander Pope. Whereas Burke, Hume, and Smith used the emergent idea of the aesthetic imagination to understand politics, society, and the economy, Pope, working as it were from the other end, made the case that contemporary poetry had become a market phenomenon.

Pope's *Peri Bathous, or of the Art of Sinking in Poetry* (1728) is a parody of "Longinus's" ancient discourse on the sublime, which was in the process of being translated into the modern European languages and was soon to spark enormous enthusiasm for the powers of the imagination as a faculty not of delusion but of transcendence.[38] Pope wasn't enthusiastic, and his brilliantly proleptic parody turns on a simple reversal. Longinus had put forth the notion that the sublime is analogous (anachronistically speaking) to the product of a physical transubstantiation achieved through alchemical sublimation, but one by which immediate sensible experience is distilled in the alembic of the imagination. Pope's speaker puts forth the opposite thesis, that modern poetry is not sublime but bathetic (thus *bathous*) largely owing to the debasing politico-economic materialism of the conditions by which it's produced.[39]

Much of the satire occurs at the linguistic level of unintentionally bathetic tropes and figures of speech drawn equally from poems and plays, but it's grounded in an attack on the modern institutionalization and mechanization of poetic production and consumption that puts quantitative measures at a premium. To those who would excel in bathos, Pope's speaker advises that "his eyes should be like unto the wrong end of a perspective glass [i.e., a telescope], by which all the objects of Nature are lessened." Expanding on the well-known Horatian dictum, Pope remarks that "if the intent of all poetry be to divert and instruct, certainly that kind which diverts and instructs the greatest number, is to be preferred" (50, 45).

Pope's crudely quantifying measure concerns both numbers of consumers and amounts of money. Of "our wiser authors," he writes, "Their true design is profit or gain, in order to acquire which 'tis necessary to procure applause by administering pleasure to the reader" (45–46). And their success is "evident from the universal applause daily given to the admirable entertainments of harlequins and magicians on our stage" (49). Johnson's means of quantifying pleasure in

Shakespeare is the winnowing effect of temporality, "length of duration and continuance of esteem." Pope's is a more opportunistic project in spatial amplification. He proposes the incorporation of the Drury Lane and Lincoln's Inn Fields theaters as one company, the addition of the Royal Academy of Music to serve as the orchestra, and the partnership of these with popular entertainments like prizefighters and rope dancers. The size of the audience for these performances is estimated at over ten thousand spectators, five times the capacity of the current Drury Lane Theater; thus, the unity of place is preserved by a physical expansion of the theater so extreme that all space might be represented there. Yet the entire project could be constructed on the site of Somerset House or (obviating the need for new building) accommodated by Westminster Hall; seating might be provided for both houses of Parliament, the legal courts, and the aldermen of the City of London. The speaker's speculation on the composition of the audience and the projected site of this "spacious building" suggest that here Pope aims at the corruptions of representative government as well as the profitability of contemporary theatrical and literary production. The audience is truly a multitude of particulars, but as a generality its judgment is so debased as to require "a Council of Six," whose office is to give signs indicating when to clap or hiss, and thereby "how far they ought to be pleas'd" (87–89).

Why does Johnson on Shakespeare come to mind? I've argued that Johnson's test of time provides a judgment of Shakespeare's greatness, one that confirms his just representation of general nature, which generalizes on the basis of a multitude of particular responses by spectators and readers. I believe this accords with Johnson's thinking; but Pope's obtrusively instrumental aim to "procure" applause by "administering" pleasure unsettlingly recalls Johnson's assurance that "pleasure is obtained," as though by mechanical extraction. The problem may be that Pope's spatial spectacle makes unavoidable what the test of time overlooks: the market. The "universal applause" for these spectacular entertainments brings too close to the Enlightenment aesthetic the capitalist universality that some critics have seen as the dark underbelly of Enlightenment universality.[40] On the model of experimental method, Dryden and Addison were already conceiving imaginative pleasure as the constant that defined the aesthetic experience and justified it as an empirically oriented mode of knowledge. Was the aesthetic attitude in danger of being subsumed by the market attitude?

Pope's vision may be fueled by the profit motive, but its remarkable prescience anticipates in its detail industrial production as much as capitalist production. The division of labor breaks down the work of making bad art and puts it in the hands of laborers in a collective "Project for the Advancement of the Bathos":

> It is therefore humbly offered that all and every individual of the Bathos do enter into a firm Association and incorporate into one regular body, whereof every member, even the meanest, will some way contribute to the support of the whole, . . . to which end our art ought to be put upon the same foot with other arts of this age. The vast improvement of modern manufactures ariseth

> from their being divided into several branches and parcelled out to several trades. For instance, in clock-making one artist makes the balance, another the spring, another the crown-wheels, a fourth the case, and the principal workman puts all together; To this economy we owe the perfection of our modern watches, and doubtless we also might that of our modern poetry and rhetoric, were the several parts branched out in the like manner. (80)

Poetry and poets are fragmented into separate tropes and specialties and described in a way that evokes both the liberties of the old craft system and shop commercialism: "Now each man applying his whole time and genius upon his particular figure, would doubtless attain to perfection; and when each became incorporated and sworn into the society . . . a poet or orator would have no more to do but to send to the particular traders in each kind." A variation on this mixture of old and new is Pope's fantasy of "a Rhetorical Chest of Drawers, . . . and every drawer shall again be subdivided into cells, resembling those of cabinets for rarities"—but the chest will have the size of a department store (81–82). Or again, "A Receipt to Make an Epic Poem" is offered, "by which any author in the Bathos may be qualified for this grand performance." Directions are given for each ingredient—fable, episode, moral, manners—although for similes and metaphors, which are easy to "gather" but difficult to apply, the poet is told to "advise with your Bookseller" (84–86).

The burden of my argument thus far has been that the early modern division of the arts from the sciences was an epochal separation that, having made explicit an opposition that would dominate modern thinking, by the same act laid the ground for overcoming that division through a campaign of conflation inspired by the recognition that what divided the two modes of knowledge might also in some fashion be shared. The campaign was vulnerable to the same degree that it was justified, because the evidence of what was shared called to mind the manifold dimensions of what was not. But in the debates on drama, the establishment of what was not held in common by scientific and dramatic knowledge laid the foundation for understanding how art shares in its own terms the empirical epistemology of scientific knowledge.

Controlling for Time, Place, and Persons: The Narrative Claim to Historicity

I've argued that the dramatic aesthetic develops in two stages. The first stage is the naive empiricism of the two unities, a doctrine that makes the most of the materiality of performance by correlating so closely the circumstances represented in a play with the circumstances of its representation that the very fact of representation will be, as it were, overlooked by its spectators. The second stage evolved from the first as the view that like scientific method, the imagination abstracts from the level of sense impressions far enough to exceed the illusion of nature's actual presence, but not so far as to sacrifice, as scientific experiment does, nature's representational image. Or rather, its double image: for the greatest pleasure of the imagination depends on its reflexivity, one's consciousness of the fact of representation. Dramatic epistemology both embraces and suspends the empirical proposition that the knower must be methodically detached from the known. We both believe in and disbelieve the actuality of what is represented; we identify with the characters even as we remain aware of our own identities.

The emergence of aesthetic epistemology in literate, prose narrative undergoes a development from the naive to the sophisticated that's similar to that of drama, but one that is adapted to the fact that by the eighteenth century, the standard medium for experiencing prose narrative was not, as in traditional oral cultures, physically embodied performance, but reading. The dramatic ideal of the two unities is a principle of decorum that aims to establish in the spectator an illusion of immediacy or spatiotemporal presence—that is, the sense that there is no ontological distance between the spectator's presence and the actuality that has been represented to the spectator. Even if this illusion were possible when a play is performed, it cannot be when it is read. What might be the rough equivalent, for literate narrative, of the illusion of presence in performed drama? Elsewhere I've called the first, or naive empiricist, stage in this narrative development "the claim to historicity," because it amounts to the pretense that the fictional characters and events one reads about have an actual existence.[41]

The claim to historicity is the most definitive formal marker of the early novel as it emerged out of older narrative genres. And in its own way, by denying the virtual status of its subject matter, the claim to historicity also asserts, like the dramatic doctrine of the unities, the immediacy of the experience it presents. True, the more the spectator is absorbed by a performance, the more unmediated the process of consuming a play can feel, whereas the very mode in which literate narrative is consumed—the process of reading what has been written—inescapably announces the fact of virtual representation, not actual presence. We might say that the claim to historicity aims to do the next best thing, promising a representation so faithful, even transparent in its use of linguistic arts, that it opens a window onto the truth of nature. But in time, the naive claim to historicity became outmoded as critics discovered that the literate arts themselves have a singular capacity to absorb the reader through a process of psychological identification that requires an experience not of immediacy but of mediacy, in which a sense of difference is the precondition for a sense of engagement.

The essence of the claim to historicity can be found often enough in the paratexts of these (in novelistic terms) transitional narratives. Aphra Behn calls *Oroonoko* (1688) and *The Fair Jilt* (1688) "true histories."[42] Of the former, her speaker writes, "I was myself an eye-witness to a great part of what you will find here set down, and what I could not be witness of I received from the mouth of the chief actor in this history"; of the latter, she affirms "that this is reality, and matter of fact, and acted out in this our later age."[43] Referring to the letters exchanged between Philander and Silvia that make up much of Behn's *Love-Letters between a Nobleman and His Sister* (1684–1687), she writes, "*These Letters were found in their Cabinets, at their house at St. Denice, where they both liv'd together for the space of a year."*[44] The title page of Daniel Defoe's *The Life and Strange Surprizing Adventures of Robinson Crusoe* (1719), which was published anonymously, contains the words "Written by Himself."[45] In the preface to *The Fair Hebrew* (1729), Eliza Haywood writes, "I have not inserted one Incident which was not related to me by a Person nearly concerned in the Family of that unfortunate Gentleman."[46] And throughout the first edition of *Pamela; or; Virtue Rewarded* (1740), Samuel Richardson represents himself as "the Editor" of these letters.[47]

These formal testimonies to the historicity of the narratives in which they appear show an empiricist influence not only in the fundamental assertion of the actuality of the texts' characters but also in the effort to conceive the texts themselves as determinate objects that have been received or found under particularized circumstances and therefore can be verified as having an objective existence—not necessarily objectivity but objecthood. No narrative equivalent exists for the quantitative criteria that are fundamental to scientific methods of controlling for the abstract nature of the object under study—although we might say that the temporal and spatial data that proliferate in the plots of these novels aim to internalize, within the novelistic object, the experimental measures that verify the natural object from without. Even the repetition of experiments is suggested by the citation of numerous eyewitnesses to different parts of the novelistic plot. The preface to Defoe's pamphlet *A True Relation of the Apparition of One Mrs. Veal* (1706) adduces no fewer than four links, mediating between the narrator and Mrs. Veal herself, in the chain of eyewitness testimonials to the credibility of her ghostly apparition.[48] Of course, the text remains an artifactual rather than a strictly "factual" entity like a natural specimen; but it is represented as the artifice not of a rhetor or an imaginative author but of one or more actual persons who have used language for the more basic and practical purposes of record keeping or information exchange. This sort of enumeration is most evident in *Mrs. Veal*, and in *Pamela*, in the form of minute timekeeping. In *Robinson Crusoe* we encounter it not only in the journal's careful (and fallible) dating but also in the record keeping of livestock and finances that punctuates Robinson's daily life on and off the island. And the authority of quantitative measure of this sort is clearly related to the strictures against rhetorical excess and the praise of the plain style heard in Sprat and Hooke.

But the most far-reaching accommodation of experimental repetition to novelistic epistemology may inhere in the way contemporaries experienced the reproductive powers of print technology. As Defoe put it, "Preaching of Sermons is Speaking to a few of Mankind: Printing of Books is Talking to the whole World."[49] Defoe's words testify to the plausibility of the hypothesis that print culture entails the establishment of a virtual or "imagined community constituted by the intuition that to read a novel is to participate in a collective experience that's repeated by myriad other readers.[50] The hypothesis is, of course, not limited to novel reading; it's implicit in the way Johnson's method of judging Shakespeare's artistic value depends on the virtuality and collectivity of a "reading public." Indeed, on the basis of this insight it's been suggested (as we've seen) that the actual experience of scientific experiment itself was enhanced by the "virtual witnessing" that print enabled.[51] Through publication, the number of witnesses who actually attended either an original laboratory experiment or one of its painstaking replications might be multiplied by the far greater number who read an accurate textual account of the experiment, which the process of mechanical reproduction ensured was an exact replication of all others. On the assumption that readers of this account gave their assent to it, the publication of experiments "controlled for" a vast, if indeterminate, range of circumstantial variables.[52] Addison, we've seen, believed that it was the experience of reading printed books that best ensured the degree of distance required for the experiments of the imagination. If the transition from the traditional category of litterae humaniores to the modern category of "literature" is fruitfully understood as the transition from a default category of written texts to a category of printed texts sharply defined by the properties of printedness, then one of those properties is surely the aesthetic.

Novelistic Plots as Experimental Hypotheses

My concern in this chapter is formal and theoretical. I'm arguing that the emergent epistemology of science, and especially experimental method, had a profound influence on the way the arts came to conceive and rationalize their relationship to the external world and to the internal psychology of their spectators and readers. But I want to shift attention for a moment from the level of form and the way it was theorized to that of novelistic content, in order to suggest how the plots of some early novels assumed the shape of scientific experiments. This shift to the level of content will also have the benefit of thickening the discursive context of this inquiry.

Broadly speaking, the genre of the novel came into being in order to engage the multitude of crises—political, religious, social, economic, familial—that arose in seventeenth- and eighteenth-century England. But in this project, the emergence of the novel was paralleled by that of other, nonliterary modes of knowledge that were focused more directly than the novel on those crises, that like the novel were deeply influenced by experimental thinking, and that therefore mediated the effect of experimentalism on the novel through their own preoccupations and specialized discourses.

In *Leviathan* (1651), Hobbes writes, "The skill of making, and maintaining Commonwealths consisteth in certain Rules, as does Arithmetique and Geometry; not (as Tennis-play) on [sic] Practice onely."[53] But for Hobbes, the scientific "rules" of policy were to be deduced by logic rather than abstracted through experiment. Critics like John Bramhall objected that the circumstantial nature of politics precluded the derivation of political philosophy on the model of sciences like arithmetic or geometry, which by their nature obtain in abstracted form: "State-policy, which is wholly involved in matter, and circumstances of time, and place, and persons, is not at all like Arithmetick and Geometry, which are altogether abstracted from matter, but much more like Tennis-play."[54] Several years after this exchange, William Petty proposed what he called the totally new method of "political arithmetic": "Instead of using only comparative and superlative Words, and intellectual Arguments, I have taken the course . . . to express my self in terms of *Number, Weight,* or *Measure*; to use only Arguments of Sense, and to consider only such Causes, as have visible Foundations in Nature; leaving those that depend upon the mutable Minds, Opinions, Appetites, and Passions of particular Men, to the Consideration of others."[55] Whatever their disagreements, Hobbes, Bramhall, and Petty concur in the belief that if politics is to become scientific, it must find a way to use quantitative measure to cut through the circumstantial and qualitative variables of time, place, person, and opinion that distort its natural foundations. Hobbes's most celebrated means to this end was the nonquantifying hypothesis of the state of nature, which forty years later Locke was to develop as an alternative way to situate political thinking on a more empirical footing.

In the *Second Treatise of Government* (1690), Locke, like Hobbes, uses the hypothesis of the state of nature to counter the traditional claim that royal sovereignty was a divinely sanctioned inheritance from Adam. Traditionally, political legitimacy was derived from on high. Locke argues, unlike Hobbes, the reverse: government acquires its legitimacy from all existing individuals, who, born in the state of nature before government of any sort existed, agree to establish an authority greater than that of any of them. But is this how governments are really constituted? To ground the hypothesis of the state of nature more empirically, Locke points out contemporary examples of what it must have been like in the distant European past. Referring not to the English colonists but to the native inhabitants and echoing the book of Genesis, Locke writes, "In the beginning all the World was America."[56] For Locke and his contemporaries, the discovery of the New World offered something like a scientific laboratory in which the universal constant of nature might be disclosed: not by using quantitative measures to strip away the circumstantial and qualitative variables that obscure nature in practice, but by observing and imagining how people actually live in the absence of custom, cultural convention, and ideological presupposition. Whether real or imagined, utopian or dystopian, this was also the promise of the travel narrative.[57]

There are several levels on which the plot of Defoe's *Robinson Crusoe* can be seen to work like an experimental hypothesis. Perhaps the most immediate is that of a political experiment resembling Locke's state of nature. Shipwreck a man on an uninhabited island (which Crusoe in fact describes at one point as "a mere state of nature" [118]), thereby isolating him from all social variables. How does government come into being? Early on and alone with his animals, Robinson indulges his droll fantasy of being "Prince and Lord of the whole Island; I had the Lives of all my Subjects at my absolute Command. I could hang, give Liberty, and take it away, and no Rebels among all my Subjects" (148). And as the island is slowly populated, Robinson transforms the Hobbesian fantasy of absolute power into a reality: "My island was now peopled," he writes, shortly before leaving it. "How like a King I look'd. . . . My people were perfectly subjected: I was absolute Lord and Law-giver. . . . We had but three Subjects, and they were of three different

Religions.... However, I allow'd a Liberty of Conscience throughout my Dominions" (241). Now, as "governor" of the island, Robinson deals wisely and justly with a rebellion against his newly established authority. So the laboratory of the desert island helps Defoe imagine how a political culture of enlightened monarchy might be justified as a natural development, from the virtuality of solitary imaginings to the actuality of society.

Other ways of thinking about *Robinson Crusoe* as an experimental narrative engage not political theory but emergent discourses of religion and economics. By the early eighteenth century, traditional moral sanctions against profit taking were being challenged by arguments and evidence that wealth is not a zero-sum game but the limitless product of market circulation and exchange; that the desire for wealth is not a vice to be overcome but a natural human aspiration to be encouraged; that the national interest, so far from being coextensive with the royal interest, is the sum of all private interests. Concurrently, the Protestant embrace of justification by faith as a means of cleansing the works—the corruptions of ecclesiastical salvation—was being complicated by the conjunction of labor discipline and the indeterminate subjectivity of the calling as a sign of grace.[58]

From this perspective we might say that Defoe takes as his experimental subject an Englishman whose nature has been corrupted by the vicious and ungodly practices of capitalist accumulation and exchange, which have led him to pursue "a rash and immoderate Desire of rising faster than the Nature of the Thing admitted" (34). Strip him of that desire; remove him from the corruptions of exchange value by placing him in a state of nature where he has no one on whom to practice his vices: "I had nothing to covet, for I had all that I was now capable of enjoying.... There were no Rivals. I had no Competitor, none to dispute Sovereignty or Command with me. I might have rais'd Ship Loadings of Corn; but I had no use for it; ... all the good Things of this World, are no farther good to us, then they are for our Use" (109–110). At the same time, subject this man to religious conversion. Allow him to see that his apparent solitude is really the society of God—"that God has made up to me, the Deficiencies of my Solitary State, and the want of Humane Society by his Presence" (96). What will happen to that man? Can the vicious proto-capitalist, once stripped of his artful depravity, obtain the natural virtue of a good Christian? Is the sociability of Christian charity consistent with the sociability of market exchange? Most of all, can the convert learn to distinguish the "secret Hints" and "Dictate" of his divine calling from the "secret over-ruling Decree" of his subjective desires (148, 14)? In this scenario, the final stage of Defoe's experiment requires that Robinson return to human society so that we can judge whether his vices return as soon as the opportunity to exercise them does—a difficult judgment that all readers are obliged to confront.

The hypothesis that chattel slavery is morally acceptable, even natural, is crucially relevant to both of these readings of *Robinson Crusoe* as a narrative experiment.[59] The most important data Defoe provides for making a judgment on this hypothesis are Robinson's treatment and sale of "my Boy *Xury*," his willingness to purchase "Negroes" to work his and his fellow planters' plantations (30, 35)—both of which are pre-conversion episodes—and his post-conversion relationship with "my Man *Friday*." Readers persist in evincing a deep conviction that Robinson makes Friday his slave despite the fact that the text doesn't support this reading. Friday's elaborate display of subservience on first contact seems to Robinson to be "in token of swearing to be my Slave for ever," but Robinson isn't so sure. First he speaks of Friday as "my Savage, *for so I call him now*." Then, "having taught him to say *Master*," Robinson describes Friday as his "Servant," followed by "a Child to a Father" (172, 174, 176). All this is consistent with racism. Friday's physical appearance, which is like a European's, pleases Robinson, in contrast to that of "negroes" and "natives of *America*." But from the outset their relationship is anything but one of enslavement, and it's tempting to interpret this habitual misreading as the product of an erroneous hindsight that attributes a capitalist-imperialist universalism to the Enlightenment universalism of Robinson and Defoe.

On the evidence of *Robinson Crusoe*, the travel narrative and its shipwreck plot may be the most compellingly literal way that contemporaries used narrative to create a laboratory—nature devoid of culture—where the truth of nature might be elicited. Where scientists build on their observations of sense data through techniques of quantification, novelistic narrative builds on observation by telling abundantly detailed stories about human crises that problematically turn what tacitly had seemed the constants of everyday life into an ambiguous compound of constants and variables, what is necessary and "natural" on the one hand and what is contingent and dispensable on the other. Richardson's *Pamela* opens soon after her mistress, who has treated her indulgently as though she were like herself a gentlewoman, suddenly dies. But Pamela is a common servant girl, and the death of her mistress means that the socially artificial circumstances under which Pamela has been bred are no longer there to support her. How will she behave toward others? How will she be taken by others? What is "natural" to her? Behind these questions lies the social crisis that had been developing for the previous two centuries. Aristocratic tradition held that birth equals worth, that inner virtue is rooted in the naturalness of noble blood. As social mobility became more common, the injustice of this ideology was increasingly recognized and challenged. The tacit belief that birth equals worth became explicit as a social and literary convention ripe for experimental testing.[60]

The metaphorical relation between socioethical behavior and experimental trial had already been imagined in reverse. Joseph Glanvill, an early member of the Royal Society, conceived scientific method as a familiar but somehow ennobled plot of male assault:

> Perhaps *human nature* meets few more *sweetly relishing* and *cleanly joyes*, then those, that derive from the *happy issues* of *successful Tryals*: Yea, whether they succeed to the answering the particular *aim* of the *Naturalist* or not; 'tis however a *pleasant* spectacle to behold the *shifts*, windings and *unexpected Caprichios* of distressed *Nature*, when pursued by a *close* and *well managed*

Experiment. And the *delights* which result from these *nobler entertainments* are such, as our *cool* and *reflecting thoughts* need not be *ashamed* of. And which are dogged by no such as sequels as are the products of those *titillations* that reach no higher then *Phancy* and the *Senses*.[61]

Mr. B.'s sexual attempts on Pamela's virtue, and Richardson's emphasis on the moral implications of clothing, give a powerful realization to the figure of scientific experiment as a stripping away of artificial variables. In search of her writings in lieu of her virginity, Mr. B. warns Pamela that "I never undrest a Girl in my Life; but I will now begin to strip my pretty *Pamela*; and hope I shall not go far, before I find them" (235). In the end, Mr. B.'s failure to corrupt Pamela may also be read as the successful revelation that virtue is her irreducible nature. Once he himself is convinced of this, Mr. B. takes care on several occasions to present Pamela to the neighboring gentry, repeating the experiment to ensure that she remains the same under all qualitatively variant circumstances. (Mr. B. aptly calls these "trials," both legal tribunals and experiments.) The more radical answer to Richardson's question about Pamela's nature—that the power of socialization renders the quest for the natural in cultural contexts elusive if not quixotic—was already being put forth by some of his contemporaries. Pamela begins her gentle apprenticeship at the age of twelve. Bernard Mandeville observed that a "girl who is modestly educated, may, before she is two Years old, begin to observe how careful the Women, she converses with, are of covering themselves before Men; and the same Caution being inculcated to her by Precept, as well as Example, it is very probable that at Six she'll be ashamed of shewing her Leg, without knowing any Reason why such an Act is blameable, or what the tendency of it is."[62] Mandeville's remark also renders uncertain the utility of cultural experimentalism.

The "shipwreck" that opens *Pamela* dictates the first half of its plot and is only the first of several. Crucial to Pamela's eventual triumph is her imprisonment in the Lincolnshire house, which Mr. B. engineers in order to have his way with her more easily, but which ironically isolates her from the variables of her customary work so as to make her not just an occasional letter writer but (in his words) a brilliantly persuasive "Novel" writer whose extended narrative transforms Mr. B. from aristocratic libertinage into a suitor of her hand (232). So the fact that Pamela is experimentally isolated at Lincolnshire ensures that her virtuous nature will not only be revealed but rewarded by an upwardly mobile marriage whose social meaning is that birth has nothing to do with worth.

But a final shipwreck is yet in store for Pamela because Mr. B.'s proud sister refuses to confirm what others have agreed is in her nature. Instead, Lady Davers sees Pamela as a social interloper who has polluted the purity of the family line, and threatens her with force if she will not serve her at table in accord with her common status. In Richardson's words, Pamela is once again a "Prisoner" (384). And although Lady Davers is soon reconciled with both Pamela and her brother, the disturbing episode raises questions of injustice that Richardson may not have anticipated. Precisely because Lady Davers's aristocratic contempt is so easily invalidated as an archaic phobia, Pamela's isolation with her discloses that what had seemed a constant may be, relatively speaking, a variable—that there are deeper reasons than the social for Pamela's subordination. Before their marriage, she was vulnerable because she was doubly subordinate, as a servant and as a woman; but the novel's intense focus on social conflict makes gender and sexual subordination relatively latent. However, once Pamela's status inconsistency is erased by marriage to Mr. B., her social status becomes a "variable" because inequality persists even in the absence of social inequality. As many readers are troubled to note, after her marriage, Pamela becomes even more deferential to Mr. B., and this is in part because she has entered into the most ancient institution of inequality, marriage. The episode with Lady Davers, who learns from her brother that sex difference is even more determinant than social difference, catalyzes our sense that there is a vital experiment that has not been and never will be performed in this novel—the experiment that would test whether the truth of nature may reside beyond sex, in the simplicity and equality of a gender-neutral human nature.

Abstractly speaking, the difference between the arts and the sciences bequeathed to us by the Quarrel of the Ancients and the Moderns is the difference between quality and quantity: between nature abstracted into a thickly figured representation that evokes its virtual presence through the very act of figural detachment, and an abstraction of nature so absolute as to enable the alteration of its present actuality. By the same token, novelistic (and dramatic) plots control for variables not by the methodical extraction of nature from culture, as with a scientific experiment, but by the cross-layered accretion of multiple experiments whose connection to each other lies in the fact that each asks us the question, Is this natural or cultural? The question cannot be asked unless both the natural and the cultural are represented.

Controlling for Time, Place, and Persons: The Novel Aesthetic, or Realism

I've argued that the dramatic aesthetic, in its emulation of scientific method, begins with the naive empiricism of the two unities, which takes the artistic or imaginative mediation of nature to be roughly comparable to that of scientific understanding. It evolves into the view that the imagination abstracts far enough from the naturalness of sense impressions to exceed the illusion of nature's concrete presence, but not so far as to sacrifice, as scientific experiment does, nature's figural image. This is why the debate over the kind of belief we invest in drama is so important. This is why Addison prefers the secondary or representational pleasures of the imagination to its primary or empirical pleasures, and why he prefers the experience of reading a play to that of watching its performance. In both cases, the greater pleasure that is enabled by taking a relatively greater distance on nature is afforded by contemplating the comparison between the sensible object and the imagined image. That is, the greatest pleasure of the imagination depends not just on the fact of artistic representation but on our consciousness of that fact, which grounds our reflexive awareness of both the artistic representation and the sensible object it evokes. This aesthetic reflexivity, what Addison calls a "new principle of pleasure," is crucial to the second stage of narrative as well as of dramatic development, and it defines the epistemology of the new novel genre. But if the novel begins with the naive claim to historicity as the evolution of drama does with the two unities, how can we describe the aesthetic stage to which the novel evolves?

The breakthrough in the development of the novelistic aesthetic, or realism, was less closely rationalized than that of the dramatic, in part because it had the latter as an exemplary precedent. The early novelists, like their contemporaries impressed by the evident truth value of empirical factuality, tended to rationalize the claim to historicity on the grounds that their readers would be more likely to take to heart the moral and religious teachings of their stories if they believed that the virtual figures they read about had an actual existence. Defoe in particular struggled throughout his career with the problems involved in claiming the historicity of his fictional characters. These were primarily ethical problems—how can the cause of virtue be served by the vice of falsehood?—but also epistemological ones. Shortly after *Robinson Crusoe* appeared, Defoe conceded that "nothing is more common than to have two Men tell the same story quite differing one from another, yet both of them eye-witnesses to the fact related."[63] The novels he published after this first one are obscure and evasive about the claim to historicity they continue halfheartedly to make. Similarly, despite Richardson's claim in *Pamela*, when its second edition came out three months after the first, he was at best careless about preserving the claim of Pamela's actual existence.

Richardson's change of heart is implicated in, and grows out of, the very logic of what it leaves behind, the claim to historicity. We can see this happening on the level of content even before Richardson abandons the formal role of editor in the second edition of *Pamela*. Although Mr. B.'s feelings have gradually been softening, until he reads the long and absorbing narrative that Pamela produces during her isolation from the circumstances of her daily duties, he sees her as a romancer—that is, at best deluded and at worst a liar (e.g., 32, 69, 93). But Mr. B. is so deeply moved by Pamela's account of the suffering he has caused her—"You have touch'd me sensibly with your mournful Relation"—that his literalistic empiricism of the senses gives way to the sentiment of imaginative identification (241). Not that Mr. B. now believes the strict factuality of all that Pamela has written about him; rather, he has become receptive to a compound standard of truth. So when Pamela says of the writings he is about to read, "All that they contain you know, as well as I," he replies, "But I don't know . . . the Light you put Things in" (239). For the reformed Mr. B., Pamela's writings no longer contain simply a representation of what happened that may be factually false; they also contain the emotional truth of the representation itself. And Mr. B.'s aesthetic reflexivity is reinforced by the way his sympathetic mode of reading provides us actual readers with a model for the aesthetic approach we too might bring to the putatively factual narrative we are reading. A century later, "realism" came to designate the specifically narrative mode of the aesthetic, and what it designates is not "the real" but something we are pleased to read as though it were real, a story that's not history but comparable to history, faithful not to this or that actuality but to the abstracted virtuality of the kinds of experiences we tend to have. At this level, it's of no consequence if Mr. B. or Pamela ever had a real existence. And in this sense, novels are experiments that capture the experience of the senses not by reproducing it in all its actual particularity but by controlling for the variables of time, place, and persons so as to reveal, as Hooke phrased it about laboratory experiments, "the ways by which Nature may be trac'd, . . . not too far removed beyond the reach of our Senses."[64] But the realist experiment removes us a good deal less far from the senses than the laboratory does. By having us confront the world that language reflects with the fact and the way it reflects it, realism achieves the superior emotional pleasure of imaginative identification that results from a detached mediation, a pleasure that is neither sensible immediacy nor abstract concept but virtual figuration.

Among the many things that Henry Fielding disliked about *Pamela* was its claim to historicity, and in *Shamela* (1741) he hilariously and mercilessly parodies Richardson's efforts to convince us not only that its plot really happened but that, through the immediacy of the epistolary mode, it somehow was happening before our very eyes. A year later, Fielding abandoned parody in order to write, in *Joseph Andrews* (1742), a positive alternative to *Pamela*. Apart from *Don Quixote* (1605, 1615), *Joseph Andrews* is probably the most relentlessly reflexive novel that had been written thus far—that is, that most draws attention to its own process of representation in the very act of doing it. In the first chapter of its third volume, Fielding also composed the first full account of realism, which, after the brief heyday of the claim to historicity, had become the definitive formal doctrine of the novel genre. So far from denying the relationship between historical factuality and the novel, however, Fielding calls *Joseph Andrews* a biography, and he pointedly asserts the superiority of its fidelity to fact over the naive empiricism of those books we commonly call "histories."

Most important for our purposes, Fielding explicitly connects the breakthrough in novelistic realism that he is now in the process of achieving with the already achieved breakthrough in the dramatic aesthetic. He frames his argument about narrative in allusion to the dramatic doctrine of the two unities, an allusion that makes clear his understanding that the solutions to these distinct narrative and dramatic problems have in common an aesthetic notion that sophisticates a naive dependence on the truth of sense impressions. Those who call themselves historians, Fielding writes, might better be termed "Topographers or Chorographers," because their chief concern is to record the facts of place and time as accurately as they can. What they ignore, Fielding continues, is the unity of action, in his terms "the Actions and Characters of Men": "Now with us Biographers the Case is different, the Facts we deliver may be relied on, tho' we often mistake the Age and Country wherein they happened."[65] This is in the spirit of the reformed reader Mr. B., who learns to read Pamela for the pleasing comparison, as Addison suggests, between her subtly abstracted self-representation and herself in the light in which he knows her. The crucial implication—for us if less so for Mr. B.—is that the truth of novels is relative not to a singular actuality but to many instances of it, a point Fielding makes acutely about his own realism: "I question not but several of my Readers will know the Lawyer in the Stage-Coach, the Moment they hear his Voice. . . . I describe not Men, but Manners, not an Individual, but a Species. Perhaps it will be answered, Are not the Characters then taken from Life? To which I answer in the Affirmative; nay, I believe I might aver, that I have writ little more than I have seen. The Lawyer is not only alive, but hath been so these 4000 Years" (164). Yet Fielding is no more oblivious here of the truth of "history" than Hooke is of the truth of nature. He uses the words "fact" and "seen" with a self-conscious amusement that aims not to subvert their empirical reference but to extend it beyond the scope required for sensibly observed and physically actual entities.

In *Tristram Shandy* (1759–1767), Laurence Sterne picks up Fielding's aesthetic reflexivity and runs with it so far as to totally subsume the pleasures of the senses within those of the imagination and content within form—or so it might seem. It's probably more accurate to say that Sterne adapts representational reflexivity to the genre of the novel even more intricately and rigorously than Fielding. And like Fielding, Sterne evinces an inclusive idea of the aesthetic by alluding to the dramatic controversies over the two unities. Nonetheless, when Tristram supposes the reader will accuse him of violating "the unity . . . of time," we are made to understand that the change in medium from drama to narrative complicates the disparity between the actual, empirical time of representation and the virtual time that's represented.[66] On the one hand, the time taken to represent *Tristram Shandy* is itself an indeterminate interplay of two temporalities, the period of writing and the period of reading.[67] And on the other, Tristram works so hard to represent this interplay with accuracy and precision that it becomes the major portion of the representation itself, exhaustively thematizing form as content and leaving no room for half of what Sterne's title page announces will be the substance of this novel, *The Life and Opinions of Tristram Shandy, Gentleman*. In fact, we do get Sterne's "life" as well as his "opinions." But the content or plot of *Tristram Shandy* is so implicated within its formal mode of narration that it takes some labor on our part to see that Sterne's form, which might be described as the failure of the narrative line, is coextensive with his story, the failure of the Shandy family line to reproduce itself owing to Tristram's overdetermined infertility—a story whose implacable narration is also responsible for the linear infertility of Sterne's form. But on another level, *Tristram Shandy* is formally more fertile than any novel had been, because in attending to the mental activity of its narrator and its putative readers it represents in unprecedentedly comprehensive terms its own process of representation.

We may be tempted to take Sterne's strategy as strictly negative, a parody of empiricism that reduces it to absurdity; but Sterne, no less than Fielding, is also clearing the ground for a positive view of novelistic realism. In fact, he is a Lockean empiricist not only in jest but also in earnest, as he claims at one point to his reader: "Pray, Sir, in all the reading which you have ever read, did you ever read such a book as *Locke*'s Essay upon the Human Understanding? . . . It is a history.—A history! of who? what? where? when? Don't hurry yourself.—It is a history-book, Sir, . . . of what passes in a man's own mind" (bk. 2, ch. 2, 66). In the second sentence of his *Essay*, Locke announces his ambition in just these terms: "The Understanding, like the Eye, whilst it makes us see, and perceive all other Things, takes no notice of it self: And it requires Art and Pains to set it at a distance, and make it its own Object."[68] Locke is in no doubt regarding the difficulty of his enterprise, in which the cardinal principle of empirical understanding, the division of the subject from the object of knowledge, would seem to come up against the reflexive interplay entailed in making the understanding "its own Object." Only two decades before *Tristram Shandy* began to be published, Hume took up Locke's problem with a good deal more explicit skepticism about the ultimate viability of the project. On its title page Hume announces that his *Treatise of Human Nature* is "an attempt to introduce the experimental Method of Reasoning into Moral Subjects." But in its introduction he warns that "moral philosophy has, indeed, this peculiar disadvantage, which is not found in natural, that in collecting its experiments, it cannot make them purposely, with premeditation" because "'tis evident this reflection and premeditation would so disturb the operation of my natural principles, as must render it impossible to form any just conclusion from the phaenomenon."[69] In the empiricism of philosophical inquiry, reflexivity is a problem because it threatens to compromise the full degree of distance required by the understanding to disembed the nature of the thing itself, in this case the human mind and its operations, as an abstract concept. In the empiricism of the aesthetic, however, reflexivity marks the crucially lesser distance that the imagination takes on its object, signifying that what is being represented is not only the constancy and invariability of the mental operations by which we seek to know that object, but also, as figuration rather than full abstraction, the formal process of its representation. In the aesthetic, the arts discover a mode of experiment, peculiarly its own, whose aim is an empirical removal from sensible actuality to imaginative virtuality that bears with it, unlike the understanding, the evidence of that removal.

However, Hume pursues so relentlessly the problem he's uncovered in the experimentalism of moral philosophy that it infects the experimentalism of natural philosophy as well. There is no empirical basis, he finds, for our knowledge of the world that lies beyond us. What we take to be the constancy of the natural object once experiment has abstracted all variables is really the constancy and invariability of the mental operations by which we seek to know that object. Hume famously compares our empirical experience of external objects to the experience of a dramatic spectator: "The mind is a kind of theatre, where several perceptions successively make their appearance; pass, re-pass, glide away, and mingle in an infinite variety of postures and situations" (bk. 1, pt. 4, sec. 6: 255).

The difference is that in empirical experience we never leave the theater because there is no outside that is accessible to this inside. Addison's fundamental distinction between kinds of knowledge and pleasure disappears. The proper term for empirical knowledge is not "understanding" but "imagination": "Let us fix our attention out of ourselves as much as possible: Let us chace our imagination to the heavens, or to the utmost limits of the universe; we never really advance a step beyond ourselves, nor can conceive any kind of existence, but those perceptions, which have appear'd in that narrow compass. This is the universe of the imagination, nor have we any idea but what is there produc'd" (bk. 1, pt. 2, sec. 6: 67–68). Elsewhere Hume paraphrases "the understanding" as "the general and more establish'd properties of the imagination" (bk. 1, pt. 4, sec. 7: 267). All knowledge is a reflexive act of self-knowledge. Where previous authors have tried to vindicate the arts as an aesthetic, hence empirical way of knowing, Hume radically reverses the process of accommodation by finding that empirical knowledge is an act of the imagination. This is not, of course, where Hume leaves his own practice as a moral philosopher, nor does natural philosophy—science—find itself painted into Hume's radically skeptical corner. If anything, Hume's stringent logic in the first book of his *Treatise* may have drawn attention to the need to understand more precisely the difference, in degree of distance from the realm of sense experience, that distinguishes scientific from aesthetic experimentalism.[70]

By the end of the British Enlightenment, literature had learned to practice and perfect its modern self-understanding as a distinctive mode of empirical knowledge. Central to literature, as to science, is the experimental process, on which both must maintain a focused concentration. What distinguishes them, the degree of distance each takes on the world, may be restated as the difference between what becomes of the experimental process in each of them. Scientific experiment abstracts from experiential data a quantitative understanding of nature that has the probability of universal sensible application, an understanding in which the data themselves, an indispensable means of reaching this point, now play no part. But in the qualitative abstraction achieved by literature, the history of the process by which experiment abstracts a probable figuration of human nature persists as its end product. In the aesthetic, the arts developed a mode of experiment that undertakes an empirical removal from sensible actuality to imaginative virtuality that also documents what has transpired in that removal. Time, place, and person, disembedded from experience by experiment, remain in the literary text as a figurative residue, both the result of the experiment and the reflexive record of how it came to be. The empirical nature of science is most importantly confirmed in the wake of experiment, in the applicability of the data it's derived from experiment to the knowledge and alteration of sensible actuality. However, the empirical nature of literature is most importantly confirmed by the thickness and density of its text, which is the history of an experimental comparison between sensible actuality and imaginative virtuality. The product of scientific experiment lies beyond the experimental process; the product of literary experiment, the dialectic of content and form, is also its immanent process.

But although this aesthetic view of literature had become firmly established in British culture by the end of the eighteenth century, it thereby also had begun to be forgotten, or misremembered, as the division between the arts and the sciences gradually came to designate a difference not of degree but of kind. For this to happen, two conditions had to be met. First, that aspect of representation that engages the world had to be subsumed under that aspect of representation that engages the way words represent the world. Second, this latter aspect of representation had to be reconceived, in mainstream thinking, as lacking empirical content by virtue of being a formal process. Reflexivity remains the signature of the literary aesthetic, but what it is now thought to coordinate and compare is two facets of formality, neither of which is rooted in the empirical senses. Or to be more precise: in the modern world, the hardening of the division *between* the literary arts and the sciences has been approximated, *within* the literary arts, as one between the mode of poetry (and especially "lyric" poetry), on the one hand, and the mode of narrative, on the other, with the mode of drama oscillating variously between these two poles. This division has reduced both categories of literature to antithetically partial versions of the idea of the aesthetic. Under the aegis of modern literary theory, the ambition of the poetic aesthetic has been influentially reconceived (e.g., by aestheticism) as confined exclusively to self-reference, while novelistic realism (if not always modern drama) has been influentially reconceived (e.g., by structuralism and poststructuralism) as a naive ambition to achieve the transparent reflection of the world.

2 From Ancient Mimesis to Modern Realism

A DIACHRONIC INQUIRY

Mimesis and *realism* are among the most commonly misconstrued categories in literary theory. More than two millennia separate their respective coinages. Both are concerned with the question of whether and how factuality and the real are to be represented in drama and narrative. My argument in this chapter will be that Aristotelian mimesis and modern realism are equivalent concepts and practices. But there has been much disagreement about their meanings, and when they're correlated, as I have done, they're likely to be similarly and reciprocally misconceived, one on the erroneous model of the other. Mimesis has been misconstrued for a long time; but because realism is a relatively recent neologism, the comparison of the two can only be modern. The most common, and reductive, approach to the relation of mimesis and realism has been that of structuralist and poststructuralist modernism. In accord with its methodological precept that structure and history can and should be separated from each other, structuralism has ignored the historical contexts and development of these categories and thereby distorted their meanings. *Structure*, like its analogue *form*, has a history that's vital to its understanding. And although the realm of content is the dimension in which the factual is manifested, the choice of whether and how to render factuality is a formal determination. Along with the two categories themselves, those that are most central to a historical approach to this question are *verisimilitude*, *probability*, and *fictionality*. I'll consider each of them in turn.

Aristotelian Mimesis

Under nonliterate orality, all official and collective discourse is "poetic," held together to mnemonic ends by techniques of repetition, recursion, echo, patterning, rhythm, formula, ritual, and the like.[1] With their objectification through literacy and then through print, these formal cues to discursive content become superfluous, and "poetry" becomes a specialized and socially marginal mode of speaking and writing characterized, unlike other discourses, by a self-conscious reflexivity, content shot through with a formal awareness. Before literacy, the relation between form and content was tacit and unselfconscious. The function of such "poetic" language to represent—to refer to—the world is latent within its primary function to represent itself so as to make memorable the knowledge of the world it refers to. As the mnemonic function of poetry ceases to dominate, its referential function, as in all language, makes an ostensive claim on our attention.

But poetry, and much modern literature, is singular in sharing the project of reflecting the world with the project of making us reflect on the means by which it does this. Aristotle writes when literacy has recently transformed the culture of Greek antiquity, and his conception of mimesis reflects the relatively new understanding that poetry's formal self-reference is conjoined with its aim to represent or imitate the world that lies beyond it.

Verisimilitude and *probability* entered theoretical discourse on drama and narrative toward the end of the sixteenth century through Italian encounters with Aristotle's concept of mimesis. In the *Poetics*, Aristotle argues that poetic imitation (mimesis) does not seek strict veracity and does not confront us with the immediate presentation of the real; it gives us pleasure by representing a similarity to or likeness of the real. It is "natural for all to delight in works of imitation. . . . Though the objects themselves may be painful to see, we delight to view the most realistic representations of them in art" (*tas eikonas tas malista ekribomenas*, literally, "the artistic images the most perfectly and exactly made").[2] In this view, imitation is based on and motivated by the awareness of a distance between the object and the act of imitation, between the spatiotemporal present and its representation. To elaborate Aristotle's celebrated distinction, history undertakes the factual description of actual events and in the order of their occurrence; poetry undertakes the virtual imitation of what might happen, reordering events to make a plot that is whole (*holos*)—that is, one that is composed of parts (actions) whose relationship to each other is probable or necessary (*eikos ē to anankaion*) (1450–1451, 1451).[3]

Verisimilitude: Italian Theory

According to Douglas Lane Patey, "Italian theorists variously render Aristotle's εικός as *verisimile* or *probabile*, but most frequently follow mediaeval rhetoric in choosing the former."[4] A sampling of texts by Bernard Weinberg confirms Patey's generalization but also documents much variation in the way *verisimile* and *probabile* are construed. Thus, with respect to every poem, Denores holds that "insofar as it is an imitation, it must be verisimilar."[5] Tasso agrees that verisimilitude must be a condition of imitation (Weinberg, 686). Zinano characterizes history and poetry as distinct kinds of truth—in actuality (what has happened) and in potentiality (what could happen). Though we might suppose that the latter partakes of verisimilitude, Zinano intends his distinction to be dichotomous, between absolute truth (*uerità*) and absolute invention or fiction (*fintione*). This suggests that verisimilitude occupies the territory between these two concepts and can even combine them (Weinberg, 670–671). For Beni, the stricter constraints on the verisimilar are evident in his argument that poets should "entrust their plot to prose" because those whose characters speak in verse "throw decorum and verisimilitude into disorder" (Weinberg, 707). An extreme instance of this literalizing tendency is Castelvetro's restriction of poetic art to the standards of the natural and historical actuality it imitates (see Weinberg, 503–504). Buonamici stays closer to Aristotle's position on the imitative distance from the presentation of the real that is required to create pleasure: "The work of verisimilitude in the spectator can never cause him—unless he is an imbecile—to mistake the thing representing for the thing represented" (Weinberg, 707, 695).

Although *probabile* is less commonly the translation of *eikos* among Renaissance Italian theorists, Oddi and Bulgarini, among others, treat it more or less synonymously with the *verisimile* (Weinberg, 653–654, 889). According to Sassetti, "A probable proposition is verisimilar, so that in order to know the nature of verisimilitude we must know that of the probable" (Weinberg, 844). Sassetti's observation might be taken to adumbrate the idea that the verisimilitude of imitation is a function of the probability of imitation. This at least may be Viperano's insight. Imitation, at one remove from the immediate presentation of what actually has happened, re-presents it virtually on the concrete model provided by probability (and necessity). This involves re-ordering an actual and contingent diversity of actions by constructing a plot that is a single action and achieves virtual unity (see Weinberg, 763–764). The importance of this insight is that it conjoins two Aristotelian fundamentals. The well-constructed plot, whose unity of action distinguishes it as qualitatively the most important part and "soul" of tragedy, provides a formal model for the singular and unified artifactuality of mimesis as distinct from the multiplicitous and chaotic factuality of the real—that is, a model for verisimilitude as distinct from veracity (Aristotle, 1450). When theorists overlook the importance of that distinction, Aristotle can appear to affirm the immediate reflection of the real in, and thereby the factuality of, poetic mimesis.

In the seventeenth century, the unity of action will figure as one of the "three unities" of French neoclassicism. Of the Italian theorists, Riccoboni and Tasso come closest to the genuinely formal implications of this quasi-Aristotelian doctrine in arguing that radical limits on the time and place represented, and correspondingly on their representation, will help ensure a plot whose action is single and unified.[6] But the two unities of time and place were also advocated for reasons other than formal. In justifying the limit on representational time, Riccoboni and Bonciani echo Castelvetro, who maintains that a disparity between representational and represented time will tax the imagination of spectators and destroy verisimilitude (see Weinberg, 69, 508–509, 540, 587). In Maggi's words, such a disparity "will absolutely produce an effect of incredibility" (Weinberg, 415). Again, by attempting to eliminate the distance between the representational and the represented, the artifactual and the factual, these theorists reveal a basic misunderstanding of Aristotle's call for verisimilitude and probability, which on the contrary enable the spectatorial experience of that distance.

Verisimilitude: French Theory

What was known to English speakers as the seventeenth-century "French heroic romance" was widely associated with the claim to *vraisemblance*. The earliest and most celebrated heroic romance was d'Urfé's pastoral *L'Astrée* (1607–1627),[7] broadly proclaimed to be *vraisemblable* even though most commonly read as a roman à clef (several keys were printed after d'Urfé died).⁸ Perhaps the indirect, allegorical historicity of a roman à clef was thought to justify taking *L'Astrée* as vraisemblable rather than simply *vrai*. In his preface, the translator of *L'Astrée* (1657), John Davies, writes, "What was before censur'd as *extravagance* of *imagination*, is now reconcil'd to *probability*, and restrain'd by *Judgement*."⁹ Madeleine de Scudéry, the most popular and prolific author of heroic romances, was widely praised for the vraisemblance of her works. But authors and theorists were becoming increasingly sensitive to the discrepancy between the romance attribution of vraisemblance and the roman à clef's indirect claim to historical vérité or factuality. In the twelfth century, romance had begun to detach from the body of the chanson de geste, and over the next several centuries, romance and history were gradually separated, then dichotomized through the analytic skepticism of that epoch's major developments: humanism, the Reformation, the scientific revolution, and the invention, then maturation, of print as a deep and permanent feature of modern culture. After 1660, history and romance had become not only opposed but also vastly unequal as vehicles of truth.¹⁰

This is despite the brilliance of *Don Quixote* (1605, 1615), which at the century's opening had made available to European readers a highly self-conscious understanding of history and romance as both antithetical and inseparable. With hindsight, many modern readers have seen Cervantes's dialectical synthesis as the first novel. But contemporary authors like Sorel, who were most immediately influenced by *Don Quixote*, can appear more focused on a partial Cervantic inheritance—the dogged historicist critique of romance—than on sustaining a reciprocity of history and romance.¹¹ Sorel's 1627 parody of d'Urféan pastoral romance, revised in 1633, was translated as *The Extravagant Shepherd. The Anti-romance: or, The History of the Shepherd Lysis* (1653). "The Author to the Reader" observes that "the most Extravagant actions of our Shepherd-Lover, have for their Presidents [*sic*] those of so many brave Hero's, whom he hath endeavor'd to imitate.... And though they have given the name of *Romance* to those charming and delightful Histories, and that his pretends more right to the title, as being nothing but charms and delight it self: Yet we have call'd him the *Anti-Romance*; and that because *Romances* contain nothing but *Fictions*, whereas this must be thought a *true* History."¹² Sorel's "imitation" of romance is, like Cervantes's, a parody. *Don Quixote* is a negation of a negation that through historicist critique supersedes romance by preserving and absorbing it as an old model for something new. It seeks fulfillment as a "true history" not in the narrow sense of the historically true (*vrai*) but as a vraisemblance reflexively aware of its doubleness, its obliquity. For Aristotle, the obliquity of parody is a defining property of imitation or mimesis itself. Lacking the equipoise of Cervantic parody, Sorel's anti-romance weights too heavily the skeptical critique of romance idealism.

As is already apparent in the popularity of the roman à clef, French authors and theorists are more inclined than their Italian predecessors and contemporaries to claim, however ironically, the factuality of history as a positive norm for their narratives. In the wake of the first voyages of discovery, the French led the way in generating scores of "imaginary voyages" that parodied the conventions of factuality in authentic travel narratives, which reasonably enough called themselves histories. No imaginary voyages achieved vraisemblance more ingeniously than those that relied on the passage of time to authenticate their apparent romances as histories in the making. According to Vairasse d'Allais (a Frenchman whose narrative was first published in English), "*Columbus* was looked upon (here in *England*, and afterward in *France*) as a brain-sick Fellow." But "the discovery of *America* . . . has sufficiently evidenced the truth of *Columbus* his Assertion. The Histories of *Peru, Mexico, China*, &c. were at first taken for Romances by many, but time has shewed since that they are verities not to be doubted of."[13] However, the doubleness of Sorel's parody (and of Aristotle's mimesis) is lost on d'Allais, because the implication is that vraisemblance will be authenticated only through its cancellation by, and its transformation into, the *vrai*.

French authors also dominated the field, at least at first, of the secret history, the *chronique scandaleuse*, and the libelous memoir. In 1690, the Comtesse d'Aulnoy confided to her readers that "[it] is not sufficient to write things true, but they must likewise seem probable, to gain belief."[14] And because she has resisted this impulse, "I do not doubt but there will be some, who will accuse me of hyperbolizing, and composing Romances." Nonetheless, she assures us that "you have here no Novel, or Story, devised at pleasure; but an Exact and most True Account of what I met with in my Travels."[15] Pierre Bayle made d'Aulnoy the occasion for a broader reflection on the problem:

> It has prevailed, as a general opinion, that her works are a mixture of fictions and truth, half romance, and half history; . . . Booksellers and authors do all they can to make it believed that these secret Histories have been taken from private manuscripts . . . [because] such like adventures, please more when they are believed to be real, than when they are thought to be mere fables. From hence it is, that the new romances [*les nouveaux romans*] keep as far off as possible from the romantic way: but by this means true history is made extreamly obscure.[16]

Testimonies like these suggest that whether or not veracious, the claim to historical factuality is usurping the authority, or absorbing and altering the meaning, of vraisemblance. Increasingly, the claim to factual historicity is being marked explicitly so as to replace, or at least to supplement, the questionable, traditionally implicit and unmarked, claim to verisimilitude. At the turn of the eighteenth century, the claim to historicity—the assertion that fictional narratives tell the stories of actual people—gaining in popularity, also anticipates the same stance in the early novel.[17]

One sign of this development is the way the unweighted Aristotelian distinction between "history" and "poetry" is being conceived as one between *histoire* and the pejorative *roman*. Bayle's phrase *nouveaux romans* designates narratives that overwrite their verisimilitude with marks of historicity. But because French has no separate word for what English calls romance, *roman* had to do double service, at times signifying a narrative norm (as in *roman héroïque* and roman à clef) and at other times a critique of contemporary narrative (as in Bayle's *nouveau roman* and Sorel's *anti-roman*). D'Aulnoy's English translator uses both "romance" and "novel" pejoratively; in the French source text, "roman" would have been ambiguous and rhetorically counterproductive. In English, the clear pejorative was "romance," whose generic status by the end of the seventeenth century had swelled to epistemological proportions and engrossed everything from the exaggerated, idealized, fabricated, erroneous, impossible, incredible, and deceptive, to falsehood and outright lies. Perhaps, in its negative application, "roman" evoked the English romance. During the 1660s, however, a genuine shift in terminology was in progress, and for a while sustained. The term *nouvelle* came into use to designate an actuality-grounded and politically subversive alternative to the traditional noblesse culture of both the old romans and the old *histoires*, and it claimed historicity in a variety of ways.[18]

These experimental shifts in usage testify to a diminished investment in the distinctive meaning of Aristotle's verisimilitude. In the *Poetics*, verisimilitude expresses the aim of imitation or mimesis to capture a heightened form of the truth of things "as they might be" by exploiting the distance entailed in representation. Toward the end of the seventeenth century, vraisemblance had come to seem a weak gesture at direct presentation, perhaps supplemented by the illusion of "historical" or "factual" immediacy—an effort to present the *vrai* that is doomed to mere *semblance*. Some French theorists lose touch with the formal significance of vraisemblance and advocate it to rhetorical and persuasive ends. In Rapin's words, "Even the truest things should not be related if they seem unbelievable or extraordinary, unless you give them an air of truth or at least the coloring of verisimilitude."[19] In fact, "*vraisemblance* is whatever conforms to the opinion of the public."[20]

The greatest impact of seventeenth-century French theory, within immediate circles and beyond, was made by Corneille's "Troisième Discours," which affirms the doctrine of the three unities a good deal more boldly than do its French proponents earlier in the century, and which disregards the formal justification for the unities of time and place advanced by Riccoboni and Tasso (see the section "Verisimilitude: Italian Theory"). On the topic of the unity of time, Corneille advocates not mimetic vraisemblance but the empirical equivalent of the *vrai*: "The dramatic poem is an imitation, or rather a portrait of human actions, and it is beyond doubt that portraits gain in excellence in proportion as they resemble the original more closely. A performance lasts two hours and would resemble reality perfectly if the action it presented required no more for its actual occurrence."[21] Corneille's famous construal of Aristotle diminishes as far as possible the crucial distance between representational virtuality and represented actuality that defines the imitative nature of poetic vraisemblance. That this is the term Corneille candidly employs here to identify the aim of mimesis even as he describes that aim as the immediate reflection of the real makes clear how far vraisemblance has diverged in meaning from Aristotle's *eikos* (e.g., 105, 109, 110, where *vraisemblance* is translated as "probability").

Of the unity of place, Corneille also maintains that "we ought to seek exact unity as much as possible" (113). But reproducing the empirical equivalent of place seems to entail more difficulties than does that of time, and this may be why Corneille frankly describes spatial adjustment more emphatically than he does temporal adjustment as a way to "deceive the spectator" (114). But deception, once named, has a powerful justification. The pleasure the spectator takes in dramatic representation requires it: "His mind . . . must not be hindered, because the effort he is obliged to make to conceive and to imagine the play for himself lessens the satisfaction which he will get from it" (108). By obscuring discrepancies between the representational and the represented, "deception" ensures that the greater deception entailed in maintaining the two unities, and hence the mental absorption of the spectator, on which pleasure is thought to depend, will not be disrupted. Later in the discourse, Corneille returns to this topic: "Most spectators [are] warmly intent upon the action which they see on the stage. The pleasure they take in it is the reason why they do not seek out its imperfections lest they lose their taste for it" (114). And here Corneille allows that the spectators themselves, supposedly deceived, knowingly play a role in maintaining their pleasure—"they do not seek out its imperfections lest they lose their taste for it"—paradoxically by self-consciously avoiding the self-conscious awareness that what they experience is a representation and not actually present. Sorel provides an instructive counterpoint to Corneille. In his parodic deployment of imitation, what is avoided in the experience of representation is not the potential consciousness of a fissure between representation and the represented; on the contrary, it is the unconsciousness of it, of the separability of the virtual and the actual. Corneille condemns his spectators to the bad faith of self-deception. Sorel denies them the pleasures of romance credulity. Mimesis, a mean between these extremes, is left by the wayside.

In the end, Corneille's approach to the unities, because it veers away from what Aristotle means by mimesis, throws into high relief and raises to the level of debate some of the crucial categories that would preoccupy theorists in the next few years: pleasure, deception, and consciousness.

Probability: English Theory

Perhaps even more than the French, a powerful strain of naive empiricism polarized English debates on the horns of the factual versus the false, "(true) history" versus "romance." Limits on space allow no more than citational sampling from my own research to support this generalization, one whose texts range from 1654 to 1727 and take in devotional, casuistical, "literary," and "scientific" discourse, collections of documents, political allegories, travel narratives, and books of wonders (McKeon, *Origins*, 57, 70, 88–89, 111–112, 102, 115, 433n.73, 438n.114, 438n.115). Printedness could be seen both to confirm the documentary truth of the text and, less often, to exemplify the deceitful rhetoric of romance (46, 48). An increasingly pervasive language of "fact" and "matter of fact" testified to the truth of, among other things, "Scripture-History," the Resurrection, and witchcraft. But factuality also might be subjected on occasion to caveats like the following: "*Facts* unably related, tho with the greatest Sincerity, and good Faith, may prove the worst sort of Deceit" (82, 85, 117).[22] What we would call the positivist view of "fact" is most significantly refuted by Fielding's satiric usage in what amounts to the first theorization of realism, *Joseph Andrews* (1742), book 3, chapter 1.

Before the theory of realism challenges strategies of factualizing and historicizing they continue to dominate, culminating in the signature trope of the "claim to historicity," the assertion that the fictional figures and events depicted in a narrative have, or have had, an actual existence. The claim could be made most obtrusively on title pages and in paratexts, but also throughout texts themselves, by insinuating characters' extratextual activities. I'll assume the reader's familiarity with the claim to historicity in Behn, Defoe, Haywood, Richardson, and others.[23]

However, a second feature of English theory and practice that distinguishes it even more decisively from that of Italy and France moderates this naive empiricism to such a degree that by the middle of the eighteenth century, the claim to historicity, having dominated narrative for several decades, begins to be superseded by realism. After 1660, English discourse greatly favors "probability" over "verisimilitude" (not to mention "vraisemblance").[24] This striking difference between French and English terminology can't be attributed to a single cause. However, one factor must be that by the latter decades of the seventeenth century, English literate culture, arguably more than French, had become suffused with the excitement and controversy generated by the new philosophy and, among other things, its reconception of probability. Bacon's program, innovative though it was, had as its premise the same goal of certainty that had grounded earlier and very different systems of knowledge. The experience of his experimentalist followers soon led them to revise that goal from certain to probable truth, and the means of attaining natural knowledge from axioms to hypotheses. For Bacon, probability still had its ancient association with opinion and rhetoric. But by the middle of the seventeenth century, the distinction between knowledge and probability was waning, and the concept of persuasion was being used not simply to designate rhetorical success but also to discriminate degrees of assent to propositions based on the evidence of the senses, reason, and testimony.[25]

Around 1660, methods of statistical quantification and computation took off, transforming the concept of probability (see especially Hacking). These developments in the theory of natural knowledge bear an evident relation to those we've been tracing in the theory of literature. We can hear this in Locke's terminology: in maintaining that the *"highest degree of Probability"* pertained to a "matter of fact" that, "consonant to the constant Observation of our selves and others, in the like case, comes attested by the concurrent Reports of all that mention it, we receive it as easily, and build as firmly upon it, as if it were certain Knowledge."[26] Newton, a committed experimentalist with a famous distaste for hypothesis, warned around 1704 that "if without deriving the properties of things from phaenomena you feign hypotheses . . . your system will be little better than a romance."[27] Both the new philosophy's turn from certainty to probability and the contemporaneous narrative turn toward claims to historicity, distinct as they may be on the spectrometer of skepticism, evince the broad and implacable wave of empirical epistemology that had been gathering for the past century or so.

The claim to historicity seeks to achieve by other means what's sought by the doctrine of the unities: the seamless accord of narrative form and content, the representational and the represented, the virtual and the actual. It's the earliest and simplest narrative technique of emulating the new-philosophical principle that all knowledge, all access to truth, is a function of experience, which is to say of our sense impressions. For a while, the claim to historicity was widely made and disseminated. But Bacon knew that the defects of the senses, obvious in individual experience, require that the knowledge of nature be detached, abstracted, and generalized from the many variable circumstances of particular sensations, and to this end his followers developed experimental models for abstracting from experience. After 1660, the Royal Society began to sponsor such trials, which was around the same time that the concept of probability was becoming more sophisticated through innovations in theory and techniques of quantification. This is also when the doctrine of the two unities was beginning to be actively challenged on the grounds that the tight fit of form and content only frustrated the pleasures of artistic experience. In significant cases (as we'll see), these challenges were made in implicit or explicit comparison with scientific modes of knowledge, and through thought experiments that recurred to Aristotle's resonant remarks about mimesis.

As formulated by members of the Royal Society, experimental method was a recognizable, if rudimentary, means of controlling for variables. "Experience" is the product of the senses as they're deeply embedded in the spatial and temporal contingencies of social practice; "experiment" names the protracted and wide-ranging effort to disembed experience, to detach what's generalizable—nature as such—from the diversity of concrete instances. Our normal knowledge of nature is conditioned by our experience. Experiment seeks to "free" nature from these conditions by treating them as variables that can be controlled for by methods of quantification. That is, variable conditions can be recognized for what they are, and their effects can be neutralized by means of a process of distantiation that involves multiplying and averaging the number of observations, observers, experiments, and experimenters. This process allows one to isolate the constant "nature" that can be seen to persist, invariably, across a range of artificial variations. The ambition of experiment is to replicate and refine sense experience; the ambition of the unities is to erase it.

Realism

Intellectual history deals with both terms and concepts. The use of the terms "verisimilitude" and "probability" has guided us toward an understanding of their conceptual meaning as it evolved over time. The term "realism" offers no comparable guidance because it was coined around the turn of the nineteenth century—in philosophy, in 1797; in literature, in 1817 (*OED*)—that is, after literary realism had begun to be practiced in the eighteenth-century novel. To contend that a concept has pre-existed what later emerges as its accepted term is by no means unusual. To be plausible it requires the demonstration of a pre-history that connects the emergence of the term with conceptual developments that approximate and anticipate their semantic fulfillment in that term. The importance of verisimilitude ultimately owes its authority to its rendering of Aristotle's concept of mimesis; but in long-term usage that authority has proved uncertain in capturing Aristotle's rather straightforward meaning. Perhaps "seeming truth" lent itself too easily to the careless shorthand "truth." "Probability," for a long time less favored, comes into its own primarily in English usage in proximity with new-scientific usage, where early on the absolutism of certainty was replaced by the skepticism of probability. By returning to the Aristotelian meaning of mimesis, I'll pick up the thread that ties it to eighteenth-century realist theory and practice as well as to the epistemology of the new science and its language of probability. I'll then turn to two notable and opposed ways that realism has been construed after its coinage.

Dryden's dialogic *Of Dramatic Poesy* appeared eight years after Corneille's discourse on the unities was published, and Corneille is cited throughout on key matters of imitation and representation. One of Dryden's speakers begins with a panegyric to "these last hundred years," in which "almost a new nature has been revealed to us" through discoveries in "optics, medicine, anatomy, astronomy."[28] However, English poetry has languished in comparison not only with that of the Ancients but also with French poetry, this speaker continues, because it hasn't maintained, as these have, the unities of time and place. Another speaker criticizes the English practice of presenting onstage, rather than narrating in the French mode, actions that "can never be imitated to a just height": "For what is more ridiculous than to represent an army with a drum and five men behind it . . . ? When we see death represented, we are convinced it is but fiction; but when we hear it related, our eyes (the strongest witnesses) are wanting, which might have undeceived us" (51).

The central problem of English dramaturgy in this Corneillian view is that it draws attention to the gap between the how and the what, the form and the content, of representation, a gap that destroys credibility. The normative status of visual witnessing betrays the perspective of naive empiricism. A third speaker, commonly seen as Dryden's spokesman, questions the critique of a staged army in battle by arguing that the testimony of the senses is always subject to the influence of another powerful faculty: "for why may not our imagination as well suffer itself to be deluded with the probability of it, as with any other thing in the play"—like the premise that the actors are "kings or princes" (62). And soon both speakers who earlier defended the two unities allow that we participate to some degree in our own theatrical deception. One, apparently persuaded by some of what he's just heard, remarks, "For a play is still an imitation of nature; we know we are to be deceived, and we desire to be so; but no man ever was deceived but with a probability of truth" (79). The language of delusion and deception recalls Corneille's tentative gesture toward self-deception but explicitly affirms it, positing a conscious agency and underscoring a distance between the apparent facticity of what's represented and the audience's awareness of its representational source. The role of the imagination is not to close the gap but to subtend it, suggesting that the imaginative adjustment of the representational to the represented is an integral feature of mimesis and its probability. I ask the reader's indulgence in my recapitulation of this crucial argument in the following four paragraphs.

In 1712, Addison extended Dryden's proto-realist insight by explicitly comparing the imagination to the empirical or scientific understanding with regard to their shared, if unequal, distance from the realm of the senses. Addison shows that these two mental faculties, although their products differ greatly, are closely comparable in their experimental methods of abstracting from sensible experience and controlling for variables. Whereas the extreme abstraction achieved by the understanding transforms sense impressions into concepts and numbers, the imagination's detachment stops, as it were, halfway and produces images or representations that provide a virtual resemblance to the actual object.

Addison is at pains to describe three degrees of imaginative distantiation from the spatiotemporal presence of sense impressions. One of these stipulates the superiority of reading—even plays—over the modes of intake proper to all other media owing to the abstracted nature of written language. Another, the distance of virtual images from what they actually represent, is the key to the peculiar pleasures of the imagination because it introduces "a new Principle of Pleasure, which is nothing else but the Action of the Mind, which *compares* the Ideas that arise from Words, with the Ideas that arise from the Objects themselves."[29] The comparison of ideas presupposes their separation and enables the pleasure of reflexive reference by which the self-conscious mind moves back and forth between the two similar but different ideas or images.[30] So, Addison's analysis allows him to restate Neander's defense of drama in a yet more positive register. There's no need for a close approximation to actual time and place in order to maintain the belief of the dramatic spectator. In fact, that would be detrimental to the kind of belief and pleasure that are appropriate to drama, and to art in general. Addison now invokes Aristotle on mimesis: if pity and fear are the emotions proper to tragedy, he asks, why is it that "such Passions as are very unpleasant at all other times, are very agreeable when excited by proper Descriptions"?[31] By this stage in his discourse, Addison has already answered that question by comparing the understanding to the imagination, a comparison that likely was inspired in turn by the ongoing revolution in empirical epistemology and the insight that all knowledge, whether scientific or literary, must be both grounded in the actuality of sense impressions and abstracted from that grounding.

Like Dryden and Addison, Edmund Burke in his *Philosophical Enquiry* (1757) and Samuel Johnson in his "Preface" to *The Plays of William Shakespeare* (1765) explicitly recur to Aristotle's touchstone mimesis, and like their predecessors they remark on the benefit artistic mimesis would derive from having access to something like scientific quantification. Henry Fielding pursues the Aristotelian topos from the dramatic into the narrative mode. His broad refutation of the doctrine of the unities facilitates the first articulation of the theory of realism.

Fielding's commentary, in the middle of his novel *Joseph Andrews* (1742), is, first of all, a rebuttal of the claim to historicity as practiced by Richardson in *Pamela* (1740). Most historians, Fielding writes, are so preoccupied with getting the empirical facts of time and place right—if possible by quantitative measure—that they may as well be called "Chorographers" and "Topographers."[32] Fielding sees himself as a "Biographer" because he is concerned instead with the faithful representation of Aristotle's unity of action and what Fielding calls "the Actions and Characters of Men" (162). He gives the term "fact" a satiric twist by applying it not to the quantitative measures of time and place but to this qualitative component of historical narration: "The Facts we deliver may be relied on, tho' we often mistake the Age and Country wherein they happened" (162). But his sober implication is also that, as in scientific experiment, factuality matters as a means to an end. By the same token, empirical quantification plays a minor role in assessing an individual fact, but a vital one in abstracting from multiple facts, which for Fielding is the means by which character is best represented. "I question not but several of my Readers will know the Lawyer in the Stage-Coach, the Moment they hear his Voice. . . . I describe not Men, but Manners; not an Individual, but a Species. Perhaps it will be answered, Are not the Characters then taken from Life? To which I answer in the Affirmative; nay, I believe I might aver, that I have writ little more than I have seen. The Lawyer is not only alive, but hath been so these 4000 Years" (164). By proclaiming that he's represented not an individual but a species—a generalized composite of many individuals—Fielding not only rejects the claim to historicity (which even if true would be no better than basing his representation on a single sense impression) but also replaces that claim by the implication that his abstracted lawyer, divested of extraneous variables, represents a characterological constant: the general type of the lawyer species. Fielding would not have us understand this in the tradition of the static type as a wittily entertaining Theophrastan "character." As his words suggest, his is rather a dynamic characterization that generalizes a virtual and probable model from the empirical observation of many actual particulars.

The growing importance of probability at this time in both scientific experiment and literary narration underscores their common methodological commitment to abstracting from a broadly inclusive range of data a "statistically" probable knowledge of their respective objects of study. In accord with Fielding's focus on literary narration, the probability of his plot is achieved by selecting and reordering its events to represent not what is but what might be. But the virtuality of what might be is also achieved through the self-consciousness of reflexive reference. The narrator's intrusion into the narrative, which here takes up the entire chapter, is typical of Fielding's technique in that it interrupts the reader's ongoing experience of the representation of events on the level of content by making her conscious of its representational process or form. This is reflexive reference, the self-conscious experience of form as content, whereby the reader takes in a representation that is similar to the actual while at the same time being reminded of its representational virtuality. Through this experience the reader is given the means of comparing the virtual with the actual, which creates the Addisonian pleasures of the imagination.

What makes this case atypical of Fielding's technique is that the substance of the narrator's interruption is an explanation of just this phenomenon of reflexive reference or self-conscious verisimilitude. And so the experience of a doubled consciousness, the actual compared with the virtual, is in this instance reinforced or redoubled by the account of how "several of my readers," like the actual readers of this account, might compare the actual lawyers they have known with the narrator's virtual lawyer. But the atypicality of Fielding's technique can also be understood in terms of probability. For this chapter, as an "event" that interrupts and reorders what Aristotle might call the "historical" narration of what is, reinforces narrative probability by explaining explicitly the technique of narrating what might be that it also exemplifies.

After the 1740s, the realist technique of narratorial intrusion underwent creative development.[33] A case in point is free indirect discourse, which can be seen as a substantial refinement of Fielding's intrusive technique. True, Burney (in her third-person narrations) and then Austen forgo Fielding's obtrusive embodiment of his reader within his text (although the less obtrusive invocation of the reader remains for them an occasional strategy), instead temporarily locating the reader function within one or another character through that character's focalization. They transform Fielding's punctual moment of intrusion into an extended temporal process that conflates, then re-separates, narrator and character, a process whose dialectical delicacy sustains the momentary illusion of interior depth. The reflexive effect of free indirect discourse, if plausibly continuous with that of Fielding's interruptive intrusions, is so subtly achieved that the negligent reader can miss the ruffling of the narrative surface and project onto the author a deceptive claim to transparency. But if so, the repudiation of realism for this supposed deception represents a failure not of the author but of the inattentive reader.

Free indirect discourse extends, deepens, and perfects the doubled state of consciousness that Fielding's realism inherits from Aristotelian mimesis. On reading Radcliffe, one reader writes that "the reader experiences in perfection the strange luxury of artificial terror, without being obliged for a moment to hoodwink his reason, or to yield to the weakness of superstitious credulity."[34] Here the account of a doubled consciousness acutely anticipates Coleridge's "willing suspension of disbelief."³⁵ This famous phrase has been seen as descriptive of the way readers respond according to the emergent modern notion of the aesthetic. The phrase also describes readers' response to realism, which is rightly understood to be the narrative version of the aesthetic. In the words of another reader, "The illusion is lasting, and complete. . . . I interrupt the unhappy Clarissa, in order to mix my tears with hers: I accost her, as if she was present with me. No author, I believe, ever metamorphosed himself into his characters so perfectly as Richardson."³⁶ This response describes the celebrated and seemingly paradoxical achievement of novelistic identification, which requires of the reader not the feeling of a character's immediate presence but, on the contrary, the sense of a distance, hence difference, sufficient to establish a sympathetic proximity.

Recourse to Aristotle on mimesis, and therefore to realism, is not confined to the English. I offer as an example Du Bos, whose understanding of realism was informed by reading Addison.³⁷ Du Bos interprets the difference between our response to what is re-presented, on the one hand, and to what is temporally and spatially present, on the other, as equivalent to that between the artificial and the real, art and nature: "Painters and poets raise those artificial passions within us, by presenting us with the imitations of objects capable of exciting real passions. . . . Here then we discover the source of that pleasure which poetry and painting give to man."³⁸ Then, having quoted Aristotle on the pleasures of mimesis, Du Bos echoes both Aristotle and Addison: this "is a pleasure free from all impurity of mixture. It is never attended with those disagreeable consequences, which arise from the serious emotions caused by the object itself."³⁹

So, modern literary realism sustains the essential import of classical mimesis. Yet, realism (like mimesis) has also been subject to widely divergent interpretations, particularly during the twentieth century. In its early decades, for example, three critics of different national cultures and theoretical approaches—José Ortega y Gasset, György Lukács, and Mikhail Mikhailovich Bakhtin—conceptualized the form of the novel in ways that are strikingly similar in their attention to the central element of self-conscious reflexivity.⁴⁰ At midcentury, however, the structuralist movement coalesced and generated approaches to mimesis, realism, and the novel that exerted a powerfully negative influence on their accurate understanding.⁴¹ For several decades, Gérard Genette's misreading of Plato and Aristotle provided the foundation for the theory of narrative (narratology).⁴² There Genette falsely attributes to Plato, a dialectician, an investment in dichotomous opposition—that is, in the structuralist position that diegesis and mimesis, narration and imitation, or "telling" and "showing" stand in dichotomous opposition to each other. He does this by suppressing Plato's recognition of a third or mixed mode that combines diegesis with mimesis and that dominates Homer's epic narration. As a consequence, Genette erroneously finds in Plato a reduction of mimesis to dramatic dialogue, and on this basis incorrectly takes Plato's text to be a critique of mimesis. Moreover, Genette wrongly attributes this same inaccurate reduction of mimesis to Aristotle, who, Genette falsely claims, criticizes diegesis in comparison with mimesis. By these multiple misconceptions, Genette holds that, for Plato and Aristotle, narration enables us to apprehend its object through the distancing mediation of a narrator, whereas imitation would delude us into the belief that we apprehend its object immediately and transparently. But in Aristotle, mimesis and diegesis cannot be compared or contrasted in this fashion because they occupy different orders of classification. For Aristotle, all poetry is mimetic. This isn't a qualitative judgment about the superiority of mimesis; it's an analytic judgment about the nature of poetry, including narrative.

Genette is right to treat realism as the modern equivalent of classical mimesis; but because his understanding of mimesis is defective, his assessment of realism is also defective. Drawing on a well-known essay by Roland Barthes, Genette glosses the "feeling of literal fidelity" putatively created by mimesis as a "referential illusion," an illusion that language is referring to something beyond itself. In this theory, the realist illusion is created by adding to narration words that have no structural "function" or "purpose" in achieving its narrative ends of telling, and therefore, by the logic of the opposition, must aim to show (i.e., to illusively refer).[43]

The normative opposition between diegesis and mimesis is the micro-version of structuralism's macro-dichotomy of structure and history. Yet on both levels, the criteria for the distinction, theoretically self-evident, are perhaps inevitably obscure. On the micro-level of the sentence, linguistic rules of signification purport to render the distinction systematic. But in fact Genette sometimes applies the rules of signification to actual language use with a nonsystematic looseness and flexibility, even an offhanded liberality.[44] Barthes's essay is for the most part a seemingly searching inquiry into what the criterion for structural signification might be—"Is everything in the narrative meaningful, significant?"—as well as an argument that the "rhetorical" and "aesthetic" functions of language (like the signifieds of "characterization, atmosphere, or information") impose the same sort of "constraints" on the generation of detail and description as structural signification does (12, 14). The result comes closer to the New Critical standard for interpreting a poem "in its own terms" than to the strict rules of signification internal to the language system. And for this reason, the indeterminacy of what qualifies as truly "useless detail" and "description," and the hermeneutic rather than structural basis for such judgments, come close to seeming the inadvertent standpoint of this essay.

But when Barthes turns to realism, the strict rules are in full force. For one thing, its "details" and "descriptions" have a suspect aura that's absent elsewhere in the essay and conveyed here by Barthes's assignment of a motive to realism, the motive to deceive (compare Genette's "referential illusion" and, before the age of "realism," Corneille's "deception"). Realism chez structuralism has none of the features that the preceding history shows it shares with probability and verisimilitude. Barthes's realism has no aesthetic function (e.g., the "aesthetic plausibility" Barthes finds in Flaubert [13]). "Pretending to follow" the real "slavishly," its "intention" is to close the gap between representation and presence so as to create "a pure encounter between the object and its expression," a "*direct* collusion of a referent and a signifier." Consequently devoid of reflexive self-consciousness, realism "looks like a resistance to meaning" (14, 16). Barthes's realism is thus a double deception: it proclaims the unmediated presence of the real, but this is no more than "pretending," "intention," what it "looks like," because language can't refer outside itself.

In the preceding chapter, I compared the work done by scientific method and novelistic narrative as complementary experiments in knowing nature by abstracting from it, experiments that became intelligible in these terms in the immediate wake of the early modern division of knowledge. One aspect of this comparison is the contrast between the absolute abstraction of nature undertaken by scientific method, and the partial abstraction achieved by the novel, which leaves a thickly figured representation of nature that evokes its virtual presence.

In Barthes's account, what I've called narrative experiments are no more than details and descriptions that are not simply superfluous but illusory because they don't function to narrate a story; rather, they represent the complex interfiliations of nature and culture. Historical discourse is for Barthes the model for realist narratives that fill their structural spaces with details. "What does it matter that a detail has no function in the account as long as it denotes 'what took place'?" In entering into a brief history of vraisemblance at this point in his essay, Barthes must in his own terms be seen as entering into historical discourse, a brief history of vraisemblance, and we may wonder if the details in this history refer illusively. There aren't many of them. Classical culture, Barthes observes, made a sharp distinction between the *vrai* and its *semblance*, "nourished by the idea that there could be no contamination of the 'vraisemblable' by the real" (15). However, he continues, "there is a break between the old 'vraisemblance' and modern realism." We've seen how impoverished Barthes's version of realism is by its will to deceive. Here he pursues his history by characterizing realism as "any discourse which accepts statements whose only justification is their referent" (15–16). But like his reading of realist reference, Barthes's historical reference to the nature of realism must be illusory, not only because it's erroneous but also because, by structuralist standards, language can only tell and can't show or refer to something beyond itself. Perhaps the emptiness of Barthes's detail about realism is intimated by the tautological fallacy that predicates his history on an assumption it purports to document, the break between verisimilitude and realism. In contrast, the narration I've been engaged in, whatever its shortcomings, has adduced a good deal of noncircular evidence ("evidence" is the word for detail in historical discourse) for the continuity between mimesis and realism. One such detail absent from Barthes is the naive empiricist claim to historicity, truly a *"referential illusion"* that virtual characters have an actual existence (16), and illusory not in using language to refer beyond itself but in confounding virtual representation with actual presence. Confused by Barthes with realism, the claim to historicity played a crucial role (as we've seen) in provoking the emergence of realism in explicit refutation of that claim. Barthes, oblivious to historical details, appears to collapse this dialectical process into a single term, absorbing within the naive empiricism of the claim to historicity its realist antithesis, which in Barthes's structuralist version of history never comes into being in its own right.

So, the structuralist understanding of narrative's relation to the real comes to a halt at the claim to historicity, which is also the moment of the two unities. Corneille, acknowledging that the "deception" of the audience entailed in the unities approaches a knowing self-deception justified by their (supposed) production of pleasure, comes close to discerning in the unities an instigation to realist self-consciousness. Barthes, constrained by structuralist dichotomy, shuts his eyes to the realist demonstration that language can simultaneously signify within its own system and refer beyond it. The hallmark of this evidence is realist reflexivity, the distance language takes on its own internal operations as structurally registered by the self-conscious replication of form on the level of content, which marks in turn the distance between presence and representation.

The Rise of Fictionality?

What's the relation between mimesis and realism, on the one hand, and fiction, on the other? When did the assumption of fictionality become a convention of literary narrative? In recent years, some critics have argued that literary fiction emerges only in the eighteenth century and under the aegis of the novel: according to Catherine Gallagher, "the novel discovered fiction."[45] This is a disarmingly simple claim. What does it mean? Gallagher's evidence for it is that novels feature characters who are "nobodies." "Nobody was the pivot point around which a massive reorientation of textual referentiality took place," she writes, "and the location of this pivot was the mid-eighteenth-century novel."[46] That is, evidence for the novel's "discovery" of fiction at this historical moment can be seen in the replacement of traditional narrative claims to extra-textual reference by the novel's acknowledgment that it is about "nobody." Halfway through her book, however, Gallagher writes that "there was no sudden novelistic revolution that purged English narrative of somebody and replaced him or her with nobody. Nevertheless, in the middle decades of the [eighteenth] century, fictional nobodies became the more popular and respectable protagonists" (*Nobody's Story*, 165). Gallagher's equivocal stance on this matter is reflected in her difficulty in defining the difference between narratives about somebodies and those about nobodies, or in affirming the chronology of this change, without including substantial qualifiers that vitiate the coherence of both the textual and the chronological opposition (see Gallagher, *Nobody's Story*, 165). To go no further, the notion that pre-novelistic narrative is devoted to extra-textual reference is belied by Aristotle's account of mimesis.[47]

Both before and after the statements I just quoted, Gallagher trains our attention in *Nobody's Story* on narratives whose content, and sometimes whose form, raises interpretive questions about the relation between embodied and disembodied personhood and between referential and nonreferential naming. We're left in no doubt about the importance of these matters. But as the quoted statements suggest, Gallagher must be aware that she's given us no plausible basis for associating disembodiment or nonreference with the emergent novel, or either of these with the emergence of fictionality. Equally puzzling is Gallagher's acknowledgment that, in fact, all sorts of prenovelistic narratives are devoid of actual reference and therefore may be by her criterion called fictional (*Nobody's Story*, xvi; "Rise of Fictionality," 338). That is, even as she pursues the incidence of nonreferential naming as evidence of fiction, Gallagher clarifies that what she refers to in claiming that the novel discovered fiction is the "modern *concept*" of fiction. But this doesn't really clarify her argument.

For one thing, Gallagher immediately adds that this concept "developed slowly in early-modern Europe" and therefore can't have been discovered by the novel ("Rise of Fictionality," 338). More important, I think Gallagher is mistaking the fact that the concept "had not been explicitly theorized" until the seventeenth century for evidence that it "had no existence in European culture" until then. The "modern" concept was also the traditional concept, what goes without saying or theorizing, an assumption "that is customary in the tacit practice of story-telling and -hearing and made explicit only when challenged."[48] This challenge came to seventeenth-century England with the massive, culture-wide, and unprecedented force of empirical epistemology, which solicited of traditional discourses a defense of their own access to the truth of the senses. The literary response differed from the traditional view not in kind—we credit fictions—but in the analytic precision it brought to describing "the psychological state of 'believing' a fiction, that is, 'believing in' a plausible character without believing his or her actual existence."[49] Gallagher takes the absence of this critical focus on the credibility of fiction as the absence of fiction rather than as the absence of the crisis that evoked this epistemological scrutiny. Soon this refined sense of fiction was sufficiently internalized in modern consciousness to obviate its frequent articulation, and what had been the tacit understanding became explicit.

So, Gallagher's conviction that the novel and fiction are coterminous requires of her a historical argument that evidently can't be made. The problem, I think, is that her central concern with "nobody" and its implication of disembodiment is not fruitfully coordinated with the category of fiction, which largely points in a different direction. Going by the kinds of interest Gallagher brings to her authors, the semantics of "disembodiment" are extremely various: generality, publicness, absence, absence of personal name, anonymity, allegorical evasion of libel, typographical reproduction, exchange value, literary property, legal nonentity, public credit, mutilation, blackness (Gallagher, *Nobody's Story*, 8; see "Index," s.v. "disembodiment"). And the thread that connects most of these is not fictionality but virtuality, which implies a dialectical relation to actuality, a movement between these two categories, and thereby a sense of seventeenth- and eighteenth-century historical process that becomes a permanent feature of the form. By this I mean that the intense and unprecedented awareness of empirical actuality was the precondition for the discovery of its virtual dimension in mentality, which contemporaries processed both as the antithesis and refutation of naive empiricism, and as its refinement and extension.[50] What became explicit in the mid-eighteenth century is not fictionality as such but the potential of virtuality as an instrument of knowledge whose inspiration and momentum derive from contemporary impulses toward humanist, empiricist, historicist, and analytic scrutiny of the actual. It's the self-conscious worldliness, the realism, of literary virtuality that gets—not so much "discovered" as purposively shaped—to serve as a technique of emulating the methods under development for exploiting the actuality of the material world. Unlike fictionality, realism works as a double consciousness. It enjoins the willing suspension of disbelief in the virtual to achieve the productivity of an Addisonian comparison with the actual. Before this period, many habits of thought, whether or not narrative, "went without saying" and were "taken for granted" because they were deeply embedded in social and material practice and did not require external standards of veracity to win assent. Like all other forms or bodies of thought that sought the status of knowledge, literature now became explicitly equipped with the mental capacity of epistemological distance through its powers of virtuality.

In her later essay Gallagher may affirm that what distinguishes the modern from the premodern practice of fiction is the fact that it had to be explicitly acknowledged and defended, hence explicitly conceptualized in these terms. The traditional prose narrative genres—epic, romance, allegory—had been experienced tacitly as mimetic fictions, virtual representations of the actual that gave pleasure in part by improving on what in actuality was painful, arbitrary, or simply humdrum. We might expect that when historical and empirical truth began to be accorded a newfound privilege in the early modern period, the term "fiction" would be subjected to critique, its resources of virtuality discredited as incompatible with a newly narrowed standard of truth. We encounter instances of this turn in the seventeenth century (e.g., see Sorel, section on "Verisimilitude: French Theory"). But as Sorel himself (or his translator) makes clear, the critical term of choice was, overwhelmingly, not "fiction" but "romance." Natural philosophy was in the process of reconceiving the certainty of common experience and deductive logic as the probability born of the experimental life, a reconception that self-consciously acknowledged the skepticism that must underlie the pursuit of knowledge in an analytic age. After the false start of the claim to historicity, the novel discovered that to make its truth acceptable in the modern world required that its knowledge be grounded in actuality at the same time that its virtuality was embraced, not by advertising the nonexistence of its subjects but by building into its formal procedure the claim to its own species of probability. This was achieved through the practice of realism. Toward the end of the century, as romance, ultimately under the aegis of romanticism, was being positively revalued, the concept "fiction" began to assume its blander function in the modern world of authorizing virtuality as an autonomous category severed—or freed, if you will—from dialectical connection to actuality.

3 The Historicity of Literary Conventions

FAMILY ROMANCE

> *The beginner who has learnt a new language always translates it back into his mother tongue, but he has assimilated the spirit of the new language and can produce freely in it only when he moves in it without remembering the old and forgets in it his ancestral tongue.*
> —Marx, *The Eighteenth Brumaire of Louis Bonaparte*

In its more recent history, the ancient convention of family romance made a signal contribution to the emergence of the novel, the genre of modernity. The root meaning of "convention," which suggests a tangibly shared sociability, helps pose the question. How can the forms of thought that bind together the like-minded constituents of a common culture persist in expressing the collective mentality of a disparate culture? How and why did the convention of family romance enter into the formation of the novel in seventeenth- and eighteenth-century Britain? The novelists I'll focus on in the latter part of this chapter are Richardson, Fielding, Burney, and Austen. However, some answers to these questions may be suggested by readings of the selected narratives that precede them.

The History of a Convention?

The convention of family romance was given its name by Sigmund Freud, who observed that it was extraordinarily common not only in literary works, such as romances and novels, but also in less consciously regulated fictions: folktales, fairy tales, daydreams, and nocturnal dreams. To Freud, this gave evidence that family romance possesses a universal fascination, which was confirmed for him by what seemed the abiding, even universal, significance of its content. Liberation from parental authority being essential to normal development, family romance plays an important role in facilitating this separation by expressing a young child's earliest capacity to distance himself (Freud's paradigm is male experience) from them. The form taken by the child's critical detachment is a "feeling of being slighted" (*Zurücksetzung*), a dissatisfaction with his parents for being poor, vulgar, distracted, or in other ways inadequate to the child's sense of self-importance and to his wish to be closely attended to and cared for. Over time the child becomes convinced that these inadequate and unworthy figures cannot be his real parents, that he must have been adopted by them or at least must be no more than their stepchild. The feeling of being slighted is expressed through "a phantasy in which both his parents are replaced by others of better birth." One day the real, "new and aristocratic" parents, resplendent in every way, will appear or be discovered, and they will free their child from the undeserved mediocrity of its existence. Developmentally speaking, this is the first stage of the family romance. As yet, the child knows nothing of how children are produced, although "the influence of sex" is already evident in the boy's greater hostility toward and greater need to be freed from his father than his mother. The fantasy that defines the second stage of family romance is marked by sexual awareness. Now the boy imagines that his father alone is an impostor and soon to be replaced: his mother is authentic and the boy's adulterous progenitor, immoral but also the object of his own sexual desire.[1]

In his interpretation of this second stage we can see how the family romance helped Freud concretize his theory of the Oedipus complex. And in the name that he gave to this ancient narrative, Freud, of course, embedded a profound interpretation of its meaning. I'll continue to use "family romance" to name that story but will also use, as frequently, "discovered parentage" as a more neutral description of just what all these narratives and narrative fragments have in common.

For thousands of years before Freud wrote his essay, family romance was being put to varied purposes, the earliest of which serve to single out, unlike Freud's modern and universalizing reading, extraordinary figures as the rightful founders of tribes, races, and communities. In these ancient versions, the feelings and wishes of the child are of little interest; what matters is the fact that they have been chosen by a higher power to do great things and therefore must be taken up into great families. But to speak of family romance specifies the discursive form of romance, which, whether we regard it as a convention, a genre, or a mode, imposes a structure on the myths of ancient gods, kings, and heroes, marked for singular achievements by the discovery or contrivance of elevated kinship.[2] The term applies more loosely to rationalized myths concerned with seasonal death, revival, and regeneration personified in successions of divine and heroic figures.[3] What we call the family romance of discovered parentage has the ordered shape of a story that has been disembedded from the vast cycles of oral myth, whose principal function is mnemonic, and whose principle of organization is therefore the repetition of actions, themes, and motifs that are metaphorically and metonymically connected to each other. The figure of Oedipus, for example, weaves in and out of mythic material in which discovered parentage mixes with child abandonment, banishment, entombment of the living and survival of the dead, patricide, matricide, incest, suicide, and metamorphosis between gods, humans, animals, and monsters.[4] The story of Oedipus, after which Freud named his theory of early psychic development, has the structured form neither of myth nor of family romance but of Sophoclean drama, which radically rationalizes the myth by providing the hero with an independent will that leads him to substitute his own wishes for the will of higher powers, thereby unwittingly substituting for his supposedly low parents his fantastically elevated but actual ones.

Lending support to Freud's claim of its universality, family romance pervades not only pagan but also monotheistic faiths. The oldest religion in the West is based on the story of the infant Moses, hidden by his mother to avoid persecution but found and adopted by the Egyptian royal family and destined by the Hebrew God to do great things. The Christian Gospel renounced the patriarchal tradition of paternal lineage that Moses had established, and instead encouraged true believers to forsake their kinship ties and to embrace their spiritual father in heaven. But this spiritualization of family romance was anthropomorphized in turn. Jesus himself, seemingly a child of the lowest descent, is discovered by marks and signs to be the son of the King of Kings and ascends at the end of his lowly life to assume his proper place beside his true father.

This quick review reminds us of the convention's antiquity. How did it become central to the modernity of the novel genre? And given the range of uses to which it was put over the intervening centuries, can we really speak of it as the same convention? The answer to the first question, at least, lies most immediately not in England's Judeo-Christian character but in the Norman Conquest and its consequences.

Literary Convention as Social Convention

The Norman Conquest disrupted Anglo-Saxon England first of all by creating the demographic chaos of mass migration. Within two decades the Anglo-Saxon earls and thanes were almost entirely displaced by an alien aristocracy, and the heterogeneous peasantry was conglomerated within the single category "serf."[5] But the great demographic shift caused by the conquest's migrations also brought with it the more subtle and long-term social disruption wrought by the advent of feudalism. With the breakup of the ancient Mediterranean world, Europe underwent a process of feudalization whose regional variations had in common the basic result of decentralized power and authority. Local rulers maintained the possession of their territories through military forces bound to their service by grants of land and a customary and legal system of reciprocal rights and obligations. Analogous but hierarchical levels of land and knight tenure loosely held the system together, allocating authority from the top down by personal bonds of homage and fealty, but also at each level through patrilineal inheritance practices.

Because feudal services to the lord were seen as indivisible in nature, partible methods of inheritance were deemed unacceptable for the passing on of the fief.[6] In England, patrilineage replaced the customary partible practices of the past, which had dispersed estates along relatively equal lines, with a stricter standard that allocated heritable property through the paternal line. The relatively hierarchical character of patrilineal practices was crowned by the rule of male primogeniture, whose long-term legacy was the intrafamilial rivalry between the heir and his younger brothers. In the immediate aftermath of the conquest, this rivalry fueled romances of disinheritance and exile. In the twelfth-century *Havelok the Dane*, the young princes are obliged to wander in anonymity until their inner worth, demonstrated by noble deeds, confirms their status as rightful heirs to their kingdoms. In the fourteenth-century *Gamelyn*, the eponymous hero's treacherous oldest brother enforces primogenitural disinheritance on him against their dying father's wishes for an equal partition of the estate. But in the end Gamelyn proves his worth and is rewarded by being made heir to the estate of the middle son. Over time the rivalry between the male heir and his younger brothers would become conventionalized as a socially resonant conflict between a priori privilege and unacknowledged merit. More striking in post-conquest England is the way this problematic conflict internal to the logic of familial inheritance was both contained and recapitulated at a higher level in the disparity between the criteria governing elevation and ennoblement in patrilineage, on the one hand, and in feudalism, on the other—the disparity, that is, between the predetermined honor of blood relations and the demonstrated achievements of tenurial service.

So one effect of the Norman Conquest was the inauguration of an extended and searching, although for the most part inexplicit, debate about the nature of nobility and aristocracy. The convention of family romance clearly participated in this debate, but to do so its form had to be regularized well beyond what had been achieved by earlier adaptations of myth to the conditions of literate objectification. On the one hand, the medieval romances I've been discussing maintain a focus on the discovery of true parentage as a means of vindicating sociopolitical and ethical claims that have been introduced or challenged by historical circumstance. On the other, they retain within their narrative dilations a connection to elements that have been, like the convention itself, disembedded from the older mythic substratum but rearranged in quasi-linear sequences. Ideologies of transformation that both explain the past and project the future link social to other modes of change in complex and unstable chains of signifiers for natural-cultural transformation. The most powerful and perdurable of these were generated by twelfth-century elaborations of courtly love and a concept of love service rooted in feudalism, from which issued not only the upwardly mobile chivalric challenge, the neoplatonic critique of carnal love, and the *cor gentil* of *fin amor* as well as its *stilnovist* spiritualization, but also theriomorphic descent and its sartorial disguises, demonism, and madness. The difference I'm describing is intelligible as a matter of both literary and social conventionality. That is, it can be understood both in formal terms—as a difference between myth and romance—and in terms of the long-term historical consequences of the Norman Conquest. The ongoing tendency was to figure status in terms of the social. But within this increasingly social framework, the representation of change was obscured by the static social framework of aristocratic ideology, in which family romance had an important role to play.

Family Romance as Ideology

Much of medieval romance is suffused with the supernatural and incompletely committed to syntactic continuity, but in comparison with myth romance aspires to provide a relatively lineal sequence and a texture of explanatory rationale and motivation. This formal development took place at a time when patrilineal principles of inheritance were gaining greater legal, socioeconomic, and cultural ascendancy, solidified through an "aristocratic ideology" dedicated to the conviction that social status depends on the possession or nonpossession of honor, a quality that points both outward and inward. On the one hand, honor is a function of ancestry, lineage, and the indivisibly genealogical and biological element of noble blood, and it's likely confirmed by other external conditions like wealth and political power. On the other, honor is an essential and inward property of its possessor to which the conditional or extrinsic signifiers of honor refer, and in this respect honor is equivalent to an internal element of "virtue" implicitly coextensive with "merit." The belief that birth equals worth, that honor is a unity of outward manifestation and inward essence, is the most fundamental justification for the hierarchical stratification of late medieval society by status, and its grounding in blood and lineage promises a stabilization of social identity.

But aristocratic ideology was vulnerable to the facts of life. One of these is that a patrilineal system of inheritance isn't able to generate a male line that will be continuous and self-sufficient over time. This is because demographic constraints ensure that in a stationary population, 40 percent of all families will fail to produce a male heir. Attrition in the direct male line is therefore a complication that aristocratic ideology is obliged to accommodate by several means of "patriline repair," like surrogate heirship and name changing.[7] Another fact of life is the occasional but ineluctable rise of the extraordinary to great wealth or political power. The royal grant or sale of fictitious genealogies and titles of nobility to ignoble families, if judiciously restrained from overuse, to some extent might reassert the integrity of honor by reuniting status with wealth and power. But the commonplace "true nobility" was also needed to buttress the laws of correspondence by more frankly allowing for their lapses, because it gave sanction to the rise of the humble to worldly eminence by acknowledging that rise to be an expression of singular ability and virtue. Thus true nobility, when invoked with moderation, provided a sort of social safety valve that endorsed the infrequent exception to the rule without really challenging it.[8] And the upward mobility that might result from such social anomalies could be justified in exceptionalist terms comparable to, if more naturalized than, those that in former times had explained the birth of the hero. So like playing cards, the deck of lineal inheritance could be kept in order by prudent expedients like these. But the wild card in the deck was the rule of primogeniture—or more precisely, the younger son whom it displaced, possessed of noble blood but deprived from birth of its external signifiers.

It's fair to say that in England aristocratic ideology reached its ascendancy in the seventeenth century. It's also fair to say that for a number of reasons—demographic attrition, political corruption, religious reform, economic innovation, social mobility, intellectual skepticism—the tacit belief that birth equals worth underwent unprecedented assault during this same period.[9] Ideological ascendancy can have a contradictory character, explicitly affirming what formerly had been taken tacitly to be true and right but thereby opening it up to searching historical and scientific analysis. In 1700 Daniel Defoe looked back to the Norman Conquest in expressing his grave doubts about the historical continuity of the great English patrilines:

> Thus from a Mixture of all Kinds began,
> That Het'rogeneous Thing, *An Englishman*:
> . . . .
> A *True-Born Englishman*'s a Contradiction,
> In Speech an Irony, in Fact a Fiction.

But his scorn was even greater for the idea that honor was biologically inherited through noble blood, "as if there were some differing Species in the very Fluids of Nature or some Animalculae of a differing and more vigorous kind."[10] William Sprigg argues that because miraculous births of the hero have ceased, the laws of nature should take precedence over arbitrary human law:

> The younger Son is apt to think himself sprung from as Noble a stock, from the loyns of as good a Gentleman as his elder Brother, and therefore cannot but wonder, why fortune and the Law should make so great difference between them that lay in the same wombe. . . . [Would it not be more charitable] to expose or drown these latter births . . . then thus to expose them like so many little *Moses*'s in Arks of Bulrushes to a Sea of poverty and misery, from whence they may never expect reprieve, unless some miraculous Providence (like *Pharoahs* daughters) chance rescue them into her Court and favour?[11]

The reform of inheritance law was less accessible than the reform of social convention. If the difference between the deserts of the firstborn and those of the younger son was subject to rethinking, so too might be the difference between the deserts of the younger son and those of mere true nobility. Edmund Bolton's advice to humble fathers was the same as his advice to the gentle fathers of younger sons: "Put your children to be *Apprentises*, that so as God may blesse their iust, true, and virtuous industrie, they may found a new family, and both raise themselues and theirs to the precious and glittering title of Gentlemen." According to Defoe, it "was said of a certain tradesman of *London*, that if he could not find the ancient race of Gentlemen, from which he came, he would begin a new race, who should be as good Gentlemen as any that went before them." Defoe refers to the practice of searching for one's family heraldry, or more likely purchasing it new. The two methods by which parentage is thereby "discovered" are radically different, but to Defoe it doesn't really matter because what's being discovered—uncovered—is a patriline of merit, not honor.[12]

And at a time when social justice and social stability vied for primary importance, legal reform was also possible. Toward the end of the seventeenth century, the legal device of the "strict settlement" sought to stabilize the landed estate by ensuring the descent of the entail in the male heir, but it also guaranteed provisions for daughters and younger sons. Scholarly debate about the ideological weight of the strict settlement has been lengthy and heated. Perhaps the most that can be said is that by attending closely and explicitly to the mediation of distinct family interests, strict settlement helped make explicit and active the intrafamilial tensions that until now had been perennial but tacit. Along with other developments of the period, it signaled the double-edged ascendancy of aristocratic ideology and thereby raised the question: What is the source of the gentle family's gentility? Of the narrative strategies for engaging this question, I'll focus on three sorts of family romance that are particularly significant in extending the convention through the confrontation of lineal and true nobility.

True Nobility in the Service of Patrilineal Nobility

In the first of these extensions, the subversive potential of true nobility is exploited in discovered parentage stories that aim to support aristocratic ideology by confirming that, in the end, birth really does equal worth. The paradigm case involves a young man or woman who is patently possessed of moral virtue but is also recognizable, despite years of penury or strategies of disguise, as possessed of high estate through inexpungible physical marks. In Thomas Deloney's *Thomas of Reading* (1600), the beautiful Margaret is obliged to forsake her "birth and parentage" and to enter domestic service. Although she pretends humble birth, she is so striking in appearance that she comes to be known as "*Margaret with the lilly white hand.*" In his family memorials twenty years later, Gervase Holles writes that his noble kinsman the Earl of Clare happens upon a young fellow "as he was playing in the street one day amongst poore boyes" and charitably decides to bring him home. The servants naturally set the young Francis to turning the spit in the kitchen. But as soon as Gervase sees that the boy has "a very good face and a pure complexion," he digs more deeply and finds not only that Francis belongs to his own extended family but also that he descends from a line that elevates him even higher than the Earl of Clare himself. But both stories end badly. Plagued by misfortune, Margaret renounces all worldly status and enters a monastery, while Francis proves true to his degraded upbringing rather than to his pedigree, and the once-bound apprentice steals from his master and runs away.[13]

As the case of Francis Holles makes clear, family romance was not confined to fiction. In 1651, two years after the beheading of his father, Charles Stuart was decisively defeated by Oliver Cromwell at the Battle of Worcester, and for the next few weeks wandered the countryside in disguise to avoid capture. The several royalist accounts of this episode relate that the young prince concealed himself first as a "Country-Fellow" and then as a "Serveing-man" and a "Woodcutter." The whiteness of his skin he obscured with coarse gray stockings and with a distillation of walnut rind. But despite these expedients, more than once his true identity was suspected and discovered by loyal subjects—"majestie being soe naturall unto him that even when he said nothing, did nothing, his very lookes . . . were enough to betray him."[14]

In 1660 Charles's majesty was collectively and ceremonially rediscovered. But the later years of the Stuart dynasty were fraught with challenges to the aristocratic version of discovered parentage. In 1649 Charles's father had been executed because of the disjunction between his birth and his worth—between his patrilineal sovereignty and his penchant for absolutist politics and crypto-papist religion. Charles II ruled with greater circumspection, but his younger brother, James, Duke of York, threatened to continue his father's policies so flagrantly that Parliament attempted to exclude him from the succession. In 1680 York's status as legitimate heir to the throne was challenged by the putative discovery of true parentage in a secret black box that contained documentary proof that Charles's son James, Duke of Monmouth, supposedly a bastard, was truly next in line to succeed his father because at the time that he was born to Charles and one Lucy Walter they were legitimately married. Neither the evidence of that marriage nor the effort to exclude York carried the day. But in 1688, three years after James had ascended the throne, it was announced that the queen had given birth to the Prince of Wales, heir to the throne as well as, presumably, to his father's popery. In an inversion of the replacement conventional in family romance, the king's opponents discovered that the baby's true parentage was not high but low: that the little prince was suppositious, the issue of commoners, and that he had been smuggled into the queen's bedchamber in a warming pan. This discovery, too, failed to find official confirmation (both sides rejected it as "romance"); but by then plans were underway to depose James and replace him with a dependably Protestant heir whose "true nobility" was thus far more important than the fact that he was only fifty-seventh in line for the throne. True, William's wife Mary was the deposed king's daughter and his legitimate lineal heir. But as a married woman her legal being was subsumed under that of her husband, whose weak lineal legitimacy therefore had to be loudly affirmed. It's not hard to see the Glorious Revolution as a parodic performance of patriline repair on the royal succession itself.[15]

True Nobility as Female

In the second kind of family romance that deserves special attention, the ideological implications of the discovery that birth is equal to worth are obscured by the fact that the discovery depends entirely on the worth of a female mediator. The sixteenth-century ballad "Lord of Learne," in the tradition of *Havelok the Dane*, tells the story of a boy who is alienated from his inheritance through the perfidy of a steward who forces him to serve as a stable groom. The "bonny" but docile Lord of Learne eventually regains his lost status through the enterprising influence of the Duke of France's daughter, who is instrumental in discovering his parentage, but more important—in fact, the question of the lord's parentage oddly fades into the background—in confirming his virtue by nobly maintaining her own constancy to him ("& as I am a true Ladie / I willbe [sic] trew vnto thee"). In the contemporaneous ballad "The Nutt browne mayd," not only the eponymous heroine but we as well are ignorant of the hero's noble birth until the ending discovery. All we know is that he is an outlaw and the beloved of the nut brown maid. She pursues him into the forest, reminding him that "of anceytrye / a Barrons daughter I bee, / & you haue proved how [I] haue loved / a squier of a Low degree." On the face of it, this is a poor choice on her part and proves, more tellingly, that her birth and worth are incompatible. In fact, her beloved confronts her on the unlikelihood of her choice, not to derogate it but to test her constancy to him. And once her virtue is confirmed by her constancy to his virtue, he carelessly remarks, "Thus you haue woone the Erle of westmoreland sonne, / & not a banished man."[16]

Both of these texts associate the question of nobility with a theme that is new to this inquiry: the constancy of the noblewoman. The theme itself is traditional to aristocratic ideology. The rule of female chastity (or constancy, its moralized enlargement) is the female equivalent of male honor because it ensures the direct transmission of honor and property in the male line. What's new here is, first, the momentary implication that female constancy has the power to validate nobility even in the absence of noble parentage; second, the scope and meaning of true nobility are altered. No longer the rare exception that proves the rule (nor therefore a social safety valve), true nobility becomes what is in the capacity of the noblewoman to recognize and affirm through her own internal worth.

As a social convention of patrilineal inheritance, female chastity is defined by its quality of passive forbearance. But already in these texts female constancy has become an active virtue, and in others with which they're contemporary, the theme undergoes a proleptic sea change. There the attribution or discovery of the woman's external birth is beside the point because female constancy has become the property of a commoner, and her spirited resistance to the nobleman's seductions fully demonstrates her internal worth, especially given the moral corruption with which noble lineage is increasingly associated. Here are two exemplary texts from the same period as the ballads.

Robert Greene tells the story of Calamus, "a noble man ... of parentage honorable, as allied to the blood Royall," whose "voluptuous appetite" is whetted by the sight of a "countrie huswife" named Cratyna. She resists his efforts to corrupt her and resolves "rather to taste of any miserie, then for lucre to make shipwracke of her chastitie." Calamus uses every means to break Cratyna's will—she and her husband are his tenants at will and his means are great—but her constancy is so unshakable that Calamus is reformed by her example. Ashamed of "offering violence to so virtuous and chast a mynd," the nobleman instead endows "her with sufficient lands and possessions, as might very wel maintayne her in the state of a Gentlewoman." Chaste love is the true nobility of the rustic housewife, whose constancy to virtue is rewarded by being reconciled with wealth consonant with noble birth. But Cratyna's constancy is to virtue and to herself, not to the purity of a male lineage, and the actuality of elevated status has no force in her story. The other story is that of Mercy Harvey, the sister of Edmund Spenser's friend Gabriel Harvey, who wrote but never published an account of her attempted seduction by a married nobleman. Although Mercy lacked the university education of her two brothers, she was more than literate, and her pert facility is shared with later, novelistic heroines who are greatly overqualified (like overeducated younger sons) for their modest employments. The main events of Harvey's narrative are much the same as those of Greene's, and like Greene, Harvey underscores the contrast between the incorruptibility of the "plaine cuntrie wench" and the "great dishonor" of the nobleman. At a certain point Mercy finds herself in greater danger than Greene's Cratyna ever does. But the whole affair comes to an abrupt conclusion when one of the lord's letters is misdirected to Mercy's brother Gabriel. In both narratives, dynamic constancy is the property of common women, defined against the values of patrilineal inheritance and emblematic of the honor that has been alienated from, but is still pursued by, a corrupt male aristocracy.[17] The convention of discovered parentage has no role to play in this scenario.

True Nobility as Puritan

The third kind of seventeenth-century family romance that exemplifies innovative experiment with the convention is thoroughly anti-aristocratic in ideology. Here we're concerned less with fully articulated narrative than with the elaboration of a familial metaphor we saw earlier in the Gospels and that's now brilliantly extended by Calvinist Protestantism into spiritual kidnapping. In 1640 Thomas Hooker wrote that "we are alive . . . as a child taken out of one family and translated into another, even so we are taken out of the household of Sathan, and inserted into the family of God." Many Puritans, looking back to the language of the Gospels, saw the deep relevance of family romance tropes to the terrifying experience of sacred rapture. Caught up in spiritual crisis, the Baptist John Bunyan "did compare my self in the case of such a Child, whom some Gypsie hath by force took up under her apron, and is carrying from Friend and Country." For orthodox Calvinists, good works or virtuous behavior counted for nothing in attaining salvation; divine grace was an unearned virtue, a predetermined and gratuitous gift of God. So when Calvinists counted those who were chosen by divine election within the "aristocracy of grace," they both imitated the doctrine of aristocratic nobility and criticized it—as being like grace, arbitrary and undeserved, but unlike grace, lacking the only sanction of value. According to Thomas Edwards, "It is not the birth, but the new birth, that makes men truly noble."[18]

But if an internal state of grace could not be earned by external works or circumstance, whether Roman Catholic penance or noble birth, the good one did in one's calling glorified God and seemed to confirm the soteriological significance of one's second birth. One paradox of the doctrine of the calling is that its arbitrary basis in the inscrutable will of a higher power harks back to discovered parentage in pagan antiquity, yet the calling also posits an intimate relationship with God lodged in the believer's conscience and susceptible to the moods and rhythms of subjectivity. And although explicitly denied by the doctrine of predestination, the godly service of labor discipline, fed by the stream of tenurial service to one's "Lord," also helped construct the secular belief that not inherited birth but demonstrated merit was the true index of worth.

Novelistic Parody of Patrilineal Nobility

One benefit of tracing the convention of family romance, however briskly, across centuries of usage is the lesson that even an epochal literary-historical event like the emergence of the novel can be understood as a difference not only in kind but also in degree. Parody, imitation with a critical distance, is a useful concept for conceiving this doubleness. Yet the question still needs to be asked: When does difference in degree become difference in kind, and how is that decisive distinction to be made? For example, how do we understand the way the divinity that drove the ancient convention of discovered parentage was superseded by the modern deus ex machina of self-representation? Does the latter preserve that conventionality or supersede it?

Samuel Richardson's *Pamela* (1740) offers a test case. Prefigured by those Elizabethan tales of female constancy in which the possibility of discovered parentage plays no part, Richardson's novel tells the story of a truly noble common woman through which the thread of that possibility nonetheless weaves a delicate skein. Early on Richardson primes our expectations by recourse to the aristocratic micro-convention we've already seen. One of the neighboring ladies, observing the adolescent servant girl, remarks: "See that Shape! I never saw such a Face and Shape in my Life; why she must be better descended than you have told me!" As a lady's maid, Pamela has learned from her benevolent and loving mistress all the accomplishments she would have taught the daughter she never had. Wearing the cast-off clothing her mistress has urged upon her, Pamela's external graces seem to match her internal worth so well that noble birth surely will be found to complete the picture. The novel opens soon after Pamela's mistress has died.[19]

As smart as she is beautiful, Pamela is so beset by her new master's lust—quickly unleashed after his mother's death—that she soon resolves to return to her humble home from the great house where she's been laboring as a servant. Keeping alive the intimation of discovered parentage, Mr. B. sneers at this news: "It would be Pity, with these fair soft Hands, and that lovely Skin . . . that you should return again to hard Work." Outraged, Pamela replies: "I'd have you know, Sir, that I can stoop to the ordinary'st Work of your Scullions, for all these nasty soft Hands. . . . If I could get Needle-work enough, I would not spoil my Fingers by this rough Work. But if I can't, I hope to make my Hands as red as a Blood-pudding, and as hard as a Beechen Trencher, to accommodate them to my Condition." Pamela turns on its head the aristocratic ideology of family romance since her point is that it's not noble blood that gives one soft hands; it's being relieved of common labor that makes one look nobly born. "Here, what a sad Thing it is!" Pamela reflects. "I have been brought up wrong, as Matters stand." We come by our appearances through nurture, not nature (69, 70, 76, 77).

But although Richardson's heroine fits comfortably into the model of Protestant labor discipline, it transpires that Pamela's great work is self-representation. *Pamela* is an epistolary novel composed of letters written almost entirely by Pamela to her humble parents. But once her master frustrates her resolution to return home by imprisoning Pamela on his estate and depriving her even of the physical mobility entailed in domestic service, she can envision no means of delivering her letters to her parents, and her style modulates into a continuous, expansive, and emotionally affecting novelistic mode. Much later, after Mr. B. has been converted to Pamela's pristine standards of ethical propriety, the only obstacle to marriage is their vast difference in social status. And when Mr. B. secretly summons Pamela's beloved father and arranges a highly theatrical scene of discovery, we find ourselves viewing a fully enacted parody of discovered parentage that both brings to a head and finally puts paid to hints that we are reading a family romance. Mr. B. prepares Pamela (and us): "You shall see . . . a Man that I can allow you to love dearly; tho' hardly preferably to me." Then, "lifting up my Eyes, and seeing my Father, [I] . . . threw myself at his Feet, O my Father! my Father! said I, can it be!—Is it you? Yes, it is! It is! O bless your happy—Daughter!" Pamela's mock-discovery is that her real parent is her actual parent (289, 294).

So Richardson disposes of the fantasy of discovered parentage with the tautology of modern life: things are what they seem. At the same time he employs other conventions of family romance to focus our attention on how, if not by gentle birth, the barrier of status inconsistency might be overcome. While still imprisoned, Pamela, strolling one day with her servant guard, is approached by "a Gypsey-like Body" who offers to tell them their fortunes. By invoking the most familiar literary gypsy trope, Richardson augments the demotic alterity of the one we have already encountered—the gypsy as baby swapper, the human embodiment of extra-human narration and causation. Examining Pamela's hand, the gypsy says, "I cannot tell your Fortune; your Hand is so white and fine, that I cannot see the Lines." The gypsy rubs Pamela's hand with the dirt on a tuft of grass. "Now, said she, I can see the Lines." The gypsy then tells a distressing fortune: Pamela will never marry and will "die of your first Child." But she also makes known to Pamela that she has hidden what turns out to be a "Bit of Paper" in another tuft, which Pamela retrieves and finds is an anonymous warning that Mr. B. plans to trick her into a sham marriage (223–225).

The gypsy episode recurs to the trope of fair skin as a signifier of noble blood, but only to deny it: to become legible, Pamela's hand, and its genealogical "lines," must be returned to the condition that signifies her truly common status. On the matter of marriage, the written "fortune" does not differ greatly in substance from the traditional, spoken one, but its detailed specificity removes it from the realm of irresistible necessity. And while the paper fortune omits direct reference to childbirth, in this context it alludes to an alternative solution to the problem of status inconsistency. For some time now Pamela has been conducting a secret correspondence with Mr. Williams. In order to hide the, Pamela has been secreting on her body the fast-accumulating papers filled with her novelistic account of things (the following day she writes that the latest packet "I still have safe, as I hope, sew'd in my Under-coat, about my Hips") and periodically leaving them under pre-designated garden plants for the parson to find and transport to safety. The location of Pamela's papers suggests a metaphorical childbirth that's antithetical to the traditional serviceability of the gentlewoman to the noble patriline. Preparing to lay a packet of papers beneath a sunflower, Pamela earlier writes: "How nobly my Plot succeeds! But I begin to be afraid my Writings may be discover'd; for they grow large! I stitch them hitherto in my Under-coat, next my Linen." Of course her writings do get discovered. Constant in her resistance to the traditional plot of serving nobility by ensuring the purity of its lineage (a fiction she at one point explicitly refutes), Pamela is also constant in her alternative resolve to create herself by writing her own story and thereby discovering her own parentage of herself. "Published" clandestinely, Pamela's self-representation persuades its first reader, Mr. B., to reconceive the generic plot they are in the process of living as not a romance but a novel, and the solution to status inconsistency as not a noble birth but the demonstration of true nobility and upward mobility through marriage (227, 130–131).[20] Richardson's parody of family romance fundamentally revalues the convention; is it thereby repudiated? Or is its conventionality a precondition for, even a fundamental component of, the formal revision Richardson conceives? Is the preservation of the convention not alternative to, but coextensive with, its supersession?

Although Henry Fielding found many things not to like in the style and morals of Richardson's novel, the parody of family romance was not one of them. And by preserving rather more of its micro-conventions than *Pamela*, *Joseph Andrews* (1742) supersedes family romance more definitively. Early on, Fielding gives us signs that his two amatory protagonists, virtuous commoners who love each other to distraction, will be found to be of higher birth. Like Pamela, Joseph and Fanny have the beautiful skin that portends the discovery of a birth equal to their worth.[21] But in creating the expectation of a climactic revelation of gentle parentage, Fielding goes a good deal further. Halfway through their adventures we meet a trustworthy gentleman, Mr. Wilson, who narrates with pain his loss of his infant boy many years ago, "stolen away from my Door by some wicked travelling People whom they call Gipsies; . . . he should know him amongst ten thousand, for he had a Mark on his left Breast, of a Strawberry" (195–196). And at the end of the story, in a bewildering series of revelations and reversals, it appears that the two lovers may be brother and sister and their match therefore unthinkable. But it turns out that Fanny, too, had been abducted—by the same gypsies—and is therefore discovered to be the daughter of Joseph's humble parents. But the infants were switched in their cradles, and Joseph, strawberry mark and all, is revealed in turn to be the son of the gentleman Mr. Wilson.

So on the face of it, Fielding's novel would appear to recapitulate the aristocratic version of family romance by representing how worth really does bespeak good birth. But Fielding has deeper motives. Throughout this novel, and in opposition to Richardson's pretense that *Pamela* is the documentary history of an actual person, Fielding's highly intrusive narrator has made it clear that the document we're reading is the author's total fabrication. Amid the incredible double discovery with which the novel ends, Fielding's narrator remarks that Joseph and Fanny "felt perhaps little less Anxiety in this Interval than Œdipus himself whilst his Fate was revealing." Now, while Sophocles is no doubt the instrument through which works the tragic hand of fate, he takes no responsibility for the causation he only represents. But when Parson Adams remarks to Mr. Wilson that "Fortune hath I think paid you all her Debts in this sweet Retirement," and Wilson replies, "I am thankful to the great Author of all things for the Blessings I here enjoy," it's hard not to hear Fielding inviting us to recognize that in this universe, the role of Fortune is played by himself (295, 195).

Since this story consists of one plot after another hatched by vicious characters to victimize the virtuous, each plot foiled only in the nick of time by equally incredible contrivances, readers are obliged to see that the family romance ending has no real-world implications. Novels are fictions that human authors create in order to achieve the sort of poetic justice scarcely ever meted out in reality, whether by fate or human law. But if this is true, we're not invited to see family romance as being any greater contrivance than the many other literary and social conventions thrown into relief by Fielding's skepticism. *Joseph Andrews* is a revolutionary, ground-clearing manifesto about the nature of aesthetic experience whose point cannot be reduced to, but is congruent with, the caveat that art should not be confused with life. It rubs the reader's nose in the conventional as training for future encounters with conventions that seek to efface their conventionality, their aesthetic nature.

A parody of family romance, *Joseph Andrews* is celebrated more particularly as a parody of *Pamela*. Fielding's premise is that Joseph is the younger brother of Pamela and a pious imitator of her gendered constancy. Although defensibly rationalized as a Christian rather than an aristocratic virtue, Joseph's constancy still seems a bit silly. This is because in the century between 1650 and 1750, gender difference underwent a revolutionary dichotomization, in part through the emergence of what a later age will call (male) homosexuality, a category that helped concretize the opposition between masculinity and femininity through the mediation of what was at once both and neither.[22] Fielding makes nothing of Joseph's "fine skin" in this respect, but that micro-convention of aristocratic family romance had become vulnerable to the hypothesis that the contemporary corruption of the nobility was the generation of sodomy.[23] The author of a satirical tract of 1747 writes of the male type of "the pretty gentleman": "Observe that fine Complexion! Examine that smooth, that Velvety Skin! View that *Pallor* which spreads itself over his Countenance! Hark, with what feminine Softness his

Accents steal their Way through his half-opened Lips! Feel that soft Palm! . . . The *Pretty Gentleman* is certainly formed in a different Mould from that of Common Men, and tempered with a purer Flame. . . . It looks as if Nature had been in doubt, to which Sex she should assign *Him*."[24] In this economical formulation, the "pretty gentleman" is distinct from "common men" in the sense of both social status and gender difference. Fine skin, increasingly debunked as a sign of nobility, is validated, as in Richardson, as a sign of something else entirely.

Discovery Within

The literary and social developments I've been describing can be understood in relation to long-term changes in attitudes toward the nature and value of the family. By discovering the true, elevated parentage of the obscure and lowly, family romance marks first the sheer wonder of how higher forces—fate, the gods, divine Providence—intervene in human affairs, and then the symmetry of human greatness, the ultimate correspondence of worth and birth. In medieval and early modern England, the family's vital role in the upper social tiers was the perpetuation of the patriline, the honor and property embodied in the male heir and passed on to future generations. And for this reason great value was accorded to the ties of blood—in the language of kinship, to consanguinity. Toward the end of the eighteenth century these traditional norms were beginning to be replaced by the modern norms of conjugality, which over time value the perdurability of the family less than the affective depth of present family relations created through marriage.[25] This shift is related to another. The novel comes into being with Western modernity, when the imagination of anthropomorphic extrahuman powers is waning and the creative force of interiority—human authorship, mentality, imagination—is gaining credit. And if novel plots tend to trace a rising trajectory (as the Bildungsroman often does) in which protagonists attain an eminence that was not evident earlier as their just deserts, it's less likely to be because they've always been possessed of an external condition that's only now disclosed and more likely to be the result of a change internal to their characters. Yet the discovery of parentage, even if its causal finality is diminished and its very presence obscured or displaced, remains central to novelistic representation.

Frances Burney's *Evelina* (1778) is ostentatiously committed to preserving the archaism of family romance, but with a parodic obliquity. We and Evelina know from the outset that she's the daughter of Lord Belmont. But we also know that his marriage to Evelina's mother was clandestine and that the marriage certificate has been destroyed. For most of the novel we're therefore asked to condemn Belmont for his cruel disregard of his daughter. But we and she learn toward the end that he's been deceived by an ambitious nursemaid (whose intrusive household authority modernizes the more traditional alterity of the gypsies) who switched the infant Evelina with her own child. So Evelina, having moved to London from the country, learns the ways of city sophistication as a beautiful heiress condemned to subsist on the meager allowance of her rural guardian.

Burney depicts a London teeming with a heterogeneous mixture of "strangers." Suggesting how physical mobility and urbanization have contributed to the centripetal shrinkage of the modern conjugal family, some of these strangers include her own "relations" (her maternal grandmother and cousins), whom she "discovers" for the first time and with whom she has nothing at all in common.[26] Evelina values the affective strength of traditional kinship terms, and she soon learns to award them on the nongenealogical basis of sympathetic proximity—and to no one more confidently than her guardian, whom she insistently addresses as her "father" (26, 131, 126, 266). This is the principle that guides the convention of discovered parentage in Evelina: not lineal filiation but emotional affiliation.[27] Burney writes under the spell of the cult of sensibility, and over the course of the novel Evelina learns to renounce her traditionalist dependence on male protection and to be guided instead by her own acute sense of the vices and virtues of those around her, whose manners and countenances she learns to read with extraordinary sensitivity. And this is a good thing because the men she encounters, from aristocrats to parvenu shopkeepers, are to a man predatory, hypocritical, or at best irredeemably vulgar. An exception is Lord Orville. As he and Evelina fall in love by passionately and wordlessly reading each other's minds in their countenances, we witness a prime instance of the elasticity of conventions. Aristocratic family romance had turned on the evidence of nobility that was visible on the subject's face and body. Burney preserves but supersedes this romance trope by turning visibility into deep legibility, not a recognition of social value on the surface of the body but an internal communion, through the body, with another's mind and soul. Female constancy has become a faculty of psychological insight.

Reading minds is like reading letters; but as Evelina becomes increasingly expert in the former her skill at the latter lags, perhaps because, for Burney, documents—language itself—are relatively crude and deceptive instruments of communication. Under the false impression that Orville has written her an improper letter (really a forgery), Evelina anxiously anticipates their next meeting with a display of sensibility that is microscopically acute: "Should the same impertinent freedom be expressed by his looks, which dictated his cruel letter, I shall not know how to endure either him or myself.... Surely he, as well as I, must think of the letter at the moment of our meeting, and he will, probably, mean to gather my thoughts of it from my looks.... If I find that the *eyes* of Lord Orville agree with his *pen*,—" But very soon she learns, by confidently reading Orville's mute response to other people's words and actions, that she has misread the offensive letter: "I should have been quite sick of their remarks, had I not been entertained by seeing that Lord Orville, who, I am sure, was equally disgusted, not only read my sentiments, but, by his countenance, communicated to me his own" (277–278, 288).

Although Evelina has come to realize that family members don't deserve their family names, Burney wants it both ways, and she arranges her novel's closure in a series of scenes that includes both the inheritance of external values (family title and fortune) and the confirmation of internal values (a deep and mutual sympathy). Still, the sequence of revelations leaves us in no doubt about which values have priority. Orville declares his love for Evelina before the romance trope of the switched infants and her rightful inheritance are revealed. And even here priorities are carefully ordered. Two maternal tokens have come into Evelina's possession: a family locket and a letter proving her identity. But once Belmont sees his late and deeply lamented wife in Evelina's face and his tears of recognition show the true motives of his heart, he receives these material and documentary tokens of parentage almost as an afterthought. Evelina's true parentage has been discovered through the lineage of feeling, and by this means she's become the subject of family romance—but in a manner that feels decidedly less romance than romantic.

My final author, Jane Austen, picks up as in other ways where Burney leaves off. For a century or more, the parodic distance taken from the convention of family romance has increasingly been expressed as a distance between birth and worth, in which the value of internal nobility is a given, and external nobility, dependent on the discovery of external parentage, is in several different scenarios unlikely to be disclosed or even highly valued. Perhaps the conclusion that worth is not entailed in birth is foregone in a culture committed to the explicit analysis of the tacit assumption that it is. For such a culture, worth or true nobility has an ethical grounding that's defined by its autonomy of external conditions and considerations like birth—that is, defined by its subjective integrity. Austen takes us further in this direction by relocating the opposition "external birth / internal worth" one level down, where the playing field belongs to one of the adversaries and the contest is between two different species of interior will or motive. In *Pride and Prejudice* (1813) these are most commonly expressed as the opposition "(social) design / (individual) feeling," whose permutations figure in all of the novel's amatory relationships. Birth remains an important category, but its former wholeness has become fragmented. The value of titled rank itself can be expressed in terms of the amount of money it usually accompanies, and the assumption of worth has become not only a joke but also, in the empty pride of Lady Catherine de Bourgh, an old joke.

One part of Austen's purpose, in fact, is to check the emergent counterassumption that low birth equals worth, which becomes evident in her heroine's prejudiced regard for Mr. Wickham. Elizabeth falls for Wickham not only because of his charm and beauty but also because he presents himself as the victim of a frustrated family romance. As he tells the story, Darcy's father "was my godfather, and excessively attached to me.... He meant to provide for me amply" by giving Wickham a clerical living. However, Darcy senior dies before the living becomes available, and his son—*our* Mr. Darcy—jealously refuses to make good on his father's promise: "His father's uncommon attachment to me, irritated him I believe very early in life. He had not a temper to bear the sort of competition in which we stood—the sort of preference which was often given me." In this telling, Wickham is the spiritual younger son cheated of a patrimony that would have declared him the good son in all but birth.[28]

So far from possessing true nobility, Wickham turns out to be a rank opportunist who in the end finds other means to scheme his way into Darcy's family. But *Pride and Prejudice* is itself a family romance, the story of a young woman who comes to believe that her mother and father cannot be her real parents. Elizabeth already feels this about her crassly acquisitive mother when the novel opens. Her father is a different matter: Elizabeth has learned to value his coolly amusing cynicism about the social conventions Mrs. Bennet vulgarly embraces. If Elizabeth ever marries, it will be for love and not for externals as her best friend Charlotte has done, sacrificing (in Elizabeth's words) "every better feeling to worldly advantage" (96). But as the relationships that solicit Elizabeth's most acute attention—Charlotte and Collins, Jane and Bingley, Elizabeth and Wickham, Elizabeth and Darcy—develop and overlap in complex ways, the easy opposition between design and feeling and their cognates becomes increasingly difficult to maintain, and she's compelled to revise the confident judgments she'd made about some of the key players in her circle once her perspective on them becomes multiple.

Austen borrows from Burney the illuminating juxtaposition of reading letters and reading characters, but what Elizabeth learns from this is less a reassuring contrast between the stable truth-values of each than the diversity of point of view. Pemberley augments the relativity of judgment mandated by a multiplicity of perspectives: observing the outlying grounds through the house's windows, wandering through its interior, seeking out the one familiar face in the long consanguineal arrangement of the portrait gallery and finding that she's able to coordinate his point of view—she "fixed his eyes upon herself"—with her own. Soon after, Darcy himself suddenly comes into view, and Elizabeth, "overpowered by shame and vexation" at her presence there, impulsively flees into his emotional interior in a similar act of sympathetic identification: "How strange must it appear to him!" (189, 191). Elizabeth thus sees herself through Darcy's eyes, a rare moment of self-recognition prefigured by Darcy's proposal and the angry confrontation it precipitates.

In *Evelina*, the suspect nature of documentary words is captured by the forged letter from "Orville" that Evelina must read twice before she can reconcile its existence with the sensible presence of the man himself. Elizabeth's two readings of Darcy's letter allow her to see the "forged" quality of her part in their face-to-face confrontation, which now goes inward: "She grew absolutely ashamed of herself. . . . 'I have courted prepossession . . . Till this moment, I never knew myself.'" Elizabeth's initial prejudice against Darcy, reinforced by a blinkered reading of his behavior, has become a habituated "design" masquerading as "feeling," the psychological equivalent of the prepossession that external birth determines internal worth. This moment of self-recognition requires a double perspective, the self reflecting on the self, and it leads her to reflect on the nature of her feelings for Darcy with a cautiously empirical self-consciousness: "She certainly did not hate him.... There was a motive within her of good will which could not be overlooked. It was gratitude.... She respected, she esteemed, she was grateful to him, she felt a real interest in his welfare" (159, 201).

Many readers see Austen as seeking a reconciliation of social conflict, even the ideological conflict between birth and worth, through the courtship and marriage of Darcy and Elizabeth. If this includes what Elizabeth refers to above as the "courtship" of subjective states, I agree. But it is this internal courtship, and the act of reconciliation within Elizabeth's mind—better, the disclosure of psychological conflict in need of reconciliation—that most commands our attention, and the true reconciliation can begin only when the simplistic "birth vs. worth" formulation has been rejected. Nonetheless, its conclusion requires that family romance rise to the surface in the Bennet family narrative through Wickham's parodic courtship of Elizabeth's sister Lydia.

True, family romance might be said to surface much earlier than this. The paradigmatic characterizations of Mrs. and Mr. Bennet as exemplars, respectively, of social design and individual feeling are masterfully established in the first chapter. Mrs. Bennet's characterization alters little over the course of the novel, and her husband's view of her (and therefore his views in general) coincides with and is validated by that of the narrative voice (3).[29] How and why do we come to know Mr. Bennet's defects? This is a surprisingly difficult question to answer. The whole of volume 2 narrates only two relatively minor instances of his improper behavior (77, 85–86). In volume 2, Darcy's letter to Elizabeth charges that apart from Jane and herself, a "want of propriety" is betrayed by all the females in the Bennet family, "and occasionally even by your father." Pondering this letter, Elizabeth painfully reviews in her mind "the unhappy defects of her family," including her father's failure to correct her sisters' manners. Hoping to persuade him to forbid Lydia's impending trip to Brighton, Elizabeth soon after warns Mr. Bennet that the family's "importance, our respectability in the world, must be affected by the wild volatility, the assurance and disdain of all restraint which mark Lydia's character." Mr. Bennet listens sympathetically but demurs. And in the opening of the final chapter of volume 2, we read at some length that Elizabeth "had never been blind to the impropriety of her father's behavior as a husband," a defect that includes his habit of "exposing his wife to the contempt of her own children" (152, 163, 176, 180–181). Propriety is related to property. But although we're told early on the crucial fact that in default of a male heir the Bennet estate is entailed out of the immediate family, not until halfway through volume 3 does the narrator address Mr. Bennet's chronic failure, and his own awareness of that failure (he "had very often wished, before this period of his life"), to provide financially for that possibility (20, 233–234).

Two points are worth making. First, Austen's narrator withholds from us the knowledge and degree of Mr. Bennet's defective parentage (and reciprocally, the rational basis for Mrs. Bennet's marital anxieties), of which the family members themselves have long been aware. Second, the revelation of these defects is precipitated by Darcy's letter and Elizabeth's reading of it. The result is that in

Austen's hands, not only Mr. Bennet's paternal defects but also Elizabeth's feeling of being "slighted," although hinted at earlier, are brought to the level of narrative consciousness by being brought to Elizabeth's consciousness by Darcy's viewpoint. Why should Darcy be the agent of this?

Elizabeth first hears of Lydia and Wickham's elopement in two distressed letters from Jane, which firmly establish the importance of epistolary communication in maintaining family connections during this multicounty crisis. Elizabeth's anguish is extreme. Impatient early on, like her father, with the practical imperatives of family designs, Elizabeth has learned, through both Lydia's "susceptibility to her feelings" and her own, that design has its place (215). Apparently Mr. Bennet, having gone to London to aid in the search for the eloped couple, has learned this too. But his family waits in vain for a letter from him and has to rely instead on bits of news sent by Mr. Gardiner, Mrs. Bennet's brother, a London lawyer of means who with his wife has enjoyed taking Elizabeth under their wing. Even on his return to Longbourn, Mr. Bennet is quite incommunicative, and when he receives a letter from his brother-in-law, he diffidently hands it to Elizabeth to read aloud. From this we learn that Mr. Gardiner has located the couple and persuaded Wickham to accept an outrageously generous marriage settlement, a modest and official amount to be paid by Lydia's father and a much larger, unofficial one to be financed by Mr. Gardiner. All that's needed is Mr. Bennet's permission "to act in your name," which is to say to act as a surrogate father in default of Mr. Bennet himself. As Mrs. Bennet exults, "I knew he would manage every thing" (230, 232).

In the latter chapters of the novel, the semantic interchange between "design" and "feeling" is rivaled by the polysemy of "family connections," a single term whose elastic power of designation shifts back and forth between patrilineal and affective propriety. Reading Darcy's letter, Elizabeth comes to see that his "feelings" regarding "the inferiority of your connections" concern—or have come to concern—less the Bennets' genealogy than their crude and unfeeling behavior (148). From a mindless remark by Lydia succinctly representative of Bennet crudeness, Elizabeth is astonished to discover that Darcy, "a person unconnected with any of us," was present at Lydia's marriage to Wickham (243). And from Mrs. Gardiner she learns that Darcy had so strenuously insisted that he, rather than Mr. Gardiner, take on the marriage settlement, that the parentage Elizabeth has discovered might justly be said to be not avuncular but that of Darcy himself. Incidentally, although Darcy bargains down Wickham's anticipated payoff, the support he provides reverses his earlier denial of support in the form of the clerical living that Darcy senior was said to have promised Wickham. So Darcy is "discovered" to be the "father" of Wickham as well as Elizabeth.

Of the several family romances I've discussed in this chapter, only the eighteenth-century versions suggest that the cause responsible for discovered parentage, as much as it might have a transindividual, genealogical-ontological origin, resides in the mind and will of the protagonist. The mysterious core of the phenomenon is to be sought not beyond but within. And it's only Austen's version that fully transforms the convention that the exteriority of marriage is a significant confirmation of interiority by interiorizing that confirmation itself at the level of psychic discovery. This discovery has a crucial ambivalence, which Austen represents through a doubled narrative perspective. On the one hand, her narrator makes us aware from the outset that Elizabeth's parentage is psychosocially problematic; but her father's role in this appears to be no more than reactive to the defects of her mother. On the other, at the moment that Elizabeth reads Darcy's letter and learns his motives we begin to realize that the problem is equally her father's behavior—both through the medium of Elizabeth's voice, which focalizes the problem in her consciousness, and through the medium of the narrator's voice, which informs us that Elizabeth (and to some extent Mr. Bennet) has been aware of it for much longer. This differential—between the narrator's voice and Elizabeth's voice and between the past and the present—marks for us Elizabeth's emotional engagement with Darcy's perspective on her family as the moment her unconscious begins to become conscious. The micro-process by which Elizabeth's unconscious becomes conscious is the same as the macro-process by which Austen's plot reveals to us the deep truth about the Bennet family. Austen's narrative creates the conditions for our identification with her central character by reproducing the stages of her coming to knowledge in the stages of the plot structure by which we come to know it. In the dynamics of Austen's family romance, Darcy is the initial agent of Elizabeth's emotional alienation from her father, the final agent of her financial alienation from him, and the discovered father who will become her marriage choice. As in the second stage of Freud's family romance, the actual mother remains known and defective, while the virtual father is found to be the ideal image and model of her husband.

Conclusion

I'll conclude with some thoughts about how the historicity of a convention might shed light on the way we conceive literary periods and how we do literary history. Although much in this chapter suggests how differently the same convention can take form in different contexts, the nature and scope of a convention are more particular and delimited than those of a genre or discourse. Attending to the life of a convention encourages us to think across categories, about how different genres and discourses deploy the same convention, which can open up the field to a pattern of interconnections that suggests a different way of thinking about how periods might cohere and how the movement from one to another might be conceived.

There is, of course, a straightforward and unproblematic meaning to the idea that the eighteenth-century novel has a futurity, and it would be rewarding to pursue the family romance convention into the nineteenth-century novel. Dickens alone—I'm thinking of *Oliver Twist* (1838), *Bleak House* (1852–1853), and *Hard Times* (1854), to go no further—wrote striking variations that would richly extend the life of the convention. What reward justifies having chosen instead to investigate the anteriority or prehistory of eighteenth-century fiction?

It's salient to this question that it's not entirely accurate. Freud's version of discovered parentage, with which I began and which by consensus gives an umbrella name to the convention, itself exemplifies the futurity of eighteenth-century fiction, having been shaped not simply by Sophocles but by the modern turn toward psychic interiority that's significantly fueled by, among other things, the eighteenth-century novel. It's not surprising that the conventionality of family romance in *Pride and Prejudice*, the most modern of our texts, should be amenable to Freud's reading of it. This is evident not only in the fact that discovery has been internalized as a matter of bringing the character's unconscious knowledge (Elizabeth's feeling of being slighted by her father) to consciousness, but also in the fact that this process of character development is paralleled by a process of narrative development that coordinates the reader's coming to consciousness with that of the character.

Hypothetically speaking, we might expect the internalization of discovery (if not also the coordination of discovery in character and reader) to be broadly shared by other modern versions of the convention. By the same token, is it not shared by the pre-eighteenth-century versions I've discussed?

Freud authorizes the internalization of family romance in two distinct senses. First, true parentage is discovered, as in *Pride and Prejudice*, by a subject's realization, through their close attention to empirical and emotional evidence rather than through external agency or revelation, that those who claim parenthood are unworthy of it. Second, true parentage is affirmed as the subject passes through a psychic fantasy, with the implicit sense that it's been "worked through" in that passage. For Freud, the first exemplifies the manifest content of a common narrative, within which the second provides a latent psychosexual meaning. But Freud posits this latent content not as modern but as universal in all cultures, and in support of this claim he finds the paradigm case in the ancient character of the Sophoclean Oedipus, whose discovery, incidentally, the playwright coordinates with that of the audience.

Freud's universalization of family romance in the second sense of the term might invite us to posit something like a transhistorical human mind that censors its own unconscious. The twenty-first-century consensus may be that Freud's family romance is a compelling modern and Western reading whose plausibility, even for this sample, depends on interpretive evidence. But the question of universality remains even if the thesis of a psychic totality is rejected, because it inheres in the idea of an integral "convention." Is the conventionality of family romance continuous across its many versions of discovered parentage despite the apparent discontinuity, at the level of both action and contextual meaning, between the mythic, the Christian, the post-conquest, the feudal, the aristocratic, the Protestant, and the novelistic? Is the convention of discovered parentage elastic enough to encompass supernatural fiat, the naturalization of mass migration, the rationalization of worth as an entailment of birth, the material accommodation of spiritual conversion, the reward of worth with the metaphor of kinship, and a crucial stage of psychosexual development? Over the course of this remarkably *longue dureé* of transmission, do we feel a balance between the elements of imitation and criticism that compose the engine of parody that powers it? Do the successive versions of family romance preserve or supersede what precedes them?

To approach the question of the historicity of conventions in this way may also unsettle assumptions about the special nature of the novel genre. We're accustomed to seeing the novel as unusually dynamic in form, singularly given to experiment and innovation compared with more traditional and stable kinds of imaginative writing. On this basis we might expect the novelistic version of family romance to push the convention to its richest development and thereby fulfill its parodic potential. But is the parodic richness of the novel genre any greater over its three-hundred-year history than romance has been over two millennia? Is the novel perhaps simply the next stage of romance?

By this way of thinking, family romance in the eighteenth-century novel is the inventive parody of aristocratic romance, but no more a culmination than is the modern formation of the family. In this chapter, moreover, I've been generalizing about the novelistic convention of the family romance in the eighteenth century as a totality. But as we've on the evidence of *Pamela, Joseph Andrews,* and *Evelina* alone, even within that period the convention is not a single, self-identical form but a series of widely variant instances. Is the historicity of a convention nothing more conventional—that is, collective—than the singular version on which we choose to focus our attention? Or is the nature of a convention to be traced, as Freud does, to a universal human motive, like hunger, that lies beyond all specificity and generates all formal instances? These two extremes—of absolute continuity and absolute discontinuity—determine the territory of historical study.

4 The Historicity of Literary Genres

PASTORAL POETRY

This book is based on the understanding that anything that has historical coherence will display both the continuity of an integral entity and, within that continuity, the discontinuity that confirms its existence over time and space, its capacity to change without changing into something else. In the previous chapter I asked how continuously a literary convention might persist in use over a long span of time, across a broad range of genres and social orders, and therefore in service to a great diversity of beliefs and ideologies, without being judged discontinuous. In the present chapter I return to this inquiry into the historical existence of literary forms, but in different terms. Genres deploy conventions, but as literary forms they're far more complex than the elements, like conventions, they're composed of. Like conventions, genres are responsive to historical change; but for this reason we might expect them to be less adaptable to it. My choice of pastoral as the specific genre of inquiry owes in part to the fact that within the range of genres, pastoral is singularly self-conscious about the role of conventionality in literary form.

What Is Pastoral?

It's evident that ancient pastoral is defined thematically by its celebration of rural life and rustic values, and that pastoral praise of the country is informed by the counter-standard of the "urban," the negative pole of values in opposition to which pastoral praise acquires its meaning. This basic oppositional structure, grounded in a spatial or geographical antithesis between country and city, rural and urban, yields a familiar series of value-laden extensions: simplicity versus sophistication, innocence versus corruption (or experience), contemplation versus action, contentment versus ambition, private retirement versus public activity, *otium* versus *negotium*, peace versus war, communal cooperation versus individual competition, and so forth. At the most fundamental level, these analogous articulations are mutually translatable as the abstract opposition between nature and artifice (or simply art).

From this perspective, pastoral is also an ancient form of satirical or "political" poetry, because the praise of one term always carries a reciprocal, if sometimes only implicit, critique of the latter. But as the need for doubling (Is it corruption or experience? Artifice or art?) suggests, the political charge of pastoral, the basic direction of its critique, is less predictable than this implies. Doesn't pastoral also reflect on the rude and uncultured way of life from the more refined and valorized vantage point of cultivation? Received wisdom, referring us to the exemplary case of Virgil, would argue that this perspective is the normative posture not of "pastoral" but of "georgic." At the beginning of his career Virgil wrote "eclogues," which embody the basic value system I've just described and which posterity learned to call "pastorals." The *Georgics* are the work of Virgil's midcareer, as distinct (in this view) from the *Eclogues* as labor is from leisure.[1]

There's no doubt that the very purpose of the *Georgics*, which aim to provide rustic folk instruction in the science of productive husbandry, enjoins a different relationship to nature than the humble modes of life endorsed by the *Eclogues*. Virgil conceived the *Georgics* as an experimental poetic enterprise implicitly analogous to the technological experiments that are the subject of his poem (see *Georgics* I, 40–42). The *Georgics* and the *Eclogues* differ less in theme—respectively, land cultivation and animal herding—than in viewpoint and purpose: practical instruction versus tranquil description (*Georgics* III, 284–566, advises herders of sheep and goats). However, both also operate within the same basic scheme of oppositions, and each may be felt periodically to enact a value reversal that runs counter to what appears to be its more customary commitment. This can be seen in the space of a single book of the *Georgics*. The second book begins with cheerful instructions for the industrious reader-farmer on how to master nature and her lore, to domesticate and improve the wild through hybrids, cuttings, grafts, transplants, and the like (II, 35–82). By the end of the book, however, the terrifying specter of war has transformed the normative farmer into one who would shun the unnatural luxuries bred by foreign intercourse and the seductive perils of urban and courtly ambition. The point is not to condemn culture and the mastery of nature's lore but to validate as an equally blessed alternative a life lived at peace with a bountiful nature and her gods, a *locus amoenus* or "pleasant place" of uncultivated plenty that Virgil compares to life in the Saturnian Golden Age (II, 458–542).[2]

This georgic vision recalls the famous fourth eclogue, the rapt prophecy of a restored golden age predicated on the return of Saturn and Astraea, perpetual peace, and the autoproductivity of an unforced nature. And the reversal of values can be seen to operate within the eclogues as well. In the second eclogue Virgil impersonates the love-mad shepherd Corydon, whose naive complaint to his beloved Alexis voices the amused disdain of the sophisticate for the bumpkin:

> If only paltry woods and fields could please you!
> We would dwell in lowly cottages, shoot deer,
> Drive herds of goats with switches cut from greenwood.
>
> Corydon, you country boy! Alexis scorns
> Your gifts—nor could they match Iollas'.[3]

In fact, these familiar topoi of the complaint and the contest remind us that a species of ambition and *negotium* is inseparable from pastoral values, and that the *Eclogues* are insistent in their thematization of the normative "artistry" of emulation, competition, and craftsmanship. Already in Theocritus, the capacity for artfulness was central to the characterization of natural humanity.

For these reasons, I think it's important to recognize that the *Eclogues* and the *Georgics* are opposed to each other in a way that is not dichotomous but continuous and dialectical. So, when I speak of pastoral in this chapter, I should be understood to take in both the eclogue and the georgic unless I'm explicitly distinguishing between them. Recollecting his own youthful exercise in pastoral song, Virgil in fact ends the *Georgics* with the opening line of the *Eclogues*. And this has significant implications for the basic oppositional structure that provides the foundation for pastoral poetry. To speak (as I've done) of a periodic "reversal of values" in pastoral suggests that we need to complicate our view of the function of the genre—the celebration of rural life and rustic values—by acknowledging how pastoral also works on occasion to satirize these values according to the positive standard of urban cultivation. But my brief reading of ancient pastoral suggests that a more fundamental complication of values is also at work in these poems. In disclosing the art—of song, husbandry, emulation, identification—of which these artless herdsmen are capable, ancient pastoral does not so much devalue nature as partition what's thought of as a unitary category into a range of more or less "natural" embodiments.

In the first eclogue, Virgil introduces his two herdsmen to the difference between the country and the city, which they soon find isn't as simple as it seems. Tityrus, returned from Rome to his rural village, tells Meliboeus what his trip has taught him:

> The city they call Rome, my Melibee,
> I like a fool thought like our own, where shepherds
> Drive down the new-weaned offspring of their sheep.
> Pups are like dogs, kids are like mother goats
> I knew, and thus compared great things and small.
> But she, among cities, holds her head aloft
> As cypresses among the creeping shrubs.
>
> —I, 19–25, pp. 10–11

Tityrus has discovered that the difference between urban metropolis and rural village isn't only one of size, and the gratitude he feels in returning to country ways and values is very great. Meliboeus, evicted from his farm and facing exile abroad, has learned a different sort of lesson:

> Ah, but we others leave for thirsty lands—
> Africa, Scythia, or Oxus' chalky waves,
> Or Britain, wholly cut off from the world.
> Shall I ever again, within my country's [*patrios*] borders,
> With wonder see a turf-heaped cottage roof,
> My realm, at last, some modest ears of grain?
>
> —I, 64–69, pp. 14–15

Both men are country folk and share country values, and the elevation of perspective would seem to confirm the proportional relation that great things may indeed be compared with small. For Tityrus, metropolitan Rome is to the countryside as, for Meliboeus, metropolitan Italy is to one or another foreign province. But the elevated perspective is confusing, because it unites in the greater term—Italy—what in more local terms are opposed. The great doesn't compare with but contradicts the small. And we hear this in the language of the rural—the turf-heaped roof, the ears of grain—that Meliboeus uses to describe Italy, "my country's borders, my home." Were this a proportional relation we would expect to see the hinterlands as a pleasing rustication rather than as a loss. And we wouldn't expect the paradoxical implication that to leave Italy, the hub of civilization, is to leave the rustic farm and homestead, the locus of country values.

On this basis one might say that Virgil's first eclogue teaches the lesson that the meaning of "nature" is always from a perspective, within a certain context. A similar lesson structures more explicitly what may be for eighteenth-century readers the most influential of Horace's pastorals, the second epode. All but the last few lines of the poem are dedicated to the description of an idyllic rural retreat whose "georgic" investment in honest, strictly domestic, husbandry is preceded by the famous "pastoral" invocation of a life devoid of negotium:

> Happy the man who, far from business and affairs
> Like Mortals of the early times,
> May work his father's fields with oxen of his own,
> Exempt from profit, loss, and fee.

But the end of the poem abruptly sets a framing context for this vision:

> Now with these words the money-lender Alfius,
> Soon, soon to be a country squire,
> Revoked all mid-month loans at interest—
> But plans relending on the first.[4]

From this perspective, the genial georgic *otium* of the rural retreat (the epode's celebrated first line is *Beatus ille qui procul negotiis*) is suddenly rendered continuous with—financially dependent on and morally inseparable from—the urban *negotium* of the parvenu moneylender. If the ostensible reflection is on Alfius the moneylender, who lacks even the courage of his effrontery, the underlying (and rather more powerful) critique is of the simplicity with which "pastoral" oppositions between country innocence and city corruption are conventionally affirmed.

But my point is that pastoral works both to affirm and to suspend such oppositions—to conceive them, that is, not dichotomously but dialectically. Pastoral opposes nature and art in such a way as to intimate simultaneously their interpenetration. This is recognizably the structural or presentational premise of the genre. As Frank Kermode remarks, "The first condition of Pastoral is that it is an urban product."[5] An artful impersonation of nature, pastoral deploys the sophisticated technology of poetic culture to represent its absence, and it's in the self-consciousness of this paradox that we recognize the characteristic complexity of the genre.

In Theocritus, and then quintessentially in Virgil, this is first of all a complexity of form and tone, a layering of lyric, dramatic, and narrative modes whose resulting multivocality both articulates and conflates the voices of which it's composed. By these means pastoral is felt to be inseparably "about" both nature and the poetic technique by which nature is enclosed and represented. But the formal and tonal complexity of the genre is the means by which its characteristic complication of geographical, cultural, and axiological relations is also ensured. Pastoral is the supreme poetic form of conventionality, not only because it presents itself as a critique of (social, political, poetic) convention or because it (inevitably) elaborates this critique in conventional ways, but because, in seeking to be mindful of both of these conditions at once, it takes as its subject the problem of conventionality itself. The instability of pastoral is therefore not an adventitious accident or a historical accretion but congenital and constitutive of it as a genre. Pastoral is a cultural mechanism whose poetic and ideological function is to test the dialectical fluidity of dichotomous oppositions.

Pastoral and Periodization

If the argument of pastoral is fundamentally one of location and geography, it's also, by a familiar and resonant extension, one of temporality and time. Pastoral's temporal dimension can be felt as a subtly emotional inflection of spatial detachment, the evocation of an immediacy that's nonetheless elusive, perhaps irreversibly unavailable. Like the *locus amoenus* of unmotivated—and therefore endless—delight, the pastoral countryside and its innocent dramas feel charmed into timelessness by the round of seasons that freeze nature apart from our flux of culture and change. Thus informed in a general way with the aura of a perpetual past "when life was simpler," pastoral also may render temporal detachment explicit, through a framing retrospection to the time when Daphnis still sang, or to the time before war and trade corrupted the land, or to the Age of Gold or the Garden of Eden. In all such retrospects, it's the past that's given the normative charge, even if it's "the past" as it's felt still to suffuse our present. The most ancient source of this thought is Hesiod's *Works and Days* (c. 700 BCE), a devolutionary periodization from the earliest golden race that lived in a *locus amoenus* and was free of labor, to a silver and a brazen age, to the age of heroes Homer sings of, to our own, fifth race of iron, rent by vice and evil.[6]

Yet the tacit implication of the temporal within the spatial is also available in a contrary, urbanist register, as in the opposition between "backwardness" and "development." And this suggests the way the temporal opposition in pastoral becomes hospitable to the sort of dialectical complication characteristic of its spatial analogue. If the *locus amoenus* is "now," how were things different "then"? In the fourth eclogue the initially intelligible distinction between past and present is quickly clouded not by the mildly paradoxical prospect of a golden age of the future—*redeunt Saturnia regna*—but because the narrative logic of this prospect leads Virgil's account of how we get there to run simultaneously both forward and backward through the history of civilization. The iron age both dies and converges with the golden, and the temporal borders erected to distinguish innocence from guilt, hope from desperation, helplessly bleed into each other. Just as ancient "pastoral" demonstrates its ready incorporation of "georgic" values, so this logic reveals the genre's capacity to celebrate at once the antithetical norms of a primitivist and a progressive historiography.

The fourth eclogue is also the supreme and concentrated instance of the more diffuse pastoral tendency to challenge the powers of normative periodization not through skepticism but through a kind of supersaturation. The multiplication of retrospects and ruptures, some personal, some historical; the competition between alternative temporal divides, all of compelling authenticity for disparate speakers: these temporalizing projects need not accompany in any precise way the destabilizations of spatial opposition that I've already described as fundamental to pastoral, but they reinforce its basic dialectical tendency. The effect is to relativize periodization even as it's promoted. The sense of time as an apocalyptic watershed coexists with the sense of time as history, as a dialectical construct in which the past acquires meaning as a projection of the present's understanding of its own alterity. Although most pastoral poetry doesn't complicate its treatment of temporality to this degree, it's in this respect that I want to suggest that the genre takes as its subject the problem of periodicity itself.

There's another way Virgil's fourth eclogue paradigmatically enacts pastoral's concern with periodization. Here the concern is an "extrinsic" feature of the poem's interpretation that parallels the "intrinsic" preoccupation with temporal divisions that I've just discussed. The Christian allegorization of the fourth eclogue reconceived it for a new epoch according to the subtle teleology of typological thought. By this reading, pagan pastoral is subjected to a normative transvaluation, annulled and revived at a higher level: Nature / Art becomes Grace / Nature. The interpretive history of the fourth eclogue as proleptic sacred prophecy therefore recapitulates the history—of past as future, of the golden age as the time to come—it narrates. Once again, however, the fourth eclogue only concentrates a pervasive tendency of pastoral interpretation to repeat, in its generic histories, a temporalized version of the genre's constitutive instability. Theocritus is the unequaled founder of the genre, but Virgil imitates him with such surpassing skill that he reinvents—or "institutionalizes"—the genre in a new form. In this familiar view, Theocritean origins are associated with a "natural" and relatively immediate rusticity that's both subsumed and preserved by the idealizing and sophisticated artifice of Virgil. And although this view invites us to oppose the nature of Theocritus to the art of Virgil, it also presupposes their unity under the aegis of a common pastoral purpose. Indeed, the opposition is recognizably a periodization of the singing contests whose modest emulativeness ruffles the rural surface in both poets. A yet subtler evocation of their debate may be sensed in the elegiac mode that sometimes colors those contests: Virgil's Menalcas is to his Daphnis not only as Theocritus's Thyrsis is to his Daphnis but also as Virgil is to Theocritus and as the Roman present is to the Greek past.[7]

Of course, the problem of periodicity is central to any essay in literary history that takes its task seriously. My aim here is not to claim its centrality to the interpretation of pastoral in particular, but to exploit the striking way pastoral thematizes such disputes in order to illuminate what happens to the genre in the early modern period. I'll approach this question by contrasting the viewpoints of two recent, powerful readers of early modern and Enlightenment pastoral.

Focusing on Renaissance texts and concluding with Andrew Marvell, Frank Kermode's anthology of English pastoral poetry represents by its very selection the view that the great tradition comes to an end after the middle of the seventeenth century. What the Renaissance poets knew, Kermode says, is that artifice is vital to pastoral: close attention to its empirical accuracy misconceives its central purpose. According to George Puttenham, the eclogue was devised not "to counterfeit or represent the rusticall manner of loues and communication: but vnder the vaile of homely persons, and in rude speeches to insinuate and glaunce at greater matters."[8] In this view Samuel Johnson's complaint at the artificiality of *Lycidas* (1638, 1645) betrays his age's indifference to this central purpose, one of whose implications is that what pastoral poets imitate is less "nature" than the conventionality of their predecessors. Of *Lycidas* Johnson writes: "Its form is that of a pastoral, easy, vulgar, and therefore disgusting"—which, despite Johnson's syntax, seems to refer to the poem, not the genre. His central criticism isn't of pastoral's conventionality but of Milton's conventionality in performing the genre's well-known conventions. One such complaint, about the poet's representation of his youthful friendship with Edward King, puts us in mind of Puttenham: "We know that they never drove a field, and that they had no flocks to batten; and though it be allowed that the representation may be allegorical, the true meaning is ... uncertain and remote."[9] Against such criticisms and to argue his periodization, Kermode wittily employs one of the most celebrated pastoral conventions of all, the invocation of the golden age: after Marvell "the true impulse of rustic Pastoral petered out; it was something the Giant Race had understood." And he adds: "The eighteenth century excelled in the mock-Pastoral, which is a kind of pantomime following the great play" (42; see also 11–13).

For Raymond Williams, pastoral poetry owes its vitality to the tension the poet's effort to see "the real social conditions of country life" imposes on the poetic tendency toward abstraction and idealization.[10] In Williams's history of pastoral, the Renaissance constitutes not the consummation of the golden age but a fall into relatively uncomplicated artifice. The rural setting comes to be taken as no more than an allegorical mirror for an urban and courtly aristocracy—or for an emergent agrarian capitalism—and the ambition to see the countryside clearly is obscured by the counter-ambition to turn "simple" matter to other, "higher" ends. This may be only to fulfill Kermode's insight that "the first condition of pastoral is that it is an urban product." But it also turns his critique of Enlightenment pastoral against itself because it reduces rural and common life to mockery, a mere "pantomime" of greater matters. The point at which this fall is reversed isn't precisely specified in Williams's literary history—for him, Pope only extends the neoclassical idealizations of Renaissance practice—because it enacts in a more concentrated chronology the aim of the British Enlightenment to criticize the Renaissance project of treating common life as devoid of importance and therefore as signifying the significance it lacks. Williams associates the parodic obliquity of much Enlightenment pastoral not with a devolutionary "mock-pastoral" but with a "counter-pastoral" impulse to supersede the past by preserving it at a critical distance, which can be summed up as the will to describe what the countryside is really like.

There's a sense in which both of these apparently incompatible views of pastoral are right. Williams is to Kermode as Theocritus is to Virgil, or as "pastoral" is to "georgic." That is, they schematically occupy alternative and partial positions on a pastoral continuum that's defined not by the dichotomous opposition of nature to art but by the fluidity with which that differential may be variously enacted. Kermode, rightly insistent on the way "art" lies secreted at the heart of this putatively "natural" form, elevates Renaissance artifice; Williams, rightly mindful that the reflexive conventionality of the form exists to enable an account of the natural order of things, elevates Enlightenment "realism."[11]

Nonetheless, these two critics agree that in the period from 1650 to 1800, pastoral poetry undergoes a fundamental change that's related to a material transformation of the English countryside. Although he's not committed to a strictly generic focus, much of Williams's book is dedicated to disclosing, with consummate intelligence, the complex and powerfully determinate connections between a changing literature and a changing way of life. Kermode's aims are introductory and very different;[12] still, he too remarks at one point that "certain things of importance had reduced the relevance of the old Pastoral. London had lost the country; its maypole, as Pope observed, had been taken down" (Kermode, 42). In Kermode's remarks there's the nostalgic implication that early modern change—Kermode doesn't specify material change, but this is surely part of it—rendered pastoral anachronistic.

Capitalism Began in the Countryside

Although it would represent not "culture" but "nature," pastoral inevitably presupposes people: voices speaking singly and in dialogue, figures populating the countryside in labor and leisure. What we take to be "natural" about these people is not an essential attribute but the way they live in relation to nature and one another. As Williams and others have observed with respect to Virgil, the depiction of these pastoral relations doesn't preclude rural disturbance and social change (Williams, 16–17). But the conventionality of the form after the Roman poets silently tends to assume a static social order against which more local and individual evocations of disorder—ambition, rivalry, death—may emerge with clarity. What does it mean to speak of fundamental material change in the early modern period, and how might such change be related to the contemporary depiction of pastoral relations?

The capitalist revolution of English modernity began not in the industrial nineteenth century but in the "preindustrial" seventeenth-century countryside. During the past fifty years or so, the consolidation of this crucial revisionist insight has made clear as well that the intricate and overdetermined story of the capitalist revolution can't be told in any linear fashion—or with any certainty of where to begin. Using modern techniques of quantification developed during the Enlightenment, we can make explicit (although at the most abstract level of analysis) the experience of social change that for contemporaries was relatively tacit. These yield a set of striking demographic figures. In the early modern period, England's population rose by 280 percent, the urban percentage of its population quadrupled, its agricultural productivity more than doubled, and the proportion of its rural population that was engaged in agriculture fell by more than 50 percent.[13] These figures, all of which are exceptional when compared with those for other major European countries and for England's previous development, have an evident interdependence that can be rationalized in different ways. One example: the increase in the national population, especially in the urban sector, created an unprecedented demand for food. The resulting rise of a national market spurred both agricultural productivity and the growth of nonagricultural activities in the countryside—those directly associated with the agricultural market itself (like transport systems and commercial exchange), but also those stimulated by the availability of labor formerly concentrated in food production (small manufactures, specialist craft work, service industries). Yet urbanization and the general level of population growth could have been sustained only by increased rural productivity both inside and outside agriculture.

What are the implications of these developments for the relations between people viewed at a less elevated level of abstraction? First, at the beginning of this period the proportion of rural agricultural to rural nonagricultural employment was four to one; at the end these labor sectors were about equal.[14] In other words, industrious activities once experienced as relatively anomalous and marginal to the traditions of country life had come to be as unavoidable as herding and farming themselves. Second, the growth of a national commercial infrastructure brought rural England into intimate proximity and unavoidable interaction with elements of a burgeoning urban culture. Third, increased productivity required that agriculture be commercialized on a scale never before experienced. The ideology of "improvement" ensured that the technological "arts" of modernized husbandry took ostentatious root within the "natural" countryside of early modern England.

This brief account broaches two distinct but related questions. First and most immediately, how did this convergence of industry and agriculture affect the transformation of the pastoral genre from its Elizabethan to its Enlightenment form? On the one hand, we can view this convergence in the familiar terms of a challenge to the opposition of art and nature. However, I've argued that this challenge, although of relevance to pastoral, is not a challenge to pastoral form but a crucial component of it and therefore compatible with its historical continuity. On the other, we can see this convergence as the symptomatic origin of a material transformation of the countryside that's unprecedented in English history in its rapidity and extremity. Capitalism emerged in England in this place and at this time and is an Enlightenment phenomenon. Did it complement the genre's characteristic dialectic of art and nature and thereby sustain the continuity of the genre? Or might the difference of degree—between earlier conditions of the pastoral dialectic and this material change, which radically transformed the nature of modernity—have amounted to a difference in kind and left pastoral in its wake, as Kermode and others have suggested?

The first question, regarding the history of the literary genre, evidently begs the second question, regarding material history. What do we mean by the emergence of capitalism? If the Enlightenment is rightly understood in the broad terms I've used in this study—as having rendered the tacit explicit through the analytic partialization of traditional wholes—we'd expect both the material and the generic transformations to be intelligible by this model. And if so, either the correspondence of material and generic change might have an equilibrium that would support their dialectical relation and the continuity of the genre, or the coming of capitalism might so overbalance that relation as to render pastoral obsolete. I'll begin with the second question, of material change, and then turn to the question of generic change.[15]

The terms in which we conceive the transition from feudalism to capitalism offer a template for the transition from traditional communities bound by customary ties, duties, and commitments to modern communities of mobile and relatively autonomous individuals. In premodern England, physical mobility beyond the immediate circle of daily routine was limited. Social relations were local and face-to-face, between people who knew each other as fellow members of a relatively closed community through which the passage of strangers was unusual. People thought of themselves less as singular, autonomous, and mobile individuals than as constituent parts of a greater whole, and whose being was defined by and inseparable from their social roles. The feudal economy, in this respect akin to the Roman Catholic Church, was hierarchically stratified into status groups, each of which had prescribed, but reciprocal, relations with those above and below them. Reciprocity depended on the understanding that what characterized each group was qualitative in nature and relative to the quality of other groups on a differential scale that was common to them all. Inferiors deferred to superiors and were obligated to them, through land service or knight service, as their superiors were mutually obligated to afford them protection in return. Payment in these exchanges was in kind—that is, in goods and services. The ultimate authorization of hierarchy came from a nonphysical God and God's nature; its ultimate experience was visible and palpable.

In such a system, social, economic, and political relations were embedded in daily life, interwoven into a single fabric whose wholeness conveyed a sense of existence as a tacit givenness, what goes without saying. In the system that replaced it, these relations were disembedded from their common substratum, separated out, and felt to need and assume their own distinct rules of operation, all of which tended to abstract and mobilize what before had been experienced in more concrete, personal, and static terms. This account of the transition from feudalism to capitalism can evoke the nostalgic retrospect for an absolute prelapsarian existence whose relativity Raymond Williams unmasks through the figure of a diachronic escalator taking us back through the multiplicity of falls from an ideal "natural economy" that stops only at Eden, or Hesiod's Golden Age (9–12). But the distinction I've made is obviously schematic. "The vast majority of cultures make some space for exchanges which display many of the features which are sometimes, as in our own society, associated with monetary exchange (a degree of impersonality, considerable scope for individual gratification and a concern for pure instrumentality, for example)."[16] This caveat is in keeping with the distinction between tradition and modernity as it's employed in this study, a methodological necessity whose overarching schematism must be assessed at every point in terms of specific levels of analysis and evidence. At the same time, it must be kept in mind that of these several features my focus is on impersonality alone, and in the specific sense of the virtualization of actual embodied relationships.

One of the most important results of the early modern disembedding of feudal relations was the separation of the economy from the polity. At the beginning of the seventeenth century, the terms "state" and "estate" were used interchangeably because the political state was inseparable from the king's economic estate.[17] By the end of the century, the monarch had ceased to own the kingdom as the feudal fee or public estate of his body political and became instead the supreme administrator of the public state, against whose protectionist interference the liberty of private property owners came to be defined. The elite nobility's feudal obligation of land service to English monarchy gradually waned in the sixteenth and early seventeenth centuries, affording great landholders absolute ownership of their property and full autonomy to use and invest it according to their own economic interests. It became popular to refer to this sort of investment in landed property as the "improvement of the estate," exploiting the ambivalence of the term to suggest that to render private ownership profitable as a matter of self-interest fulfilled a higher moral end.

After the king had been defeated in civil war, the devolution of royal absolutism to absolute private property was officially ratified in 1646 by the parliamentary abolition of feudal tenures. Daniel Defoe thought that the English gentry thereby held and inherited "their lands in capite, absolutely and by entail. . . . All the knight's service and vassalage is abolish'd, they are as absolutely possess'd of their mannours and freehold as a prince is of his crown."[18] Those who worked the land of the great, no longer remunerated in kind or participants in face-to-face reciprocity, increasingly were paid in wages, the abstract, quantifiable, and therefore universal medium of exchange for qualitatively different sorts of products and services. The circulation and exchange of commodities translated the qualitative nature of actual things into the abstract virtuality of quantitative sums.

The transition from the "actual" social relations of feudalism gains a more material specificity when understood, in the formulation of Robert Brenner, as a transition from a "direct" mode of appropriating the produce of agrarian laborers. Before capitalism, or in early modern states like France, where the breakup of feudal jurisdictions hadn't proceeded as far as in England, the property of peasant owners was directly ceded to landlords or states in the form of rent or taxes. Following Marx, Brenner describes this as an "extra-economic" or "politically-constituted" mode of property relations, in contrast to the "indirect," "economically-constituted" relations that already were emerging in England, where propertyless laborers sold their labor power in exchange for wages determined by market levels of exchange value.[19] Wage payment virtualized—abstracted and universalized—labor, which no longer was tied of necessity to the same actual relations. The traditionally static nature of rural life was transformed by the mobilization of laborers and the creation of a mobile labor market. Brenner's contrast of the direct and the indirect to characterize the transition from feudal to capitalist socioeconomic relations accords with the transition from tacit to self-consciously explicit knowledge that oversees the argument of this study.

Over the course of many centuries, the market had undergone a complex development in denotation and connotation, from an actual marketplace in proximity to human settlements and physically frequented for the purpose of different sorts of social exchange, to buying and selling according to the price or exchange value of goods and services, to the governing concept of commodity exchange for the primary purpose of capital accumulation. Already by the end of the eighteenth century, "the gradual separation of the generality of a market process from the particularity of a market place" had led to the locution "market overt" to refer to the original sense of an actually situated locale.[20] The transformation of agrarian production is reflected in the breakdown of the domestic economy that accompanied the rise to dominance of the virtual market. The household was traditionally the major unit of production, largely for the subsistence of the household itself but to some degree also for sale at the actual marketplace. Capitalist innovation and "improvement" rendered the customary sexual division of labor and property use-rights unprofitable and subsistence conditions untenable. And as the domestic economy became more thoroughly intertwined with production for "the market," household labor that was once the flexible province of wives was transformed into "housework," the exclusive domain of women and increasingly denigrated not only for its unproductivity on the market but also for its nonremuneration.[21]

The "Financial Revolution" of the 1690s established those instruments and institutions—the Bank of England, the National Debt, Public Credit—that both responded to and enabled the virtualization of economic activity. Visiting the Royal Exchange in 1711, Joseph Addison's Mr. Spectator was struck "to see so many private Men, who in [past] Time would have been the Vassals of some powerful Baron, Negotiating like Princes for greater Sums of Mony than were formerly to be met with in the Royal Treasury[,] . . . thriving in their own private Fortunes, and at the same time promoting the Publick Stock."[22] Like Defoe, Addison imagines the autonomy of private men lately liberated from the actual "vassalage" of feudal dependence into efficient investment practices on the virtual "market." Mr. Spectator puts the virtuality of economic exchange in the best possible light. But less upwardly mobile commoners were undergoing the more painful process of having to substitute, for their tacit and personal trust of actual creditors who were also friends, a speculative and suspect trust in the abstract notion of a virtual "public credit" guaranteed not by personal reputation or by supernatural sanction but by the Bank of England. But again, the substitution was by no means absolute: for the network of private credit and debt continued to enmesh men and women in relationships with actual people where trust was based on personal reputation.[23]

Contemporaries became aware of these changes on several levels. For years, the national revenue had been thought to be primarily a joint function of land and trade, which were understood to be opposed to each other along the ideological lines of hereditary gentility versus upstart commoner, the unchanging countryside versus urban mobility. By the end of the seventeenth century this formulation no longer seemed adequate. Land and trade, the traditional opponents, had come to be seen as having more in common than not, and the traditional terms of conflict had been superseded by the emergent conflict between the "landed interest," which possessed "real" estate, and the financial "monied interest," whose virtual possessions seemed to many not only insubstantial but imaginary. Jonathan Swift wrote that "the Wealth of the Nation, that used to be reckoned by the Value of Land, is now computed by the Rise and Fall of Stocks." He supported the Property Qualifications Act of 1711, which sought to restrict parliamentary membership to landowners, because he thought it would ensure that "our Properties lie no more at Mercy of those who have none themselves, or at least only what is transient or imaginary."[24] Defoe, an enthusiastic supporter of both trade and credit, was at least ambivalent about what he calls the "Power of Imagination" that increasingly ruled the modern world of exchange value. For those who created "imaginary Value" by playing the stock market, Defoe had only contempt. But he was deeply preoccupied by the abstract virtuality of public credit, "the great Mystery of this Age," "neither visible [n]or invisible," "a Being without Matter, a Substance without Form." Defoe expresses his bemusement here through the most virtualizing mode of figural re-presentation, an allegory of Lady Credit. Addison records his dream of public credit as the allegorical figure of a "beautiful Virgin." In 1720, the material consequences of immaterial imaginings were brought home by the world's first stock market crash, the South Sea Bubble.[25]

To abstract from the preceding account, the coming of capitalism to the countryside had the effect of virtualizing actual relations—not only economic but also social and political relations. How can this material change be consistent with a generic change aimed at reforming the artifice of Elizabethan idealization through a representation of nature more attentive to empirical actuality? The argument of this book is that the Enlightenment found in traditional thought an affirmation of what was tacitly self-evident, an actuality not empirically known but deduced from premises that were conceptually preordained. The paradox central to rendering the tacit explicit is that only when categories are separated out from each other do their traditional relations become actual in the sense of being available to view, analysis, and alteration. Capitalist virtualization, like that related Enlightenment phenomenon experimental method, cleared a space amid the traditional idealisms of the actual—feudal relations, social rank, patriarchal dominion, theological dogma, the artificialization of nature, traditional wisdom itself—a space where categories, once inseparable parts of a greater whole, were now fully separate and susceptible to empirically justified conflation. In Marx's resounding words: "All fixed, fast-frozen relations, with their train of ancient and venerable prejudices and opinions, are swept away, all new-formed ones become antiquated before they can ossify. All that is solid melts into air, all that is holy is profaned, and man is at last compelled to face with sober senses his real conditions of life, and his relations with his kind."[26]

In the difference between superstructure and infrastructure Marx separates out the parts, the "forms" and the "forces," of production, creating a terminology for the difference between the generic and the material and for assessing their relationship by the measure of macro-historical change. According to Marx and Engels, in most epochs the infrastructural forces of production are mediated, represented, or expressed by superstructural forms of thought, consciousness, or ideology that correspond, more or less seamlessly, to their respective forces. Epochal change occurs when the forms of production fall out of sync with their corresponding forces, a moment of "uneven development" when forms are self-consciously experienced as both facilitating and "fettering" production.[27] This is the unpredictable and indeterminate dynamic that generates capitalism itself and in time replaces it by a new stage of historical development. The question follows: Is the evident change in the genre of pastoral during the Enlightenment adequate to facilitating the material change entailed in the emergence of capitalism, or is pastoral, although evolving, insufficient to that end? And is it therefore a fetter upon capitalist development, undergoing the decomposition of genres that have outlived their historical viability?

From Forms to Fetters?

How do forms become fetters? At every stage in what with hindsight we see as a period of fundamental change (like the transition from feudalism to capitalism), it's possible to analyze at a microscopic level the language contemporaries use that reflects a sense of change without an evident awareness of it. In a well-known essay, E. P. Thompson undertakes this kind of analysis with respect to the latter decades of the British eighteenth century.[28] Among his insights is the idea that some usages, whether words or acts, suggest a kind of pre-awareness, without signs of detachment or interrogatory intent, that Thompson characterizes as social "theater," less role-playing than occupying a discursive space metaphorically enclosed by scare quotes. The effect is related to that of parody, which closely imitates another discourse while taking a certain distance on it. We expect parody to be criticism, but it's also epistemology and historiography, the preservation of the past as the necessary means to supersede it. Yet the notion that change in both material and literary history has a parodic quality may also suggest an obstacle to the analogy. One reason other disciplines find literary terminology useful in their own thinking—for example, Thompson's "social theater"—may be that discourse about literature is more attentive to form, in all its intricacies and ramifications, than the discourse that develops around other human products. And "genre" or "kind" may be the most responsive of all literary concepts to the challenge of accounting for both the range and the particularity of formal structures, implications, and effects.

But the obstacle can be overemphasized: the vivid figure of forms and fetters comes to us not from literary critics but from political theorists Marx and Engels.[29] I turn now from the emergence of capitalism to the analogous and contemporaneous transformation of pastoral poetry. What follows is a diverse and extensive range of evidence that both the idea and the practice of pastoral, the ancient genre whose attention to conventionality was fundamentally intrinsic, was itself undergoing a self-conscious examination of its own conventionality. It may be plausible to read this evidence as suggesting a hypothesis that enabling forms are in the process of becoming constraining fetters. And this might return us to a question I broached in the introduction to this volume: Is the terminological continuum of anti-pastoral, mock-pastoral, counter-pastoral, neo-pastoral, and post-pastoral useful in concentrating attention on how this generic development is best interpreted?[30]

Pastoral Poetry: Changing Places

I've argued that the coming of capitalism may be seen as having rendered the tacit explicit, and thereby the qualitative in the terms of quantity, through the analytic partialization of traditional wholes. In 1713, Thomas Tickell devoted a series of essays in the periodical the *Guardian* to the question of how far imitations of the ancient pastorals may be naturalized to a modern English setting. Tickell instanced Jacopo Sannazaro's piscatory eclogues as the negative limit case, his impropriety consisting, in Tickell's words, in having "changed the Scene in this kind of Poetry from Woods and Lawns, to the barren Beach and boundless Ocean." Having drawn this line, Tickell is pleased to assure his reader that "I shall now direct him where he may lawfully deviate from the Ancients." To think self-consciously about the laws of deviation is, of course, already to deviate from tradition.[31]

The trope of a generic "law" suggests how much further than Sannazaro Swift had gone several years earlier in his well-known "descriptions" of London. They appeared in the *Tatler*, Steele's periodical predecessor to his *Guardian*. Steele praises both the anonymous author and his verse for their innovative and highly particularized empirical accuracy. These days, Steele writes, we're "tormented" by the conventionality of "Easy Writing," like "Sonnets on *Phillis* and *Chloris*."[32] This author "has, to avoid their Strain, run into a Way perfectly new, and describ'd Things exactly as they happen: He never forms Fields, or Nymphs, or Groves, where they are not, but makes the Incidents just as they really appear. For an Example of it"; Steele continues, "I stole out of his Manuscript the following Lines: They are a Description of the Morning, but of the Morning in Town; nay, of the Morning at this End of the Town."[33]

In my dialogue between Kermode and Williams I reminded readers that pastoral, like epic, is a genre that was ostentatiously parodied in the early eighteenth century—for Kermode a sign of its triviality and deliquescence, by inference for Williams a sign of its vitality, its empiricist impatience with artifice, which was expressed in a variety of ways. Swift's parodic technique is more complex than we might at first appreciate. His deviation lies in both his empiricism and, in this spirit, his focus on the city, describing in realistic detail scenes in the daily life not of rustic folk but of commoners going about their city affairs. Even the dialectical conflation of nature and art is more complicated than usual, in that it's not artifice but nature (the rising sun, a torrential shower) that throws the simplicity and quiet of the scene into action and confusion. The sense of a basic conflict between city and country values is preserved but transvalued in a way that displays the mutual vulgarity of their subjects. Echoing the actual convergence of agriculture and industry in the English countryside, Swift virtually transports the country to the city, preserving pastoral's complex semantics but also superseding its social geography. Is this mock-pastoral or neo-pastoral?[34]

"Urban pastorals" and "town eclogues" or "city eclogues" were popular subgenres in the coming years, although perhaps none had the offhand inventiveness of Swift's descriptions.[35] We can see in the will to "change places," to detach pastoral geography from its traditional value system, the basic Enlightenment impulse to pressure tacit distinction into separate parts and to observe more closely their features and qualities. City dwellers self-consciously examined the actual experience of urbanity in ways that called up country topoi. For John Evelyn this was a matter of sheer practicality. Four years before the Great Fire razed the old city and laid the scorched ground for a new, modern London, Evelyn published a seemingly prescient tract deploring the effects on the City of burning sea coal, "spoyling" and "corroding" the "aer" with "horrid Smoake" that "corrupts" all things, "insinuating it self into our very secret Cabinets, and most precious Repositories." The "City of London," Evelyn concludes, "resembles . . . the Suburbs of Hell" and thereby imagines the filth that insinuates itself into us as sin.

The plan of "Improvement" Evelyn proposes is to construct a vast pattern of fields stretched across London, enclosed by fences and planted with "the most fragrant and odoriferous Flowers, as are aptest to tinge the Aer upon every gentle emission at a great distance," so that "the whole City, would be sensible of the sweet and ravishing varieties of the perfumes." And as an aid to concretizing the proposal, Evelyn lists scores of herbs and flowers that are known for their fragrant and penetrating odors. Like the reverse case of agricultural industry rusticated for the purpose of efficiency, Evelyn's early project in urban renewal is a harbinger of dialectical mixture in the material world occasioned not by formal or cultural forces but by the capitalist spirit of "improvement" and the need to mitigate its worst consequences. The image of land plots dedicated to the flourishing profusion of wonderful plants also calls to mind—Evelyn describes the transformed city as "one of the most pleasant and agreeable places in the world"—a pastoral *locus amoenus*, a pleasant place.[36]

Milton's detachment of place in *Paradise Lost* is a special case in this chapter because it's a formal necessity of his entire poetic project, the Christian accommodation of nonempirical spirit to human sense perception; nonetheless, it's of interest in this context. *Paradise Lost* makes frequent accommodating use of what might be called relatively "generic" scenes of the countryside and conventions of pastoral poetry. But in at least one case, Milton figures the country in opposition to the city in specific terms that evoke Evelyn's contemporary London. This is the moment when Satan, coasting down to earth, spies Eve in the Garden, surrounded by flowers and herbs and "Veil'd in a Cloud of Fragrance," and the narrator turns to epic simile:

> Much hee the Place admir'd, the Person more.
> As one who long in populous City pent,
> Where Houses thick and Sewers annoy the Air,
> Forth issuing on a Summer's Morn to breathe
> Among the pleasant Villages and Farms
> Adjoin'd, from each thing met conceives delight,
> The smell of Grain, or tedded Grass, or Kine,
> Or Dairy, each rural sight, each rural sound;
> If chance with Nymphlike step fair Virgin pass,
> What pleasing seem'd, for her now pleases more,
> She most, and in her look sums all Delight.
> Such Pleasure took the Serpent to behold
> This Flow'ry Plat, the sweet recess of Eve
> Thus early, thus alone . . .[37]

Eve's prelapsarian innocence of sin is figured as a "recess" within the recess of Eden, which in turn is figured as a stroll in the countryside; Satan's fallen state is figured as perdition in Hell, which in turn is figured as life in a contaminated city. Heaven is to Hell as Country is to polluted London.

Addison's imagination of the country in the city redeems the latter as a technological improvement on the former. At the Royal Exchange, Mr. Spectator prides himself "as I am an *Englishman*" on the scene before him, "so rich an

Assembly of Country-men and Foreigners . . . making this Metropolis a kind of *Emporium* for the whole Earth." Truly the epitome of the modern city, the exchange gathers together the traders and commodities of the entire world as never was possible before the global economy had coalesced in the past few decades. As expressed by Addison, "I look upon High-Change [the Royal Exchange] to be a great Council, in which all considerable Nations have their Representatives. . . . I am infinitely delighted in mixing with these several Ministers of Commerce, as they are distinguished by their different Walks and different languages."[38] And yet there's an uncanny resemblance between this account and, more fully than in Evelyn, the ancient topos of the *locus amoenus*, where bountiful nature anticipates our alimentary desires and obviates our labor. Here's Marvell's rendition:

> What wondrous life is this I lead!
> Ripe apples drop about my head;
> The luscious clusters of the vine
> Upon my mouth do crush their wine;
> The nectarene, and curious peach,
> Into my hands themselves do reach;
> Stumbling on melons, as I pass,
> Insnared with flow'rs, I fall on grass.

In tradition, the source of this unmotivated and unearned wonder is nature itself, or divinity, as in prelapsarian Eden. Its modern source, also wonderful, is very different and is explained by Addison with Enlightenment discernment and practicality: "If we consider our own Country in its natural Prospect, without any of the Benefits and Advantages of Commerce, what a barren uncomfortable Spot of Earth falls to our Share! . . . Our Climate of it self, and without the Assistance of Art," never could have produced "our Melons, our Peaches, our Figs, our Apricots, and Cherries," which we owe rather to "this mutual Intercourse and Traffick among Mankind."[39]

Retreat

So, the Enlightenment impulse toward the explicit and the analytic also fueled the impulse toward dialectical conflation in the face of opposition.[40] Another topos of rural otium that urbanites were transplanting to the city was the pleasure of retreat. Mr. Spectator, having spent a month in retreat from London, writes that it's "high time for me to leave the Country, since I find the whole Neighbourhood begin to grow very inquisitive after my Name and Character. . . . I shall therefore retire into the Town, if I may make use of that Phrase, and get into the Crowd again as fast as I can, in order to be alone."[41] Horace Walpole asks Horace Mann more pointedly: "Would you know why I like London so much? . . . There is no being alone but in a metropolis: the worst place in the world to find solitude is the country: questions grow there, and that unpleasant Christian commodity, neighbours." The young Boswell, too entranced by society to value retreat from it in any form, turns the topos in another direction: "There is a great difference between solitude in the country, where you cannot help it, and in London, where you can in a moment be in the hurry and splendour of life." Departing from the topic of London for a moment, the growth of the British spa town exemplifies a more specialized and consciously motivated strategy to urbanize rural conventions and values. The presence of hot springs and the remains of Roman baths gave Bath the authentic aura of the natural, which was fully exploited in the eighteenth century by the transformation of this important provincial town into the flagship of spa resorts, resorted to as an urban center of not labor but leisure. Or rather, Bath was able to sustain this new kind of otium because it was, paradoxically, a phenomenon of negotium, and exemplary of what's been called "the commercialization of leisure."[42]

An ingenious "advertisement" that appears in a *Tatler* of spring 1710 may go as far as possible in the opposite direction, bringing the city to the country not only as a matter of literal transportation but fully and amusingly as a platform for marketing the product. Here the urban authorship of pastoral poetry isn't a covert challenge to its rural character but the explicit condition for a system of poetic production and consumption:

> *These are to give Notice, That the proper Time of the Year for writing Pastorals now drawing near, there is a Stage-Coach settled from the* One-Bell *in the* Strand *to* Dorchester, *which sets out twice a Week, and passes through* Basingstoke, Sutton, Stockbridge, Salisbury, Blandford, *and so to* Dorchester, *over the finest Downs in* England. *At all which Places, there are Accommodations of Spreading Beeches, Beds of Flowers, Turf Seats, and Purling Streams, for happy Swains; . . . And for the Conveniency of such whose Affairs will not permit 'em to leave this Town, at the same Place they may be furnished, during the Seasons, with Opening Buds, Flowring Thyme, Warbling Birds, Sporting Lambkins, and Fountain Water, right and good, and bottled on the Spot, by one sent down on purpose.*[43]

The artlessness of country values is processed through a marketing approach that packages nature in poetic tropes and schedules the poet's trips to preselected locales with a shockingly modern tone of salesmanship and commodity fetishism.

A different kind of ingenuity in reversing the traditional retreat from the city to the country is evident in John Philips's explicit parody of the archetype, Horace's *beatus ille*, an epode that ends with the ironic turn whereby the urban money lender decides against retiring to the country. Philips begins his poem with the same declaration as Horace does, but not for long: "Happy the Man, who Void of Cares and Strife, / In Silken, or in Leathern Purse / retains a *Splendid Shilling:* . . ." The retreat this urbanite would make is from the cares not of making money but of lacking it.[44]

Locational Pastoral

Besides urban pastorals, town eclogues, and the poetry of retreat, several other subgenres flourished in this period that scholarship tends to group together because they have a common thread. The loco-descriptive poem, the topographical poem, and the prospect poem are terms that were used inconsistently if at all by contemporaries; modern scholars have tried to apply them to poetry that has a family resemblance, with mixed results. They show the miscellaneous influence of Virgilian georgic and pastoral, and although various in their interests and emphases, they share the "locational" trope of describing a landscape that's viewed from, or near to, an actual and empirically fixed place in the countryside. Broadly speaking, the topographical poems of the earlier Enlightenment use allegorical and emblematic techniques to evoke local politics and history; later ones provide instruction in agrarian methods and in local crafts and industries. In different ways they all make a formal commitment, if sometimes no more than a minimal framing, to the empirical purpose of viewing and recording the reality of a certain time and place. Here I'll describe two important representatives of these developments in topographical poetry.

In his vastly influential topographical poem *Coopers-Hill* (1642, 1655, 1668), John Denham assumes a firmly fixed view point at the summit of Coopers Hill. From there he looks down first on St. Paul's Cathedral, the highest point in the City of London, then on Windsor Castle, St. Anne's Hill, the river Thames, and finally the meads and floodlands from which rises Coopers Hill itself. In this visual descent, Denham's speaker explicitly marks each successive stage downward ("Exalted to this height, I first looke downe / On *Pauls*," ll. 14–15; "So rais'd above the tumult of the crowd / I see the City," ll. 27–28; "*Windsor* the next [. . .] above the valley swels / Into my eie," ll. 49–51; "Here could I fix my wonder, but our eies, / Nice as our tastes, affect varieties; [. . .] So having tasted *Windsor*, casting round / My wandering eye, an emulous Hill doth bound / My more contracted sight," ll. 141–142, 145–147; "Parting from thence [. . .] My eye descending from the Hill survaies / Where Thames amongst the wanton valleys strayes," ll. 183, 185–186).[45] These place names track the poem's movement downward, reminding us that the poetic surveyor's geographical perspective, his locational focus, and the sequence from one place to the next, have a concrete empirical grounding. Yet as the language I've quoted suggests, the speaker's visual instrument of perception is uncertain and distracted ("swells into," "affect varieties," "wandering eye," "contracted sight"). Compounding this effect is our sense that most of the poem's discourse involves descriptive and narrative detail that departs, sometimes through counterfactual and prophetic imaginations, from the empirical account of the places themselves. Freely associating to circumstances that are evoked by these places but take us somewhere else, this discourse amounts to a radically miscellaneous body of knowledge about different aspects of England's history.

Because these details have been generated by associations from different places that are topographically but not chronologically related, they're unlikely to comprise a meaningful historical sequence. However, they have a thematic similarity that may suggest, in the focus the speaker brings to bear on or the filter through which he reads, the particularity of the poet's preoccupation with the history of England. This theme is the recurrent and volatile imbalance of power between monarch and subject. *Coopers-Hill* takes a very long view of England's past. It envisions the signal occasion of Magna Carta and Runnymede, but also goes back and forward through confrontations when monarch or subjects display (in Denham's view) an overweening appetite for power only to provoke a comparably extreme reaction in the other. This repeated pattern of excessive ambition and its reciprocal provocation is the cyclical movement Denham traces through English political history up to the present moment of 1642 and the outbreak of civil war. Denham's speaker supposes that Charles I, now goaded into asserting his authority, will vanquish his subjects, and the poem ends in this anticipation. But the actual fortunes of war favored first the king, then parliament, and reached a climax with the victory of the king's subjects, the execution of the king, and the rule of Oliver Cromwell.

A second version of *Coopers-Hill* was published in 1655 in the middle of Cromwell's rule, and we might expect Denham to have felt that he must now account for this stunning reversal in the balance of powers, which confirmed his reading of history but confuted his abiding royalism.[46] And he does: but so subtly that the revision requires close reading to discern the silent excisions and emendations that distinguish the 1655 from the 1642 text. Perhaps most striking is Denham's retention of allegorical and emblematic tropes—the cure that worsens the disease, the wants that increase desire, the discord bred by harmony, the hunted stag, the river banks overflown—whose political valence is almost imperceptibly reversed. So, the similarity between the crises of 1642 and 1655 is the most immediate and undeniable instance of the principle of analogical recurrence that organizes Denham's reading of history. Perhaps the royalist Denham's will to deny change accounts for the minutely redoubling character of the 1655 version. In any case it makes the principle of historical recurrence inescapable and suggests a view of history as a sequential movement counteracted by the denial of movement. This counteraction of linear temporal motion by stasis recalls the interruption of linear spatial movement by mental association we experience in the poem's topographical process. In other words, the topographical/geographical logic of *Coopers-Hill* both generates and is overtaken by a comparable chronological/historical logic, whose movement of cyclical recurrence submerges each stage of the empirical movement, from the height to the floodlands of Coopers-Hill's, in an aggregation of events whose relation is one of analogy not contiguity.

The first lines of the poem, which initially may seem agreeably "metaphysical," now provide a more practical key to what follows:

Sure we have Poëts, that did never dreame
Upon *Pernassus*, nor did taste the streame
Of *Helicon*, and therefore I suppose
Those made not Poëts, but the Poëts those.
And as Courts make not Kings, but Kings the Court;

> So where the Muses, and their Troopes resort,
> *Pernassus* stands; if I can be to thee
> A Poët, thou *Pernassus* art to mee.
> Nor wonder, if (advantag'd in my flight,
> By taking wing from thy auspicious height)
> Through untrac't waies, and airie paths I flie,
> More boundlesse in my fancie, then my eie,
> Exalted to this height, I first looke downe
> On *Pauls*, as men from thence upon the towne.
> —ll. 1–14

The unequal comparison between the poet's powers of eyesight and fancy sets the stage for the contest between geographical and historical movement that organizes *Coopers-Hill*. Denham, a late Renaissance poet under early Enlightenment influence, writes in 1642, a moment when political and social change are gaining an implacable momentum. "History," becoming less intelligible through emblematic equipoise, solicits explanatory inquiry into the phenomena of sequence and development. Denham's preoccupation with the chronological scope of English history exemplifies this impulse, yet takes the form of analogical correspondence. The topography of *Coopers-Hill*, fueled by the empirical impulse of the eye, is also thwarted by the dominion of historical fancy over the empirical historical eye. What structures the poem at the most general level is not this dialectic of geography and history but the dialectic of fancy and the eye, which is the key to the dialectic of art and nature that gives Denham's poem its pastoral character.

In the topographical poetry of the later Enlightenment, nature is more likely to be represented in its empirical and developmental detail. In the opening of the Pindaric Ode version of John Dyer's prospect poem, *Grongar Hill* (1726), Denham's influence is clear where, on the hill's "lonely Eminence," the power of *"Fancy"* issues "thro' the Eye" but makes "Thought," "Sense," and "all worldly Things" its own. However, the contest of virtual and actual vision that we see in *Coopers-Hill* never materializes. The pastoral opposition itself is well articulated by conventional contrasts of country and city images and values. But both this Pindaric version and the octosyllabic version of the poem give a far more empirically detailed account than Denham does of both the speaker's location on the hill and what he sees from it.[47]

Dyer's four-book *The Fleece* (1757) illustrates at great length and with enormous energy the amount of discursive territory the topographical poem might cover without abandoning its conventional georgic-pastoral associations. *The Fleece* is a patriotic poem. Monarch and subjects have found a political balance that can be expressed in traditional pastoral tropes: George II is "the people's shepherd" (61). *The Fleece* celebrates Britain's stadial achievement, narrating a long chain of rationally divided labors, from shepherding ("happy at your ease") and sheep shearing ("We think the golden age again return'd") (67) to the international commerce that's made this famously British product, and Britain, known throughout the world. Even if there are "gardens black with smoke in dusty towns" (69), urban industry is an art without artifice, continuing the work of nymphs and swains now partnered with merchants. The present continues the past: productive Leeds is our modern Carthage; the music of paradise is still heard by the heart, and "the first happy garden" is seen again in our "flow'ry scenes" (68). Perhaps we've lost these delights in a moral or fabled sense, like the myth of the Golden Fleece that's narrated in book 2 or the recollection of the first eclogue. They have the status of stories that found the ancient traditions of our craft, and they exist, one feels, on a different plane from what our current labors achieve and fulfill. Or better, the fanciful stories coexist with, without challenging, the empirical descriptions and histories—as well as the actual corruptions of city values.

Taking the Measure of the City

Pastoral's self-conscious attention to the city was evident in campaigns to integrate rural pleasures within its walls. But it was also subtly implicit in the preoccupation of commentators, many of them pastoralists, with the incomparable magnitude and heterogeneity of the capital city London. Between 1600 and 1800, the population of Paris grew from 400,000 to 550,000, at a rate of 38 percent. In the same period, the population of London grew from about 200,000 to 900,000, at a rate of 350 percent.[48]

London's size and rate of expansion at this time were unprecedented, and they required that the concept of the city be explicitly rethought in a modern register. In the early modern period, urbanization was becoming more varied in both sources and motives. London was seen increasingly as a copious collection of types and "characters," whose diversity invited attention to what made people different, singular, idiosyncratic—especially as their coexistence and enforced sociability made comparison inescapable. The multitude of character types went along with a multiplication of urban institutions—places to eat, drink, and smoke, entertainment venues, markets, hospitals, prisons, churches, parks, and other public spaces—where particular kinds of people might be encountered. Ned Ward's *The London Spy* (1703), a voluminous prose account of London places, describes them and their habitués in the old-fashioned style of jest books, cony-catching pamphlets, and rogues tales, characterized by crude vulgarity, heavy-handed witticisms, and casual brutality. But *The London Spy* also has the loose sense of place of a walking guide, of how to get from here to there, noting districts and street names with some regularity, and taking account of the city's major sights and landmarks—Bedlam, the Royal Exchange, Gresham College, Bridewell, the Monument to the Great Fire—as though promoting London for the purposes of popular tourism. And the sequential articulation of these separate parts arguably gives the whole a new coherence.

As a label for printed pieces, "spy" mediates at this moment between the nearly outdated buzz of illicit secrets revealed by an illicit source and an emergent and more neutral emphasis on the dependably empirical observation of a site or scene of general interest. John Gay's *Trivia: or, the Art of Walking the Streets of London* (1716) conveys in its title a more self-conscious focus on physical process. Gay explicitly celebrates the "art" of walking as first and foremost the topic of his poem, and comments that arise in the course of this perambulation suggest that walking the city streets may have a charged relation to the use of carriages, partly expressive of a difference in social status.[49] But Gay's posture in *Trivia* is hardly one of complaint against an elite. Unlike Ward's prose *Spy*, the poem is written in heroic couplets and punctuated by learned allusions: thus "trivia" alludes to the *trivium* of the liberal arts and to Sophocles's tragedy. Still, the more active association may be with "trivial." Gay's muse is Trivia, who although a goddess also rambles through the city streets. Can this degree of parody really authorize itself by claiming classical roots?

Throughout *Trivia*, in fact, there runs a mildly parodic undertone that shadows without negating its epic and georgic frame. And it could hardly be otherwise: Gay's epic arming is with shoes, coat, and cane, and the urban Theseus is warned against depending on the guidance of Ariadne, who's probably a pickpocket. Seasons no less than days of the week are distinguished by commercial as much as by natural activities. Natural signs of how to read the weather, a georgic staple, extend to ladies' fashions, and even to the signs that advertise shops because they swing with the wind in rainstorms. At one point, the mire that smears the walker's shoes leads Gay's speaker to digress (a common practice here) on Cloacina, goddess of the sewers and of the bodily excretions they circulate. Both the digression and the accompanying pedantic note recall the Scriblerian satire that Gay contributed to.

But if Ward suggests a postcard tour of the vulgar sites, Gay's gently parodic style gives his urban excursion a historical depth that places London among the great centers of culture. This propinquity would sink *Trivia* in the depths of satire were Gay not assiduous in evoking the culturally thick details of everyday life in London. All the familiar places are there, but often lacking Ward's forthright place names because layered with the language of local custom, habit, history, and ritual, in the poem as well as in the comprehensive index. The density of this language argues the incremental foundation and the long persistence of this modern city. It justifies the classical comparisons: to Rome, for example, although as a walking city, London also compares favorably with other modern places—Paris, Amsterdam ("Belgia"), Naples, and Venice.

But London was incomparable. It was the stronghold of science, which was also the only means of conveying its incomparability. "God made the country, and man made the town," declared the pastoralist William Cowper, asking where science finds her "implements exact / With which she calculates computes and scans / All distance, motion, magnitude, and now / Measures an atom, and now girds a world?" and answering, "In London."[50] To convey the great city, Defoe had recourse to these same implements. In *A Tour Thro' the whole Island of Great Britain* (1726), the reader is warned to anticipate a problem that isn't present in the rest of the book.[51] Writing "in manner of a Letter, and in the Person of an *Itinerant*,"

Defoe remarks that "London, as a City only, and as its Walls and Liberties line it out, might, indeed, be viewed in a small Compass; but, . . . I speak of *London*, now in the Modern Acceptation" (presumably what we mean by "greater London" and which he later gives as London, Westminster, and Southwark). "And how much farther it may spread, who knows?" "It is the Disaster of *London*," Defoe continues, that it hasn't spread according to a rational scheme of central planning but "is thus stretched out in Buildings, just at the pleasure of every Builder, . . . and this has spread the Face of it in a most straggling, confus'd Manner, out of all Shape, uncompact, and unequal; . . . Whither will this monstrous City then extend? And where must a Circumvallation or Communication Line of it be placed?" This is a literal question; and Defoe's answer is to propose *"A* LINE *of Measurement, drawn about all the continued Buildings."* Once more, Rome is the classical touchstone. And Rome, too, was "a Monster for its Greatness"; but it was more or less round. London is a disaster because of its shape.

Defoe's project touches on our concerns at several points. First, taking the measure of London is for him a project in quantification, in accurately measuring its size and dimensions according to the strict criterion of "continued buildings." To measure the size of the city requires knowing its dimensions; but a line, however long (and its running dimensions are given precisely in miles, furlongs, and rods), isn't a dimension. However, Defoe is able to speak of the "Circumference" of the continued buildings when his measurement reaches the point where it began, and he gives it as thirty-six miles, two furlongs, and thirty-nine rods. "Were it possible to reduce all these Buildings to a compact Situation," London's circumference is thought to be about twenty-eight miles.

Second, the separateness of country from city is retrospectively affirmed by the notice that they're no longer separate: "We see several Villages, formerly standing, as it were, in the country, and at a great Distance, now joyn'd to the streets by continued Buildings." "*Deptford* is no more a separated Town, but is become a Part of the great Mass, and infinitely full of People also." Again, how much farther London may spread, who knows? Defoe takes this oscillation between parts and wholes as inevitable, and if at all measurable, not by space but by time.

Greenwich, he writes, *"might be also called a Part of this Measurement; but I omit it, as I have the towns of Chelsea and Knights Bridge on the other side, tho' both may be said to joyn the Town, and in a very few Years will certainly do so."* What's nonetheless uncertain, however, is how long this will take, going by the unregulated growth of London that has prevailed thus far. But Defoe suggests this may change. "This great Mass of Buildings . . . is now" much greater than what "was within the Circumference of a few Years past" because it "has been generally made in our Time." After the fire of 1666, all rebuilding was prohibited until Parliament could "regulate and direct the Manner of Building, and establish Rules" for future construction. The implication seems to be that it was the Great Fire that occasioned this architectural modernization. But a keynote of modernity is that city planning, like so much else, became systematized (whether with good or bad results) according to estimates of its importance, rather than taking for granted things as they are until sudden necessities promote ad hoc, haphazard accretion. If this is the case, the Great Fire was an accident not only in its immediate occurrence but also as it happened to coincide with the emergence of what I'm calling an Enlightenment way of thinking, which helped rationalize its aftermath.

Space and time carefully measured converge again in a number of the *Spectator* that narrates a trip to the cities of London and Westminster that spans only twenty-four hours.[52] Steele departs by boat from Richmond at four in the morning and returns at 2 in the morning the following day. Traveling mainly by coach, he assumes the persona of Mr. Spectator, for whom the greatest delight lies in "speculation": the pleasures of virtual experience, stimulated by the actual and internalized largely by vision, which, like financial and conceptual speculation, in their purest state please through their freedom from actual fulfillment. Mr. Spectator narrates a number of such sights in the city: saluting strangers, taking in the industrious sale of fruits and flowers on the shore of the Thames, indulging in the spectacle of (virtual) window-shopping, and everywhere "agreeable young Women," "pretty Hands" folding ribbons, "dear Creatures" vending their wares at shop counters and asking him what he wanted, and he, truly a window-shopper, can do no more than imagine his reply: "only *To look at you*." Yet throughout the day and evening, all of this artificial activity takes place in actual named streets, lanes, squares, and landings, and we're left in no doubt about what time of day it is, situationally but sometimes also by noting the hour. From Spenser to Gay, the pastoral calendar was concentrated from months of the year to days of the week. It's tempting to see Steele's times of day as the next reminder that the conventionality of pastoral punctuality is subject to the same degree of change as other features of the genre. But for the most part, Steele's urban circuit seems only dubiously aware of the pastoral convention. With this exception: at the moment when carts and hacks begin to mingle with showy equipages, the speaker implies such an awareness by inviting us to read that event as not cultural but natural, like the sun rising: "The Day of People of Fashion began now to break."

In his account of a single day spent wandering and speculating through the streets of the city, Steele seems to have concentrated our temporal and spatial attention so minutely as to claim first prize in taking the measure of London. But another contender, identified as one Thomas Legg, has arguably outdone him. Legg, a proponent of time management, selects Sunday as the experimental sample in his close analysis of London life in order to guard against exaggeration: "If such be the Mismanagement of Time on this sacred Day, hardly can it be expected, that the other Six begin or end in a more exemplary Manner." Legg's analytic procedure is clear. What's less clear is what he means by "mismanagement," or time's "misemployment," and therefore his rationale for this analysis.[53] The survey has a moral basis. At present, London is "utterly absorbed by Places of Entertainment, and Inventions," and its "People" "have left no Hour unemployed"—in "Debauchery, Luxury, or yawning Stupidity." They "have ingeniously contrived to murder not only Common Time" but that portion of it devoted to divine worship. "Common time" is a musical term for equal rhythms, and especially 4/4 time. Is its "murder" the metaphorical destruction of a moral "regularity" or "balance" by indulging in ungodly activities? In eighteenth-century discourse, to be "employed" often stands metaphorically for "to be used"; but does it here literally denote labor on the day of rest (Legg, iii)? And who are these people? Not just Londoners but "common" people, "low-lifes" whose time is "common" and who are now exposed in print to the better half of English people? Yet the subtitle of the text designates a much more inclusive population, and the behavior described within it isn't confined to commoners—although they themselves are almost entirely engaged in labor. Have the better sort been oblivious to—have they taken for granted—the emergent lower classes?

Legg dedicates his tract to William Hogarth, whom he claims as his greatest influence, instancing especially "The Four Times of the Day" (morning, noon, evening, and night). Like Hogarth, Legg organizes his day in a temporal sequence, and he's obviously inspired by the artist's skill in cramming his canvas with a tightly packed and diversified range of figures, plausibly varied by "religion, nation, circumstance, and understanding." Less predictably, Legg briefly contrasts the media he and Hogarth use, thereby adumbrating an aspect of his writing style that's absent from (for example) Steele's. In Hogarth's "The Four Times of the Day," Legg remarks, there "are many Things made visible to the Eye in the most elegant Colours, which are here only recorded" (v). Explicit reflection on the relation between spatial form and temporal form, which the classical *ut pictura poesis* of Horace is not inclined to separate, was increasingly inviting to Enlightenment analysis. On the one hand, one thinks of Lessing's argument for separation. On the other, Scottish Enlightenment thinkers like Adam Ferguson were interested in pursuing what would be theorized as a new dimension of historicity, a part that completes the whole formerly constituted by chronology alone.[54] Legg's "recording" is to "visibility to the eye" as diachrony is to synchrony, and as the temporal series is to the simultaneity of the individual atemporal moments that compose it.

Legg seems to think that his microscopically analytic "recording" of a dynamic temporal series is nonetheless unable to make "visible" the static moments of that series, but his grammatical usage suggests otherwise. "I have attempted to deliver the Actions of every Hour," Legg writes, "as they really pass; omitting nothing, however trifling it may seem, which is the Subject of that Hours Employment or Abuse" (v). Accordingly, the hours of the day succeed each other in time; but within the space of any given hour, actions really pass not sequentially but simultaneously because they're conveyed by present participles. Here's a representative passage from the fourth hour of the day:

> The Men and Boys who live at the Cow-Keepers about the Villages adjacent to *London*, hallowing about the Fields to get their Kine into the Cow-Houses to be milked. Bawds, Whores, Thieves, Cullies, Fools, and Drunkards, fighting

under the Piazzas in Covent-Garden, surrounded by a Number of daring Pick-Pockets, fearful Passengers and frighted Constables, whose Staves are hardly of Authority sufficient to prevent them from being beaten. Fools who have been up all Night, going into the Fields with Dogs and Ducks, that they may have a Morning's Diversion at the noisy and cruel Amusement of Duck-Hunting. Poor honest Women who are waiting in their Apartments for the coming home of their drunken Husbands from Night-Cellars or Bawdy-Houses, are mending Stockings and Shirts, ironing Linnen, washing Infants Apparel, or performing some other Act of Good-housewifry to pass away the Time till their return. Pigeon Fanciers preparing to take long Rambles out of *London*, to give their Pigeons a Flight, that they may know how to pair them, for having the best Breed of the quickest Flyers. Young Maidens who have been awake two-thirds of the Night, kicking and sprawling as they lie in Bed, and praying for strong-back'd Husbands, no matter of what Nation, Religion or Occupation. (19–20)

The actions themselves are of the greatest diversity, the actors vary in social status, sex, generation, and occupation, and the scene of action contracts and expands from an urban apartment to the open countryside (and in other passages beyond, "to all Parts of *Great-Britain, Ireland*, and other Places in his Majesty's Dominions" [7]). The hours pass, but with the singular thickness and depth of Hogarth's images, inviting readers to concentrate for a moment on one or another micro-action, which, like Hogarth's, are self-contained little worlds each energized by private purpose or desire. Legg's style, it might be said, aims to achieve the spatial expansiveness of painting, as well as the synchronic dimension of historicity.[55] Only the novel experience of London life might have motivated Hogarth's and Legg's efforts to achieve this spatial and temporal density of description.

Renaissance Pastoral Parodied

The best-known Enlightenment minority heir to the Renaissance emphasis on art over nature in pastoral was Alexander Pope: "Pastoral is an image of what they call the Golden age. So that we are not to describe our shepherds as shepherds at this day really are, but as they may be conceiv'd then to have been; when the best of men follow'd the employment." Johnson makes the best-known majority rebuttal: according to Virgil, he writes, pastoral is "a poem in which any action or passion is represented by its effects upon a country life." The reader will observe, Johnson adds, "that there is no mention of the golden age." Moreover, "pastoral admits of all ranks of persons because persons of all ranks inhabit the country."[56]

It's of great interest that the most subtle and successful Enlightenment parody of Renaissance pastoral takes as its evident target the extraordinary poem that, although in service to its socially elevated allegory, most anticipates the Enlightenment turn toward actual common life. Even in its title, John Gay's

The Shepherd's Week (1714) appears to parody Spenser's *The Shepheardes Calendar* (1579), whose intentionally archaic English and rural dialect aim to imitate the simplicity of Theocritus, the first pastoralist. Gay's direct target is Ambrose Philips, his contemporary, who figures in the *Guardian* debates and, like Spenser, also imitates the language of Theocritus, whom Philips and others take to depict not a fancied golden age but authentic rusticity.

Gay's Proeme, implicitly in the voice of Philips (although signed by Gay), is explicitly parodic of both Theocritus and Spenser's exhaustive commentator E. K.[57] This poem (Gay refers to his own Proeme) is written *"after the true ancient guise of* Theocritus," "*that ancient* Dorick *Shepherd*" who knew nothing of a "Golden Age." Gay's deeper dig is at English Theocriteans, and less clearly at Spenser than at the Spenserian Philips. He promises a true picture of England *"just as thou mightest see it, didest thou take a Walk in the Fields at the proper Season"*—"*our own Fields*" and not those of Sicily or Arcadia. Here you'll see no wolves, because in England "*there are none*, as Maister Spencer *well observeth*" (but Philips, says Gay's footnote, does not). It's worth noting that the similarity between Gay's language here, parodic of Spenser and Philips, and Steele's language in the *Tatler* in reference to Swift suggests, despite their differences, the proximity of Steele, Gay, and Philips (and even Spenser's rusticity) in the primary aim to do justice to pastoral's proper subject, the actuality of English rural culture. Encounters like these sometimes can make parodic imitation and criticism indistinguishable.

In the eclogues that follow and compose the body of *The Shepherd's Week* Gay continues in a parodic mode, borrowing the names of Spenser's and Philips's rural clowns and mixing the speech of his own with mildly crude vernacular and naively inflated diction. Moreover, Gay's notes are rich with the antiquarian pedantry that distinguishes some Spenserian pastoral commentary (like E. K.'s glosses). We recall that Puttenham, Spenser's contemporary, thought that the primary purpose of pastoral is to allude to "greater matters" "under the veil of homely persons." Although in propria persona Spenser is silent on what might be the allegorical significations of his rustic figures, E. K. alludes several times to their "secret" reference and sometimes provides it. However, Gay's rustics, liberated from Spenser's allegorical artifice, are truly rustics, filled with proverbial and folk wisdom and superstition, and transported, with seeming spontaneity despite the pentameters, by the primary passions of anger, love, jealousy, and emulation. Their innocent emotions, while amusing, elicit our sympathy, especially in "Friday," the pastoral dirge that imitates Theocritus's first idyll and Virgil's fifth eclogue and that becomes genuinely moving (Gay, I, 113–118).

Finally, a distinctive aura of English "authenticity" arises from the enormous wealth of detail about food, work, clothing, customs, and daily routine that feels fully integrated into description rather than there for its own sake. Of Gay's eclogues Goldsmith later writes: "They were originally intended, I suppose, as a burlesque on those of Philips; but, perhaps without designing it, he has hit the true spirit of pastoral poetry. In fact, he more resembles Theocritus than any other English pastoral writer whatsoever."[58] Goldsmith captures one crucial sequence in the greater dialectic of parody. *The Shepherd's Week* begins, reportedly at Pope's urging, in parodic criticism of poetry that's so partial to the imitation of the past that it appears ludicrous and lost. But in adapting outworn conventions to present conditions in this spirit, Gay becomes fascinated by the details of common rural life, finding that close attention to them positively revalues those old conventions, which, from being fetters, now become enabling forms once more.

When "Philips" promises at the end of the Proeme to *"annex"* his *"Glosses,"* his reference apparently would be only to the parody of E. K.'s pedantic notes, were it not that their concern is said to be *"uncouth* [unfamiliar] *Pastoral Terms,"* a phrase that aptly describes not the glosses but a four-page addendum to the poem: the "Alphabetical Catalogue, of Names, Plants, Flowers, Fruits, Birds, Beasts, Insects, and other material things mentioned in these Pastorals" (I, 123–126). This catalogue has no counterpart in Philips, Spenser, or Theocritus and is in effect an index: a list, keyed to eclogue and line number, of "material things" in the poem that includes, besides the above, personages, foods, locales, equipment, tools, clothing, activities, ballads, holidays, and seasons. As we saw, Gay adopts and develops this device in *Trivia*. But it seems to me that in *Trivia* both the index and the text itself are less successful than their country counterparts. *Trivia* lacks a long tradition of the urban walking poem, and despite its close attention to the details of London life, *Trivia*'s formal allusiveness depends on epic and georgic conventions and is unable to sample the range of its own generic richness to achieve what can be done in the parody of pastoral.

Gay's two indexes, common in contemporary discursive publications, are unusual in literary texts like these, and their self-conscious use here bespeaks the basic Enlightenment conviction that to know something is to divide it into its parts and to make them systematically accessible and intelligible in their own right. In concert with its aim to amuse, *The Shepherd's Week* aims to suggest that pastoral poetry represents the actuality of rural life in all its dimensions: that nature and country people are the subject matter of pastoral, and that the art of the pastoral poet lies in large part in the sympathetic sincerity with which she or he regards the empirical reality of the English countryside. Art is a human activity, and the tacit belief that common people have literary value only as they serve to signify their betters is one that permeates traditional literary culture. As other chapters in this study testify, Enlightenment thought on a number of fronts is dedicated to rendering this belief explicit in order to reject it.

Enlightenment impatience with Renaissance pastoral marks a watershed in the history of the genre. I argue at the outset of this chapter that in its classical origins pastoral poetry celebrates nature and the countryside against artifice and urbanity, with an understated awareness that no humanity is devoid of artifice and that poetry is itself an instrument of art. Over time, this proviso had evolved from a subtle acknowledgment of an existential truth to an affirmation of artful sophistication and decorum, buttressed by skepticism about the capacities of common people, rural and otherwise. This belief in a ranked social order contributed to a broader tendency to idealize nature, and in reaction encouraged in Enlightenment authors a more realistic perspective, in particular a parodic impulse, deflating what had come to seem normative in the tradition by bringing it down to earth. A heightened mode of imitation, parody reveals the distance between reality and its representation, and thereby returned pastoral to a rudimentary version of its original project, which in the parodic practice of a poet like Gay could resurrect in the genre the subtle oscillation between nature and art. For other poets, what seemed necessary was a direct attack on what had become of the tradition, and therefore on the dominance of art's ideals over the reality of nature.

Explicit Critique of the Pastoral Tradition

Enlightenment pastorals that would seem unambiguously to merit the label of "counter-pastoral" are self-consciously metapoetic critiques aimed at the idealizing conventions of the pastoral tradition. For example, Mary Leapor's "*On WINTER*" qualifies her powerful censure only by its seasonal specificity, focusing on the painful and closely observed suffering of "Shepherds," "Nymphs," and "Swains" during the cruelest season of the year. She ends her poem reflexively:

> Say, gentle Muses, say, is this a Time
> To sport with Poesy and laugh in Rhyme;
> While the chill'd Blood, that hath forgot to glide,
> Steals through its Channels in a lazy Tide:
> And how can *Phoebus*, who the Muse refines,
> Smooth the dull Numbers when he seldom shines.

George Crabbe seems at first to allow for the truth of the tradition, and to condemn only our modern efforts to extend it:

> Fled are those times, when, in harmonious strains,
> The rustic poet praised his native plains:
> No shepherds now in smooth alternate verse,
> Their country's beauty or their nymphs' rehearse;
> Yet still for these we frame the tender strain,
> Still in our lays fond Corydons complain.

This misimpression is quickly corrected; the shepherd's song was always a dream:

> On Mincio's banks, in Caesar's bounteous reign,
> If TITYRUS found the golden age again,
> Must sleepy bards the flattering dream prolong,
> Mechanic echoes of the Mantuan song?
> From Truth and Nature shall we widely stray,
> Where VIRGIL, not where fancy leads the way?

Crabbe's "The Village" is a comprehensive indictment of the entire genre, and for this reason its status as a parody is questionable. In parts of the poem Crabbe employs phrases that echo Gray and Goldsmith to achieve limited but tactical parodic effect, and he invokes nymphs and swains in default mode; but in "The Village," criticism of pastoral far outweighs imitation.[59]

Crabbe's explicit and intractable truth is that nature and poetic art bear no relation to each other: "Then shall I dare these real ills to hide, / In tinsel trappings of poetic pride?"; "I paint the cot [cottage], / As truth will paint it and as bards will not:"; "Can poets soothe you, when you pine for bread, / By winding myrtles round your ruin'd shed?"; "Where are the swains, who, daily labour done, / With rural games play'd down the setting sun . . . ?"; "own that labour may as fatal be / To these thy slaves, as thine excess to thee" (I, 47–48, 53–54, 59–60, 93–94, 152–153). Crabbe's rhetorical questions lend his denunciation the force of the undeniable. And as even these few lines suggest, both his speaker and its implied auditor shift from stanza to stanza, giving his accusations a comprehensive coverage. Still, the closest Crabbe gets to explicitly identifying the actual position of the auditor most responsible for the oppression of the poor is the virtual evocation, above, of "thy slaves."

Most striking is the way "The Village" proceeds in an Enlightenment mode as though by experimental method, methodically ruling out, by granting, mitigating objections as though they were variables that only obscure the essential misery. "I grant" that the countryside has charms for those who own it—but not for those who work it (39). Grant that some land is blighted and defies the pleasures of improvement; but elsewhere, "Where Plenty smiles—alas! She smiles for few" (36). Grant that, denied wealth, the rural poor at least are "amply paid in health" (140)—but Crabbe's speaker refuses this in a remarkable series of empirical imperatives: "Go then! And see them . . . ," "See them . . . ," "Behold them . . . ," "See them . . . " (142, 144, 146, 148). And then, for the sake of argument "Yet grant them health, 'tis not for us to tell, / Though the head droops not, that the heart is well" (164). Grant that the picturesque cottage may look peaceful, like the sonnet that celebrates it; but "Go look within" and see the human suffering (175). Grant the existence of parish charity—the house for poor relief, the parish doctor, the parish priest (228–229, 286–287, 298–299); but these either are shockingly inadequate or show a shocking indifference, disdain, or contempt for their charges.

Throughout the poem, Crabbe is implacable in exposing the reality of country life and relentlessly visual in forcing us to gain an empirical knowledge of what our pastoral poetry is content tacitly to take for granted. He insists on a radical partialization, a separation of our pastoral art from nature, of the virtual from the actual, and therefore of country life itself from its conventional associations with simplicity, innocence, and otium.[60] The result is counter-pastoral, not without art but with an art informed by realism, an ambition to represent the real without benefit of tacit knowledge. Or in the terms I used regarding Enlightenment partialization, counter-pastoral precludes a return to the tacit belief in qualitative wholes but sanctions the explicit and self-conscious creation of new wholes both within and through the conflation of former parts. It seems unlikely that "The Village" is a "lawful deviation" from traditional pastoral by Tickell's standards. But it's worth asking by what standards counter-pastoral might be deemed lawful and whether this has some bearing on the question of how forms become fetters.

Object as Subject: Laboring Pastoral

Both questions benefit from thinking about Stephen Duck's "The Thresher's Labour" as a counter-pastoral.[61] The first condition of pastoral, we recall, is that it's written by urbanites and is therefore an artful impersonation of nature that deploys the sophisticated technology of poetic culture to represent its absence. In other words, the virtual rustic object of pastoral representation could not serve as its actual subject author. This principle was routinely violated in the eighteenth century when actual rustic laborers began to write and publish pastorals, a violation far more "unlawful" than Crabbe's. Duck, patronized by contemporaries as the Thresher Poet, was the first and most celebrated of these figures. On the precedent of Virgil's *Georgics* and like Crabbe's poem (which praises Duck's), "The Thresher's Labour" reflexively takes not only rural labor but also the "labor" of writing pastoral poetry as its topic. But Duck goes one step further than Crabbe because he is not only doubly the subject of critique but also doubly its object. To recapitulate, my present effort to assess the Enlightenment transformation of pastoral poetry was initiated by the following question: Was there a prevailing correspondence between this generic change and material change, or did the capitalist transformation of the countryside so outstrip pastoral's traditional form as to turn form into fetter, rendering it obsolete or/and transforming its remains into a new genre? Thus far the evidence suggests to me that the formal resources of the pastoral tradition transfigured, while sustaining, its generic identity. In "The Thresher's Labour" we encounter a poem so self-consciously attuned to the capitalist forces of material change as to address them even on the level of content.

From Theocritus onward, rustics have been known for their song. That Duck can speak of "we" in the following line accurately expresses his singular status as a laborer-poet, and therefore perhaps the identity of his customary rustic song with the pastoral poem we're reading. "Nor yet," Duck writes,

> Can we, like Shepherds, tell a merry Tale:
> The Voice is lost, drown'd by the louder Flail.
> . . . .
> Our Eye beholds no pleasing Object here,
> No cheerful Sound diverts our list'ning Ear.
>   The Shepherd well may tune his Voice to sing,
> Inspir'd with all the Beauties of the Spring.
> No Fountains murmur here, no Lambkins play,
> No Linnets warble, and no Fields look gay . . .
>   —ll. 48, 50–51, 54–59

Why is it important for Duck the thresher to distinguish his labor from that of the shepherd? Most evidently, to emphasize how onerous his work is compared with the animal herder's, whose labor is more otium than negotium. But there's also a suggestion that the difference between the herder shepherd and the agricultural thresher is one between the golden age ideal and reality, and perhaps between the tacit tradition of the past and the self-conscious present of 1730. One particular product of Enlightenment partialization sheds light on the importance of this difference. Before the end of the eighteenth century, empirical observation and an emergent statistical ethnography had led to the formulation, of which I've already spoken, of the proto-social scientific hypothesis that came to be known as stadial theory. This theory hypothesized for all human cultures a historical development through the same four stages based on these modes of subsistence: hunting and gathering, herding and animal breeding, agriculture, and commerce. A three-stage version loosely correlated with this pattern: savage, barbarian, and civilized.[62] Duck's account of the thresher's labor captures the third and relatively "evolved" stage of early, agricultural, capitalism: a complex division of labor quantified for productivity in all its dimensions, the institution of absolute private property, and a rationalized system of economic and social organization. From the laborer's viewpoint, this material evolution entails not only an assault on the senses but also a profound devolution of the spirit.

Feudalism, however mystified by posterity's idealization of personal reciprocity, operates through the actual, face-to-face exchange of consumable goods for tangible services. In schematic form, the capitalist exchange between owner and laborer abstracts the service of labor in the virtual form of wages, which quantify services for impersonal exchange on the market; and it abstracts the goods or use values produced by labor for circulation on the market, the generation of surplus value, and the owner's profit. So, the capitalization of production, in transforming the relationship between serf and lord into that between laborer and owner, partializes an actual relationship into its actual and its virtual dimensions. And because exchange has been abstracted from the actual site of labor to the virtual site of the market, the actual relationship between laborer and owner (or overseer) represented in "The Thresher's Labour" is one not of exchange but of supervision and surveillance, which make labor more efficient through several different methods of quantification.

The brilliance of Duck's poem lies in its power to analyze and disclose within a 1730 agricultural setting a condition and experience that we associate with a much later industrial capitalism. This power inheres equally in Duck's objective and subjective qualities of attention to the work of quantification. At corn harvest, the overseer watches the laborers closely, and if he spies "One charitable Ear, he grudging cries, / 'Ye scatter half your Wages o'er the Land.' / Then scrapes the Stubble with his greedy Hand" (242–245). At winnowing time, "He counts the Bushels, counts how much a Day: / Then swears we've idled half our Time away" (72–73). Both work and time are subjected to the strict quantification of "Day-works" so as to ensure for the owner the "Profits of the Year" (16–17). To this end, Protestant labor discipline is reduced to quasi-military regimentation: "He calls his Reapers forth: Around we stand, / With deep attention, waiting his Command. / To each our Task he readily divides, / And pointing, to our diff'rent Stations guides." "Divested of our Cloathes, with Flail in Hand, / At proper Distance, Front to Front we stand: . . . Down one, one up, so well they [the flails] keep the Time, / The Cyclops' Hammers could not truer chime" (29–30, 38–39).

Quantification fueled the capitalist revolution. Here "keep the time" refers not only to the military mode of marking time but also to the regularity of clock time in measuring the rate of production by the number of bushels produced in a given period. Attentively keeping the time was essential both to the overseer's record keeping and to the efficiency of the laborer, whose awareness of this standard as the measure of his labor, like the payment of wages, was internalized over time as the measure of his worth. To "idle" time away is pastoral otium seen from the near side of the capitalist revolution, which negates otium into negotium. How much is enough? Broadly speaking, the traditional measure of sufficiency was the amount needed to sustain a person or family for a limited period of leisure from work until supplies ran out and the cycle of production and consumption began again. So, from the perspective of traditional culture, the subsumption of leisure time into work time was as unnatural as a year unpunctuated by the rhythm of the seasons.[63]

The cycle of the seasons lends structure to "The Thresher's Labour." The poem begins when, after harvest, the farmer "divides" the "reapers" for their next task, which is to store the wheat and barley in their different barns (17, 19). Threshing and "winnowing" follow, until "Winter" gives way to "*Spring*" and "*Summer*," when "SOL begins his longest Race to run" and mowers turn their "scythes" to the "ripen'd Grass" (69, 82, 84, 86–87, 89, 109). The grass is dried in the sun by the "Hay-makers," "cut," and fashioned into "Cocks" and "Ricks" (173, 200, 202). Soon enough it's "Harvest" time, and the "Reapers" set to work again (212, 222).

Duck frames this seasonal cycle in words that evoke the Virgilian tag *Volvenda dies* (*Aeneid*, 9): "each revolving Year"; "the Year's revolving Course" (8, 281). And it would make sense to see this temporal cycle as the natural antithesis that's negated by the artifice of clock time, which is driven by the desire for endless accumulation rather than the naturally limited rhythms of subsistence. But Duck's poem is a pastoral, and it obscures the antithesis of art and nature in the very process of depicting it. The repetitive pattern of the revolving seasons is inevitably overlaid by the repetitive pattern of labor and its specialized instruments for managing it. Clock time isn't the opposite of natural time: it quantifies temporality, giving its cycle the semblance of linearity and partializing its tacit unity into equal parts. By 1730, the otium of tradition has become no more than a work break. Even so, "Time flows" for a moment; but soon: "We often . . . view the Sun; / As often wish, his Tedious Race was run" (142, 146–147). Is there a subtext to passages like this that asks, Can this really be a new experience, a new wish? Beneath the unfamiliar tedium of rationalized labor is there yet an ancient tedium of labor? In Marx's view, the transition from the qualitative feudal relation of serf and lord to the quantitative capitalist relation of lower and upper class makes conscious the conflict of classes that always tacitly existed. Does the candor of "The Thresher's Labour" confirm that there never was a golden age?

Duck's poem raises a related question about the consequence of the laboring poet's balance between the embeddedness of the innocent pastoral object and the detachment of the knowing pastoral subject. Insofar as Duck speaks with the detached voice of the artful poet, does he also run the risk of seeing with the detached eye of the cultivating employer? The issue comes to a head as Duck observes and records the spectacle of female hay-makers.

> Soon as the rising Sun has drank the Dew,
> Another Scene is open to our View:
> Our Master comes, and at his Heels a Throng,
> Of prattling Females, arm'd with Rake and Prong;
> . . . .
> Ah! Were their Hands so active as their Tongues,
> How nimbly then would move the Rakes and Prongs!
> —160–163, 168–169

The thresher might find a class ally in these women, who enforce custom and resist the regimentation of the work week by setting their "tongues" against their "hands," their otium against their negotium. However, the thresher's posture as poet leads him instead to speak for, and to identify with, the owner: to transform the nascent pastoral opposition between natural laborer and artful owner into one between cultivating men and unproductive women. Class solidarity, a giant step from commoner collectivity, isn't learned quickly. Here the unaccustomed detachment of the speaker encourages him to fall back on the ancient and ongoing dominance of male over female.

Women's Pastoral

However, the separation of the pastoral subject from the pastoral object, the principle that Duck violates, could also be violated by working women. Duck's denigration of female labor received a trenchant refutation by Mary Collier, a washerwoman whose close reading of Duck's poem reveals, among other things, his grammatical erasure of their work.[64] Collier's larger argument is that the work expected of, and done by, women like her is fourfold: agricultural, domestic, child care, and post-harvest charring for ladies. Implicitly, female laborers are to male laborers as male laborers are to owners.

If the conventional subject matter of pastoral poets is the natural existence of rustics both male and female, a common representation of that existence figures it as specifically female. This was true at least as early as the *Georgics*, which sometimes gender the inseminating cultivator male and nature as fecund female. And in an easy and traditional extension, the art of husbandry might be analogized to the art of poetry. Yet eighteenth-century pastoral is unusual in having been written not only by rustics but even by female rustics, who played self-consciously with the double irregularity of their artifice. The extension of authorship to commoners and women at this time is, of course, part of a larger movement whereby authorship as such began to be institutionalized in the modern terms of print culture and the literary marketplace. In this context as in others, commoners and women were accorded an analogous significance by an eighteenth-century elite culture apprehensive both of their deficiencies and of their incipient challenge.

Pastoral provided contemporaries with a mechanism for thinking about the limits of gender difference.[65] Like their precursors, eighteenth-century pastoralists were preoccupied not simply with the orthodox correlation of male with culture and female with nature but also with its complications. On the one hand, the normative charge of the gender opposition was positively weighted toward the female by virtue of her normative naturalness. On the other, if female is predominantly nature, it's also significantly art. This contradiction is evident whenever social cuts across gender opposition, as in the artifice of female aristocracy when contrasted to the simplicity of the commoner. More broadly, the association of the female with art or culture appeared in the paradigmatically negative artifice of Eve: superficiality, deceit, corruption, and the lust for knowledge as power.

Pastoral experiment, attentive to the changing face of agrarian production, exploited this contradiction. Over the long term, the participation of women in agricultural labor was greatly reduced and women's household labor in the domestic economy became unproductive "housework."[66] The increasingly unequal sexual division of labor made men (even more than before) the principal visible inhabitants of the rural landscape and established them as heirs apparent to the role of pastoral personage whose natural authenticity had been most persuasively gendered female. However, women, less visible on the land than before, for that reason were less tainted by the industrious corruptions of modern productivity and better equipped to mediate the older, land-centered virtues. Yet the leisure of the emergent figure of the "housewife" was not easily conflated with the otium of the pastoral maiden. If, as contemporaries recognized, the market was driven by the engine of consumption, it seemed the singular social role of the unproductive housewife to sustain the cycle of exchange by the perpetual desire for consumer goods and by the satisfaction of that desire.[67] This social role was understood to capitalize on women's contradictorily natural thralldom to the artifice of appearance, ornamentation, and fashion. In the tradition of the Roman goddess Fortuna, the volatile instability and corruptibility of the capitalist market were often figured as female in the eighteenth century.[68] And an important contribution to this richly overdetermined figuration was made by the contradictory insight that the negotium of male marketplace activity was inseparably dependent on the otium of the retired housewife and her enforced leisure. At the same time, the depreciation of women as agricultural cultivators was inseparable from the inflation of housewives' powers in the domestic cultivation of their churlish husbands and civilizing the natural brutishness and savagery of men.

In summary, the question that pastoral helped to ask is: What's the relationship between men and women under contemporary conditions of work and leisure? Behind this query, however, lies the yet more fundamental question: What, under such conditions, is the "nature" of men and women?

Recalling the *Guardian* numbers on pastoral poetry, the "deviation" most common among female pastoralists was to corroborate the founding opposition of art to nature as the opposition of men to women. In "The Golden Age" (1684), Aphra Behn offers an exhaustive account of the beginning of the world when innocent nature flourished, unimpeded by the corruptions of human art and artifice—war, trade, monarchy, laws, religion, property, right, and the tyrannical rule of honor. The speaker then calls for the return of the golden age in the present, and most of all for the end of honor, revealing only in the final lines that this poem is not a celebration of innocence and freedom by a female persona but, addressed to "Sylvia," a poem of seduction by a male speaker in the style of Donne.

That the topos of retreat called for revision by women may be in part a reaction against the male imagination of retreat as the prelapsarian garden without Eve. In "The Petition for an Absolute Retreat" (1713), Anne Finch, Countess of Winchilsea, describes the place of her desired retreat in classically Edenic detail, then names as the person she'd have join her the female friend to whom she dedicates the poem. At the age of twenty-one, Lady Mary Pierrepont, convinced her father will never approve her marriage to Edward Wortley Montagu, conceives her elopement as a "Retirement" from "Town" into the country; and, because of Edward's diplomatic ambitions, into the country of Italy, where Naples will serve as their "Garden of Eden." A lifetime later, Lady Mary Wortley Montagu, her marriage long since a failure, finds herself actually living in Italy, conceiving her country estate there as an Edenic garden where the "Solitude" of "retreat" entirely depends on her being in a single state, without a man. The blessings of pastoral retirement have remained vital in validating woman's lot as "natural," but the state of matrimony has shifted from embodying to hindering those blessings.[69]

In the present context, it's notable that Leapor, whose "On Winter" I've briefly discussed, was a laboring poet who served as a kitchen maid and wrote self-consciously as a pastoralist, a worker, and a woman. That poem ends with the metapoetic passage I quoted; it begins with two metapoetic couplets that may intimate female authorship given their figuration of seasonal change in bluntly gendered terms: "What Pictures now shall wanton Fancy bring? / Or how the Muse to *Artemisia* sing? / Now shiv'ring Nature mourns her ravish'd Charms, / And sinks supine in Winter's frozen Arms" ("On Winter," ll. 1–4). Leapor's "*Complaining DAPHNE. A PASTORAL*" (1748) attains its status as a gendered poem of retreat with contrasting indirection. Like Behn's paean to the golden age, it undertakes a formal shift, but unlike Behn's (which shifts from a pastoral framework to a gendered conceit of seduction), Leapor's modulates between two standard topoi within the pastoral frame, thereby evincing a subtle sense of how the genre may be partialized and reassembled to create a new plot logic.

Ultimately modeled on Virgil's second eclogue, the poem begins with the topos of the love complaint. The nymph Celia, wandering sadly through a "blooming Grove," observes "blooming *Daphne*," whose "secret Sorrow" evokes a "plaintive Song" addressed to all the elements of this *locus amoenus* and seeking their solace. But suddenly Daphne breaks off, all at once aware that formulaic "Tales of Love" like hers are unbefitting: Cynthio is "replete with Guile," and her complaint about him simply "foolish." At this moment Daphne recalls the days when she would wander in a grove like this one with her mother, who to while away the hours would tell her a "mournful Tale" of seduction and abandonment, which "always ended—*Child, beware of Man*." This memory, a temporal retreat to the golden age of maternal care before the fall into adolescent fantasy, might appear to extend Daphne's tale of love; but instead it revalues her present solitude as a liberating escape from male artifice into the natural devotion of women. "Complaining Daphne" modulates from a complaint about male inconstancy to a retreat in the faithful company of women, her remembered mother and the "Sylvan Sisters" "Content" and "Rest."[70]

Pastoral Internalized: Micro-pastoral

At significant points in her poem, Leapor figures Daphne's pastoral drama as a specifically mental activity. In this way, the physical seclusion entailed in pastoral retreat is recapitulated, as it were one level down, as a "micro-pastoral" withdrawal into the mind. The impulse toward partialization characteristic of the Enlightenment conceives mentality, one part of human existence, as a whole susceptible of partialization and pastoralization. This deviation into the landscape of the mind was most memorably achieved in Marvell's "The Garden." The speaker is lushly embedded in the garden's *locus amoenus*.

> Meanwhile the mind, from pleasures less,
> Withdraws into its happiness:
> The mind, that ocean where each kind
> Does straight its own resemblance find;
> Yet it creates, transcending these,
> Far other worlds, and other seas;
> Annihilating all that's made
> To a green thought in a green shade.
> . . . .
> Casting the body's vest aside,
> my soul into the boughs does glide . . .
>
> —41–48, 51–52

Marvell's poem raises the following question for his experimentalist successors: Does the detachment of the mind-soul from its body liberate it to extend the process of partialization by which its own autonomy has been engendered?

James Thomson's *The Seasons* ([1726] 1746), forward in its modernization of ancient pastoral settings, is bold in their internalization. The speaker of "Winter" vows to "lay the meddling senses all aside." Poetry of retreat commonly solicits retirement with a single friend; Thomson can depict multiple companions because in a number of important passages his retreat is imagined, not actual. In the following passages from "Winter," Thomson's "rural, sheltered, solitary, scene" is quickly transformed into a mental screen on which are projected a train of ancient heroes and poets, seen in the mind's eye.

> Now, all amid the rigours of the year,
> In the wild depth of winter, while without
> The ceaseless winds blow ice, be my retreat,
> Between the groaning forest and the shore,
> Beat by the boundless multitude of waves,
> A rural, sheltered, solitary, scene:
> ....
>   There studious let me sit,
> And hold high converse with the mighty dead;
> Sages of ancient time . . .
> ....
> Roused at the inspiring thought, I throw aside
> The long-lived volume; and deep musing hail
> The sacred shades that slowly-rising pass
> Before my wondering eyes.
> ....
> Thus in some deep retirement would I pass,
> The winter-glooms, with friends of various turn,
> ....
> Hence, larger prospects of the beauteous whole
> Would, gradual, open on our opening minds;
> And each diffusive harmony unite,
> In full perfection, to th' astonish'd eye.[71]

As we see in these passages, the internalization of pastoral retreat as a micropastoral mental landscape is achieved through a double act of imagination. The speaker's external retreat is of course not "actual" but an imagined poetic representation of an actual setting; and within that representation his imagined retreat takes the form of a psychological projection inward. The effect of this doubleness is a subtle transvaluation whereby the external subject, the speaker, is felt to be internalized as the object of knowledge. Achieved by a different means, the result is unexpectedly comparable to the transvaluation of the speaker, the object turned subject, in "The Thresher's Labour."

In *The Deserted Village* (1770), Oliver Goldsmith famously pursues Leapor's personally temporalized mode of micro-pastoral internalization by conflating the recent history of the English countryside with the poet's own life history. Ostensibly, the problem the poem sets out to document and mourn is, in Goldsmith's words, the actual "depopulation" of the land, the desertion of the village under the pressures of large-scale social change. And he anticipates the internalization in this dedicatory acknowledgment, to Sir Joshua Reynolds, that others have said of his poem "that the depopulation it deplores is no where to be seen, and the disorders it laments are only to be found in the poet's imagination. To this I can scarce make any other answer than that I sincerely believe what I have written."[72] It's because of this large-scale change, Goldsmith writes, that he is now unable to experience the Horatian *beatus ille*, the return ("how happy he"!) to the "seats of my youth" (6, 99):

> In all my wanderings round this world of care,
> In all my griefs—and God has given my share—
> I still had hopes my latest hours to crown,
> Amidst these humble bowers to lay me down;
> . . . .
> O blest retirement, friend to life's decline,
> Retreats from care, that never must be mine,
> How happy he who crowns in shades like these
> A youth of labour with an age of ease;
> Who quits a world where strong temptations try
> And, since 'tis hard to combat, learns to fly.
> —83–86, 97–102

Yet the crucial change, we come to see, is not in the land and its inhabitants but in the subjective history of the poet himself. And the crucial depopulation is his own personal and irreversible removal—not only from the physical "seat" of his youth but, more fundamentally, from his youth itself. The poet's subjective experience of temporality is projected as the impossibility of objective pastoral retreat. So, the truths of nature are seen to be an effect of the truths of culture—that is, of human nature.

Insofar as the poet finds he *can* go home again, it's because he sympathetically repopulates the landscape with the memories of those he mourns, even in the act of mourning them. The swain and his milkmaid, the village preacher, the village schoolmaster: these are the objects of pathos—so objectionable to Crabbe—by whose sympathetic recollection Goldsmith's speaker would imaginatively reclaim the innocence of his childhood. Like Thomas Gray in *Elegy Written in a Country Churchyard* (1751), to which much of *The Deserted Village* is an inspired allusion, Goldsmith sadly clears the land of its rustic personages only to re-people it with figures of his own imagination. In both poems, the natural retreat therefore is found ultimately in poetic artifice, which retrieves what nature cannot. This amounts to a pastoral deviation that circles back to the first principle of pastoral, the indispensability of poetic culture to the experience of the natural. And from this perspective, Enlightenment (and Romantic) micro-pastoral might be said to repeat, in sociological or psychological terms, the Renaissance substitution of other personages for the representation of actual inhabitants of the countryside. Looked at another way, however, the internalization of pastoral retreat amounts to a striking modernization, the transformation of one part to a new whole. In naturalizing the inmost recesses of human artifice, it helps facilitate the uniquely modern conviction that the source of normative value is to be found in individual subjectivity.

Pastoral Externalized: Macro-pastoral

Macro-pastoral extends the locational deviance entailed in "changing places" from the national scale of the Swiftian urban eclogue (from country to city) to an international scale (say, from Britain to Africa). Some contemporaries saw Virgil's first eclogue as an authoritative precedent: thus William Collins's *Persian Eclogues* (1742), Thomas Chatterton's *African Eclogues* (1770), Edward Rushton's *West-Indian Eclogues* (1787), Robert Southey's *Botany-Bay Eclogues* (1797). These poems transport the perspective of the speaker from the familiar rural setting to a new and unfamiliar locale, a far-flung place or nation. But first, they're less concerned to transport specifically pastoral conventions and values than to use a loose eclogue format as a peg on which to hang exotic scenes and heightened emotions that aren't recognizably pastoral. Second, because the transport of perspective from the national to the international is total, it lacks the formal transvaluation that occurs in Virgil's first eclogue, the overlap of the speaker's national perspective on its international application. The first eclogue doesn't transport the terms of pastoral from a national to an international level; it extends pastoral opposition from national to imperial dimensions, a process that's felt to be contradictory because it represents both dimensions simultaneously, both the pastoral opposition of city and country in the national dimension and their macro-pastoral dialectic as mutual components of "city" values in the imperial dimension. Rome is to the Italian provinces, city is to country, as metropolitan Rome, both city and country, is to its colonial empire.

The form of macro-pastoral is analogous to that of micro-pastoral. Micro-pastoral turns inward from the pastoral norm of art versus nature by conceiving that dichotomy in terms of body versus mind, wholes that are then dialectically transvalued into component parts of mind that replay there the opposition of body and mind, of which they're now micro-versions. Macro-pastoral turns outward from the pastoral norm of art versus nature by conceiving that dichotomy in its locational terms of city versus country values. These locational wholes are then dialectically transvalued into component parts of the national whole, which replicates, in its macro-relation to the imperial whole, the same opposition that obtains between city and country. Like micro-pastoral, in other words, but through a different dialectic, macro-pastoral transvalues the pastoral dichotomy: the domestic countryside is opposed to both the city and, in the imperial extension, one part of the greater metropolitan unit. Imperialist discourse has a macro-pastoral character to the degree that it raises this contradictory transvaluation to the level of textual consciousness. Unlike micro-pastoral, however, macro-pastoral has ancient precedent in Virgil, which makes clear that the macro-pastoral deviation is not an invention of Enlightenment self-consciousness. As in the emergent Roman Empire, the emergence of Great Britain as a national entity and an imperial power generated a discourse that is closely and intricately interwoven with the discourse of pastoral, setting the metropolitan unit of Britain against the "underdeveloped" rusticity of the colony. So, macro-pastoralism may be seen as a method of cultural imperialism that's aligned with the capitalist expansionism that is the engine of imperialism in the material sense of the term.[73]

The North-South Axis

With the "Voyages of Discovery" to the New World, Europe became the Old World and began to project the aura of pastoral rusticity and Edenic innocence onto the Americas, at first onto their native population and then also onto their European settlers. From the perspective of the colonial trade, however, the experiential basis for that aura—the difference between the English city and the countryside—was invisible. By midcentury the Navigation Acts of 1651 and 1660 had constrained the economic productivity of the colonies enough to provoke resistance and revolution against what was perceived as a unified system of metropolitan exploitation.

Contemporaries believed the slave trade to be the most profitable branch of English commerce. The capture of Jamaica in 1655 provided a base for its operations. The War of the Spanish Succession at the turn of the century won for England the monopoly of supplying slaves to the Spanish American empire; the South Sea Company was founded in 1711 to trade with that empire once peace had returned. The ultimate instance of the commodification of labor, slavery afforded a brutal analogy for capitalist employment that some English people, nurtured in the republican language of anti-slavery, were not slow to see. Even with respect to sheer physical situation, enslaved people and wage laborers might be seen to share the fate of having been uprooted from their lands. Of course, the georgic aim of human "improvement" helped rationalize the temporary debasement of people who seemed patently inferior, although both domestic employers and colonial planters knew on pragmatic grounds to resist the educational "cultivation" of their workers. Yet in any case the analogy between slave and wage labor cut across social identities.[74]

At the "pastoral" level of domestic relations, indignation at the "enslavement" of the laboring poor was complicated enough for those who found themselves in what was increasingly recognized as the "other" class, and pastoral discourse could always be made to construe impoverishment as freedom from care. But within the international, "macro-pastoral" context, even the laboring poor could be persuaded to regard colonized people as their essential Other, uncannily familiar in their subjection yet necessary both for economic reasons and as a negative ground against which the vaunted "English liberty" might be positively valued. Of course, the alterity of native-born class abjection was very different from that of alien enslaved Africans. It has been argued that the slave trade was a cause, not the consequence, of color racism in England. In the eighteenth century, Black people began to share the obloquy traditionally reserved for the (colonized) "black Irish."[75] The anti-slavery movement became an effective force only when England's special, colonial relationship with the Americas was in the process of being annulled. However, the indignation of pastoralists who were long since fed up with unselfconscious imitative parody may have fueled the anger of abolitionists, and vice versa.

Ireland was the prototypical English colony. Precisely because it shared with England a broad frame of cultural reference, Ireland's linguistic, religious, and ethnic departures from the English norm aroused an absolute enmity, and the Irish were physically close enough (unlike the Americans) to suffer a perdurable policy of colonial exploitation. Solidified under Charles II, this policy was briefly suspended at the Glorious Revolution but rigorously reinforced thereafter through trading prohibitions and absentee landlordism. Yet physical proximity, because it made the process of exploitation so visible, also made the macro-pastoral ideology of a priori difference hard to sustain. This in turn aggravated the difficulty, inherent in the extension of pastoral ideology to the macro-level, that what is locally viewed as innocence and corruption—small proprietorship, for example, versus unscrupulous rack-renting—might be revalued as backwardness versus development when displaced onto the larger scene. On the evidence of Jonathan Swift's *The Drapier's Letters* (1724), this revaluation was not inevitable.

Scotland's story was very different. Bound to English political culture by a diversity of ties—the royal house of Stuart, but also the Solemn League and Covenant—Scotland enjoyed a free trade with England under Cromwell that was restricted under Charles II but restored in 1688 and ultimately codified in the Act of Union of 1707. The relationship of Scottish to English nationality had long exemplified one classic but contradictory version of pastoral opposition along the north-south axis.[76] The union of England and Scotland as "Great Britain" sought to dissolve the old quasi-colonial opposition within a singular national unit. In fact, it had mixed results: the Scottish remained "North Britons," both familiar with and estranged from English identity. And within Scotland the English connection helped ossify the rivalry between the highlands and the lowlands into an internalized version of nationalist opposition, redolent of pastoral meaning: the highlands were to the lowlands as Scotland was to England. With the highlands stood "nature," the customary clanship relations of feudal hierarchy, and a "backward" way of life; with the lowlands stood "art," capitalist improvement, and modernization. Jacobitism and the defeats of 1715 and 1745 provided a pastoral theater in which was enacted the inevitable corruption of nature by art, of the past by the present, engendering nostalgia for a golden age enriched by the aesthetic distance of its political and cultural relics. Yet at the macro-level, the putative simplicity of England's northern neighbor was profoundly complicated by the authentic aura of cultivation conferred by the Scottish Enlightenment.

Much of this is played out in William Collins's remarkable unfinished poem of midcentury, "An Ode on the Popular Superstitions of the Highlands of Scotland, Considered as the Subject of Poetry." Unfinished, its title bears the signs of both incompletion and self-conscious deliberation. With hindsight we can see in the latter consideration a germ of the insight that the idea of the aesthetic, currently in cultural circulation but not yet fully formulated, is the key to answering the question, compelled by the power of empirical epistemology, of what sort of truth poetry delivers. Addressed to John Home on his return to Scotland, Collins's ode urges his cultivated friend to emulate the native Highlander in order to recover in Scotland what can no longer be found farther south: "Nor thou, though learned, his homelier thoughts neglect; / Let thy sweet muse the rural faith sustain."[77]

It's significant that Collins associates "the rural faith" not with religion but with popular superstition. Scotland is to England as the country is to the city not only in ethos but also in the highly temporalized sense that it represents an archaic mode of belief whose authority resides in its very anachronism. Sheltered from modernity and its cultural overdevelopment, the Highlands are still populated by notional beings—fairy people, old runic bards, wizard seers, pigmy folk—who bespeak not religious but poetic spirituality. Spatial distance facilitates the aura of historical distance, which in turn underscores the aesthetic distance required to conceive Highland culture as an imaginative construct and therefore (paradoxically) more natural than our own. Insistently theatrical, Collins's exhortations also insist upon the aesthetic mechanism whereby the acknowledgment of artifice only promotes the feeling of the natural, which is also the ultimate answer to pastoral's great question of how the truth of nature can be best served by art:

> Nor need'st thou blush that such false themes engage
> Thy gentle mind, of fairer stores possessed;
> . . . .
> Proceed, nor quit the tales which, simply told,
> Could once so well my answering bosom pierce;
> Proceed, in forceful sounds and colours bold
> The native legends of thy land rehearse;
> To such adapt thy lyre and suit thy powerful verse.
>
> In scenes like these, which, daring to depart
> From sober Truth, are still to Nature true . . .
> —171–173, 183–189

Here poetic is to empirical truth as nature is to art. To aestheticize the past is to frame it as a pleasingly self-conscious fiction, serviceable to present reality by virtue of its very detachment from it. The antiquarian excavation of a native English past during the eighteenth century was tinged with this aesthetic regard, and it contributed importantly to the growth of modern English nationalism. In the middle of the seventeenth century English or British "nationality" was still a manifold and contradictory idea, rooted as deeply in the sense of a strictly alternative past—or of a radically oppositional outpost of the present—as in the reigning institutional embodiments of sovereign authority and power. By the end of the century a series of distinct but mutually reinforcing developments had laid the ground for the modern conflation of the "nation" and the "state." The Hanoverian settlement propounded the British constitution as an all-purpose explanatory myth plausible enough to suspend the disbelief of those several interests crucial to the settlement compromise. In the space of two generations the Whig "opposition" had engineered an efficient and enduring working relationship with the monarchy and the fledgling financial forces of the city without entirely sacrificing its public persona as defender of English liberties. Finally, the spectacular growth in taxation, public deficit finance, and the vast bureaucratic infrastructure of fiscal administration in the early eighteenth century centralized state power on the unprecedented scale required to finance Britain's ostentatiously "national" military, commercial, and imperial enterprise.[78]

The effect of these developments was to enforce the sense of Britain as a homogeneous "nation-state" whose very diversity testified to the perpetually inclusive consensus of its "Englishness." Thus cultural aberration and regional recalcitrance might be read as the colorful precondition for an irresistible and enlivening absorption, and the moldering remains of ancient alterity could be figured as the enduring and legitimating sign of national permanence—as "England's ruins"—rather than as a more ostensible emblem of the transience of all things.[79] Yet the complicating pastoral countertendency was never absent. Even as antiquarian scholarship facilitated the sentimental accommodation of the Celtic, the Anglo-Saxon, and the "gothic" past to the English present, it inevitably unearthed evidence of an ineluctable and unassimilable strangeness, an alien barbarity evocative of precisely that national foreignness against which the homogeneity of the English national tradition was seeking to define itself. The effect is that of the uncanny—the repressed made familiar, the past made uneasily present—an effect that Freud historicized as an Enlightenment phenomenon.[80]

The East-West Axis

Along the east-west axis, eighteenth-century England's most significant foreign acquisition, in both material and symbolic terms, was India. Only toward the end of the century did England undertake the full governmental and administrative responsibility that stamped the face of Victorian India with an anglicized veneer. In the earlier period the East India Company exercised a trade monopoly that facilitated what contemporaries and historians agree in calling the "plunder" of India. The word bears a host of contradictory associations. Supine and defenseless in its natural feminine languor, the Orient was seen to submit to the piratical depredations of a criminal virility. India also bore a metonymic relation to the female. More than any other, the India trade dealt in articles of leisure and conspicuous consumption, exotic luxury goods whose "plunder" accentuated John Bull's hard-nosed practicality by indulging the splendid superfluousness of his women. But so far from being "raw material" extracted by European ingenuity from a native and primitive land, this Eastern plunder most famously consisted of the exquisitely artful fabrications of an ancient civilization. In these terms it was as though the rude hinterlands had plundered the metropolitan center of culture. In confronting the East, the West confronted not nature but an alien mode of cultivation: devious, "mysterious," unfathomable, yet possessed of an arcane wisdom that exposed to the West its own guileless innocence and vulnerability. From this perspective the Orient (India, Persia, Turkey, and to a lesser degree China) was the venerable artifice of urbane corruption—autocratic tyranny, diplomatic perfidy, religious hypocrisy, sexual perversity.

Ripe for exploitation, the East was by the same token seductive of English innocence—a means simultaneously of English aggrandizement and exculpation. "The East" was, in short, a way in which the English regulated their contradictory sense of national and imperial identity, and it bespoke in turn the contradictions of domestic, "pastoral" experience. As we've seen, however, the macro-pastoral did not reflect the pastoral in any direct and consistent way. On the contrary, the structural effect of macro-pastoral was, as in Virgil's first eclogue, to unhinge the logic of pastoral opposition by expanding and imploding its terms: London is to its countryside as England is to the world. Thus the nabobs of the East India Company, laden with the fabled wealth of the East, returned to metropolitan England to purchase a seat in Parliament like parvenu City stockjobbers buying a country seat in rural Kent. Ultimately, macro-pastoral argued the evaporation of difference at the level of the international market, where everything—all nationality, all "natural" utility—seemed convertible and equalizable through the exchange mechanism. But macro-pastoral experience also sensitized English people to the indefinite internalizability of the north-south and east-west axes, their stealthy pertinence to the putatively irreducible, "micro-colonial" localities of the intranational domestic scene. In Tobias Smollett's *Humphry Clinker* (1771) this sensitivity is registered in the way incremental travel northward is experienced as a continuous chain of stereotypical movements from "south" to "north," each link plausible in itself but also radically relativized by its placement in a more comprehensive series.

"Macro-pastoralism" is a term that aptly captures both material and cultural imperialism; but they didn't necessarily go together. A case in point is Johnson's Juvenalian satire *London* (1738), which contrasts the corruptions of the English metropolis to several alternative and increasingly far-flung realms of the rural: the wilds of Kent, the shores of Wales, the rivers of Hereford and Staffordshire, the rocks of Scotland.[81] Despite their regional and even national disparateness, all these British locales figure in some fashion a natural innocence that stands in contrast to the monolithic artifice and corruption of London. Partway through these classic passages of pastoral opposition, however, Johnson's focus temporarily takes leave of this intranational territory and crosses the channel to the international opposition between Britain's London and France's Paris, and the opposition is suddenly transvalued.[82]

> London! The needy villain's gen'ral home,
> The common shore of Paris and of Rome;

> With eager thirst, by folly or by fate,
> Sucks in the dregs of each corrupted state.
> Forgive my transports on a theme like this,
> I cannot bear a French metropolis
>
> —93–98

It's not that London loses its own artifice and corruption. It's rather that London is the sewer of France and Europe, innocently duped by foreign vices and a mere metonymy for Britain, the land of gullible bumpkins seduced and exploited by the libertine sophistication of her traditional antagonist, metropolitan France:

> Obsequious, artful, voluble and gay,
> On Britain's fond credulity they prey.
> . . . .
> These arts in vain our rugged natives try,
> Strain out with fault'ring diffidence a lye,
> . . . .
> For arts like these preferr'd, admir'd, caress'd,
> They first invade your table, then your breast;
> Explore your secrets with insidious art,
> Watch the Weak hour, and ransack all the heart.
>
> —11–12, 152–155

Johnson's poem is a brilliant variation on the Virgilian model of macro-pastoral. The crucial locale here is not the countryside, transvalued in Virgil by becoming part of the imperial whole of metropolitan Rome, but the capital city of Britain, which is transvalued from being the oppressor of rural innocence to being the home of rugged natives' fond credulity.

I've argued that the traditional form of the pastoral entails a dichotomous relationship between art and nature, city and country and their variants, but also complicates it with a self-consciousness subtle enough to raise without answering the question of conventionality: How far is nature from its artful representation? The pastorals of the Enlightenment pursue the same strategy, but with a more explicit insistence that's conveyed through a variety of techniques suited to the empirical study of nature as it really is at the present moment. For this reason, it's been useful along the way to ask how parody operates in specific instances; to keep in mind the spectrum of potential descriptors, from pastoral to neo-pastoral, counter-pastoral, mock-pastoral, and anti-pastoral; and to assess if and how far the forms of pastoral have become fetters on it.

A final example of macro-pastoral comes once again from *The Seasons*. The salient theme now is not the contemplative interiority of "Winter" but the expansive abundance of the other seasons. The macro-pastoral elements in Virgil are necessarily available in Thomson—city is to country as nation (city + country) is to empire—but the contradiction stemming from that overlap is not exploited. It seems to me that Thomson's project as both a pastoralist and an imperialist lacks the contradictory element of transvaluation that's central to the Virgilian inheritance, and if this is so it would argue that Thomson's text is, at least within the body of poems I've discussed, an anomaly. *The Seasons* is a long poem, composed, published, and revised over two decades. Its seasonal seriality invites comparison with the monthly and weekly series of Spenser and Gay and also can seem at times to invite correlation with historical diachrony, which Thomson alludes to from time to time. The following discussion cannot begin to do justice to the richness and complexity of *The Seasons*, and even my focus on the immediate matter at hand must be highly selective. Nonetheless, this interpretation has a salience within the context of this chapter's argument about the relationship between pastoral and macro-pastoral and between generic and material change.

Beginning with Virgil's fourth eclogue, trade often figures in pastoral as an expression of city values. Near the opening lines of Thomson's "Spring" there appears the following heroic simile addressed to Britons, describing the relationship of foreign trade and farming. The opposition of city and country values is a familiar one, as is the alliance of pastoral and georgic forms and themes, as here, in the representation of country values:

> As the sea,
> Far thro' his azure turbulent extent,
> Your empire owns, and from a thousand shores
> Wafts all the pomp of life into your ports;
> So with superior boon may your rich soil,
> Exuberant, nature's better blessings pour
> O'er every land, the naked nations cloath,
> And be th' exhaustless granary of a world.
> —"Spring," 68–74

Thomson's simile describes a deceptively classic exchange of rural raw materials for urban manufactures, deceptive in that the usual terms of exchange are reversed. For the raw materials, in the form of agricultural produce, are exported from metropolitan Britain to its far-flung colonies, while "all the pomp of life" is imported into the metropolitan center from its underdeveloped colonies. The import/export reversal makes explicit the necessity of the natural countryside to the arts of commercial and imperial exchange. However, the reversal only heightens the theme of the entire passage. The country values of national farming are not contradicted by a transvaluation to the urban values of imperial trade because in Thomson's scheme, neither nature nor art has a value that conflicts with the other. British farming and trade make complementary contributions to its imperial welfare, and by implication to its national welfare. Farming, as an element of the country at the national level and of the metropolitan at the imperial level, has the same value at both levels. "Ye generous BRITONS, venerate the plough," for it will sustain your empire ("Spring," 65).

Other important sections of *The Seasons* support the implications of this one. In a central passage of "Summer," Thomson celebrates "Happy *Britannia!*" and the natural richness of its soil and climate, which favor "thy mountains flocks" and "the mower's scythe." "Thy country teems with wealth, / And *Property* assures it to the swain." "Full are thy cities" with "trade, and joy," and "Thy crouded ports, / Where rising masts an endless prospect yield" ("Summer," 541, 545, 545–546, 549, 550, 553–554). The theory that all cultures evolve through the same stages—savage, barbarian, and civilized—was a product of the (civilized) Scottish Enlightenment and was endorsed by many in neutral, descriptive terms. In "Autumn," Thomson seems to anticipate stadial theory in a long passage whose terms, if not neutral, all apply to Britain at different stages in its cultural development.[83] Here he tells the story of *"Industry,"* source of "the soft civility of life" and "Raiser of human kind," from "sad barbarian" and "rugged savage" "To pomp, to pleasure, elegance, and grace;" and, "breathing high ambition thro' his soul," humankind gains "every form of cultivated life." Now "the city rose;" and "Commerce brought into the public walk / The busy Merchant" ("Autumn," 43, 47, 57, 69, 93, 94–95, 110, 114, 124–125). In sum, this is the story of how "lavish Nature the directing hand / Of Art demanded" ("August," 75–76). It's as though the story is Thomson's reduction of the Virgilian progression—from pastoral to georgic to imperial epic—to a stripped-down georgic without tears.

How can we explain the absence of a macro-pastoral transvaluation in *The Seasons* comparable to the micro-pastoral shift earlier described? Thomson is aware of, and recurs to, a number of familiar conventions over the course of his poem: the golden age, Hesiod's golden and iron races, the *locus amoenus*, the Horatian *beatus ille*, rural retreat from the vices of the city, the affirmation of the country values of innocence and contemplation, the criticism of the city values of trade, ambition, and luxury. But with respect to macro-pastoralism he treats pastoral conventions principally in thematic terms and as a body of commonplaces that communicate a rural ethos detached from the logic of form—from the dominance of dichotomy, but also from its self-consciously dialectical supersession. However, this is less to explain than to re-describe one's sense of Thomson's relation to pastoral. His commitment to the empirical description of nature in its seasonal variations is perhaps as great as that of any other poet. And this so fully accords with the Enlightenment impulse toward a descriptive and analytic engagement with the sensible that the formal counterpart of empirical attention—the dialectical transvaluation of terms—is likely in some fashion to shape his macro-pastoralism. I suggest that what we see in *The Seasons* is not an absence but an extreme instance of the pastoral logic of form. Thomson has gone so far in subjecting the pastoral dichotomy to dialectical conflation as for the most part to obscure or suppress the dichotomous foundation of pastoral form—the separation of art from nature, of city from country values—and therefore also to obscure or suppress the conflation of these categories as an explicit and self-conscious act. Art and nature, city and country values coexist and interpenetrate not in subtle dialectical disclosure of their relation but as coextensive parts of a greater whole. This is the nature of macro-pastoralism in *The Seasons*: a reciprocal transvaluation whereby the human subject and its natural object can't be distinguished. As a result, the form of pastoral ceases to energize the genre through its dynamic tension and becomes instead a fetter on it, seamlessly representing the national will. The working parts of the genre are greased into sheer fluidity, and the smoothness of the representation encourages us not to look too closely into its coherence.

Is Thomson's mode of macro-pastoralism in *The Seasons* simply anomalous, or does its formal attenuation suggest an extended fettering of the future representation of imperialism in relation to ongoing material change? To conceive imperialism as macro-pastoralism yields the basic insight that the appropriation of foreign lands has a model and precedent in domestic experience. Empire is in this sense uncanny, a collective adventure into the unknown that recapitulates and contains, in both senses of the term, a familiar internal opposition. If this tension subsides, has pastoral form become a fetter, or has generic change thereby adjusted to and continued in sync with a material condition in which inequality, both domestic and foreign, has become an acceptable second nature?

The answer to this question lies far beyond the scope and competence of this inquiry. My less ambitious aim has been to inquire into the correlation of pastoral poetry with the capitalist transformation of the countryside, which marks the material difference between Elizabethan and Enlightenment England and encouraged such strikingly different versions of pastoral. Enlightenment pastoral took as its task the description of that transformation in its empirical effects through a deep and extensive investigation of the country and the city as a dialectical relationship. Their shifting boundaries, actual and virtual; the emergence of absolute private property; the quantitative analysis of their spatial and temporal extent and extensions; the change in their populations in anticipation of and response to the changing demands of agrarian labor, the sexual division of labor, and the displacement of status by class characteristics; the utility of pastoral conventions in opening up the internal and external dimensions of experience: all of this participated in the ongoing change in the nature of pastoral poetry. Elizabethan pastoral displays an exquisite and pervasive art whose intensity owes something to its disregard for the material and the actual. Enlightenment pastoral takes responsibility for the actual materiality of rural and urban life. Overdetermined by a number of influences besides material change, these differences nonetheless owe a great deal to it. Yet pressured by the impulse to achieve its difference, Enlightenment pastoral inevitably evokes, and with a heightened self-consciousness, the artifice of its attention to the actual. The eighteenth-century development of the aesthetic attitude, an unprecedented equipoise of the artful and the empirical, is one of the great achievements of Enlightenment thought. It's worth reflecting on the profound and period-specific affinity of pastoral and the modern idea of the aesthetic. Is the aesthetic neo-pastoral?

5 Political Poetry

COMPARATIVE HISTORICIZING,
1650–1700, 1930–1980

What is political poetry? Throughout both volumes of this study my aim has been to argue that the Enlightenment inaugurates the modern period by explicitly analyzing the tacit wholes of traditional thought into parts that constitute new wholes, which are subjected in turn to further analysis. Another way of saying this is that where tradition conformed to a top-down hierarchy in which the quasi-metaphysical integrity of the higher category was taken to authorize the subordination of those below it, Enlightenment thought pursued the modern supposition that the authority of the most general principle or institution derives from its particular parts. Schematically speaking, this is a movement from distinction to separation and then to conflation. The aim of this chapter is to test this proposition with respect to the case of "political poetry," a case that invites this inquiry because the period of the Restoration and early eighteenth century is commonly "credited" with being the golden age of political poetry in English literary culture. This is the period whose greatest poets—Milton, Marvell, Dryden, Pope—took politics to be self-evidently worthy of poetic treatment. I use scare quotes because as I document in the introduction to this volume, in the eyes of posterity, political poetry is anything but golden. With the Romantic movement and thereafter, politics came to be judged as inimical to poetry. In the terms of my project to historicize the Enlightenment, does it follow that the years 1650–1700 represent the traditional view, that politics and poetry are distinguishable but not separable? To answer this question I'll need to begin at the end of the chronological comparison that is the focus of this chapter.

The Modern Problem of Political Poetry

In 1975, I wrote that "it is a fact of some relevance to the way we understand poetry of the past that in the contemporary climate of academic criticism, 'political poetry' is a particularly troublesome phrase, one which approaches the status of a contradiction in terms. This has not been so in other times and places—most significantly, for the purposes of the present study, in the England of the late seventeenth century."[1] More specifically, even by the end of the eighteenth century, British culture was turning broadly and increasingly toward the view that politics and poetry are incompatible. This generalization can of course be challenged by evidence that in some texts following (and even within) the Romantic movement, the opposition between politics and poetry has at times been resisted and refuted with a force and logic bred of vital causes and circumstance. But this very force betrays the far greater force of what it resists and refutes, and its highly self-conscious insistence on its own anomaly is the identifying hallmark of "political poetry" in the modern age. In the first part of this chapter I'll illustrate this quality of reflexive insistence through examples taken from the poetry of 1930–1980, whose striking self-consciousness I discuss not as typical but as making explicit what was broadly accepted to be the problem of political poetry in this period (and beyond). I'll then turn to poetry of the years 1650–1700.

Politics

In our time, the destiny of man presents its meaning in political terms.
—Thomas Mann

How can I, that girl standing there,
My attention fix
On Roman or on Russian
Or on Spanish politics?
Yet here's a travelled man that knows
What he talks about,
And there's a politician
That has read and thought,
And maybe what they say is true
Of war and war's alarms,
But O that I were young again
And held her in my arms![2]

The paradoxical sense in which W. B. Yeats's famous lines cohere as a political poem is broadly characteristic of modern political poetry as a form. "Politics" is a political poem by virtue of its wishing it weren't. Ruefully entertaining Mann's authoritative dictate, Yeats takes it to entail a drastic reduction of focus. Politics is war and war precludes love—except as it makes us regret what it precludes. The sharpness of the separation is disparately enforced by the requirements of space, time, and rhythm. The palpable presence of "that girl standing there" distracts from the demands of distant countries accessible only to "a travelled man." At the present moment—"in our time" of impending war and ineluctable aging—what once was possible in life and verse is available only to memory. Yet the prose epigraph gives way to an irregular meter whose modulation into the evenness of alternating iambic tetrameters and trimeters counterpoints this devolution with the idea that distance may become presence, that the past may be made present, that "poetry" can be written under the sway of "politics"—if only as an imaginative longing. The virtuality of "Politics" as a love poem is proportional to that of the aged poet as a "young" lover. But our enforced recollection of Maud Gonne, Leda,

Helen, the Countess Markiewicz, and Crazy Jane also actualizes that potential: Yeats has always been a political poet.

In an elegantly structured Italian sonnet, Gwendolyn Brooks's imperatives impose on the simultaneity of contradictory resolves the form of chronological sequence.

> First fight. Then fiddle. Ply the slipping string
> With feathery sorcery; muzzle the note
> With hurting love; the music that they wrote
> Bewitch, bewilder. Qualify to sing
> Threadwise. Devise no salt, no hempen thing
> For the dear instrument to bear. Devote
> The bow to silks and honey. Be remote
> A while from malice and from murdering.
> But first to arms, to armor. Carry hate
> In front of you and harmony behind.
> Be deaf to music and to beauty blind.
> Win war. Rise bloody, maybe not too late
> For having first to civilize a space
> Wherein to play your violin with grace.[3]

As the sonnet's caesuras slip from division to a greater regularity, poetic form at the level of the line shows how disorder can be reconciled and resolved. However, in the stanzaic order of the sonnet's form, the reversed insistence in the respective demands of octave and sestet may contradict this resolution.

Bertolt Brecht's resolve to set aside poetic topics in a time of disorder proves difficult to fulfill:

> Solely because of the increasing disorder
> In our cities of class struggle
> Some of us have now decided
> To speak no more of cities by the sea, snow on roofs, women
> The smell of ripe apples in cellars, the senses of the flesh, all   5
> That makes a man round and human
> But to speak in future only about the disorder
> And so become one-sided, reduced, enmeshed in the business
> Of politics and the dry, indecorous vocabulary
> Of dialectical economics   10
> So that this awful cramped coexistence
> Of snowfalls (they're not merely cold, we know)
> Exploitation, the lured flesh, class justice, should not engender
> Approval of a world so many-sided; delight in
> The contradictions of so bloodstained a life   15
> You understand.[4]

Political disorder is a condition of reduced reality that dictates a reduced range of linguistic reference. When order is overtaken by disorder, the poetic language of the senses (4–5) that makes us ordered ("round and human") must be replaced by the "dry, indecorous vocabulary" of politics—of "dialectical economics" (9–10)— by which alone our "one-sided, reduced" disorder (8) can be expressed. Why must this be done? For reasons not only of accuracy but also of ethics: for to speak now of "a world so many-sided" is to risk "approving of" its complexity and repletion (14) and so ignoring, even condoning, the political disorder that's visible only in the singlemindedness of a deliberately partial view.

Or so the logic of the poem would seem to run. In fact, Brecht muddies the waters by gesturing toward the collapse of his own distinctions. The "political" vocabulary of dialectical economics (12–13) doesn't obliterate the poetic fullness of a usually ordered life. It redescribes that fullness so as to disclose a more fully "round and human" existence—a "cramped coexistence," charged with material motives and agency—than that available through what we customarily take to be the (poetic) language of the senses. To be reduced to this political vocabulary is to be reduced to "the contradictions of so bloodstained a life," to the round and human disorder of the world at large. Properly understood, times of "order" are always also times of "disorder"; the "one-sided" view gives way to the "many-sided" view; to speak narrowly of one thing is the path to speaking of many things. By the same token, ordered poetry and disordered politics bleed together. Brecht's disordered, unpunctuated, and increasingly ambiguous syntax affords something like the discursive equivalent of a dialectical experience of reality.

Political poetry is problematic because it appears, on the face of it, to entail a contradiction in terms. The topos of a radical break between two orders of time, the poetic and the political, can temporalize this contradiction as the result of one's poetic habit (things as usual) having insensibly persisted into the exceptional realm of political change. This is especially clear in a poem of the watershed year 1968 by Nikki Giovanni, which begins and ends in the following way:

> i wanted to write
> a poem
> but revolution doesn't lend
> itself to be-bopping
> . . . .
> perhaps these are not poetic
> times
> at all[5]

The logical result of such a persistence will be either poetry as politics or politics as poetry, anti-poetry or anti-politics. The actual result often will be an effort both to evoke and to frustrate what the author contracts with us to conceive as representatively poetic and political discourse. Here is Muriel Rukeyser's "In Our Time":

> In our period, they say there is free speech.
> They say there is no penalty for poets,
> There is no penalty for writing poems.
> They say this. This is the penalty.⁶

On the one hand, Rukeyser's diction is flat, her syntax prosaic, her evident purpose unapologetically didactic. On the other, line length is blocked in a fashion that suggests not simply meter but a fully accentual-syllabic regularity. Moreover, Rukeyser's "message" is counterproductively difficult of access: gnomic; incantatory ("they say . . . they say . . . there is . . . there is . . . they say"); marking its political contradiction (the penalty is that there's no penalty) by a medial caesura ostentatious in its "poetic" dependence on typographical form.

In "Poetry: I," Adrienne Rich temporalizes the contradiction of becoming educated in how to read poetry and learning to forget that poetry teaches us how to live in the world:

> Someone at a table under a brown metal lamp
> Is studying the history of poetry.
> Someone in the library at closing-time
> Has learned to say *modernism*,
> *Trope, vatic, text.*
> She is listening for shreds of music.
> He is searching for his name
> Back in the old country.
> They cannot learn without teachers.
> They are like us what we were
> If you remember.
> In a corner of night a voice
> Is crying in a kind of whisper:
> *More!*
>
> Can you remember? When we thought
> The poets taught how to live?
> That is not the voice of a critic
> nor a common reader
> it is someone young in anger
> hardly knowing what to ask
> who finds our lines our glosses
> wanting in this world.⁷

Like Rukeyser's, Rich's caesuras are crevices in the lines of a poem that tries to overcome the inevitability of the process it describes—learning to read poetry—that it shares with time itself. The paradox of poetic criticism is that the more sophisticated it becomes at glossing the meaning of a text, the more it glosses over what's really important.

In the very short space of Lucille Clifton's poem, her speaker's sense of remembered time is so economically compressed that the self-conscious register of contradiction is anticipated and forestalled by the pre-conscious poetics of her imagination, which finds a potent political figure for the otherwise unstated politics of her actual world.

> At last we killed the roaches.
> mama and me. she sprayed,
> i swept the ceiling and they fell
> dying onto our shoulders, in our hair
> covering us with red. the tribe was broken,
> the cooking pots were ours again
> and we were glad, such cleanliness was grace
> when i was twelve. only for a few nights,
> and then not much, my dreams were blood
> my hands were blades and it was murder murder
> all over the place.[8]

The twelve-year-old speaker's world of Black urban poverty is focused on an experience whose utter familiarity begins to be estranged through nothing more than the literal action itself. As the ceiling is swept, the domestic world is turned upside down: the kitchen becomes a battlefield, the insects become an indigenous and "underdeveloped" third-world "tribe," and the speaker becomes, absurdly but irresistibly, a colonial invader. The reversal is complete: oppressed slum dwellers "attacking" their poverty are imaginatively transformed into murderous soldiers attacking "oppressed" natives. Only the fantastic figure gives us access to the disturbing relativity of the literal through the power of identification. Like Americans in Vietnam ("at last" experiencing, in 1974, its own belated liberation), the speaker has a childish ideology ("cleanliness was grace") that comes close to justifying the genocide—were it not for her dreams.

But what are the politics of Clifton's poem? Does it diminish the sociopolitical rectitude of "mama and me" or deepen it through the recognition that what feels to the speaker like a murderous complicity is rooted in her empathy for a comparable victimization? The politics of the poem turn on such questions of identification and difference—not only between the speaker, the roaches, and the natives, but also between the adolescent speaker and the adult speaker (for the poetic viewpoint is in fact—and crucially—that of an adolescent consciousness re-created retrospectively), and between both of these and us. Does the distance between the speaker's underdeveloped unconscious and her more knowing narration deprive the former of its truth value? Or does the latent content of childhood dreams pierce adult consciousness like the shrapnel of a yet-unblunted, unsocialized revelation?

The temporalizing topos—then versus now, unconscious versus conscious—is only one means among many for articulating the contradiction of political poetry. Both of the following poems by Amiri Baraka individually forgo that topos even as their striking differences from each other enact it across the chronological divide of the 1960s. The first was written in 1961, the second six or seven years later:

> Political Poem
> (*for Basil*)
>
> Luxury, then, is a way of
> being ignorant, comfortably
> An approach to the open market
> of least information. Where theories
> can thrive, under heavy tarpaulins   5
> without being cracked by ideas.
>
> (I have not seen the earth for years
> and think now possibly "dirt" is
> negative, positive, but clearly
> social. I cannot plant a seed, cannot   10
> recognize the root with clearer dent
> than indifference. Though I eat
> and shit as a natural man. (Getting up
> from the desk to secure a turkey sandwich
> and answer the phone: the poem undone   15
> undone by my station, by my station,
> and the bad words of Newark.) Raised up
> to the breech we seek to fill for this
> crumbling century. The darkness of love,
> in whose sweating memory all error is forced.   20
>
> Undone by the logic of any specific death. (Old gentlemen
> who still follow fires, tho are quieter
> and less punctual. It is a polite truth
> we are left with. Who are you? What are you
> saying? Something to be dealt with, as easily.   25
> The noxious game of reason, saying, "No, No,
> you cannot feel," like my dead lecturer
> lamenting thru gipsies his fast suicide.⁹
>
> Black Art
> Poems are bullshit unless they are
> teeth or trees or lemons piled
> on a step. Or black ladies dying
> of men leaving nickel hearts
> beating them down. Fuck poems   5
> and they are useful, wd they shoot

come at you, love what you are,
breathe like wrestlers, or shudder
strangely after pissing. We want live
words of the hip world live flesh &
coursing blood. Hearts Brains
Souls splintering fire. We want poems
like fists beating niggers out of Jocks
or dagger Poems in the slimy bellies
of the owner-jews. Black poems to
smear on girlmamma mulatto bitches
whose brains are red jelly stuck
between 'lizabeth taylor's toes. Stinking
Whores! We want "poems that kill,"
Assassin poems, Poems that shoot
guns. Poems that wrestle cops into alleys
and take their weapons leaving them dead
with tongues pulled out and sent to Ireland. Knockoff
poems for dope selling wops or slick halfwhite
politicians Airplane poems, rrrrrrrrrrrrrrrr
rrrrrrrrrrrrrrrr . . . tuhtuhtuhtuhtuhtuhtuhtuh
. . . rrrrrrrrrrrrrrrrr . . . Setting fire and death to
whities ass. Look at the Liberal
Spokesman for the jews clutch his throat
& puke himself into eternity . . . rrrrrrrr
There's a negroleader pinned to
a bar stool in Sardi's eyeballs melting
in hot flame Another negroleader
on the steps of the white house one
kneeling between the sheriff's thighs
negotiating coolly for his people.
Agggh . . . stumbles across the room . . .
Put it on him, poem. Strip him naked
to the world! Another bad poem cracking
steel knuckles in a jewlady's mouth
Poem scream poison gas on beasts in green berets
Clean out the world for virtue and love,
Let there be no love poems written
until love can exist freely and
cleanly. Let Black People understand
that they are the lovers and the sons
of lovers and warriors and sons
of warriors Are poems & poets &
all the loveliness here in the world
We want a black poem. And a

> Black World.
> Let the world be a Black Poem
> And Let All Black People Speak This Poem
> Silently
> or LOUD[10]   55

Both of Baraka's poems are self-consciously (as the earlier one calls itself) "political poems," but they are so in very different ways. The first is cerebral and intensely introspective, a singular voice overheard as it meditates on its own estrangement, a parenthetical opening out that, like the "open market" (3) and the thought initiated at line 7, never attains closure. On the evidence of his bodily functions a "natural man" (13), the speaker is nonetheless estranged from his nature by intellectual and technological rationalization. He suffers the "luxury" (1) of useless knowledge that satisfies unnecessary needs. He produces theories as though they were plants and concepts as though they were the things they refer to. He consumes food like a technocrat (14) and information like a starving man. The poem is "political" in the peculiar sense of being a protest whose futility is ensured in advance: to confront the problem through articulation is to give it being. Hence the poem is perpetually "undone" (15, 16, 21), unachieved, and uncompleted by the very effort to do it, and it doesn't so much conclude as peter out in the solipsism of private reference. This is political poetry as Sisyphean labor, a vain exercise in pushing away self-spun cobwebs, a poem that demonstrates even as it declares the impassable gulf between mind and matter, thought and action, poetry and politics.

"Black Art" is "Political Poem" put through the wringer of the sixties. The alienated "I" has become collective and implacably desirous: "We want . . ." (9, 12, 19, 50). Highly literate sobriety has become oral performance: "Let All Black People Speak This Poem" (53). Private self-doubt has been gleefully projected out onto an ecumenical spectrum of collectivized and stereotyped others: abject "niggers," "owner-jews," "mulatto bitches," Irish cops, "dope selling wops," "halfwhite politicians" (13, 15, 16, 21, 24–25). Most important, poetry has shed its tautological introspection and become a dangerous weapon: a penis (5–9), a fist (13), a dagger (14), a gun (21), an airplane (25), steel knuckles (40), poison gas (41). The solution to the problem of "Political Poem" (the gulf between poetry and politics), like the solution to the problem of "In Our Time" (the penalty of no penalty), is to write a poem that causes physical damage and therefore can't be met with tolerance and "indifference" ("Political Poem," 12). Not a "love poem" (43), "Black Art" is on the contrary a hate poem, a "bad poem" (39) filled with "bad words" ("Political Poem," 17). Bad poetry is "bad" not only in the antithetical sense of Black slang or in how its hate words hurt and violate in a way that suspends the opposition between verbal discourse and physical action, but also because it forces the question of normative evaluation. What's the relationship between "good" poetry and "good" politics? What's the overlap between "good" politics in the ethical sense of humanitarian sentiment and "good" politics in the rhetorical sense of conducing toward political action? Yet to read/hear "Black Art" in the rationalizing mode of "Political Poem"—to justify its violence on poetic or political grounds—would be to make it palatable, consumable, tolerable. On the other hand, to read/hear it without appreciating the amusingly utopian grandiosity of its ambition—"Put it on him, poem"! (38)—is to miss something of its value as both poetry and politics.

Audre Lorde's "Power" begins:

> The difference between poetry and rhetoric
> is being
> ready to kill
> yourself
> instead of your children. 5
>
> i am trapped on a desert of raw gunshot wounds
> and a dead child dragging his shattered black
> face off the edge of my sleep
> blood from his punctured cheeks and shoulders
> is the only liquid for miles and my stomach 10
> churns at the imagined taste while
> my mouth splits into dry lips
>
> without loyalty or reason
> thirsting for the wetness of his blood
> as it sinks into the whiteness 15
> of the desert where I am lost
> without imagery or magic
> trying to make power out of hatred and destruction
> trying to heal my dying son with kisses
> only the sun will bleach his bones quicker. 20
>
> The policeman who shot down a ten-year-old in Queens
> stood over the boy with his cop shoes in childish blood
> and a voice said "Die you little motherfucker" and
> there are tapes to prove that. At his trial
> this policeman said in his own defense 25
> "I didn't notice the size or nothing else
> only the color." and
> there are tapes to prove that, too.
>
> Today that 37-year-old white man with 13 years of police forcing
> has been set free 30
> by 11 white men who said they were satisfied
> justice had been done
> and one black woman who said
> "They convinced me" meaning

> they had dragged her 4'10" black woman's frame 35
> over the hot coals of four centuries of white male approval
> until she let go the first real power she ever had
> and lined her own womb with cement
> to make a graveyard for our children.
>
> I have not been able to touch the destruction within me. 40
> But unless I learn to use
> the difference between poetry and rhetoric
> my power too will run corrupt as poisonous mold
> or lie limp and useless as an unconnected wire
> and one day I will take my teenaged plug 45
> and connect it to the nearest socket
> raping an 85-year-old white woman
> who is somebody's mother
> and as I beat her senseless and set a torch to her bed
> a greek chorus will be singing in 3 / 4 time 50
> "Poor thing. She never hurt a soul. What beasts they are."[11]

Lorde's poem is about how to gain the power to "touch" and to channel the "hatred and destruction" "within me" (18, 40). The first stanza might seem to suggest that poetry and rhetoric are different ways of doing this; but it's hard to see what their enigmatic, existential epithets have to do with power.

"Yourself instead of your children":

"I," trapped in a dreamscape, embodies her Black son dying of gunshot wounds and fails to make a healing power of the hatred and destruction that have killed him. Is this the language of poetry?

With quantifying objectivity, the white policeman who shot a Black boy and the white male jury that acquitted him are described in the blind color hatred they share, while the single Black woman juror, "convinced" by domination (34), fails to use her power to testify against advancing the destruction of Black children from the past into the future. Is this the language of rhetoric?

Thus hatred and destruction, natural to white power, are deadly pathogens that have been transmitted to the bodies of Black people and made them impotent. "I" now returns to ask how she can transform this sickness into a power that can heal her body of the white disease. Otherwise they will corrupt her power with the pathology of reverse color hatred, and she will come to embody a Black youth who, noticing "only the color," is empowered not to heal but to destroy a white woman (27).

The question also returns: What is "the difference between poetry and rhetoric"—or rather, how to "use" that difference (41, 42). What does this word add? It suggests that the point of learning their difference isn't to enable a choice between them but to know how to exploit their differences. Moreover, the poem suggests that there isn't a choice between poetry and rhetoric, because whether to heal or to destroy, we embody our children. The question also reminds us that this is a poem about the power of discourse, not action, even if discourse can lead to action. True, unlike poetry, rhetoric aims to incite action, like destroying a white woman. The voice that reminds us that this woman is destroyed for her color, not her person, also reminds us of the lesson of Aristotelian tragedy, that we feel pity and fear because we know poetry imitates the real but isn't, so to protest that characters don't deserve their plots confuses art with life. Yet the voice disregards that lesson by sliding from art to life, and although the protest about the deserts of those destroyed by color hatred arises over the imagined white woman, the tone of voice—"What beasts they are"—betrays its source in the pathology of white power, which has taken hatred and destruction as its guiding light (51).

The difference between art and life invites us to think about the difference between poetic and rhetorical discourse. If the drily dispassionate account of the cop and his trial is the rhetoric of persuasive description, it's also about the rhetoric used to "convince" the Black woman of what she lacked the power to be unconvinced of. And if the speaker's nightmare of passionate identification with the murdered boy is poetry, it's also about her effort to experience it as a tragic catharsis whose power purges her of the terrible passions she is forced to suffer. Lorde's poem is about the difference between poetry and rhetoric, but does it also find in that difference a contradictory key to political poetry?

Politics as Form

The problematic nature of political poetry depends for its meaning on the cultural dominance of the notion that poetry and politics are antithetical entities: at the most extreme, discourse versus action; less extreme but still decisive, poetic discourse versus political discourse. The most accessible understanding of this discursive opposition is content based. Poetry concerns itself with both private and transcendent themes, politics with the middle range of the public; so political poetry diverges from the poetic norm by taking up issues of institutional and social power. But to retain a recognizable status as poetry, it also has to sustain a self-conscious relationship to the indispensable hallmark of poetic discourse, poetic form. In attaining its effects, political poetry therefore is theoretically confronted by a basic choice between a strategy of "politicizing" form—turning it to political ends—and (since form as such is "poetic") one of eschewing form altogether. Needless to say, neither alternative is easily undertaken. And because the content of language is inevitably informed, a common recourse of political poetry is to the language of literal description, documentation, and news report, stripped of all but empirical reference.

We've already seen some examples of how the fundamental elements of poetic form—rhythm, rhyme, verse form, voice, figures of speech—can be exploited for (as it were) anti-poetic, political purposes. Pablo Neruda's "I'm Explaining a Few Things" begins with a frankly reflexive repudiation of poetic language that bears the metaphorical suggestion of the kind of political action of which it falls short:

> You are going to ask: and where are the lilacs?
> and the poppy-petalled metaphysics?
> and the rain repeatedly spattering
> its words and drilling them full
> of apertures and birds?
>
> I'll tell you all the news.
>
> —1–6[12]

Neruda's turn now from a declarative to a narrative mode, although it might seem to promise a demystifying Brechtian "one-sidedness," in fact begins a story that's filled with both figurative and literal flowers. The actual change in diction occurs suddenly, in the middle of things, with the temporal rupture of civil war:

> And one morning all that was burning,
> one morning the bonfires
> leapt out of the earth
> devouring human beings—
> and from then on fire,
> gunpowder from then on,
> and from then on blood.
>
> —39–45

Rather than evacuate his poem of figures, Neruda now concentrates their former plurality into a single-minded insistence on the relentless images of fire and blood:

> Treacherous
> generals:
> See my dead house,
> look at broken Spain:
> from every house burning metal flows
> instead of flowers . . .
>
> —59–64

Under totalitarian conditions, Neruda seems to explain, poetry must totalize. His poem ends:

> And you will ask: why doesn't his poetry
> speak of dreams and leaves
> and the great volcanoes of his native land?
> Come and see the blood in the streets.
> Come and see
> the blood in the streets.
> Come and see the blood
> in the streets!
>
> —71–78

Political Poetry 167

As figuration, so line length; the monotonous implacability of Neruda's explanation seems to say: slice it any way you want, it still smells the same.

The association between poetry and flowers receives a more consistently Brechtian treatment in Zbigniew Herbert's "Five Men":

I
They take them out in the morning
to the stone courtyard
and put them against the wall

five men
two of them very young   5
the others middle-aged

nothing more
can be said about them

II
when the platoon
level their guns   10
everything suddenly appears
in the garish light
of obviousness
the yellow wall
the cold blue   15
the black wire on the wall
instead of a horizon

this is the moment when the five senses rebel
they would gladly escape
like rats from a sinking ship   20

before the bullet reaches its destination
the eye will perceive the flight of the projectile
the ear record a steely rustle
the nostrils will be filled with biting smoke
a petal of blood will brush the palate   25
the touch will shrink and then slacken

now they lie on the ground
covered up to their eyes with shadow
the platoon walks away
their buttons straps   30
and steel helmets
are more alive

than those lying
beside the wall

III

I did not learn this today 35
I knew it before yesterday
so why have I been writing
unimportant poems on flowers

what did the five talk of
the night before the execution 40

of prophetic dreams
of an escapade in a brothel
of automobile parts
of a sea voyage
of how when he had spades 45
he ought not to have opened
of how vodka is best
after wine you get a headache
of girls
of fruit 50
of life

thus one can use in poetry
names of Greek shepherds
one can attempt to catch the color of morning sky
write of love 55
and also
once again
in dead earnest
offer to the betrayed world
a rose[13] 60

The three-part division of the poem throws its logic into relief. Herbert begins his account of an execution with language that's radically purified, stripped down to the brutal, empirical truth of things so as to justify, with an outrage whetted—like Lorde's two stanzas of "rhetoric"—by being unspoken, the prohibition against saying more. But in making predications "about" the five men (8), the speaker has only broached the empirical imperative from an external perspective. The second part of the poem, while seeming to evade the prohibition with which the first part ends, in fact respects it by pursuing the empirical approach into the realm of the senses. The facticity of the world gives way to its sensible immediacy at the very moment of execution, accessible to the speaker through an imaginative projection into the sense perceptions of the five subjects. Personified, the senses take on the aura of allegory, figuratively if discontinuously standing for the five men and thereby justifying the figurative phrases—"like rats" (20), "steely rustle" (23), "biting smoke" (24), "petal of blood" (25)—that now begin to deepen the empirical truth of things.

And yet the senses, no less than the men they personify, are mortal and must die. This ultimate fact generates the question with which part three of the poem begins—"so why have I been writing / unimportant poems on flowers" (37–38)—and that's answered by another question: "what did the five talk of / the night before the execution" (39–40). If "nothing more can be said about them," much can be imagined of what they said. The catalogue that succeeds and answers both questions, Herbert suggests, is an anthology or a *florilegium*, a bouquet of flowers gathered through an act of poetic imagination whereby stating the bare truth of executed men demands a sensual projection, an identification with their collective subjectivity.[14] The revitalizing "rose" that blossoms from the poet's fancied petal of blood is offered less as the consolation of "the betrayed world" than as its figure of defiance (59–60). The importance of poems on flowers lies in their capacity to say more where nothing more can be said—a poetic, pressured to the condition of a political, capacity.

The only alternative to this kind of dialectical reversal would seem to be the pursuit of Herbert's opening language of empirical description to its bitter end, a pursuit that must entail a radical change of form. Carolyn Forché's poem "The Colonel," an account of her interview with a Nicaraguan colonel in the 1970s, is one example:

> What you have heard is true. I was in his house. His wife carried   1
> a tray of coffee and sugar. His daughter filed her nails, his son went
> out for the night. There were daily papers, pet dogs, a pistol on the
> cushion beside him. The moon swung bare on its black cord over
> the house. On the television was a cop show. It was in English.   5
> Broken bottles were embedded in the walls around the house to
> scoop the kneecaps from a man's leg or cut his hands to lace. On
> the windows there were gratings like those in liquor stores. We had
> dinner, rack of lamb, good wine, a gold bell was on the table for
> calling the maid. The maid brought green mangoes, salt, a type of   10
> bread. I was asked how I enjoyed the country. There was a brief
> commercial in Spanish. His wife took everything away. There was
> some talk then of how difficult it had become to govern. The parrot
> said hello on the terrace. The colonel told it to shut up, and pushed
> himself from the table. My friend said to me with his eyes: say   15
> nothing. The colonel returned with a sack used to bring groceries
> home. He spilled many human ears on the table. They were like
> dried peach halves. There is no other way to say this. He took one
> of them in his hands, shook it in our faces, dropped it into a water
> glass. It came alive there. I am tired of fooling around he said. As   20
> for the rights of anyone, tell your people they can go fuck them-

selves. He swept the ears to the floor with his arm and held the last
of his wine in the air. Something for your poetry, no? he said. Some
of the ears on the floor caught this scrap of his voice. Some of the
ears on the floor were pressed to the ground.[15]   25

Rather than write a poem, Forché will, like Neruda, "tell you all the news," but in a different form. "The Colonel" has the tone and pace of investigative reporting, telling a story in the first person that provides factual details in accounting for how a piece of news has been put together. The personal nature of the story has the quality of hearsay but goes beyond and confirms it: "What you have heard is true" (1). Figures of speech proliferate as they will in accounting for real life, although at times they may require acknowledgment: "They were like dried peach halves. There is no other way to say this" (17–18). The sense of literal-descriptive neutrality devoid of affect is achieved instead by a minimalist syntax that creates a paratactic sequence of things that are related not by any other narrative logic than the order of narration, which is generated by the description of a single setting. Its force comes from the grotesque incongruity that the interview with this military butcher takes place in his domestic family setting, replaying the contradictory nature of political poetry in a different key. The familiar details of family life are shockingly defamiliarized by the ambience of an American situation comedy. In fact, the TV features an American product of cultural imperialism, an apt reminder that the Somoza dictatorship was sponsored by American money.

In Giovanni's words, "these are not poetic times at all," and Forché forgoes meter and line length, turning to the prose of what is literally journalism in order to report this day in the life of a murderer. But having recourse to figuration, she allows to germinate a symbol whose utopian extravagance far exceeds the bounds of investigative reporting in its surreal imagination that the ears can hear. The mundane "sack" of "groceries" bears witness to the colonel's brutality and occasions the vindication of the poet in the reporter. His question to her is scornfully rhetorical, but the poet replies with this piece of disciplined prose that also turns the colonel's political atrocity into poetry.

Mike Gold's "Examples of Worker Correspondence" revises letters sent by workers to the Communist Party of America datelined like news dispatches.

Flint City Jail, Mich.
Arrested as a picket in a recent strike
I have found my cellmate here an Indian chief
His name John Thunder of the Ottawas.
Once his father owned America
But now after ten years at the Buick plant   5
Working under Mr. Crowder as an expert fender finisher
Chief Thunder is destitute and can find no job.
His family scattered, his children in the orphanage
So the Chief worried and was low in mind

> And drinking in a saloon fought a Ku Kluxer   10
> And beat up the 100 percent American
> So now is in jail waiting his sentence.
> He talks of days when his fathers owned this land
> The buffalo days when food was shared by all
> When no one was hungry and there was no rich   15
> He has asked me to write and tell his tale
> He wants us to remember the deep wrongs of the Indian
> I have given Chief Thunder a pamphlet by Lenin.[16]

Gold's localizing caption melds the prose form of the news dispatch with that of the personal letter but departs from both in the variant line lengths of verse. In this particular poem, voice is also explicitly an amalgam, a "tale" told by another ("the Party," or like Forché, a poet doing nonpoetic service?), its subjective authority underwritten by its documentary authenticity (16). The Party's frank didacticism is, unironized, also that of the poem and anathema to modern standards of aesthetic value. This may be true as well of the Chief's naive retrospective utopianism, a literal conviction unmediated by the anticipatory surrealism of Forché's fantastic ears. If the sentiment also attaches to the Party, it bespeaks either a similar naivete or unabashed propaganda, utilitarian oil that repels the purposeless water of poetry. Gold's poem lacks the reflexivity of these other poems because it doesn't articulate the contradiction of political poetry so much as perform it, but without the self-consciousness of Baraka's "Black Art." Is this because Gold's poem approaches the status of political poetry from (why is this?) the direction of politics rather than poetry? If so, we might be tempted to say that in the case of this text, the problem of political poetry is absent because it's clearly not poetry but politics. Or does it pose the problem of political poetry with greater force than the others for this very reason: because it relieves the pressure of that contradiction by evading it?

Tradition: The Tacit Distinction of Politics and Poetry

I began this chapter with a passage from an earlier book in which I claim that political poetry, whose contradictory status in the modern period is my present subject, is unproblematic during the Enlightenment. By this line of thought, we might extrapolate, political poetry had always existed until that moment. But if political poetry has always existed, why do we associate it with the Enlightenment in particular? Moreover, to see the poetry of 1650–1700 as continuing and culminating the traditional view—that politics and poetry are distinguishable but not separable—runs counter to the broadest hypothesis of this study. Other chapters in this volume make the case that a highly innovative idea of the aesthetic emerged at this time. One implication of this might be that the idea of politics, too, was separated out in this period from its traditional cultural embeddedness as distinct but inseparable from other bodies of thought and understanding.

In the realm of politics, the great watershed was the English Civil War. The traditional view that politics was grounded in metaphysical and moral principles of justice, reason, and grace had been permanently challenged by the Italian Renaissance unmasking of politics as "reason of state," the "mysteries" of rule, or *arcana imperii*, whose autotelic end is the maintenance of governmental power itself.[17] In 1642, Charles I warned that if the House of Commons is ceded the authority it seeks,

> so new a power will undoubtedly intoxicate persons who were not born to it, and beget not only divisions among them as equals, but in them contempt of us, as become an equal to them, and insolence and injustice toward our people, as now so much their inferiors, which will be the more grievous unto them, as suffering from those who were so lately of a nearer degree to themselves . . . till . . . at last the common people . . . discover this *arcanum imperii*, that all this was done by them, but not for them, and grow weary of journey-work, and set up for themselves, call parity and independence liberty, devour that estate which had devoured the rest, destroy all rights and proprieties, all distinctions of families and merit, and by this means this splendid and excellently distinguished form of government end in a dark, equal chaos of confusion, and the long line of our many noble ancestors in a Jack Wade or a Wat Tyler.[18]

Charles foresaw the decay of hierarchy that would accompany a general disenchantment with the fictions of lineage and succession that traditionally buttressed the power of the dynastic English polity with sovereign legitimacy. Over time this demystified and pragmatic understanding of what politics amounts to became the modern view.

As the notoriety of the dramatic figure "Machiavel" makes clear, Renaissance England felt the direct influence of the Italian unmasking. A more permanent expression of it (although vastly overdetermined) was the emergence of civil society over against the state that transpired in the years of the Civil War and in its aftermath.[19] This didn't reinforce, but rather cut across, the separation of "the state" as such from the private realm of elite gentility and property owners that civil war brought to a head, but both developments helped define and throw into relief, against the rich spectacle and distractions of traditional courtly culture, the state's focus on naked interest and power. After the Civil War, political theory and practice turned away from the assumptions of royal sovereignty, monarchal succession, and absolutist rule and toward contractual models of political authority and systems of representative democracy. The experience of civil war, the internal division of a presumptive whole, made absolute terms of opposition untenable, at least in domestic politics, but it laid the ground for the emergence of party politics and the concept of a "loyal opposition," which, although at any given time lacking the authority to rule, would not try to subvert the ruling government because even in opposition it was committed to being part of the government. The category of nobility and the justice of social status lost credit over a longer term, but with comparable finality.

In the broadest terms, the transformation of politics in the early modern period can be understood by reference to the emergent doubleness of the "public": on the one hand, the traditional authority of the state and its apparatus; on the other, the authority of civil society, "the people," and the private institutions—paradigmatically religion, trade, and the press—that shared with the people their separateness from absolute state control.

In the light of this context it becomes problematic to associate the Enlightenment with a simple belief in the compatibility of politics and poetry, whether retrospectively as the golden age of political poetry or even in the minds of contemporaries. My view now is more circumspect. I suggest that this is the moment when the genre itself emerged, coalescing around and defined by the sense of a crucial space between the political and its poetic mediation that's absent, in general, from earlier poetry written on political themes. In its Enlightenment inception, "political poetry" represents the first stage in a movement, from tacit assumption to explicit concept and language, that we see across the entire range of Enlightenment innovation. The singular becomes specialized and requires modifiers (political as distinct from other kinds of poetry, poetic as distinct from other political manifestations). Two distinct categories are sufficiently dislodged from their tacit conjuncture to be separated and conjoined in active usage. At this early stage, the self-conscious character of political poetry isn't the explicit reflexivity of twentieth-century political poetry, whose content notably entails a formal recognition that its project is contradictory in nature. But it's recognizably self-conscious nonetheless.

If the preconditions for political poetry were laid down by the Civil War, the emergence of civil society, and the coalescence of a virtual public, its more proximate conditions were created by the gestation of party politics in the wake of the Restoration, the Exclusion Crisis of the early 1680s—the campaign to disqualify the Duke of York from the royal line of inheritance—and the legal vacuum opened up by the lapsing of the Printing Act in 1694.

The seventeenth-century entrenchment of print culture brought with it an intensified apprehension of libel or written defamation. By defaming public officials, seditious libel amounted to a direct challenge to the authority of the state; but libel against private persons was also subject to public prosecution, and it was a far more prevalent problem. Legal strategies to stamp out libel were largely unsuccessful. On the one hand, for a number of reasons the requirement that the names of authors and publishers be included on libelous publications fell short of its aims. On the other, publications were libelous if they aimed at actual persons, but authors were often able to obscure the identity of those they referred to just enough to thwart prosecution by the state but still allow identification by their readers. Contemporaries cite many techniques of concealment: nicknames, initials, stars, dashes, circumlocution, insinuation, innuendo, historical parallels, allegory, and the like. The state's counterstrategy was to prove the presence of "innuendo" by clarifying the reference of suspect language so as to reveal its defamatory nature.[20]

Dryden's political poetry is the great exemplar of political poetry, and *Absalom and Achitophel* (1681) the most exemplary of his poems and the most distinguished contribution to the Exclusion Crisis. Defending Charles II in a confrontation comparable to that faced by his father forty years earlier, *Absalom and Achitophel's* virtuousity lies in the way it deploys the tropes of royal sovereignty with an experimental skepticism that sustains a benign and intelligent detachment from what it defends in the way that it defends it. Dryden makes his case by interweaving several threads of argument based on the traditional legitimacy of succession—spiritual, political, literary, social—so as both to disclose their vulnerability on rational grounds and to affirm their pragmatic efficacy for the task at hand.

Spiritual, political, literary, and social. *Absalom and Achitophel*, about the politics of the contemporary moment, is framed with self-conscious indirection as an account of an episode of Old Testament history so as to present the English crisis as the typological fulfillment of an artfully partial reading of that history. Both the spiritual and the historical truth entailed in typology are parodied so amiably that the force of its advocacy is conveyed despite its irrelevance to the English case at hand. Dryden refutes the challenge to the royal succession mounted by the opposition by indulging its weakest and ignoring its strongest claim (which was ratified eight years later by the deposal of Charles's brother James II). Multiple allusions and echoes throughout *Absalom and Achitophel* invite us to see Dryden as seeking a place for the poem in the literary line of heroic poetry, or perhaps that of mock epic, and suggesting a special proximity to *Paradise Lost*. But these allusions have a way of undermining each other, and Dryden's attitude toward Milton's poem is as ambivalent here as it is in other of his writings.[21] Most important, when Dryden undertakes to defend royal sovereignty by the measure of Adam's lineage, he argues not the spiritual truth of Charles's patriarchal descent from Adam but the logic of analogy: our present subjecthood is entailed in Stuart sovereignty as our original sin is entailed in Adam's fall. Dryden's argument for Charles's sovereign succession is consistently rational, conditional, and interrogative in this fashion; but he goes even further. With an ironic deference Dryden now shifts gears to a prudential and instrumental register:

> Yet, grant our Lords the People Kings can make,
> What Prudent men a settled Throne would shake?[22]

Although he liberally employs the tropes of metaphysical ascription in *Absalom and Achitophel*, Dryden plants them in what with Edmund Burke and Samuel Johnson will become the soil of modern conservatism: the affirmation of traditional principles not for their essential but for their pragmatic value. Not that political poetry is necessarily, or even likely to be, conservative. What it shares with modern conservatism, and with much else that's modern, is the force of a self-conscious mode of belief that inheres in what Coleridge was to call the willing suspension of disbelief. This is the mode of aesthetic response that was first theorized in Enlightenment England and that Dryden crucially helped establish.[23]

Dryden's skeptical detachment from the principles he espouses gently adumbrates his espousal with a shade of persuasive purpose. If we can assume that a persuasive purpose inheres in all political discourse, I suggest that it now comes to the surface when, fueled by the danger of a return to civil war and the coalescence of a political party in explicit opposition to Stuart rule, Royalist advocacy had for the first time to negotiate its relation to an absolutism that as a principle formerly had gone without saying, whether or not monarchy was actually ascendant (as for much of midcentury it was not). The alternative option, a royalism whose rhetorical investment might remain implicit, was disappearing. A late example may be seen in Richard Lovelace's love lyric "To Lucasta, Going to the Warres," which was published in 1649, a year that with hindsight would turn out to have been the climacteric when the world changed utterly:

I.
Tell me not (Sweet) I am unkinde,
   That from the Nunnerie
Of thy chaste breast, and quiet minde,
   To Warre and Armes I flie.

II.
True; a new Mistresse now I chase,
   The first Foe in the Field;
And with a stronger Faith imbrace
   A Sword, a Horse, a Shield.

III.
Yet this Inconstancy is such,
   As you too shall adore;
I could not love thee (Deare) so much,
   Lov'd I not Honour more.[24]

Lovelace's stance may be set off by contrasting it with a modern poem whose message is ostensibly the same. In "First fight. Then fiddle," Gwendolyn Brooks insists so tenaciously that political fighting must come before artful fiddling that the inversion of this sequence in the respective attention paid to them in octave and sestet, if it weakens the imperative mood, still bolsters a sense of sequence and order. In Lovelace's title, the opposition, although also temporal, is absolute. The poem is about what comes "first"; "then" doesn't even enter into it. Yet the effect isn't devastating, because the opposition is absorbed within a greater whole, and what reads like the personal valediction of a lover to his beloved is inseparably the affirmation of a "stronger faith." Where Brooks confronts the opposition between politics and poetry on the level of how to write a poem that's both political and poetic, Lovelace tells a story that explains why it proceeds as it does by evoking the rule of royalism and aristocracy that encloses it and preordains its end. The speaker's inconstancy is a higher form of constancy, as love of a woman is love of honor, because male honor is a higher version of female chastity since the wife's chastity underwrites the inheritance of honor in the husband's patriline. The poem is built on a set of distinctions: honor is distinct from chastity, men are distinct from women, chasing the first foe in the field is distinct from chasing Lucasta, war is distinct from love. But the elements that are distinguished are inseparable because they're parts of a greater whole, and to write a love poem is also, implicitly, to write about politics. In the world of Nikki Giovanni and her contemporaries, politics may sometimes dictate that times are not poetic. In the waning world of Richard Lovelace, the times are always poetic, as well as political. Speaking poetically, "To Lucasta" is structured on a single metaphor. Speaking politically, its metaphorical structure is that of the world and goes without saying.

State Poetry: The Enlightenment Emergence of "Political Poetry"

In justifying the deposal of James II in 1688, the rupture of the patriline at the highest level was deemed providential on the grounds that it pragmatically ensured "a Setled possession of the Throne."[25] And beginning in 1689, immediately after this "glorious revolution" and continuing until 1716, a series of miscellanies was published that collected a large body of political poetry under the omnibus title *Poems on Affairs of State*. These are the years when English people are becoming accustomed to the innovative notion of a civil society that coexists with a newly autonomized state. *Poems on Affairs of State* self-consciously christens political poetry as "state poetry."[26] The early, Whig-inspired miscellanies, published soon after James II had been deposed, represented their contents as state secrets now triumphantly brought to light. "The Design of Collections of this kind," says the "Preface" to the edition of 1703, "is to afford some assistance to History; the Spirit of the Several Parties in the Nation being to be discover'd hereby, as much, if not more, than from any other sort of Writing." The 1697 "Prefaces" are more outspoken. Praising the variety and pleasure of the poems to follow—including, in a likely allusion to Milton's headnote on "The Verse" of *Paradise Lost*, their "rough Cadencies"—the author writes that

> there is no where a greater Spirit of Liberty to be found, than in those who are Poets. . . . When all *Europe* is engag'd to destroy that Tyrannick Power, the mismanagement of those Times, and the selfish evil Designs of a corrupt Court had given Rise to, it cannot be thought unseasonable to publish so just an Account of the true sourse [sic] of all our present Mischiefs; which will be evidently found in the following Poems, for from them we may collect a just and secret History of the former Times. . . . Take off the gawdy veil of Slavery, and she will appear so frightfull and deform'd that all would abhor her; for all Mankind naturally prefer Liberty to Slavery.

The state poems give "the best *Secret History* of our late Reigns, as being writ by such great Persons as were near the Helm, knew the Transactions, and were above being brib'd to flatter, or afraid to speak truth."[27]

These early prefaces portray the state poetry they collect as clearly opposed to the state in both what they say and how they say it, celebrating liberty against tyranny and slavery and dispelling the mysteries of state in a plain style free of disguise and illusion and imbued with honesty and truth. Needless to say, this oppositional relation, so far from intimating a contradiction in terms, expresses the capacity of discourse, and perhaps of poetry in particular, to engage directly and forcefully in the criticism of politics. The prefaces associate state poetry with the "secret history" of Procopius, whose second-century *Anecdota*, recently translated into English, was gaining celebrity as a model for the public revelation from below, by minor functionaries, of scandal in the high corridors of power that was suppressed in official accounts of state affairs.[28] The association of state poetry with the secret history was opportunist but rhetorically apt. In fact, the authors of the state poems were highly diverse in position, stature, and circumstance, and relatively few of them are likely to have been anywhere "near the helm" of government. But the notion that state poets were disaffected state officials sustained the opposition between poetry and the mysteries of state because they publicized apparently confidential information that subverted the historical account as it appeared in official organs like royal proclamations and the *Gazette*. This may be implied in the dismay of Samuel Pepys, himself an important state official, at the "fourth *Advice to the painter*, . . . that made my heart ake to read, it being too sharp and so true."[29]

However, viewing the state poetry as secret histories also puts them and the state in a relation of apposition. Most obviously, these putative poet-officials were closely proximate to the state, which was their immediate source of knowledge. More important, state poetry resembled mysteries of state because it shared their aura and aim of secrecy. The state poems did not simply dispel secrecy by disclosing what had been private to public view. In order to avoid state prosecution for libel, they had to maintain their secrecy not only by obscuring their own authorship—the vast majority were anonymous—but also by using techniques of innuendo that veiled the precise identities of those they disclosed even in the act of disclosing them. Addison wrote a parody of a libel that employed many of these obscuring devices: "It gives a secret Satisfaction to a Peruser of these mysterious Works, that he is able to decipher them without help, and, by the Strength of his own natural Parts, to fill up a Blank-Space, or make out a Word that has only the first or last Letter to it."[30] In other words, the obscurity of the state conditioned the obscurity of the state poems whose ambition was to dispel the obscurity of the state. The grounds of their opposition to the state were also the grounds of their apposition. And royalist poets, equally vulnerable to prosecution for libel, also had recourse to the obfuscating techniques of innuendo. As *Absalom and Achitophel* attests, Dryden made brilliant use of historical parallels. *The Duke of Guise* (1683), coauthored with Nathaniel Lee, was held back from performance on the complaint that, in Dryden's words, "some Great Persons were represented or personated in it." (But "it is not," he added, "a Parallel of the *Men*, but of the *Times*. A Parallel of the *Factions*, and of the *Leaguers*.") Thomas Shadwell charged *Absalom and Achitophel* with being a libel, and John Dennis later named it as among the "Libels which have pass'd for Satires."[31]

And despite the retrospective emphasis on opposition in the early prefaces, the *Poems on Affairs of State* themselves were as much preoccupied with the affinities between, the delicate apposition of, statesman and poet, which is evident also in poetry that didn't appear in these miscellanies:

> The forward youth that would appear
> Must now forsake his Muses dear,
>   Nor in the shadows sing
>   His numbers languishing.[32]

> Nor think the Kindred-Muses thy Disgrace;
> A Poet is not born in ev'ry Race.
> Two of a House, few Ages can afford;
> One to perform, another to record.[33]

A second quality shared by state poetry and the state, one that also, like secrecy, has complex ties to the emergence of civil society, is artifice.

In response to civil war, contract theory evolved to rationalize the creation of state and civil society as the product of a collective decision of proto-citizens to abandon the state of nature by sacrificing certain rights so as to ensure the preservation of others. In the Lockean version of the contract fiction, the state serves at the will of civil society; in the Hobbesian version, the state, once created, becomes the seat of an absolute sovereignty that, no longer what goes without saying, is expressly justified as the will of the people. The Lockean view of the contract provides a model for the Habermasian theory of the public sphere as the domain in which the private citizens who compose civil society join together in a public body to engage in critical discourse that contributes to state policy. For others, the Hobbesian view may dovetail with noncontractual theories of royal absolutism.

From both perspectives, government might become or be seen as "statecraft," analogous to the mechanic crafts and trades in possessing and preserving its own proper "mysteries." All lesser arts—including the art of poetry—are subservient to the great ends of the art of the state. "'Tis a fine Age, when Mercinary Poets shall become Politicians, and their Plays business of State."[34] Describing the environs of the Drury Lane Theater in Covent Garden, Samuel Garth wrote:

> The Politicians of *Parnasssus* prate,
> And Poets canvass the Affairs of State.

Describing common discourse in the coffeehouses, bastions of the public sphere, Nahum Tate wrote:

> Look, look, the sovereign people here dispense
> The laws of empire to an absolute prince.[35]

Another poet situated the coffeehouse absorption with public, state affairs within the more general tendency in modern times for commoners to ignore their own trade mysteries in favor of those of their betters:

> In former days, when men had sense,
> And reason rul'd both peer and prince;
> When honesty no crime was thought,
> And churchmen no sedition taught;
> When soldiers for their pay would fight,
> Without disputing wrong or right;
> When each mechanic kept his trade,
> Ere tailor's yards were scepters made;
> Before each coffee club durst prate,
> Or pry into affairs of State.[36]

By this account, the public interest in properly public state affairs is something like an occupational deformation, an engrossment of the political "profession" by amateurs. But the dynamic apposition of "poems" and "affairs of state" slid easily into and out of a variously weighted opposition. These lines might also be taken to suggest that when "amateurs"—that is, citizens—become politicians, it's in response to the fact that politics has already become (in Fielding's phrase[37]) "pollitrics": not politics in the traditional sense of the term, rightly left to "peer and prince" and what goes without saying, but its modern deformation, state politics. Poets must criticize state affairs when state affairs impinge too closely on the inherently poetic province of artifice. At such moments,

> the Arts of Priest-Craft and the Tricks of State
> Did for the angry Muse large Themes create.[38]

This is the perspective from which "there is nowhere a greater spirit of liberty to be found than in those who are poets." At its most aggressive, the art of state poetry aims to disclose, with superior artifice, the art of the state—and thereby to lay bare the anterior authority of civil society:

> Here, Painter, rest a little, and survey
> With what small arts the public game they play.
> For so too Rubens, with affairs of state,
> His labouring pencil oft would recreate.
> The close *Cabal* marked how the Navy eats,
> And thought all lost that goes not to the cheats,
> So therefore secretly for peace decrees,
> Yet as for war the Parliament should squeeze.[39]

Jonathan Swift praises his mentor the diplomat Sir William Temple for his ability to unmask the illusions that lie hidden by political theater:

> The wily Shafts of State, those Juggler's Tricks
> Which we call deep Design and Politicks
> ....
> Methinks, when you expose the Scene,
> Down the ill'organ'd Engines fall;
> Off fly the Vizards and discover all,
> How plain I see thro' the Deceit!⁴⁰

The traditional poetic genre to which state poetry was most often assigned is satire. Despairing of "the Defectiveness of our Laws," Swift suggested that "it was to supply such Defects as these, that Satyr was first introduced into the World; whereby those whom neither Religion, nor natural Virtue, nor fear of Punishment, were able to keep within the Bounds of their Duty, might be withheld by the Shame of having their Crimes exposed to open View in the strongest of Colours, and themselves rendered odious to Mankind."⁴¹ This view of satire would seem explicitly to synthesize the oppositional and the appositional relations of state poetry and the state: state poetry criticizes the state by supplementing, even replacing, the work of the public polity by the analogous and virtual work of the public sphere. Others also proposed this notion; but it was complicated by the recognition that in performing this function, satire, including state poetry, broke the laws against libel and thereby flaunted the laws whose defects it might be said to remedy. This double capacity of state poetry had a profound bearing on the debate that engaged some of the most brilliant poets of the period—not only Swift but Dryden, Pope, Steele, Addison, Defoe, Butler, Shadwell, Congreve, and Fielding—the debate over the difference between satire and libel. Libel by definition defamed actual persons, whether private citizens or government officials. The secrecy and artifice state poetry had in common with the state were essential weapons in its libel of state officials and in its avoidance of prosecution.

A final example of state poetry shows, with brilliant concision and wit, how poetry can wield those weapons with a virtuosity that far surpasses that of the state. Some background is needed. When James II was deposed in 1688 he was replaced by the Dutchman William of Orange, fifty-eighth in the line of succession to the throne of England but a secure Protestant. He ascended to the throne in 1689 with his wife Mary, daughter of James and his lineal heir. Theirs was a dual or joint monarchy. Mary's place in the royal succession gave it the legitimacy of inheritance; William's greater authority demonstrated that English law subordinated the patrilineal rule of status to the patriarchal rule of gender. A number of the royal couple's compatriots accompanied them to England, among them Hans Willem Bentinck, Earl of Portland, William's devoted companion whose homosocial relations with his master were rumored to deviate with regularity into the homoerotic. During the first year of their reign, William and Mary spent more of their time with the royal household at Hampton Court, the suburban royal palace, than at the Whitehall palace, a rustication that encouraged Fleetwood Sheppard to conjure up a vision of the married couple in the privacy of domestic retirement:

> A Description of a Hampton Court Life
> Man and wife are all one
>   In flesh and in bone,
> From hence you may guess what they mean:
>   The Queen drinks chocolate
>   To make the King fat,
> The King hunts to make the Queen lean.
>   Mr. Dean says grace
>   With a reverend face,
> "Make room!" cries Sir Thomas Duppa,
>   Then Benting uplocks
>   His King in a box,
> And you see him no more till supper.[42]

The poem confronts the familiar mystery of the king's two bodies with the unfamiliar mystery of a monarchy made dual by marriage. How does the corporate nature of the public institution of kingship—which binds together the private, or "natural," embodiment of the monarchy of the moment with its public "political" perpetuity—incorporate the corporate nature of the private institution of marriage, which binds together two natural bodies in spiritual perpetuity? The problem is made yet more difficult (or perhaps constituted in its difficulty) by the fact that William's greater authority derives from his private role as husband, whereas Mary's lesser authority derives from her public role as heir to the throne. This is to frame the problem in the arcane and technical terms of constitutional principle. Sheppard's poem frames it in the form of a nursery rhyme, with domesticity as the key to sovereignty.

Sheppard transports us to the intimate sphere of the royal domestic arrangement at Hampton Court to follow the common round of daily life among the royals, where the public terms of state rule are eerily domesticated in the private terms of the conjugal household. Here the corporate nature of kingship persists not in the reciprocity of king and Parliament, prince and people, or even in that of the public and the private "body," but in the symbiosis of a husband and wife who, pursuing their own quotidian, gendered desires in the normal course of things, seem to exert a magical influence on each other's bodies. Sheppard evokes this strictly physical symbiosis by alluding both to the biblical account[43] of our first parents' marriage and to the nursery rhyme of Jack Sprat and his wife.[44] The sharing of sovereignty "betwixt the two of them" is then expressed by the oneness of a royal flesh that somehow manages to "lick the platter clean."

But this sort of secret sharing inevitably bears the possibility that in a pinch the one can do without, or take the place of, the other. Here the household servants play an important part. As the diurnal routine unfolds, Henry Compton, dean of the Royal Chapel, says grace, and when lunch is over, the king's intimate

"Benting" (i.e., Bentinck), Groom of the Stool and First Gentleman of the Bedchamber, "locks up" William until suppertime.[45] The uplocked "box" suggests a confinement within the domestic interior—bedchamber, cabinet, closet, closestool, nursery—and the image of the king in a box, like an element of dreamwork, has the supersaturated obscurity of overdetermination. William is put to bed, infantilized, but also put to bed, effeminated, by the concupiscent Bentinck. Like the poetic macro-form of the nursery rhyme, the micro-trope of the king in a box does the work of domestication and privatization, condensing the somatic symbiosis of the married couple to the ultimate point of sodomitical substitution, "man" taking pleasure in his own flesh and bone to the exclusion of wife.

But the displacement of government onto the household leaves a telltale trace, for Sir Thomas Duppa—the third of William's subordinates Sheppard names—isn't a servant of the royal household at all but an officer of government. Duppa is Usher of the Black Rod at Whitehall, the doorkeeper or sergeant at arms whose ceremonial duties include escorting the king to Parliament and summoning the Commons to the House of Lords. Duppa, ordering "make room" for William's uplocking in the private confines of the "house" of Hampton Court, parabolically makes room in those public "houses" of Parliament for the time-honored constitution of English sovereignty in the joining of king and Parliament. And with this association, the domestic substitution of one for two coalesces at a higher level. For centuries "the King in Parliament" had served as shorthand for the correlative and indivisible authority of monarchy and Parliament. Over the course of the seventeenth century, however, the phrase had come to acknowledge the unequal division of authority by making explicit that the king exercised his greatest power only when in Parliament.[46] (In a parallel fashion, Charles I's beheading both confirmed and demystified the doctrine of the king's two bodies by showing that the natural body could be divided from the political with no constitutional consequences.) The constitutional crisis realized in 1688 is mysteriously domesticated as a postprandial privation, a royal withdrawal from royal presence; as William makes do without Mary, so Parliament makes do without William.[47] And the muted echo of "jack-in-the-box" associates domestication with infantilization and autoeroticism, the king reduced to a knave mechanically popping up, and off, on schedule.

To summarize: in the period from 1650 to 1700, political poetry emerged in the self-conscious mode of state poetry as royal rule did in the self-conscious mode of the state or nation-state. In this process the two had a close, even symbiotic, reciprocity. State poetry learned and applied the techniques of monarchal mystification, making explicit the tacit secrecy of what goes without saying and the cynical debasement of poetry's own artistry. The oppositional relationship between politics and political poetry therefore consisted in the appositional parody of each by the other. And the reflexive self-consciousness of state poetry entailed, as a declarative element of its content, the formal display of the state's failure to conceal the impotence or outrage of its policies. Three centuries later, the relationship is very different. And this is where my former understanding of the modern division between politics and poetry now seems to me not only half right but also half wrong. I now think it's misleading to see political poetry as having "always existed." It's only at the end of the seventeenth century, when political poetry is temporarily christened state poetry, that political poetry comes into being as a genre, just as it's only in this period that the metaphysical substratum and spectacle of traditional regimes that had been inseparable parts of royalty come to be seen as epiphenomenal, and politics becomes the stripped-down pursuit of power and interest that it is in the modern world. Secrecy and artifice, potent concealed weapons in the arsenal of traditional politics, are now disclosed as its constitutive elements. By the same token, the reflexive self-consciousness of modern political poetry expresses a fundamental problem of representation, a contradiction analogous to that between discourse and action, order and disorder, love and hatred, image and reality.

A Model: Religious Poetry and "Religious Poetry"

How did this come to be? Changes in the customary character of religious belief, and religious poetry, may shed some light on this question. Marvell's "The Coronet" (writ. c. 1645, pub. 1681) provides a complex analogue to the modern political poetry we've read thus far:

> When for the Thorns with which I long, too long,
> With many a piercing wound,
> My Saviours head have crown'd,
> I seek with Garlands to redress that Wrong:
> Through every Garden, every Mead,   5
> I gather flow'rs (my fruits are only flow'rs)
> Dismantling all the fragrant Towers
> That once adorn'd my Shepherdesses head.
> And now when I have summ'd up all my store,
> Thinking (so I my self deceive)   10
> So rich a Chaplet thence to weave
> As never yet the king of Glory wore:
> Alas I find the Serpent old
> That, twining in his speckled breast,
> About the flow'rs disguis'd does fold,   15
> With wreaths of Fame and Interest.
> Ah, foolish Man, that would'st debase with them,
> And mortal Glory, Heavens Diadem!
> But thou who only could'st the Serpent tame,
> Either his slipp'ry knots at once untie,   20
> And disintangle all his winding Snare:
> Or shatter too with him my curious frame:
> And let these wither, so that he may die,
> Though set with Skill and chosen out with Care.

> That they, while Thou on both their Spoils dost tread, 25
> May crown thy Feet, that could not crown thy Head.[48]

On the evidence of Marvell's poem, modern political poetry has much in common with early modern religious poetry. In both, a reflexive critique of poetic language, launched from its own domain, inevitably re-enacts what it would eschew. "The Coronet" is a palinode, a formal retraction of the attempt to replace *amor* by *caritas*, profane love poetry by devotional garlands, which recognizes in this replacement an aggravation of the original sin. The temporal change that defines the moment of recognition ("now," 9) isn't an external event, like the rupture of war (Neruda) or the protracted experience of growing up (Clifton), but an instantaneous spiritual illumination—contrition, conversion, the onset of grace—that divides time, consciousness, and poetic practice into a before and an after. An internal change in consciousness is of course also a feature of political poetry; and so the difference between the two may rest in the fact that political poetry tends to present itself as occasioned by an objective correlative to subjective change while religious poetry does not. But the difference isn't absolute: Rich's poem challenges the restriction of "politics" to any simple objectivity, and the murky intensity of subjective focus in Baraka's "Political Poem" is close to that of "The Coronet," of which it might also be said that to confront the problem through articulation is to give it being. Moreover, there's some truth to the notion that Marvell's speaker, too, responds to an epochal event, the Fall. But the modern contradiction of political poetry conceives the inner as a response to an external condition as poetry is a response to politics, whereas in early modern religious poetry the contradiction is inseparably internal and external because it derives from the fallen nature of humanity. The contradiction that confronts the Christian poet is that between matter and spirit and therefore absolute, as that between action and discourse or hatred and love is not. Yet the possibility of its suspension posed by the doctrine of accommodation intimates a potential for mediation, modeled on the Passion, between the profane and the sacred, but also the iniquity of that desire.[49]

Even before Marvell's apostrophic prayer begins (19), "The Coronet," like "Black Art," evinces the conviction that poetry is a speech act with consequences. But Baraka's approach is performative, by turns aggressive and playful, whereas Marvell's is sober and filled, however futilely, with a sadly self-abnegating humility. And there's another obvious difference. As the speaker tries to chasten himself, Marvell is able to represent the difficulty of this process through the subtle maneuvers of a rich formal register that's customarily renounced by the blank and "free" verse of modernism and modernity. True, he shares with Neruda, Herbert, and others the poetic metaphor of the flower as a self-consciously symbolic figuration of the problem. But in these poets, the figure stands for the unflinching admission of its own vacuity, whereas for Marvell it stands for sin. The inevitability of flowers, of a figuration that signifies fame and interest, is deftly woven throughout this "curious frame" (22), as dense in its contrite conclusion as at its beginning. But Marvell also exploits rhythm and rhyme to construct the sense of a formal frame whose power is to associate by turns both order and disorder, regularity and irregularity, norm and deviation, with the decorative and evasive excess that the poem exists to retract.[50]

The order of the opening four quatrains is defined by the regularity of an alternating rhyme scheme and alternating pentameters and tetrameters. Signs of disorder appear midway through the poem, with the inverted rhyme at lines 11 and 12 and with the dropped feet at lines 13 and 16, the very point at which the devotional coronet is seen to provide protective coloration for the serpentine wreath. As the speaker now turns to address first us and then God, the curious problem of accommodation is formally enacted. The alternating line lengths give way to implacable pentameters while rhyme becomes entangled (or is it only now "disentangled"?) with the "slipp'ry knots" of deviation. This ambiguity—is the speaker's final gesture a solution or a sophistication of the problem?—is sustained by the obscurity in syntax and pronominal reference of the last four lines. With a disarming modesty that would disguise its own vanity, the speaker inadvertently turns the tables on God by offering him a choice between "disentangling" and "shattering," between rescuing and sacrificing, his curious frame.

In the Christian tradition, Marvell calls on Jesus Christ to mediate the contradiction that his duplicitous—and paradigmatically poetic—language is unable to achieve. Does the problem of contradiction in early modern religious poetry dovetail with that voiced by modern political poetry? What's become, by the end of the eighteenth century, of the religious grounds for the critique of poetry? The question solicits broad—but I think broadly valid—generalization.

The secularization of poetry in the modern era is accomplished through a contradictory process of negative and positive movements. On the one hand, modern poetry shares the demystifying detachment from religious dogma evident throughout modern culture. On the other, the special dispensation of modern poetry is to internalize and preserve, as human spirit, the divine Spirit of a theistic morality whose metaphysical reality no longer goes without saying. Political motive was traditionally framed in religious concepts. The seventeenth-century demystification of absolutist politics detached it from religion as it did from political poetry. William Blake's rhetorical question—"And are not Religion and Politics the same thing?"—depends for its insight on the fact that by the end of the eighteenth century, politics had been sufficiently separated out from religion for each category to be conflated, in its newfound autonomy, as a surprising version of the other.[51] If modern poetry internalizes the "spiritual" aspect of a religious discourse no longer authorized to oversee and adjudicate discourse as such, modern politics might be said to take on the more external and disciplinary authority that religious dogma formerly had exercised over traditional poetry (and politics). And modern poetry, itself increasingly transformed by its idealization as a secularized mode of spirituality, is therefore also newly vulnerable to political—that is, to material and empirical—critique. And to write "political poetry" is henceforth a contradiction in terms.

For the implication of the idea that early modern English people expressed politics through the language of religion is that for such people "politics" didn't possess its modern categorial integrity and identity. Of course, poetry (like religion) might have for them a "political" significance in our sense of the term, and contemporaries were willing to differentiate poetry and politics in terms we'd find recognizable. But poetry wasn't conceived as political, because politics and poetry hadn't yet been disentangled enough to permit the opposition and the apposition that presuppose not simply differentiation but full separation and conflation. Similarly, although premodern poetry was implicitly and presumptively moral, it could become "didactic"—and susceptible to critique on those grounds—only in the modern age because it's only then that poetry acquires the normatively private and self-referential character on which depends, as its dialectical antithesis, the idea of a "didactic" deviation from the norm. In traditional culture, only the immensely inclusive discourse of religion, perhaps, has the authority to impose upon experience an explicit distinction—between spirit and matter, good and evil, grace and sin, salvation and damnation—absolute enough to entail full separability. The separation of poetry from politics, and the contradictory status of political poetry that is its consequence, is a modern phenomenon whose emergence depends on the waning of (at least the tacitly overarching cultural authority of) religious absolutism. As a by-product of modern secularization, poetry "preserves" and "stores" religion's spiritual properties while politics preserves and stores religion's judicial function. And in this process, of course, both "poetry" and "politics" become something other than they'd been before.[52]

But when we take this long view of modernity as an accomplished outcome, we pass too quickly over the transformation that poetry underwent in eighteenth-century Britain through the aesthetic reconception of art as a distinct mode of knowledge. Had it prevailed, this reconception might have sustained not only the opposition but also the apposition of politics and poetry. Other chapters in this volume make the case that in their British development, the ideas of the aesthetic and realism maintained and sophisticated their grounding in empirical epistemology to a degree that balanced the imaginative representation and reflection of the virtual by the reflection of the actual that was represented by the sensible image.[53] I say British, because this development wasn't shared by the French theory of the aesthetic. In British thought, poetry, like the other arts, was conceived to be a dialectical way of knowing that mediated between the politico-empirical and the conceptual-ideational, partaking of both and reducible to neither, and therefore not susceptible to the demystifying strictures of empirical epistemology and political skepticism because it was devoid of the metaphysical claims of religious spirituality. In his indispensable epitome of poetic secularization, Coleridge writes that the aesthetic involves "that willing suspension of disbelief for the moment, which constitutes poetic faith."[54] The post-Enlightenment career of the aesthetic, and therefore of political poetry, turned in a different direction.

6   Paradise Lost *as Parody*

PERIOD, GENRE, AND CONJECTURAL
INTERPRETATION

One of the more striking oddities of literary historical periodization is our tendency to see John Milton's *Paradise Lost* as the culminating production of the English Renaissance. Framed in this fashion, Milton's epic poem is read with and against epic poems of the previous century: primarily Ariosto's *Orlando Furioso* (1516), Tasso's *Gerusalemme Liberata* (1581), and Spenser's *The Faerie Queene* (1590, 1596). This may seem the best way to appreciate the generic nature of *Paradise Lost*. But by disembedding Milton's poem from the immediate age in which it was written we actually lose touch with its form. The reason for this is that when we situate these texts in the broad generic category "epic poem," we attribute to them a formal identity whose integral coherence is misleading. The closer we get to them, the more we see that each text takes a complicating perspective on the idea of the epic poem, evoking the genre by parodying it.

Parody

By "parody" I don't mean ridicule (although this can be a major parodic effect). I mean a mode of representation that combines in variable ratios the imitation of an authoritative form, on the one hand, and an adaptive detachment from it, on the other. Parody preserves form in the very process of detaching from or superseding it, and it is therefore not only a rhetorical figure but also a model of historical change.

In fact, when we approach *Paradise Lost* with this understanding, we find that its distinctive mode of formal parody is best illuminated by comparing it not to Renaissance epics but to other works of the early Enlightenment. This is because these contemporary works also share with Milton's poem a parodic approach to literary form, but to a more explicit and insistent degree than had been common. And this gives them, and *Paradise Lost*, a family resemblance peculiar to late seventeenth-century culture and the transformation it was undergoing. Milton's ambition to write a Christian epic only enhances the resemblance. In this chapter I aim to read *Paradise Lost* (1667, 1674) alongside several long narratives, published between 1663 and 1687, by Samuel Butler, John Bunyan, John Dryden, and Aphra Behn. None of these narratives are even broadly categorized as epics. Rather, like *Paradise Lost*, they show the influence of several experimental, mixed forms that flourished during the Restoration period—some of traditional standing, some emergent, and some momentary and occasional. My concern will be not to show

Milton's influence on these other authors (although some well-known evidence of influence will arise) but to show their common formal enterprise. In other words, I hope to show Milton working among his contemporaries.

Mock Epic

Milton's best-known contribution to the ascendancy of mock epic in the period that immediately followed his own is the parodic figure of Satan as monarch, and the other devils as his heroic epigones. Book 2 of *Paradise Lost*, in which the fallen angels debate whether to foment another battle in order to regain heaven, opens with a tableau of Satan sitting in royal eminence:

> High on a Throne of Royal State, which far
> Outshone the wealth of *Ormus* and of *Ind*,
> Or where the gorgeous East with richest hand
> Show'rs on her Kings *Barbaric* Pearl and Gold,
> Satan exalted sat, by merit rais'd
> To that bad eminence.[1]

Milton's speaker warns us that Satan's eminence over other kings is "bad," hence that this tableau is not epic but mock epic. And in the following book Milton provides an alternative tableau of good eminence:

> Now had th' Almighty Father from above,
> From the pure Empyrean where he sits
> High Thron'd above all highth, bent down his eye,
> His own works and their works at once to view . . .
>
> —3.56–59

Satan's exaltation above all kings is materially measurable; God's exaltation is above all such accountability, an absolute contrast that bespeaks the absolute badness of monarchy as such. Human eminence, authentically embodied in "merit," nonetheless bears no relation to divine. We may be reminded of Milton's famous suggestion that fallen humanity comes to know good through evil: "It was from out the rinde of one apple tasted, that the knowledge of good and evil as two twins cleaving together leapt forth into the World. And perhaps this is that doom which *Adam* fell into of knowing good and evil, that is to say of knowing good by evil."[2] Milton's mock epic exemplifies how we come to know good parodically, by evil. Moreover, the dialectical nature of this method stands in formal contrast to the bad linearity exemplified by the practice of royal descent. Sir Robert Filmer's *Patriarcha* (written at the outbreak of the Civil War and printed during the Exclusion Crisis) most famously claimed that a line of legitimacy extended from God the Father to the first human father, Adam, and thenceforward authorized the succession of all future fathers and kings. Writing in refutation of Charles I's posthumous martyrology, Milton thought it mistaken to "nullifie and tread to dun the rest of mankind, by exalting one person and his

Linage without other merit lookt after, but the meer contingence of a begetting, into an absolute and unaccountable dominion over them and their posterity."³

Milton's mock epic exerted a powerful influence on his Enlightenment successors. To go no further than the most celebrated of these, ten years after *Paradise Lost* was published, John Dryden transferred Milton's trope of "bad eminence" to the sphere of literature. *Mac Flecknoe* celebrates the succession and coronation of Thomas Shadwell as the new prince and prophet of dullness: "The hoary Prince in Majesty appear'd, / High on a Throne of his own Labours rear'd."⁴ Alexander Pope extended the legacy first through Lewis Theobald in the 1729 *Dunciad Variorum* and then through Colley Cibber in the 1742 four-book *Dunciad*, in which Cibber succeeds to the throne of Theobald, Shadwell, Flecknoe, and Satan: "High on a gorgeous seat, that far out-shone / Henley's gilt Tub, or Fleckno's Irish Throne, / Or that where on her Curls the Public pours, I All bounteous fragrant Grains and Golden show'rs, / Great Cibber sate . . ."⁵ Milton is not here an object of mock-epic parody but a mock-epic master whose form and style on sacred subject matter are translated by his successors to the analogous matter of what Enlightenment culture would learn to call "literature."

By the time *Paradise Lost* was published, literary forms that can be described as political allegory—using historical and romance narratives to reflect on current political developments—had become common in English print. Together they manifest a rich variety of formal techniques of political allusion and degrees of indirection and discontinuity that, however much these owed to prudential motives, also normalized the practice of evoking English affairs by other means.⁶ Christopher Hill and others have made a strong case that the sacred matter of Milton's epic is subtly informed by allusions to contemporary politics, and in this as well *Mac Flecknoe* followed the example of *Paradise Lost*.⁷ Although printed in 1682, *Mac Flecknoe* was composed in 1676, as momentum for the outbreak of the Popish Plot was building, and a plausible case can also be made that Dryden's poem about literary history, like Milton's about sacred history, has a political subtext.⁸

Of course it wasn't only by imitating Milton that the great Enlightenment parodists brought mock epic to its highest English development. Pope in particular experimented with the idea that the parodic method of mock epic distinguished it as an authentic "comic" mode in its own right. Homer's lost *Margites* was not only "the first Epic poem" but also "the first Dunciad," and these two poems exemplify the "little Epic" and excel in "Parody, one of the liveliest graces of the little Epic."⁹ Henry Fielding became the most accomplished practitioner of mock epic, first on the stage and then, after the Licensing Act, in the novel. The sequence from Samuel Richardson's *Pamela* (1740) to Fielding's *Shamela* (1741) to Fielding's *Joseph Andrews* (1742), although not exemplary of mock epic, was the parodic paradigm of preservation and supersession that gave the new genre its foundation. Moreover, within *Joseph Andrews*, mock-epic method is central to Fielding's subtly mixed characterization of Parson Adams and to his narrator's innovatively distantiating realism (Cervantes, he insists, is his master). But Fielding comes closest to Milton's mock-epic practice in *Jonathan Wild* (1743), in which the parodic relationship between high and low, prime minister Robert Walpole and notorious criminal Jonathan Wild, achieves some of the same formal effects as that between God and the angels and the fallen angel Satan. Of course they differ greatly as well: in Fielding's novel the reference to contemporary politics is quite explicit, and the gap in status between Walpole and Wild crucially emphasizes the fact that in moral terms there's no gap at all.[10]

But for all its influence, the local satire of Satan is only a minor feature of Milton's mock-epic project in *Paradise Lost*. The entire poem is mock epic, because it derives from the poet's ambition to write an imitation of classical epic that can provide a parodic basis for a Christian epic that will far surpass the classical. Milton's ambivalence about classical epic as a model for the Christian poet is of course a thread that runs throughout *Paradise Lost*, interweaving sumptuous admiration with the reminder of its inferiority to its sacred counterpart. The fall of Mulciber, the seafaring Jason and Ulysses, that fair field of Enna: these are perhaps the best-known passages in which stylistic and substantive imitation of the classical is pointed by explicit notice of its limitations, the magnificent preservation by the principled supersession of the ancient form (1.738–747, 2.1016–1022, 4.268–272). They culminate toward the beginning of book 9, as the narrator modulates his tone to tragic in anticipation of the fall. His is a

> sad task, yet argument
> Not less but more Heroic than the wrath
> Of stern *Achilles* on his Foe pursu'd
> Thrice Fugitive about *Troy* Wall; or rage
> Of *Turnus* for *Lavinia* disespous'd,
> Or *Neptune's* ire or *Juno's*, that so long
> Perplex'd the *Greek* and *Cytherea's* Son.
>   —9.3–9

Christian Typology

Typology would seem to be eminently serviceable in reinforcing the parodic status of *Paradise Lost* as a Christian epic. It is itself a method of reading history parodically: the types of the Old Testament are both sustained and annulled, preserved and superseded by the antitypes of the New. In the "Nativity Ode," Milton already had parodied the parodic structure of typology by depicting the anticipatory types of pre-Christian beliefs as those of pagan natural religion rather than of the Jewish Law.[11] And by doing this he adumbrates an understanding of typology as cousin to mock epic and prepares the ground for his later conception of *Paradise Lost* as the Christian fulfillment of classical epic. But Milton makes no use of such a framework in *Paradise Lost*, limiting typology's explanatory force to book 12, when Michael reveals the postlapsarian future as a movement "From shadowy Types to Truth, from Flesh to Spirit" (12.303; see generally 12.300–314). In fact, Milton's Restoration contemporaries were experimenting with typology far more boldly than he was.

Dryden's *Absalom and Achitophel* (1681), only the best known of these experiments, contains mock-epic effects on the local level that are verbally and syntactically allusive to those in *Paradise Lost*, but its unorthodox use of typology as a structural frame would seem to owe nothing to Milton's influence. The "Nativity Ode" substitutes for the types of the Old Testament the pagan figures of natural religion; Dryden's poem more radically substitutes for the antitypes of the New Testament the secular figures of modern history, which therefore occupy a position that is chronologically but not spiritually conclusive. The parodic structure of typology remains, but it is itself parodied by the replacement of the New Testament, the orthodox apotheosis of sacred history, by contemporary English politics. What remains of sacred history—the Old Testament—becomes a past narrative like classical history, one that enables the disclosure not of a spiritual fulfillment but of a secular parallel with present events that facilitates their interpretation.[12] I've suggested that typology itself has a parodic double structure, analogous to that of mock epic. To recognize Dryden's unorthodoxy we therefore need to see his use of it as mock typology, because in *Absalom and Achitophel* typological fulfillment becomes a rhetorical technique of partisan reading (or, to acknowledge a Jewish perspective, a politically rather than a religiously partisan reading). Moreover, Dryden ingeniously obliges his readers to take responsibility for that reading.

Paradise Lost and *Absalom and Achitophel*, both Old Testament narratives, are also political allegories, but they exemplify that mode in different ways. In Milton's poem the evocation of contemporary politics is discontinuous and subtly allusive. Dryden, we might say, divides Milton's evocation into two distinct parts.[13] On the one hand, the preface to the poem makes clear that the political crisis the English reader of 1681 experiences is broadly implicated in the poem's reference. On the other, *Absalom and Achitophel* itself narrates a story composed of Old Testament material that is devoid of contemporary reference, and its allegorical meanings therefore depend on the reader's will to discover them there. In other words, Dryden's investment in the epistemology of typological signification has a studied ambivalence, and the speaker's self-consciously judicious impartiality in reporting Old Testament history sometimes appears to distract him from a more judicious skepticism about the typological relationship itself. At one point, for example, his careful adjudication of a report that something resembling the Popish Plot was intended by the Jebusites (i.e., the Catholics) ignores the far more patent absurdity of its anachronism:

Some thought they God's Anointed meant to Slay
By Guns, invented since full many a day:
Our Author swears it not; but who can know,
How far the Devil and *Jebusites* may go?[14]

As Dryden's first readers likely knew, this amusing mock-epic effect imitates Milton's war in heaven, in which Satan (to quote the "The Argument" of book 6) "invents devilish Engines" that "put *Michael* and his Angels to some disorder." In other words, Dryden's intentional anachronism parodies not only typological authority but also Milton's mock-epic parody, in which contemporaries may have discerned an allusion to the late Civil War. The difference is that Milton's allusion does no more than give modern warfare a plausibly satanic pedigree, whereas Dryden's anachronism sacrifices an affirmation of typological fulfillment to the cause of polemical refutation.[15]

Christian Accommodation

This brief comparison of formal technique in Milton and Dryden throws into relief the older poet's relative circumspection with respect to ancient and divine authority. Milton's Christian typology supersedes both Jewish prophetic and, like his mock epic, pagan poetic truth by preserving their authority as the basis for that supersession. Dryden by contrast occupies a more fully critical place on the parodic spectrum. But this is surely to overlook Milton's grand ambition to "justify the ways of God to men" by accommodating them to human comprehension, an ambition that Dryden's political purpose doesn't share. Milton's mock epic proceeds from profane knowledge—classical epic—to an adumbration of the sacred. His accommodation of God's ways proceeds in the opposite direction, from an apprehension of divine spirit to a profane and sensible representation of it. The representational gap between earthly and heavenly understanding had been debated from Origen and Augustine onward as a problem of the first order. Broadly speaking, the doctrine of accommodation is a kind of theological safety net that God condescends (a seventeenth-century synonym for accommodation) to cast across the otherwise impassable gulf between humanity and divinity. However, disagreement on its meaning and scope has been widespread. Milton devotes the better part of a chapter of *De doctrina Christiana* to the topic, but scholars, apart from agreeing on its unorthodoxy, are very far from consensus on his position.[16] Milton's best-known statement, apparently to be taken as a model for all human education, is strikingly confident: "The end then of learning is to repair the ruins of our first parents by regaining to know God aright. . . . But because our understanding cannot in this body found itselfe but on sensible things, nor arrive so deerly to the knowledge of God and things invisible, as by orderly conning over the visible and inferior creature, the same method is necessarily to be follow'd in all discreet teaching."[17] Milton was mindful that the powerful language of the ancient epic, unless used with the paradoxical obliquity of mock epic, pointed the path to Christian error. But to parody the divine spirit, boldly rationalizing it as justifying the ways of God to men, is a far more risky enterprise, and one in which the entire narrative of *Paradise Lost* consists.

Andrew Marvell begins the poem that prefaces the 1674 second edition of *Paradise Lost* with his misgivings at Milton's extended exercise in accommodating sacred truth to profane story:

When I beheld the Poet blind, yet bold,
In slender Book his vast Design unfold,

> *Messiah* Crown'd, God's Reconcil'd Decree,
> Rebelling Angels, the Forbidden Tree,
> Heav'n, Hell, Earth, Chaos, All; the Argument
> Held me awhile misdoubting his Intent,
> That he would ruin (for I saw him strong)
> The sacred Truths to Fable and old Song
> . . . .
> I lik'd his Project, the success did fear;
> . . . .
> Lest he perplex'd the things he would explain,
> And what was easy he should render vain.

Marvell's doubts don't persist to the end of the poem:

> And things divine thou treat'st of in such state
> As them preserves, and thee, inviolate.[18]

However, they're broadly shared during the Restoration about a variety of accommodating narratives. Four years later, in "The Author's *Apology* for His Book," which prefaces part 1 of *The Pilgrim's Progress* (1678), John Bunyan stoutly agrees that

> *solidity, indeed becomes the Pen*
> *Of him that writeth things Divine to men:*
> *But must I needs want solidness, because*
> *By Metaphors I speak; was not Gods Laws,*
> *His Gospel-laws in older time held forth*
> *By Types, Shadows and Metaphors?*[19]

In the "Conclusion" to part 1, Bunyan is more frank about the liabilities of figurative narration.

> *Now Reader, I have told my Dream to thee;*
> *See if thou canst Interpret it to me;*
> . . . .
> *Take heed also, that thou be not extream,*
> *In playing with the out-side of my Dream:*
> *Nor let my figure, or similitude,*
> *Put thee into a laughter or a feud;*
> *Leave this for* Boys *and* Fools; *but as for thee,*
> *Do thou the substance of my matter see.*
>   —155, ll. 1–2, 7–12

In a later era, to experience the failure of "sensible things" (in Milton's phrase) to accommodate divine spirit was to find oneself in the grip of a novel—at least for Coleridge, who remarked on the experience of reading *The Pilgrim's Progress* that "with the same illusion as we read any tale known to be fictitious, as a novel, we go on with his characters as real persons, who had been nicknamed by their neighbours."[20] If so, Bunyan's allegorical aims dovetailed with the efforts of early novelists to enhance their empirical credibility by grounding their plots in sensible things, and even to claim their actual historicity (I'll return to this). Others, like Bunyan aware that scripture itself uses figures that require interpretation, nonetheless chastised those whose concrete embodiment of the spirit seemed to them to invite interpretive license. The problem was that a method's promise at accommodating spiritual truth is directly proportional to the likelihood that it will subvert that truth by rendering it material.

Domestication

The Christian Incarnation and Passion, in which the Creator's Son assumes the status and suffering of a common creature, can be taken both as a sacred mystery and as an accommodation of God's merciful promise to fallen humanity, a figurative justification of the ways of God to men. The term "domestication," a seventeenth-century synonym for hermeneutic accommodation, fruitfully concretizes the warrant of divine accommodation as, in Milton's words, "the method to be followed in all discreet teaching." Metaphorically speaking, "to domesticate" is "to naturalize" or "to familiarize" the great, the noble, the public, the distant, the worldly, the strange, or the foreign by "bringing it home"—through the medium of the little, the common, the private, the proximate, the local, the familiar, or the native. Between 1600 and 1800, the traditional hermeneutic serviceability of the latter, lower rungs of this metaphorical ladder in signifying the former, higher rungs underwent a fundamental transformation occasioned by a positive revaluation of the low in all spheres of experience.

These lower realms, traditionally seen as devoid of intrinsic value and therefore of no more use than as a means to the end of figuring forth what lay above and beyond them, came to be invested, across an entire range of social, political, economic, intellectual, and emotional experience, with value in their own right. The higher realms ceased to be the exclusive province of value, and the signifying ladder of domestication lost its purpose. What remains when domestication is no longer needed might, sticking with the metaphor, be called the domestic. But it's crucial to understand that this term would refer to the entire range of experience that, newly value laden in the modern world, is no longer a means to a greater end but an end in itself. This must be said because what we mean by the experience of domesticity, although only one among several that now are taken to be ends in themselves, has a compelling relevance that otherwise might usurp the entire range of this phenomenon. With this caveat we may acknowledge that in the parodic process of historical change that I've been trying to trace, language happily conspires to represent the dialectic of preservation and supersession as one of domestication and domesticity. That is, the hierarchical relationship between the high and the low that's implicit in the process of domestication is both preserved and superseded in the institution of domesticity that's being increasingly valorized toward the end of the Enlightenment.[21]

This historical process was fed by many overlapping sources. Before it became an explicit and openly debated theory, patriarchalist belief tacitly posited the metaphorical analogy and the metonymic determinacy between divine, paternal, and royal sovereignty, a belief that found special traction in a state like England, where royal sovereignty was indexed by dynastic or familial inheritance. Over the course of the seventeenth century, attitudes toward patriarchalism underwent complex development that was superintended by the recognition that epistemological formulations can have ontological implications. Milton's rejection of the patriarchalist assumption is clear in his republicanism. In 1651 he wrote that "by calling kings fathers of their country, you think this metaphor has forced me to apply right off to kings whatever I might admit of fathers. Fathers and kings are very different things."[22] But if this is so, then paternal sovereignty is neither a domestication of divine sovereignty nor what royal sovereignty domesticates, but a free-standing institution of domesticity.

In the gospel story, Christian spirituality is articulated through a domestication to the lowly level of domesticity, the holy family. Moreover, Jesus is a child of lowest descent. He is born in a place almost theriomorphic in its humility, his disciples are drawn from the common people, and his end is that of a degraded beast or criminal. The gospel's domestication is itself related to the development of the *sermo humilis*, the new Christian style that was answerable to its lowly yet elevated substance.[23] Nonetheless, the peculiar nature and development of English Protestant teaching—especially its will toward internalization and privatization—made the intercourse between a formal domestication and a domestic content more insistent, in Protestant hermeneutics, than it had been before the Reformation. The Protestant theology of grace individualized salvation as a matter of private conviction, whether or not in alliance with the privacy of economic individualism and interest. And the long-term legacy of English Reformation history entailed the devolution of absolute authority from pope to monarch to spiritualized household and individual conscience. Given that trajectory, it's not surprising that Protestants tended to put a special premium on the humblest—the "meanest," "basest," "homeliest"—signifiers of grace.[24]

As we've seen, Bunyan was mindful that Christian accommodation entails a delicate balance. Part 1 of *The Pilgrim's Progress* so adequately domesticates its allegorical meaning as to risk becoming, itself, the self-sufficient signified. Bunyan's salvation story is figured as a narrative of physical and social mobility—not only the flight of a solitary common man from home, family, neighbors, and impoverished humility but also his rise from the disparate tyrannies of feudal custom to the centralized bureaucracy of the modern nation-state.[25] Through much of this pilgrimage, Bunyan keeps before us and Christian the poignant memory of the family he has left behind, and he punctuates his pilgrimage with ambivalent episodes of domestic and familial potential that evoke a domestication in the most literal sense of the term. To some degree, the serial ambivalence of these episodes bespeaks the contradictory status of the domesticated family within traditional Christian thought. Familial kinship ties are one of those low, sensible things that both define what the Christian must leave behind and model the Christian's alternative destination.[26]

Six years after the appearance of part 1 of *The Pilgrim's Progress*, Bunyan published a second part, in which domesticity enters the content of the allegory far more thoroughly than it had in the first because it tells the story of how Christian's solitary pilgrimage is recapitulated by that of his wife Christiana and their four sons. The difference is partly in the familial and collective nature of this second pilgrimage. But it's equally that the narration of their adventures is for long stretches so absorbed in details that play no role in signifying anything ontologically beyond themselves that the pilgrimage seems to assume the self-standing autonomy of a fully achieved domesticity.

In one of these episodes, individual salvation is represented as something like a genealogical and family affair. Christiana is advised that because her sons appear to "take after" their father she should marry them off to ensure that their posterity populate the world; and so Christiana arranges a marriage for her eldest that is also a love match, in the process bridging the conflict that will become crucial to early novelistic plotting (to which I'll return) (Bunyan, 242). Although part 1 is scrupulous in maintaining a clear relationship between material signifier and spiritual signified, the publication of the second part retrospectively qualifies Christian's status as a domestication universal in its exemplarity, augmenting instead its already powerful legibility as a story of one man's upward mobility. Complemented by the female and collectivized domesticity of part 2, part 1 vindicates even more Coleridge's experience by reading like an individual male adventure. In other words, the domesticity of part 2 can be felt to parody part 1, bringing closure to the already well advanced process of domestication in which the first part consists, and it thereby both preserves part 1 and supersedes it.

The Pilgrim's Progress, whose first part was published four years after the twelve-book edition of *Paradise Lost*, provides an instructive comparison to it. Both are accommodations or domestications of Christian doctrine that use familiar and common material figures to signify the invisible and immaterial. Both avail themselves of the accommodations that already exist in sacred scripture. Bunyan's Christian allegorizes the emotional psychology of the typical believer, buttressed by scriptural passages, in his struggles to attain salvation. Milton's Adam accommodates the Old Testament figure of the first believer in his struggles to understand and maintain salvation. And for important narrative stretches, both rely on domestications that significantly lead us to scenes of domesticity—that is, that rely on formal techniques that posit domestic contents.

Probably the best known of such domestications in *Paradise Lost* occurs in book 5 when Eve "entertain[s] our Angel guest" Raphael at "Dinner." Because Milton's narrative is not, like Bunyan's, an allegory, its spiritual meaning doesn't depend on a close correlation with material signifiers, and the culinary details of this scene are many and finely realized. Meanwhile, Adam walks abroad to meet their guest and show him to the seats and table to talk a bit, "No fear lest Dinner cool" (5.308–512). So Milton's dinner scene, like much of Bunyan's second pilgrimage, is a domestication of spiritual knowledge to a domestic setting.

Adam the gracious host doubts that the spiritual sustenance of angels can be achieved by "unsavory" human food, but he learns that in this case there's no gap between human and angelic sustenance that needs to be accommodated. For according to Raphael, just as humans are in part spiritual, so angels possess "every lower faculty / Of sense, whereby they . . . / Tasting concoct, digest, assimilate, / And corporeal to incorporeal turn" (5.410–413). In both humans and angels, Raphael continues, nutriments

> by gradual scale sublim'd
> To vital spirits aspire, to animal,
> To intellectual, give both life and sense,
> Fancy and understanding, whence the Soul
> Reason receives.
> —5.483–487

And on the basis of this account the angel speculates that

> time may come when men
> With Angels may participate . . .
> . . . .
> And from these corporal nutriments perhaps
> Your bodies may at last turn all to spirit,
> Improv'd by tract of time.
> —5.493–494, 496–498

What Adam learns is therefore not that there exists an analogy between spiritual knowing and domestic eating that accommodates the first through the second. Because humans are also a compound of matter and spirit, angels, "differing but in degree," model in reverse a process that humans too may aspire to (5.490). That is, the material process of eating is the means by which humans may in tract of time attain the ontological condition of spiritual beings, learning like angels "to transubstantiate" (5.438). The domestic scene in book 5, a remarkably confident domestication of the invisible spirit by sensible things, also substantializes that formal act in Raphael's discourse, which ups the ante by suggesting the yet more remarkable idea that angelic spirit and human sense are continuous and ultimately coextensive. In other words, Milton's consummate ease with his powers of representation has led us subtly and audaciously from the epistemological analogy between sensible and spiritual things that is the work of accommodation to the ontological transubstantiation of sensible into spiritual beings.

Soon Adam will remind us of this interchange by asking Raphael another question about the heavenly existence of angels so as to gain a rough measure of the height to which humans may aspire.[27] "The Argument" to book 5 prefaces this dialogue with the information that "God to render Man inexcusable" has sent

Raphael "to admonish [Adam] of his obedience, of his free estate, of his enemy near at hand; . . . and whatever else may avail *Adam* to know." Now we understand why. Adam has assumed an exhilarating but heavy burden of knowledge, and he is ingenuously oblivious of its purpose. He thanks Raphael for directing

> our knowledge, and the scale of Nature set
> From centre to circumference, whereon
> In contemplation of created things
> By steps we may ascend to God. But say,
> What meant that caution join'd, *if ye be found
> Obedient?*
>
> —5.509–514

And he then seeks more knowledge, now of the war in heaven. In reply to Adam's question, Raphael briefly explains that true obedience depends on free will. He doesn't explain that true freedom depends on knowledge—sufficient knowledge to avail in rendering man inexcusable of disobedience. But how is the sufficiency of knowledge to be assessed when spiritual knowledge is accommodated in material terms?

Henceforth the formal problem of the Christian poet will dovetail with the theological problem of the Fall as joint exercises in accommodation and domestication. How can, and how far should, sensible things convey the realm of the spirit? How can, and how far should, the lowly precincts of earth convey the high realm of heaven? Adam will continue to ask Raphael "to impart / Things above Earthly thought, which yet concern'd / Our knowing, as to highest wisdom seem'd," grateful for "This friendly condescension to relate / Things else by me unsearchable" (7.81–83; 8.9–10). On "Commission from above" Raphael will continue "to answer thy desire / Of knowledge within bounds," hence "if else thou seek'st / Aught, not surpassing human measure, say" (7.118, 119–120; 7.639–640). And as Adam has invoked Raphael, so Milton's narrator famously invokes the heavenly muse, "Up led by thee / Into the Heav'n of Heav'ns I have presum'd, / An Earthly Guest," and asks, condemned to earthly metaphor, thence to be safely guided down "Lest . . . on th' *Aleian* Field I fall / Erroneous" (7.12, 17, 19–20).

Yet neither angel nor narrator seems confident about the bounds and measure of human knowledge. In response to Adam's desire to learn about the war in heaven, Raphael is dubious:

> High matter thou injoin'st me, O prime of men,
> Sad task and hard, for how shall I relate
> To human sense th' invisible exploits
> Of warring Spirits[?]
>
> —5.563–566

But hasn't Raphael just been engaged, on the metaphysics of food, in this very process of domestication, as has the narrator himself by depicting this dinner scene—indeed, by narrating *Paradise Lost?* As if in acknowledgment, the problem immediately evaporates. "Yet for thy good," the angel continues, "this is dispens't, and what surmounts the reach / Of human sense, I shall delineate so, / By lik'ning spiritual to corporal forms / as may express them best" (5.570–574).

Later, at the beginning of book 9, Milton's narrator recurs to the dinner scene, now troubled, as Raphael momentarily had seemed to be, by its accommodation of heaven to earth:

> No more of talk where God or Angel Guest
> With Man, as with his Friend, familiar us'd
> To sit indulgent, and with him partake
> Rural repast, permitting him the while
> Venial discourse unblam'd.
>
> —9.1–5

Permission for that discourse is of course the province of Milton's narrator and the angel. But to call it venial might nonetheless seem to beg the question of who bears responsibility for it: the man whose mortal sin is foreknown but not yet committed, or the narrator whose bold project is to justify the ways of God to men? However we answer this question, Milton, like Bunyan, hereby draws attention to his formal method and its problematic ambivalence, thematizing it on the level of content and throwing its authority into question.

In any case, the Fall brings to an end the signifying process of domestication by which Milton has been working. Not that his sensible representation of the invisible world of the spirit has ended—fallen—with book 9. But by canceling the promise of eternal grace, the Fall has abruptly left Adam and Eve at a terrible endpoint of domesticity defined by its negative state of absolute privation. Only when Michael reveals the future to Adam will this miserable existence be tempered by the anticipation of a positive privacy, "a paradise within thee" distinct from this purely sensible condition (12.587).

Heroic Poetry

The parodic relationship of *Paradise Lost* to the great poetry of the past, plausibly framed in generic terms as "mock epic," also may be read through the lens of "heroic poetry." In his headnote on rhyme, Milton refers to *Paradise Lost* as a "Heroic Poem." Milton and his contemporaries speak of "heroic" more than of "epic" poetry, as contemporary passages and commentary I've already quoted suggest. Heroic poetry was a relatively recent synthesis of epic and romance, and it contains within itself that reflexive element of formal self-consciousness that's more directly stated in "mock epic." The ease with which modernity attributes antithetical contents and forms even to twelfth-century epic and romance was alien to medieval thinking.[28] Even when Renaissance scholars began applying the formal standards of Aristotelian epic to romance and found romance wanting, the result was not a definitive separation but rather the elaboration of the category "heroic poetry" in which the best of epic and romance might stand together.[29] But by the seventeenth century, readers were becoming increasingly preoccupied with a primarily content-based tension between epic and romance unstably schematized as one between public warfare and personal love. After the Restoration this heroic nexus was chronically suspect, its elements self-consciously distinguished although not yet fully separated out. So the experimental work of heroic poetry was to confront the emergent, modern opposition between epic and romance with the more traditional, but increasingly archaic, view of them as unequal versions of each other. I'll discuss two examples of this singular phenomenon to provide a context for conceiving *Paradise Lost* as an experiment in heroic poetry.

The first two parts of Samuel Butler's *Hudibras* appeared in print four and three years, respectively, before the first ten books of *Paradise Lost* were published in print. Butler speaks of *Hudibras* as "Heroical Poetry." Indebted as he is to Spenser and Cervantes, however, he also associates his poem with "romance"; yet he finds in that form, and displays in his poem, the contradictory relation of love and war that has become conventionally characteristic of heroic poetry. Speaking of his own poem, Butler observes that just as Empedocles claimed that the world

> was made of *Fighting* and of *Love*.
> Just so *Romances* are, for what else
> Is in them all, but *Love* and *Battels*?
> O'th' first of these w' have no great matter
> To treat of, but a world o'th' lat[t]er.[30]

Yet Butler begins the second part:

> But now t'observe Romantique Method,
> Let rusty Steel a while be sheathed;
> And all those harsh and rugged sounds
> Of Bastinado's, Cuts and Wounds
> Exchang'd to Love's more gentle stile,
> To let our Reader breathe a while.
>
> —2.1.1–6

Elsewhere in *Hudibras* Butler reflects on the literary form that most famously asserts the compatibility of love and the language of war, the "Petrarchan" love conceit, and through the wealthy Widow's response to Hudibras's highly conventional and opportunistic love complaints he makes a more single-minded criticism of the love-war nexus. "I cannot Love where I'm belov'd," says the Widow:

> *Love-passions* are like *Parables*,
> By which men still mean something else:
> . . . .
> Shee that with *Poetry* is won,
> Is but a *Desk* to write upon;
> And what men say of her, they mean,
> No more, then that on which they *lean*.
>
> —2.1.304, 441–442, 591–595

And with a cold and penetrating skepticism the Widow proceeds to demystify the figurative brutality of the *blazon*.

This is one result of the labor performed by heroic poetry. Only when war and love are experimentally separated out from each other can their conjunction be perceived and criticized as a gross incompatibility rather than experienced more or less tacitly and traditionally as a unified whole. Butler's disclosure of "war" at the heart of "love" works as a desublimation that reinforces (as desublimation often does) the disparity between the two. This critique of courtship has an analogue in the macro-critique of the late Civil War that is the moving force behind Hudibras—and not very far behind, because Butler's poem is a good deal more explicit in its political reference than is *Paradise Lost*. The analogy between Petrarchan courtship and the Civil War lies in Butler's conviction that the war was hypocritically animated by the ideals of religious faith, by the putative love of God.[31] Butler begins the famous first stanza of his poem: "When *civil* Fury first grew high," folks fought, "like mad or drunk, / For Dame *Religion* as for Punk" (1.1.5–6). The key to the analogy lies in the Widow's allegorical identity as a wealthy England courted by Interregnum suitors. *Hudibras* is a comprehensive indictment of the Civil War as a grotesque amplification of the Puritan powers of accommodation. Justifying physical violence as a low and sensible means of achieving elevated ends, religious wars are desublimated—shockingly domesticated—by Butler as a degradation of *caritas* into a whoring lust for power.[32] In short, what's wrong with heroic poetry at the most abstract level is that its conjunction of epic and romance, war and love, gives stealthy sanction to the corrupt accommodation of spirit by matter.

Aphra Behn's *Love-Letters between a Nobleman and His Sister* (1684, 1685, 1687) is also political allegory, although far more continuously so than Butler's because its dominant form is that of the roman à clef.[33] In systematically alluding to contemporary politics, Behn—ten years after the twelve-book version of *Paradise Lost* was published—picks up chronologically where *Absalom and Achitophel* leaves off, narrating the period from 1683 to 1685 in which Dryden's Absalom (James, Duke of Monmouth) continues to be a central figure, but doing so through a strictly secular signifying system—not typology but romance. *Love-Letters* begins in epistolary mode but modulates to a third-person narration in which letters are plentifully embedded. And although not a poem, Behn's narrative is, like Butler's, preoccupied with the defining question of heroic poetry: Are war and love compatible? Although political allegory ultimately aims both to conceal and to reveal, its basic fiction is that it's innocent of political reference; soon after Behn begins, her narrator insists that *"'tis not my business here to mix the rough relation of a War with the soft affairs of Love"* (10).

But this quickly turns out to be mere convention. Behn's allegory, structured by a hierarchy of semantic levels that are anything but watertight, does a good deal more revealing than concealing of actual identities. The amatory affairs and stock Italianate names give her plot a perfunctorily "low" flavor. But for one thing, these fictions stand for players actually involved in the high politics that succeed the Exclusion Crisis and eventuate in warfare between Monmouth and the king's forces. Moreover, they're not really fictions: the plot centers on the seduction of a lady by her brother-in-law, Philander (Lord Grey of Wark), who, a master of Petrarchan opportunism, is also, as one of Monmouth's main supporters, a master of proto-liberal opportunism. Behn's royalist argument about the Whig cause in the 1680s, consonant with Butler's royalist argument about the Puritan cause in the 1640s, is that Monmouth's Rebellion is the public equivalent of libertine adultery, a hypocritical power grab masquerading as high-minded principle. The political allegory on which *Love-Letters* is constructed is a reflexive tissue of interpenetrating high and low "affairs." As war is saturated by love, so love is saturated by war. Signifiers become signifieds and vice versa. And when, toward the end of *Love-Letters*, the narrator disingenuously repeats that "it is not the Business of this little History to treat of War, but altogether Love" (426) we know to read this denial as equally an affirmation. Both Butler and Behn depict their radically different texts as structured by this ambivalence, both affirming the incompatibility of war and love, epic and romance, and affirming their inseparability.

Milton calls *Paradise Lost* heroic poetry, and like Butler and Behn he considers both epic and romance hypothetical generic models for his poem. Directly after Milton opens book 9 by announcing his modulation from the pastoral friendship of man and angel to their tragic rift comes his claim, which I quoted earlier, to be pursuing an "argument / Not less but more Heroic than the wrath / Of stern Achilles," a disavowal (that is, a parodic imitation-criticism) of classical epic that is extended in turn by the disavowal of chivalric romance, which is "not that which justly gives Heroic name / To Person or to Poem" (9.14–15, 40–41). But Milton doesn't oscillate between the implications that epic and romance are compatible and incompatible, and he therefore doesn't invite us to see *Paradise Lost* as structured by such an ambivalence. Whatever their apparent differences, both classical epic and chivalric romance are fundamentally concerned with war, not love. So although this opening of the climactic book 9 may create the expectation that Milton will now confirm the status of *Paradise Lost* as heroic poetry by showing its vacillation between these two forms, the conventional trope turns out to have been something of a decoy. Heroic poetry is not for Milton an experimental inquiry into the relation between the two great narrative genres of the past at the present moment of self-conscious stock-taking. It's an experiment in a new, superior enterprise, a parody of those older forms that aims to supersede the ambivalent duality of the heroic tradition by proposing the singular and self-consistent heroism of Christian love.

That we must wait until book 4 to arrive, with Satan, in Eden and to be informed of this grand alternative only heightens its significance, as does Milton's enumeration of what Christian love is not: neither "the bought smile / Of Harlots," nor the "Court Amours, / Mixt Dance, or wanton Mask, or Midnight Ball" of romance, nor (with Butler and Behn) the Petrarchan "Serenate" (4.765–770). Christian love is "wedded Love, mysterious Law": lawful sexual coupling, which is the "true source / Of human offspring," the "sole propriety / In Paradise of all things common else" (4.750-752). During the Restoration, "propriety" still carries the connotation of "property": conjugal monogamy is the bulwark against promiscuity. But the sanctity of marriage also legitimates the sexual pleasures gained through sensible things. To this end God made the "blissful Bower" in Eden "when he fram'd / All things to man's delightful use," and here Adam and Eve perform "the Rites / Mysterious of connubial Love," "And heav'nly Choirs the Hymenæn sung" (4.690, 691-692, 711, 742-743). So Christian love, consecrated by heavenly love, promises to supersede the old tension between love and war.

Three years after *Paradise Lost* and four years before *Absalom and Achitophel*, Dryden published an opera that anticipated in full the latter poem's allusive and partial mode of Miltonic parody. As Milton did with *Paradise Lost*, Dryden called *The State of Innocence, and Fall of Man* (1677) a heroic poem, and his prefatory "Apology for Heroick Poetry, and Poetick License" ingratiates his imitation with a humility that reserves an edge of conceit at sharing a bit of Milton's sublime poetic license, and thereby achieves a certain parodic balance. This doesn't go so far as to countervail imitation with criticism. But the poem itself is alert to the sexual nuance in Milton's account of the couple's connubial love, which Dryden imitates with a degree of desublimation that adumbrates a new tension that on the eve of the Fall will threaten with a new division the resolution achieved by heavenly love.[34] In meeting this challenge, Milton has recourse to another generic formation that, like heroic poetry, gains footing during the Restoration.

Secret History

Defending the regicide in 1649, Milton had criticized Charles I as an exemplar of "how great mischief and dishonor hath. Befall'n to Nations under the Government of effeminate and Uxorious Magistrates. Who being themselves govern'd and overswaid at home under a Feminine usurpation, cannot be but farr short of spirit and authority without dores, to govern a whole Nation." Milton uses "effeminate" in the traditional sense of the word to characterize the gender ambivalence not of the man who's excessively like a woman (as in the word's modern meaning) but of the man who excessively likes women.[35] In *Paradise Lost* he returns to the topic of the male ruler besotted and unmanned by his devotion to his ambitious consort, a topic whose deep roots are commonly traced to the *Anecdota* of Procopius of Caesarea (c. 550 CE). His title literally means "unpublished things," but it came to be translated as "secret history," a form devoted to making public what never appears in the official histories: the low scandals of people in high places—in this case the emperor Justinian and his empress Theodora.[36] Shakespeare's *Antony and Cleopatra* (writ. 1606-1607?) and Dryden's reconception of it in *All for Love* (1673) are the two great English enactments of the Procopian theme. Over the course of the Enlightenment, the secret history enjoyed great popularity as a narrative technique for exhuming scandals of various kinds, but the original, Procopian kind was as compelling as any. How does the ambivalence of masculine and feminine stereotypes in Procopius's secret history engage the ambivalent relationships—epic and romance, war and love, high and low—that preoccupy heroic poetry? How does Milton's exclusive concentration on Christian love alter that engagement? I'll limit my discussion to Behn and Milton.

For Milton in 1649 the ruler in question was Charles I. For Behn it's Cesario (Monmouth), the leader of the rebellion against Charles II's younger brother. In part 3 of *Love-Letters*, Cesario falls hard for Hermione (Lady Henrietta Wentworth). Monmouth, Charles's bastard son, was the dashing and deeply charismatic embodiment of cavalier gallantry, intrepid valor, and libertine nerve. Denied what to many seemed his birthright, Monmouth became the people's culture hero and alternative heir during the Popish Plot. But by the end of Behn's romance, Cesario has come to the end of the line, desperate for recognition and, once enthralled by love, cursed by the confusion of amatory with political ambition. An associate fears he's been "perfectly effeminated into soft Woman" by Hermione's "Grace so Masculine," and in his climactic and doomed rebellion against his uncle (now ruler) he fights bravely enough, but "Love, that coward of the Mind, . . . had unman'd his great Soul" to such a degree that he forgoes the noble Roman expedient of falling on his sword. "Even on the Scaffold . . . he set himself to justifie his Passion to Hermione, endeavouring to render the Life he had led with her, Innocent and Blameless in the sight of Heaven" (Behn, 325, 434, 438).

The genre of the secret history presupposes an illuminating difference between the official history and history from below. To read *Paradise Lost* as a secret history requires that we understand Genesis, authored by God, to be the official history of the Fall; and in that account Adam's act of disobedience is scarcely motivated at all: on receiving the apple from Eve he eats it. Like Behn's, Milton's account supplements the official history with knowledge gained through his narrator's third-person detachment and his character's self-consciousness, and this greatly augments our understanding of Adam's part in the Fall.

When we first hear of Eve and Adam's relationship in book 4, the narrator affirms her "absolute" "subjection" to him (4.301, 308; see 295–311). But in book 8 Adam recounts to Raphael how, having named the animals, he doubted that their (in God's words) "low subjection" to him was an appropriate model for this human relationship; and God, agreeing, makes Eve from Adam's own body, "Thy likeness, thy fit help, thy other self" (8.345, 450). Once he sees Eve, now a "sensible thing," Adam is more than pleased with God's creation: "I now see / Bone of my Bone, Flesh of my Flesh, my Self! / Before me" (8.494–496). And once he's made sexual love to Eve, "so absolute she seems . . . , Seems wisest, virtuousest, discreetest, best; / All higher knowledge in her presence falls / Degraded." In Eden, Adam's bodily senses have given him much delight in many objects, which nonetheless "works in the mind no change"; "but here / Far otherwise, transported I behold, / Transported touch." He wonders if nature, in making Eve, "took perhaps / More than enough" from his own body. But in any case there is "an awe / About her, as a guard Angelic plac't," Adam tells Raphael, and the angel discerns in him a felt "subjection" to her (8.525, 528–530, 547, 550–552, 558–559, 570).

Has Adam's bodily transport reversed their hierarchical relation? Has Eve taken even God's place? Raphael is impatient with Adam's words: "What admir'st thou, what transports thee so, / An outside?" And he instructs Adam in the workings of the *scala amoris*, whose rungs lead us upward, from passion for sensible things to rational and heavenly love:

> Love refines
> The thoughts, and heart enlarges, hath his seat
> In Reason, and is judicious, is the scale
> By which to heav'nly Love thou may'st ascend,
> Not sunk in carnal pleasure . . .
> —8.567–568, 589–593

In response, Adam, "half abash't," struggles to describe the incomparable "change" wrought on him by his sensible love of Eve, less as a differential ascent from one to the other and more as the coextension of outside and inside, low and high, passion and reason. In defense of his rapt words, Adam denies being subjected to Eve's delights, as Raphael surmised: "these subject not; I to thee disclose / What inward thence I feel, not therefore foil'd" (8.607–608).

Raphael's account of the *scala amoris* or ladder of love recalls his earlier account of the *scala alimentorum* in book 5, when Adam, bemused by the angelic capacity for material transubstantiation, finds in angelic experience a definitive intimation of the heavenly bliss that humans might experience in tract of time, sensible things being a step upward toward spiritual being. On that occasion Adam found that the ladder of food, easily accommodated, is an ontological continuum that at each stage partakes of different proportions of matter and spirit, requiting movement both upward and downward. The ladder of love, too, combines epistemology with ontology, knowledge of what it's like to be an angel with the prospect of becoming one. There is, however, a major difference between the two ladders. On the scale of food, the comparability of angels and humans makes clear that the angelic movement upward or downward, which is empowered by the active duality of matter and spirit, will also be available to humans. But in Raphael's neoplatonic account of the scale of love, the upward movement from human love to heavenly love is a process of refinement in which material and "carnal pleasure" seem to be refined away (8.593). Perhaps this is why Adam at this point turns self-consciously to an interrogatory mode ("Bear with me then, if lawful what I ask") on the nature of his love for Eve, hoping to clarify this crucial point:

> Love not the heav'nly Spirits, and how thir Love
> Express they, by looks only, or do they mix
> Irradiance, virtual or immediate touch?
> —8.614, 615–617

We recall Raphael's three-pronged pedagogical charge from God, linking obedience, free choice, and knowledge (book 5, "The Argument"). But compared with the plainspoken clarity of the angel's earlier reply, this one is crucially obscure. "Let it suffice thee that thou know'st / Us happy," he begins, thereby conveying perhaps that this itself is sufficient to avail in rendering man inexcusable of disobedience, or in Adam's terms that it marks the bounds of the "lawful." And Raphael proceeds to affirm angelic "Love" in terms so profusely paradoxical as to sound equivocal if not downright evasive. Clarity comes only when the angel abruptly concludes with the injunction to "love, but first of all / Him whom to love is to obey" (8.620–621, 633–634).

Adam thanks the angel for his "condescension" (8.649), but the nature of heavenly love, unlike the nature of heavenly sustenance, hasn't been well accommodated.[37] Instead, Adam has been told that obedience must be prior to knowledge, not a consequence of it. But if this doesn't avail Adam to know, is he really possessed of a free estate? God would have obedience be freely chosen, but freedom of the will satisfies only one of two necessary conditions. The other condition of free choice is knowledge of the nature of what's being chosen, in this case heavenly love. Milton's confidence in his powers of accommodation should ensure that such knowledge is feasible. But perhaps the implication that angelic love is immaterial is legible enough. Or perhaps the notion of a limit to the knowledge required for choosing obedience is beyond accommodation, a contradiction in terms for a human understanding grounded in contractarianism. Whatever the case, this secret history of the Fall's preconditions suggests that God's ways have been not justified but obscured.

However, there is another reason, intimated earlier, for this apparent failure to accommodate heavenly love to Adam, one that is its consequence. As on the ladder of food, so on the ladder of love the change of knowledge entails the prospect of a change of being. The sexual love of Eve has fueled Adam's desire that transubstantiation to the spiritual bliss of angelic love not sacrifice the sensible bliss of human love. The apprehension that sexual love will be sacrificed in heaven prefigures the fatal choice that Adam soon will make, which is itself prefigured in the series of choices Milton has made in his secret history of Genesis. Sensible things are no longer the means to a higher end and ultimately expendable: they're the end itself. The implication is that the Fall occurred not because of Eve's female weakness or because of Adam's "effeminate" weakness, but as a consequence of God's will to withhold the knowledge needed for Adam to choose freely. When Adam first sees Eve, "Bone of my Bone, Flesh of my Flesh, my Self / Before me," he infers from this vision why future man "shall forgo / Father and Mother, and to his Wife adhere; / And they shall be one Flesh, one Heart, one Soul" (8.495–496, 497–499). At the moment the first man sees Eve he becomes a prefiguration of future man, who will adhere to his conjugal wife instead of his consanguineal parents and God the Father. This is perhaps intimated in Michael's closing consolation that "to leave Paradise" is to "possess a paradise within thee, happier far" (12.586–587). Satan in his spite pinpoints more precisely the sensible heart of the matter: "these two / Imparadis't in one another's arms / The happier *Eden*, shall enjoy their fill / Of bliss on bliss" (4.505–508).

So Milton's decision to postpone to the latter half of book 8 Adam's account of his earliest contact with Eve provides a highly proximate and otherwise unavailable motivation for his climactic act of disobedience, which immediately follows in book 9. Once Eve eats the fruit, Adam hears and accepts her hopeful rationales and delusions. And when she gives him the apple, Milton's narrator confirms what we already know from Adam's internal discourse (9.894–916):

> He scrupl'd not to eat
> Against his better knowledge, not deceiv'd,
> But fondly overcome with Female charm.
> —9.997–999

Disclosed as the fondly effeminate hero of a secret history, Adam is later confirmed in this role by God himself:

> Was shee thy God, that her thou didst obey
> Before his voice, or was shee made thy guide,
> Superior, or but equal, that to her
> Thou didst resign thy Manhood, and the Place
> Wherein God set thee above her[?]
> —10.145–149

For Adam the sensible power of Eve's touch has exceeded that of God's voice, and she has replaced not only Adam but even God in the hierarchy of nature, deranging if not toppling the ladder of dominion.

If Milton's secret history of the Fall confers on Adam a "feminine" sensitivity to his love for Eve, it also gives Eve a pragmatic "masculine" tenacity in pursuit of external goals. Her wish to "divide our labors" bespeaks both an industrious economy and an autonomy of choice that "domestic Adam" equates, perhaps too easily, with studying "household good" (9.214, 233, 318).[38] Once Eve eats the apple, she wonders that it's been "let hang, as to no end / Created; but henceforth my early care, / . . . / Shall tend thee" (9.798–799, 801). And in this sentiment she echoes Satan's remark about the unproductivity of "The Gods": "This fair Earth I see, / Warm'd by the Sun, producing every kind, / Them nothing" (9.720–722). Eve's unwonted masculine pragmatism even borders on a "feminist" self-interest that incidentally evokes the discourse of God and Adam concerning her place in the hierarchy. Eve's new knowledge, she speculates, might "add what wants / In Female Sex . . . , / And render me more equal, and perhaps . . . sometime / Superior" (9.821–823, 824–825).

Our access to Adam's interiority, through both first- and third-person narration, alters the official history's absolute emphasis on Adam's Fall as an act of disobedience to God by emphasizing his absolute physical devotion to Eve. Not that Milton's secret history challenges the fact or the consequences of Adam's disobedience. But it parodies that curt official story by giving the Fall a psychosubjective intention. When Raphael reproaches Adam for his seeming subjection to Eve, he replies: "I to thee disclose / What inward thence I feel, not therefore foil'd" (8.607–608). "Subjection" unfolds to express not simply a one-dimensional subordination to a higher power, but a state of multi-intentional subjecthood in relation to other subjects. This is an ultimate effect of accommodation. True, the condition of materiality subordinates human love to the transcendent spirituality of divine love. But in providing the only medium through which the spirit can be known, matter also provides the multiple vehicles of sensible relation that diversify and subtilize, beyond hierarchy, what it means to be subjected.

Reading *Paradise Lost* as a secret history also deepens our sense of it in the tradition of the heroic poem. A Renaissance synthesis concerned to elevate the increasingly dialectical tension between epic and romance to a high level of generic self-consciousness, heroic poetry was reinforced in some cases (compare Behn and Butler) by a gendered ambiguity that complements the dominant dialectic between war and love. In *Paradise Lost* that tension seems to have been entertained notionally only to be transcended by the affirmation of a unified Christian love. However, the triumph of love over war in *Paradise Lost* turns out to be short-lived—not because war as such returns but because Christian love divides against itself and reproduces the old tension in a new form. Behn's Procopian hero Cesario abandons war for love. Milton's Adam, supplied with a motive for disobedience denied him in the official history, abandons divine love for human love. The ultimate effect of accommodation is human subjectivity, which leads Adam to disobey his Father and to sacrifice the rewards of patriarchal obedience in exchange for the rewards of amatory intimacy.

Is this what *Paradise Lost* is "about"? My aim, more speculative than that, has been to read *Paradise Lost* alongside other closely contemporary texts that share some of its features in order to ask if the signs of generic instability they evince shed light on the historicity of Milton's poem. By analogy, I've argued elsewhere that the novel genre emerges in order to undertake social, political, economic, and religious problems that traditional genres, like epic and romance, aren't equipped to engage. Mixed and less stable modes like mock epic, mock typology, heroic poetry, and the secret history are formulated as part of a comparable effort to bridge the gap between forms that are known but deficient and forms that are effective but unknown. Like his contemporaries Butler, Bunyan, Dryden, and Behn, Milton self-consciously aimed to represent his subject parabolically, signifying with brilliant indirection what he thought was not susceptible to less mediated narration and description. All of these authors had recognizable motives—rhetorical, political, theological—for their indirection, but they also shared in the complex indeterminacy characteristic of a historical context that seemed more than most to require innovative methods of understanding, a context that also for the first time was learning to conceive innovation itself in positive terms. The genre of the novel coalesced at this time as well, and its earliest experiments in form and content bear an arresting relation to what these texts were variously attempting to do.

Formally speaking they have much in common. The "antiromance" movement, generated by the auto-parodic Renaissance *romanzo* and the followers of *Don Quixote*, fueled the early Enlightenment outcry against "romance," which attained not only the generic but even the broadly epistemological status of an impossible or trivial ideal, a gross error, or a lie. For Milton, the dubious compound of romance and epic of which heroic poetry consists expressed the incapacity but indispensability of traditional forms, and ultimately of all "sensible things," to accommodate the truth of divine spirit. The positive standard by which the early novel condemned romance might momentarily seem almost the opposite of Milton's—namely, the empirical and quantitative measures of truth that, championed by the permanent revolution of the new philosophy, for much of the Enlightenment were most commonly identified in narrative with the generic tag "history" or "true history." Yet we've seen how functional sensible things are in Milton's pedagogy and how far materialism is implicated in his theology; and in other respects Milton shared fully in the proto-scientific skepticism of the proto-novelists. Moreover, by the 1740s, the naive empiricism of the early novel's claim to historicity was being supplanted by an epistemology of representational "realism" that bears comparison with Milton's heterodox practice of accommodation.[39] The difference lies in the ontology of what's being evoked: on the one hand, the invisible realm of the spirit, which is inaccessible to human materiality; on the other, the pristine presence of the object, which is inaccessible to the sense perception of the subject. What's shared is the sophisticated skepticism of suspended disbelief in both representations, whose formal hallmark is textual reflexivity, the self-conscious thematizing of formal experimentation, our subliminal awareness of domestication always at work.

Obviating Accommodation, Forging Domestication, Precluding Allegory

Reading *Paradise Lost* as a secret history makes available the figure of domestication as a ladder—of food, of love—that serves the purpose of accommodation, but whose premise of an elevated goal accessible only by lower rungs of ascent can be challenged, the ladder shaken, if the implicit hierarchy of value is questioned. The figure of the ladder is equally applicable to allegorical forms in which the material or sensible level of the narrative is the signifying rung that enables ascent to the goal of the signified. What the novel doesn't share with *Paradise Lost* and the forms I've been comparing it with is their bi-leveled structure of domestication, whether theological or political. And what makes this time and these texts distinctive is precisely the tendency of the two levels to bleed into each other; or to put this differently, the uncertainty that domestication across two discrete realms is semantically required. We feel this in reading *The Pilgrim's Progress*, where Bunyan imbues the sensible things of his allegory with a materiality so powerful that readers find themselves, as it were, pushing away the domesticating ladder of allegory and discovering that what had served as signifier, the sensible thing, is actually its own autonomous signified. Bunyan was well aware of the defective epistemology with which romance was being associated. Nonetheless, the ease with which Coleridge, a century later, was able to read *The Pilgrim's Progress* "as a novel" (Coleridge, 31) has to do with the fact that its allegorical form required a figural continuity that Bunyan found not only in the seriality of the pilgrimage plot but also in the popular figures of chivalric romance: the Lord of the Hill, who possesses an ancient pedigree and gives pilgrims land to tend, or outfits them in sword, shield, and helmet; Christian's knight service for his lord against the foul monster Apollyon, who claims his fealty but is beaten back; the Giant Despair who imprisons Christians in Doubting-Castle.

Of course, to read Bunyan in this way is to misread him, to "secularize" his narrative, in the most pejorative sense of that term, as a modernizing process of radical devaluation. But it's worth conceiving the secular in the broadly neutral terms of parody, hence as preserving the moral center of Christianity while superseding its monotheistic supernaturalism. At a further extreme of domestication, *The Pilgrim's Progress* might then become the story of how the modern individual and family emerged from the protective constraints of tradition to embrace the difficult responsibility of self-sufficiency and ethical subjecthood.

Although the domesticating purpose of the roman à clef differs from that of Christian allegory, something similar becomes available in the course of reading Behn's *Love-Letters*. We begin in the imitative stealth of political allegory, which entails a manifestly uneven relationship of low signifier to high signified. But as the masquerade becomes sophisticated and habituated, its semantic force and interest are increasingly located in the realm of the signifier itself. The high–low differential remains unchallenged, but the hermeneutic key to characterization shifts from the macro-level of the allegorical mode, in which character is disclosed as a correspondence to public exteriority and actual particularity, to the micro-level, on which the personal space of character, in all its intimate interiority and virtual particularity, claims our attention. Behn's epistolary form gives way to third-person narration as the sheer documentary secrecy of letters comes to feel less expressive than the secrecy of the motives that lie behind and beneath them. The secrets of political history become less compelling, less revelatory than the secrets of the personal—the casuistical and psychological—case history. And yet the political reference of the narrative is preserved even as it's superseded.

In other words, what makes these texts unusual is the way they shake the ladder of domestication by promoting a less strictly differential interchange between the two levels of signifier and signified, and thereby also between form and content. I've argued that a similar case can be made for *Paradise Lost*. Milton is committed there to the accommodation of an immaterial and invisible world by means of sensible things that are familiar to him and to the world of his readers. But we need to be mindful that Milton's very confidence in his powers of accommodation, like Bunyan's in his allegory, tends to militate against the hermeneutics of hierarchical signification on which the religious purpose of this method depends. This is most evident in Milton's secret history of Adam's Fall, an act of disobedience motivated by his choice of sensible things, sexual and conjugal love, as an end in themselves rather than as a means to the higher end of spiritual and consanguineal love. Milton is poised on the threshold between domestication and domesticity. The sensible things of his narrative, notionally committed to bringing home the realm of the spirit in a direct if not one-to-one relation, show a tendency to float free of that accommodation and instead to represent, with an abundance and depth of detail, the mundane and familiar materiality of actual experience. It's on these grounds that I pursue the comparison between *Paradise Lost* and the novel genre.

If for a moment we imagine counterfactually that a given novel—say, Samuel Richardson's *Pamela* (1740)—originated as a bi-leveled structure of domestication, we might conclude that its ladder had been pushed away, which is to say that domestication, having nothing left to do, had yielded to domesticity. Nonetheless, this hypothetical process of domestication would have left a thickly sedimented record of its own activity. Richardson's account of the amatory struggle between Mr. B. and Pamela is in fact rich with the residual, metaphorical language of seventeenth-century political conflict (king, tyrant, jailer, traitor, rebel, prisoner, etc.). In a roman à clef, the virtual romance figure provides a key that unlocks the political identity of the actual elevated personage. In *Pamela*, the fictional figure is characterized by a political metaphor that provides a key to her ethical capacity and identifies a type of person that's susceptible to manifold elaborations and refinements. By these means, Richardson's political metaphors make a subtle contribution to his major aim to disclose within common people the qualities of mind and spirit that had been thought to exist only among the sociopolitically elevated. By the end of the seventeenth century, both the ideology and the institution of estate settlement were in dispute. In *Love-Letters*, marriages among the nobility and gentry are conceived almost exclusively as a means of settling and perpetuating the family estate. In the eighteenth century, love has become an acknowledged motive even for elite marriages, and the most insistent thematic pattern in the novel genre is a conflict between two models of marriage. The first is the "arranged" or "forced" marriage (the marriage "of convenience"), engineered by the parents with the more or less obedient subservience of the children, and dominated by the consanguineal interests of patrilineal inheritance. The cornerstone of patrilineal inheritance was the rule of male primogeniture, whose purpose was to ensure the integrity of the family estate by passing it in perpetuity to the firstborn son in the paternal line. The second model is marriage for love, motivated by the free choice of the couple and representative of the emergent, conjugal paradigm of the family. The traditional, consanguineal model conceived the family on a diachronic continuum that gave it temporal unity; the modern, conjugal family is unified according to a synchronic depth model, through affective ties within a generation or two.[40] The tension between war and love that preoccupies heroic poetry is both preserved and superseded by Milton in the tension he reveals, within love, between its divine and human fulfillments. The novel genre in turn will find, within human love, a tension between consanguineal and conjugal models of marriage. What the several stages in this sequence supersede are unequal relations of authority—ontological, generational, sexual. What they preserve is the dynamic differential of inequality.

The historical emergence of mock epic, heroic poetry, mock typology, heroic poetry, Christian epic, antiromance, roman à clef, and secret history was approximately ordered according to this chronology. Not that Milton's use or anticipation of their formal capacities has for his part any chronological or developmental significance. Rather, these several genres have a synchronic, richly layered availability for any author of Milton's time. However, when we bring to the intergeneric thickness of *Paradise Lost* an attention to the specifically parodic relations between its genres, we begin to discern a parodic pattern in their chronological progression—not a normative "progress" but a logic of diachronic succession based in the dialectic of imitation and criticism, of preservation and supersession. From distinction to separation and then to conflation: this is the logic of Enlightenment thought. The generic form of each stage in the chronological sequence coheres as a distillation or refinement of what immediately came before. Each emergent stage selects and makes central one element or part of a formal whole that previously had been in tacit tension with another part.

To return now to where I left off: human love, freed of dependence on the authority of the divine spirit, becomes subject to human authority and the domination of youth by age. This is the conflict between consanguineal and conjugal relations, which eventuates in the triumph of the rising generation over parental arrangement. Once affirmed, however, the coherence and integrity of conjugal love and the marriage choice divides once more into that most ancient inequality, obscured of late by the authority of generational conflict but now thrown into stark relief: the unequal domination of wives by husbands and of women by men. The struggle to overcome this inequality is engaged on many fronts in the modern world, among them the novel. That it's now engaged with unprecedented recognition and determination says little about the perseverance of its advocates or the likelihood of its continuance, but does owe something to the influence of unprecedented Enlightenment principles.

I've now concluded a series of readings of Restoration texts by Milton's contemporaries Butler, Bunyan, Dryden, and Behn. My aim has been to compare these texts with *Paradise Lost* in terms of their shared ambition to respond to the demands of the historical moment by experimenting with a heterogeneous array of innovative literary forms. The following and concluding reading is in this spirit; but the text itself is suppositional, a virtual parody of *Paradise Lost* rather than an actual text that deploys an array of novelistic conventions to suggest a text in the emergence of the genre but before its formation.[41] This parody has a loose precedent. In 1710 Richard Steele published a parody of Adam and Eve's quarrel just after the Fall. Steele writes that he has translated "out of Heroicks, and put into Domestick Stile" "the First Couple's" dispute. Steele's "domestic" target text evokes the ambience of Restoration comedy as mine does the early novel, and his concluding remarks complement my argument by evincing how Enlightenment thought conceived historical difference as entailing the preservation of the past (in this case the past of both Milton and Genesis) in the process of superseding it.[42]

The Novel
The True History of Adam Newton

I've been assured by an elderly gentlewoman of my acquaintance that the occurrences I am about to relate are the solemn truth and witnessed by others who will vouch for them. Neither does anyone question the gentlewoman's exact narrative, only the terms I put it in departing from hers, which is natural given our difference in age and station.[43]

The following events transpired several years ago in the county of ———.

A wealthy landowner Lord G——— was known and admired by neighboring gentry as the patriarch of an ancient family whose nobility was said to extend back to the earliest creations of William the Conqueror (this we may with reason doubt). Recently widowed, he had two sons. The eldest, Jesus, being the firstborn, was *heir* (5.720) to his father's vast estate. Adam, his *youngest son* (3.151), was in contrast to his brother a modest and uncommanding gentleman farmer. G——— himself was one of those old-fashioned landholders, familiar but increasingly singular these days, who believed that the only real estate is land, uncorrupted by innovative agricultural techniques and the modern sorcery of financial stockjobbers. Like many of his generation, G——— associated such practices with the ungodly Puritans, and he'd recently played a central role in enforcing the laws against nonconformists so as to *root them out* (6.855) of all government posts and clerical livings. G———, customarily and carelessly attired in common dress, had the appearance of a gnarled and weather-beaten old oak.

The person of Lord G———'s eldest son, Jesus, was as splendidly fashionable as his father's was lacking in propriety of rank. Jesus was nominally and by right of status Justice of the Peace for the county of C———, but he spent much of his time in London, consorting with devilish courtiers and earning a name for himself as both a model of *Manhood* and a dissolute libertine (3.314). This troubled his father, whose chief concern in recent years had been to ensure the continuity of the patriline, which seemed increasingly endangered by the wayward passion of his firstborn. By the rule of primogeniture, G———'s ambitions to perpetuate family honor and property had rightly been focused on his worldly son Jesus. But in truth it was the younger son, Adam, who showed more interest and capacity in the improvement of the estate and its ancient seat Empyreal Hall. And so the three men dwelt together, in the company of a few servants who were treated as family members.

One day the noble lord, reading in his drawing room, was approached by Mary, a maidservant for whom her departed mistress had felt a special affection, in earnest of which she had given Mary a brooch, which she usually kept in a cabinet of her most precious things, but was presently wearing. Remarking this, G——— surmised that its appearance intimated the personal nature of an appeal Mary hoped to make to him. But instead her purpose, sincere if officious, was to communicate the news that returning from the village that morning she had seen there a splendid carriage adorned with coronets, whose presence perforce announced the speedy arrival of Lady W———at Empyreal Hall. G———had arranged this visit, having invited his oldest friend's consort expressly to inform him of Lord W———'s expedition to the *New World*. His Lordship would soon return, but the motive for G———'s alacrity lay in the resolve he had come to regarding his eldest son's prospects. We will pass over the other topics entered into by these two estimable aristocrats, engaging though they may be, to attend to the matter whose conveyance so piqued G———'s interest.

He quickly gathered from Lady W———'s spirited if scattered conversation that a remarkable plantation of which her lord had intelligence had fortuitously become available for purchase, one remarkable in having proved so lushly productive of *wanton growth* that it required, unlike most homesteads in that part of Virginia, no more than energetic maintenance (4.629). Ordinarily G———would have had no more than passing curiosity about this prodigious evidence of Providential bounty, in which the New World seemed to abound. But having despaired both of his heir's dissipated existence in the city, and of his apparent distaste for his firstborn obligations in the countryside, G———hoped to interest Jesus in this compromise between patrimonial duties and the anticipation of unknown adventure. So he wrote to his eldest, explaining the singular opportunity before him, and ending: "Would that this Prospect might engage your Attention, and gratify your Hopes, for a Way of Life more satisfying than what now confronts you, I remain your devoted Father, G———."

Braced for the rebuff that came by the next post, G———was astonished to find that Adam, hearing of his brother's decision, with an easy grace inquired if he might accept the offer in the stead of Jesus. The patriarch was perplexed. His indulgence of the firstborn was not heritable by the second. Yet he also realized how suited Adam's *domestic* discipline would be to this undertaking and wondered if the entail might be translated or passed down to him, and to his colonial property, notionally re-conceived as Empyreal Redivivus (9.318).

The untimely death of the estate's owner had left a young widow, Eve, proprietor of the plantation, from whom G———planned to purchase it, and between whom and Adam he determined to arrange a marriage that would handsomely serve his own desires. "What say ye, my boy?" said father to son. "'Tis a ripe opportunity for improving the land on a grand scale. The woman's rank is of course damnably inferior, but yours will raise her. And should your undoubted success yet leave you weary of strange foliage and savage heathens, I will welcome you back to civilization." As for the woman, no need to look further into her situation: she is innocent and ignorant and will be honored to serve as Adam's docile and humble helpmeet. But in G———'s disdain for closer inquiry—his pride in his powers of foreknowledge was legendary—he ensured his ignorance of the fact that along with her former husband's wealth Eve had inherited the rebellious spirit of her father, a parliamentarian general during the late Civil War.

Eve found in Adam a gentle and thoughtful spirit, a true instance of *manly grace*, unlike the men of power she was accustomed to, and they delighted in endless conversation (4.490). On only one topic did they discover a presumed seed of disagreement. Before Adam's arrival, Eve had devoted much thought to how her plantation Eden might be developed by the latest techniques of agrarian improvement, perhaps on the model of Paradise, Eden's central *enclosure green* (4.133). However, Adam's patriarch Lord G———had just dispatched his chief gardener, Raphael, to ensure that the plantation was maintained, not improved. Even Paradise, which had been planted with exotic species and enclosed for future horticultural experiment, was subject to this prohibition, in the case of one tree in particular. Because the unique botanical properties of this tree held mysteries that, if mastered, might transform the science of artificial propagation and reproduction, Lord G———insisted that even its harvesting be forbidden.

Adam recognized in this prohibition his father's extreme antipathy toward what G———regarded as one more *devilish machination* of modernity (6.504), but he was inclined to obey the old man, if only to avoid conflict. So he traveled to Jamestown with pleasure to greet his old companion in horticulture and farming, knowing that they need not enter into dispute on this topic. Obtaining a second horse for the ride back to Paradise, Adam by chance glimpsed on Raphael's greatcoat a small decorative device that for an instant raised in him a flash of recognition that was gone before it could be examined or understood. Meanwhile, *advent'rous Eve* (9.921), raised by a father of the Independent sect and without her husband's pious subservience to authority (as she put it to Adam, he *"is thy Law, thou mine"* [4.637]), intimated to her haughty father-in-law her displeasure at this command, as much for its presumption as for its substance. Lord G———, consumed with wrath at this woman who lacked the weakness of a woman, fancied in Eve a kind of *Monster, upward Man and downward* female (*for Spirits when they please can either Sex assume, or both,* as he knew from *Fable or Romance*) (1.423–424, 462–463, 580). What began as fancy quickly became derangement: in G———'s mind, Eve was transformed into the supernatural "Satan," his imagined, malevolent, and mortal enemy.

Eve realized now that her Lord, fueled by the grandiose delusion of absolute authority, was mad and must be resisted. In Eden the next day, she planned with care a simple al fresco luncheon with her mate. Afterward, reclining with him in a bower, Eve echoed to Adam his own earlier hopes for strenuous horticultural *reform*, recalling that *the work under our labor grows luxurious by restraint. Now let us divide our labors* (9.208–209, 214; see 4.623–633). Adam feared that Eve, if left alone, would be guided by her enthusiasm rather than her reason, and he cautioned against division. But Eve, cannily echoing her father-in-law, argued against a cloistered female virtue sheltered from the knowledge of vice by protective men.

Eve had been well trained in the Puritan arts of casuistry, and once alone she debated with herself the difficult case of conscience that pitted the ethics and consequences of defying her husband and father-in-law against those of forgoing the promise of the wonderful tree. After much deliberation she resolved to take a cutting of it. Adam was shocked at Eve's *bold deed* and at the *peril great provok't* by it

(9.921, 922); but he too pondered the choice he himself now faced. Lord G———— would demand that he abandon his wife and return to England, and to a life of obedient ease on the family estate. But the crisis had educated Adam in what he really wanted. To return home would be to sacrifice the vitally present and sensible pleasures of conjugal union for a deadening loyalty to the family lineage, to a past in which he had no share and to a future exaltation bleached of humanity. When Adam first arrived in the New World, he experienced his rustication as a devastating privation, an exile from the value-generating presence of his father and Empyreal Hall. But in his time with Eve, Adam had come to experience his privation of that elevated presence as instead the positive privacy of life with a self-reflective equal. And so Adam resolved to push away the demeaning and unneeded ladder of dependence. G————, enraged, disinherited Adam and evicted them both from the plantation. No doubt honest Raphael knew about and approved this fall from the rank of colonial landowner—to what? But as they stood dumbfounded at Eden's entrance, Raphael himself all at once appeared, extending his open hand to Adam. There lay the brooch that Adam's mother, unbeknownst to him, had given her servant Mary, and that Adam had espied on Raphael's coat in Jamestown. What did it mean? Why did Raphael have it, and why was he offering it to him? But before Adam could even tell Eve the source of the amulet (for the brooch seemed now to take on an almost talismanic aura), from behind Raphael there appeared Mary herself. And now things began to be clarified.

Raphael explained that soon after he was taken on at Empyreal Hall he had fallen in love with Mary; but fearing G————would take a dim view, they had kept it secret. Raphael remained the loyal servant, at least in show, even as he became aware of the noble lord's continuing devotion to the former absolutist regime. So when G————ordered Empyreal's chief gardener to enforce the horticultural prohibition at Eden, Raphael embraced both the duty and the opportunity. Mary would accompany him on the one-way voyage to America, covertly disembarking to elude Adam's view and traveling alone to Eden, for there remained to be discovered Adam's state of mind and how to confront him. So, in asking Mary for the brooch and disclosing it to Adam, Raphael hoped to surprise him into a candor enhanced by the sentiment of maternal memory, and thereby to communicate, if it seemed congenial, his own release from paternal prerogative. But Raphael had not anticipated that Mary would actually enter into this first encounter, nor could he have imagined what she herself would add to this moment of discovery—that her mistress was also her mother, and that she and Adam were sister and brother. The brooch, purportedly a gift to a favorite, was in fact authentic proof of Mary's familial and social quality.

Knowing from experience her master's intolerance of the female sex, Lady G————had concealed from him the birth of their illegitimate daughter, and as Mary grew up in the household treated her as a beloved maidservant. All present now were astonished by this revelation, but no one so much as Adam, who was well pleased to exchange one incompatible sibling, whom he would never see again, for the sympathetic and loving Mary, who would also become the intimate companion of her sister-in-law Eve.

And so *adventurous* Eve and *domestic* Adam, accompanied by their dear companions, happily made their way out into the welcoming wilderness, bringing with them the cutting of the plant they'd come to call *the tree of knowledge* (9.751–752). *The world was all before them*; and in their westward travels together, the four friends would seed and plant the new knowledge in the New World for future generations (12.646).

Acknowledgments

I'm deeply grateful to the many critics, scholars, colleagues, friends, and family who over the years have aided my thought and writing with unflagging intelligence and generosity. Rather than acknowledge everyone who has helped me by naming them individually, I'll confine myself to highlighting those whose work has energized mine early on, in recent years, or at each stage of my intellectual development: György Lukács, Jean-Paul Sartre, Claude Lévi-Strauss, R. H. Tawney, Christopher Hill, E. P. Thompson, Ellen Meiksins Wood, Raymond Williams, Jürgen Habermas, Randy Trumbach, Ruth Perry, and Douglas Lane Patey.

Notes

INTRODUCTION

1. My complaint that the Enlightenment has been reductively misread as the culmination of tradition rather than as its critique may be vulnerable to a complaint that my version of tradition reductively misreads it as being more statically "traditional" than it really was. To assess the justice of this complaint, as of mine, depends on assessing the evidence that can be adduced to support it. These are the adventures of periodization. See my discussion in *Historicizing the Enlightenment*, vol. 1, intro. and ch. 6.

2. Walter Jackson Bate, *From Classic to Romantic: Premises of Taste in Eighteenth-Century England* (New York: Harper, 1946) (further citations appear parenthetically in the text).

3. Thomas Quayle, *Poetic Diction: A Study of Eighteenth-Century Verse* (London: Methuen, 1924), 13.

4. Harold Bloom, *The Visionary Company: A Reading of English Romantic Poetry*, rev. ed. (Ithaca, NY: Cornell University Press, 1971), xxi (further citations appear parenthetically in the text).

5. George Sherburn and Donald F. Bond, *The Restoration and Eighteenth Century (1660–1789)*, vol. 3 of *A Literary History of England*, ed. Albert C. Baugh (New York: Appleton-Century Crofts, 1948), 710, 712 (further citations appear parenthetically in the text).

6. Robert Southey, "Preface" to *Specimens of the Later English Poets*, 3 vols. (London: Longman, Hurst, Rees, and Orme, 1807), 1:xxix, xxxii.

7. Robert Southey, "Sketches of the Progress of English Poetry from Chaucer to Cowper," in *The Works of William Cowper*, ed. Robert Southey, 3 vols. (London: Baldwin and Cradock, 1836), 2:138, 141, 142, 144.

8. William Hazlitt, "Lecture VII. On the Living Poets," in *Lectures on the English Poets Delivered at the Surrey Institution*, 2nd ed. (London: Taylor and Hessey, 1819), 318–319.

9. William Hazlitt, *The Spirit of the Age* (1825), in *The Complete Works of William Hazlitt*, ed. P. P. Howe et al., 21 vols. (London: J. M. Dent, 1930–1934), 11:87, 89.

10. M. H. Abrams, "English Romanticism: The Spirit of the Age," in *The Correspondent Breeze: Essays on English Romanticism* (New York: Norton, 1984), 68–69. In fact, under the aegis of "neoclassical" authors, aesthetics had already been self-consciously leveled and transvalued.

11. See William Wordsworth, "Preface" to *Lyrical Ballads*, 3rd ed. (London: Longman, 1802), in William Wordsworth and Samuel Taylor Coleridge, *Lyrical Ballads and Related Writings*, ed. William Richey and Daniel Robinson (Boston: Riverside, 2002), 393, 397–398 (further citations appear parenthetically in the text).

12. M. H. Abrams, *The Mirror and the Lamp: Romantic Theory and the Critical Tradition* (New York: Norton, 1958), 57, vi (further citations appear parenthetically in the text).

13. René Wellek is inclined to see these as concerns of Romanticism rather than of the eighteenth century. After an exhaustive comparatist survey of controversy about the nature of Romanticism, he writes, "In all of these studies, however diverse in method and emphasis, a convincing agreement has been reached: they all see the implication of imagination, symbol, myth, and organic nature, and see it as part of the great endeavor to overcome the split between subject and object, the self and the world, the conscious and the unconscious." René Wellek, "Romanticism Re-examined," in *Concepts of Criticism*, ed. Stephen G. Nichols Jr. (New Haven, CT: Yale University Press, 1963), 220.

14. Jerome J. McGann attributes to Romanticism the modern commonplace "that poetry, and art in general, has no essential relation to partisan, didactic, or doctrinal matters. Poetry transcends these things." *The Romantic Ideology: A Critical Investigation* (Chicago: University of Chicago Press, 1983), 69.

15. See especially Maynard Mack, "The Muse of Satire," *Yale Review* 41 (1951): 80–92, reprinted in *Studies in the Literature of the Augustan Age: Essays Collected in Honor of Arthur Ellicott Case*, ed. Richard C. Boys (Ann Arbor, MI: George Wahr, 1952), 218–231.

16. George Savile, Marquess of Halifax, quoted in Derek Hirst, *England in Conflict, 1603–1660: Kingdom, Community, Commonwealth* (New York: Oxford University Press, 1999), 328.

17. David Duff, *Romanticism and the Uses of Genre* (Oxford: Oxford University Press, 2009), 37, 38 (further citations appear parenthetically in the text).

18. Bloom, *Visionary Company*, 7–15; Harold Bloom, *The Ringers in the Tower: Studies in Romantic Tradition* (Chicago: University of Chicago Press, 1971), 4, 15, 134.

19. William Rushton, *The Afternoon Lectures on English Literature* (London: Bell and Daldy, 1863), 75.

20. Northrop Frye, "Towards Defining an Age of Sensibility," in *Eighteenth-Century English Literature: Modern Essays in Criticism*, ed. James L. Clifford (New York: Oxford University Press, 1959), 311.

21. E.g., see Bertrand H. Bronson, "The Pre-Romantic or Post-Augustan Mode," in *Facets of the Enlightenment: Studies in English Literature and Its Contexts*, ed. Bertrand Bronson (Berkeley: University of California Press, 1968), 159–172.

22. Marshall Brown, *Preromanticism* (Stanford, CA: Stanford University Press, 1991), 2, 3, 6.

23. Dror Wahrman, *The Making of the Modern Self: Identity and Culture in Eighteenth-Century England* (New Haven, CT: Yale University Press, 2004), xi (further citations appear parenthetically in the text).

24. See *Historicizing the Enlightenment*, vol. 1, ch. 5.

25. Fredric Jameson, *The Political Unconscious: Narrative as a Socially Symbolic Act* (Ithaca, NY: Cornell University Press, 1981), 105.

26. Rene Wellek, "Genre Theory, the Lyric, and *Erlebnis*," in *Discriminations: Further Concepts of Criticism* (New Haven, CT: Yale University Press, 1970), 224.

27. Philippe Sollers, quoted in Jonathan Culler, "Toward a Theory of Non-Genre Literature," in *Surfiction*, ed. Raymond Federman, 2nd ed. (Athens: Ohio University Press/Swallow Press, 1981), 255–262.

28. On negative liberty see *Historicizing the Enlightenment*, vol. 1, Intro.

29. Mikhail M. Bakhtin, *The Dialogic Imagination: Four Essays*, ed. Michael Holquist, trans. and ed. Caryl Emerson and Michael Holquist (Austin: University of Texas Press, 1981), 5.

30. Sigmund Freud, "The 'Uncanny'" (1919), in *The Standard Edition of the Complete Psychological Works of Sigmund Freud*, ed. James Strachey and Anna Freud, 24 vols. (London: Hogarth Press, 1955), 17:219, 247 (further citations appear parenthetically in the text).

31. Terry Castle remarks on Freud's Enlightenment historicization of the uncanny in her perceptive introduction to a collection of her essays on eighteenth-century British literature that evoke the uncanny from different angles. I'm indebted to her insight. Terry Castle, "Introduction," in *The Female Thermometer: Eighteenth-Century Culture and the Invention of the Uncanny* (New York: Oxford University Press, 1995), 3–20.

32. F. R. Leavis, *The Great Tradition* (Garden City, NY: Doubleday, 1954), 17.

33. Clifford Siskin, *The Historicity of Romantic Discourse* (New York: Oxford University Press, 1988), 125–147.

34. Viktor Shklovsky, "The Novel as Parody: Sterne's *Tristram Shandy*," in *Theory of Prose* (1925), 2nd ed., trans. Benjamin Sher, intro. Gerald L. Bruns (Elmwood Park, IL: Dalkey Archive Press, 1990), 147–170.

35. Jens Martin Gurr, *Tristram Shandy and the Dialectic of Enlightenment* (Heidelberg: C. Winter, 1999). On Horkheimer and Adorno see *Historicizing the Enlightenment*, vol. 1, intro.

36. E.g., see Rosalind Coward and John Ellis, *Language and Materialism: Developments in Semiology and the Theory of the Subject* (London: Routledge, 1977), 47.

CHAPTER 1 — THE SCIENCES AS A MODEL FOR THE ARTS

1. Jerome Stolnitz, "'Beauty': Some Stages in the History of an Idea," *Journal of the History of Ideas* 22 (April–June 1961): 185–204. On the aesthetic, see also chapter 2 of this volume

2. Paul Oskar Kristeller, "The Modern System of the Arts," in *Renaissance Thought II: Papers on Humanism and the Arts* (New York: Harper & Row, 1965), 163–227.

3. Francis Bacon, *New Organon*, I, in *The Philosophical Works of Francis Bacon*, trans. and ed. Robert L. Ellis and James Spedding, ed. John M. Robertson (London: Routledge and Sons, 1905), aphs. 19, 82 (261, 280) (further citations of this edition appear parenthetically in the text).

4. John Dryden, *Of Dramatic Poesy: An Essay* (1668), in *Dryden: Of Dramatic Poesy and Other Critical Essays*, ed. George Watson, 2 vols. (London: Dent, 1962), 1:25, 26 (further citations appear parenthetically in the text).

5. Bernard Le Bovier de Fontenelle, "A Digression on the Ancients and Moderns," trans. John Hughes (with revisions, 1719), in *The Continental Model: Selected French Critical Essays of the Seventeenth Century, in English Translation*, ed. Scott Elledge and Donald Schier (University of Minnesota Press, 1960; rev. ed., Ithaca, NY: Cornell University Press, 1970), 362. "Cependant afin que les modernes puissent toujours enchérir sur les anciens, il faut que les choses soient d'une espèce à le permettre. L'éloquence et la poésie ne demandent qu'un certain nombre de vues assez borné, et elles dépendent principalement de la vivacité de l'imagination; or les hommes peuvent avoir amassé en peu de siècles un petit nombres de vues, et la vivacité de l'imagination n'a pas besoin d'une longue suite d'expériences, ni d'une grande quantité de règles pour avoir route la perfection dont elle est capable. Mais la physique, la médecine, les mathématiques, sont composées d'un nombre infini de vues, et dépendent de la justesse du raisonnement, qui se perfectionne avec une extrême lenteur, et se perfectionne toujours." Bernard Le Bovier de Fontenelle, "Digression sur les anciens et les modernes," in *Entretiens sur la pluralité des mondes. Digression sur les anciens et les modernes* (1688), ed. Robert Shackleton (Oxford: Clarendon Press, 1955), 166.

6. William Wotton, *Reflections upon Ancient and Modern Learning* (London, 1694), 78, 79, 340.

7. Thomas Sprat, *The History of the Royal Society of London, for the Improving of Natural Knowledge* (London, 1667), 62–63, 99 (further citations appear parenthetically in the text).

8. Robert Hooke, "A General Scheme, or Idea of the Present State of Natural Philosophy, and How Its Defects May Be Remedied by a Methodical Proceeding in the Making Experiments and Collecting Observations" (c. 1668), in *The Posthumous Works of Robert Hooke*, ed. Richard Waller, 1705; facs. rpt. ed. Theodore M. Brown (London: Cass, 1971), 61–62.

9. Aristotle, *Poetics*, in *Introduction to Aristotle*, trans. Ingram Bywater, ed. Richard McKeon (New York: Modern Library, 1947), 1450b–1451a (further citations appear parenthetically in the text).

10. Including members of the society. See Joseph Glanvill, "An Address to the Royal Society," in *Scepsis Scientifica or Confest Ignorance the Way of Science; in an Essay of the Vanity of Dogmatizing and Confident Opinion* (1665), b2v-3r.

11. John Shanahan, "Ben Jonson's Alchemist and Early Modern Laboratory Space," *Journal for Early Modern Cultural Studies* 8, no. 1 (Spring/Summer 2008): 35–66; John Shanahan, "From Drama to Science: Margaret Cavendish as Vanishing Mediator," *Literature Compass* 5, no. 2 (2008): 362–375; John Shanahan, "Theatrical Space and Scientific Space in Thomas Shadwell's Virtuoso," *Studies in English Literature, 1500–1900 (SEL)* 49, no. 3 (Summer 2009): 549–571.

12. Al Coppola, *The Theater of Experiment: Staging Natural Philosophy in Eighteenth-Century Britain* (Oxford: Oxford University Press, 2016), dustjacket.

13. I discuss contributions to this development made by other important figures later in this chapter. For Edward Young see "Mediation as Primal Word: The Arts, the Sciences, and the Origins of the Aesthetic," in *This Is Enlightenment*, ed. Clifford Siskin and William Warner (Chicago: University of Chicago Press, 2010), 396.

14. Joseph Addison, *Spectator*, no. 411 (June 21, 1712), in *The Spectator*, ed. Donald F. Bond, 5 vols. (Oxford: Clarendon Press, 1965).

15. Addison, *Spectator*, nos. 411, 416 (June 21, 27, 1712), in Bond, *The Spectator*.

16. Addison, *Spectator*, nos. 416, 418 (June 27, 30, 1712), in Bond, *The Spectator*.

17. Addison, *Spectator*, no. 411 (June 21, 1712), in Bond, *The Spectator*.

18. Addison, *Spectator*, no. 418 (June 30, 1712), in Bond, *The Spectator*.

19. Samuel Taylor Coleridge, *Biographia Literaria* (1817), ed. George Watson (London: J. M. Dent, 1965), vol. 2, ch. 14, 169. Coleridge first used the phrase, with reference to novel reading, in *Critical Review*, 2nd ser., 19 (February 1797): 195.

20. On the French versus the English attitude toward theatrical illusion, see ch. 2 in the present volume. Corneille's commitment to illusionism is sustained a century later by Diderot.

21. Bernard Le Bovier Fontenelle, *Réflexions sur la poétique* (1742), trans. David Hume (with revisions), in David Hume, "Of Tragedy" (1757), in *Essays Moral, Political, and Literary* (1777), ed. Eugene F. Miller, rev. ed. (Indianapolis: Liberty Classics, 1987), 218–219. See Fontenelle, *Oeuvres Completes*, texte revu par Alain Niderst (Paris: Fayard, 1989), III, sec. 36, 133: "Il est certain qu'au Theatre la representation fait presque l'effet de la realité; mais enfin elle ne fait pas entierement: quelqu'un entraine que l'on soit par la force de Spectacle, quelque empire que les sens et l'i magination prennent sur la raison, il reste toujours au fond de l'esprit je ne sais quelle idée de la faussete de ce qu'on voit. Cette idée, quoique foible et enveloppée, suffit pour diminuer la douleur de voir souffrir quelqu'un que l'on aime, et pour reduire cette douleur au degré ou elle commence a se changer en plaisir. On pleure les malheurs d'un Heros a qui l'on s'est affectionné, et dans le meme moment l'on s'en console, parce qu'on sait que c'est une fiction; et c'est justement de ce mélange de sentimens que se compose une douleur agréable, et des larmes qui font plaisir."

22. Addison, *Spectator*, no. 420 (July 2, 1712), in Bond, *The Spectator*.

23. Edmund Burke, *A Philosophical Enquiry into the Origin of Our Ideas of the Sublime and Beautiful*, ed. J. T. Boulton (London: Routledge, 1958), "Preface," 1 (further citations appear parenthetically in the text). On Locke's and Hume's skepticism, see *Historicizing the Enlightenment*, vol. 1, ch. 3.

24. Samuel Johnson, "Preface" to *The Plays of William Shakespeare* (1765), in *The Yale Edition of the Works of Samuel Johnson*, vol. 7, *Johnson on Shakespeare*, ed. Arthur Sherbo, 23 vols. (New Haven, CT: Yale University Press, 1968), 59–61 (further citations appear parenthetically in the text).

25. David Hume, "Of the Standard of Taste," in *Essays*, 233, 242.

26. On these see *Historicizing the Enlightenment*, vol. 1, ch. 3.

27. Compare Johnson's treatment of the two different senses of "the common" in *Historicizing the Enlightenment*, vol. 1, ch. 5.

28. William Wordsworth, "Preface" to *Lyrical Ballads* (1800), 2nd ed. (1802), in *The Prose Works of William Wordsworth*, ed. W. J. B. Owen and Jane Worthington Smyser

(Oxford: Clarendon Press, 1974), I, 119, 157, 141–142, 131, 133, 123, 124, 125. References are to the 1850 edition, which modifies the second edition of 1802 (further citations appear parenthetically in the text).

29. Although in different terms, John Bender has made a related proposal regarding the coemergence of "scientific factuality" and "manifest fictionality" in the Enlightenment. See "Enlightenment Fiction and the Scientific Hypothesis," in *Ends of Enlightenment* (Stanford, CA: Stanford University Press, 2012), ch. 2.

30. For a fuller discussion see the following chapter in this volume.

31. Edmund Burke, *Reflections on the Revolution in France*, ed. Thomas H. D. Mahoney and Oskar Piest (Indianapolis: Bobbs-Merrill, 1955), 86, 87, 88, 91, 92 (further citations appear parenthetically in the text). Coleridge first used the phrase, with reference to novel reading, in *Critical Review*, 2nd ser., 19 (February 1797): 195.

32. William Godwin, *Enquiry concerning Political Justice* (1793, rev. ed. 1798), bk. 5, ch. 15, 137. Cf. Henry Fielding, *Jonathan Wild* (1743), ed. David Nokes (Harmondsworth: Penguin, 1982), bk. 3, ch. 11, 154–155: "The stage of the world differs from that in Drury Lane principally in this—that whereas, on the latter, the hero or chief figure is almost continually before your eyes, . . . on the former, the hero or great man [i.e., the political leader] is always behind the curtain. . . . To say the truth, a puppet-show will illustrate our meaning better, where it is the master of the show (the great man) who dances and moves everything, . . . but he himself keeps wisely out of sight. . . . Not that any one is ignorant of his being there, . . . but as this (though every one knows it) doth not appear visibly, i.e. to their eyes, no one is ashamed of consenting to be imposed upon. . . . The truth is, they are in the same situation with the readers of romances; who, though they know the whole to be one entire fiction, nevertheless agree to be deceived."

33. Adam Smith, *The Theory of Moral Sentiments*, ed. D. D. Raphael and A. L. Macfie, Glasgow Edition of the Works and Correspondence of Adam Smith (Indianapolis: Liberty Classics, 1982), 29, 30, 9 (further citations appear parenthetically in the text).

34. On virtual witnessing, see *Historicizing the Enlightenment*, vol. 1, ch. 3.

35. Adam Smith, *An Inquiry into the Nature and Causes of the Wealth of Nations*, bk. 1, chs. 4 and 5, ed. R. H. Campbell, A. S. Skinner, and W. B. Todd, Glasgow Edition of the Works and Correspondence of Adam Smith (Indianapolis: Liberty Fund, 1981), 46, 47–48, 49 (further citations appear parenthetically in the text).

36. For a fuller discussion of these matters see *Historicizing the Enlightenment*, vol. 1, ch. 3.

37. For example, see Daniel Defoe, *Review* 6, no. 31 (June 14, 1709); Jonathan Swift, *Examiner*, no. 34 (March 29, 1711).

38. Martinus Scriblerus [Alexander Pope], *Peri Bathous, or of the Art of Sinking in Poetry* (1728), in *Literary Criticism of Alexander Pope*, ed. Bertrand A. Goldgar (Lincoln: University of Nebraska Press, 1965) (further citations appear parenthetically in the text). In the following reading I take seriously the conceptual implications of Pope's parody at the risk of seeming to miss the easy lightness of its humor; the two are, I think, compatible.

39. Swift had already desublimated human culture—empire, philosophy, and religion—in terms of a biological materialism that debased culture to its origins in the anal and sexual functions of the body. See Jonathan Swift, *A Tale of a Tub and A Discourse concerning the Mechanical Operation of the Spirit* (1704, 1710).

40. See *Historicizing the Enlightenment*, vol. 1, intro. and ch. 3.

41. See Michael McKeon, *The Origins of the English Novel, 1600–1740* (Baltimore: Johns Hopkins University Press, 1987), 45–47.

42. Aphra Behn, *Oroonoko; or; The Royal Slave. A True History* (1688), in *Aphra Behn: Oroonoko and Other Writings*, ed. Paul Salzman (Oxford: Oxford University Press, 1998), title page; and *The Fair Jilt; or; the History of Prince Tarquin and Miranda* (1688), in *Aphra Behn: Oroonoko and Other Writings*, 74.

43. Behn, *Oroonoko*, 6, 74.

44. [Aphra Behn], *Love-Letters between a Nobleman and His Sister* (1684, 1685, 1687), ed. Janet Todd (London: Penguin, 1996), 10.

45. Daniel Defoe, *The Life and Strange Surprizing Adventures of Robinson Crusoe, of York, Mariner* (1719), ed. Thomas Keymer and James Kelly (Oxford: Oxford University Press, 2007), title page (further citations appear parenthetically in the text).

46. Eliza Haywood, *The Fair Hebrew: or, a True, but Secret History of Two Jewish Ladies Who lately resided in London* (n.p., 1729), A2v–B1r.

47. Samuel Richardson, *Pamela; or; Virtue Rewarded* (1740), ed. Thomas Keymer and Alice Wakely (Oxford: Oxford University Press, 2001), 3–4, 7, 503 (further citations appear parenthetically in the text).

48. See the preface to Daniel Defoe's *A True Relation of the Apparition of One Mrs. Veal the Next Day after Her Death to One Mrs. Bargrave at Canterbury the 8th of September, 1705* (1706).

49. Daniel Defoe, *The Storm: Or, a Collection of the Most Remarkable Casualties and Disasters Which Happen'd in the Late Dreadful Tempest, Both by Sea and Land* (London, 1704), A2r–v.

50. Benedict Anderson, *Imagined Communities: Reflections on the Origin and Spread of Nationalism* (London: Verso, 1983), ch. 2.

51. See *Historicizing the Enlightenment*, vol. 1, ch. 3.

52. On the yet broader applications of this hypothesis, see Michael McKeon, *The Secret History of Domesticity: Public, Private, and the Division of Knowledge* (Baltimore: Johns Hopkins University Press, 2005), 106–108.

53. Thomas Hobbes, "Of Dominion Paternall and Despoticall," ch. 20 in pt. 2 of *Leviathan, or the Matter, Forme, and Power of a Common-wealth Ecclesiasticall and Civill* (1651), 107.

54. John Bramhall, *Castigations of Mr. Hobbes His Last Animadversions in the Case concerning Liberty and Universal Necessity Wherein All His Exceptions about That Controversie Are Fully Satisfied* (1657), 507.

55. William Petty, "Preface," in *Political Arithmetick, or; A Discourse concerning the Extent and Value of Lands, People, Buildings [. . .] as the Same Relates to Every Country in General* (1690), sig. a3v–a4r, a4v.

56. John Locke, *Second Treatise of Government: An Essay concerning the True Original, Extent, and End of Civil Government* (1690), in *Two Treatises of Government*, ed. Peter Laslett, 2nd ed. (Cambridge: Cambridge University Press, 1967), 319, para. 49.

57. For a different but related analysis of this section of the *Second Treatise*, see *Historicizing the Enlightenment*, vol. 1, ch. 3.

58. See McKeon, *Secret History*, 30–33; *Origins*, 189–205.

59. In *Historicizing the Enlightenment*, vol. 1, ch. 3, I argue that chattel slavery is a fundamental departure from Enlightenment, but not from capitalist, universalism.

60. See McKeon, *Origins*, ch. 4.

61. Glanvill, "Address to the Royal Society," b2v–3r.

62. Bernard Mandeville, *The Fable of the Bees* (1705, 1714), ed. F. B. Kaye (Oxford: Clarendon Press, 1924; Indianapolis: Liberty Fund Classics, 1988), 1:69.

63. Daniel Defoe, *Serious Reflections during the Life and Surprising Adventures of Robinson Crusoe with His Vision of the Angelic World* (1720), in *The Works of Daniel Defoe*, ed. G. H. Maynadier, 16 vols. (New York: George D. Sproul, 1903–1904), 3:98.

64. Hooke, "General Scheme," 61–62.

65. Henry Fielding, *The History of the Adventures of Joseph Andrews, and of His Friend Mr. Abraham Adams. Written in Imitation of the Manner of Cervantes, Author of Don Quixote* (1742), ed. Douglas Brooks-Davies and Thomas Keymer (Oxford: Oxford University Press, 1999), bk. 3, ch. 1: 162.

66. Laurence Sterne, *The Life and Opinions of Tristram Shandy, Gentleman*, ed. Ian Watt (Boston: Houghton Mifflin, 1965), bk. 2, ch. 8: 79 (further citations appear parenthetically in the text).

67. We may want to question this difference between the two media if we consider the way Buckingham's *The Rehearsal* (1671–1672) represents the two dramatic temporalities of rehearsal and performance. See Michael McKeon, "Marvell Discovers the Public Sphere," in *Texts and Readers in the Age of Marvell*, ed. Christopher D'Addario and Matthew C. Augustine (Manchester: Manchester University Press, 2018), 60–63.

68. John Locke, *An Essay concerning Human Understanding* (1689), ed. Peter H. Nidditch (Oxford: Clarendon Press, 1975), bk. 1, ch. 1, 43, para. 1.

69. David Hume, *A Treatise of Human Nature* (1739), ed. L. A. Selby-Bigge and Peter H. Nidditch, 2nd ed. (Oxford: Clarendon Press, 1978), xviii–xix (further citations appear parenthetically in the text).

70. For a fuller discussion of these matters see *Historicizing the Enlightenment*, vol. 1, ch. 3, "Extending Experiment II: Beyond Observables."

CHAPTER 2 — FROM ANCIENT MIMESIS TO MODERN REALISM

1. See Eric A. Havelock, *Preface to Plato* (Cambridge, MA: Harvard University Press, 1963).

2. τᾱς εικόνας τᾱς μαλιστα ηκριβωμένᾱς. Aristotle, *Poetics*, in *The Basic Works of Aristotle*, trans. Ingram Bywater, ed. Richard McKeon (New York: Random House, 1941), 1448b (further citations are given parenthetically in the text).

3. In passing, it's worth noticing that Plato and especially Aristotle practice the same kind of explicit analytic method that I've associated with the European Enlightenment.

4. Douglas Lane Patey, *Probability & Literary Form: Philosophic Theory & Literary Practice in the Augustan Age* (Cambridge: Cambridge University Press, 1984), 77. Liddell and Scott translate εικός as "like truth, i.e. likely, probable, reasonable." See Henry George Liddell and Robert Scott, *A Greek-English Lexicon* (Oxford: Clarendon Press, 1976), 484.

5. Bernard Weinberg, *A History of Literary Criticism in the Italian Renaissance*, 2 vols. (Chicago: University of Chicago Press, 1961), 675 (further citations are given parenthetically in the text). All translations from the Italian and Latin are by Bernard Weinberg.

6. Antonio Riccoboni, *Aristotelis Ars Rhetorica and Aristotelis Ars Poetica [and De re comica]* (Venice: Paolo Meietti, Bibliopolam Patauinum, 1579); Torquato Tasso, *Del Giudizio sovra la sua Gerusalemme da lui medesimo riformata. Le Prose Diverse di Torquato Tasso*, ed. Cesare Guasti, 2 vols. (Florence: Successori Le Monnier, 1875); see Weinberg, 587, 1057–1058.

7. Honoré d'Urfé, *L'Astrée* (Paris: Toussainct du Bray, 1607–1627).

8. Roman à clef: Erica Harth, *Ideology and Culture in Seventeenth-Century France* (Ithaca, NY: Cornell University Press, 1983), 38–41. Vraisemblable: Harth, 39–40nn.5, 6. Harth cites Charles Sorel, *La Bibliotheque françoise* (Paris: Compagnie des libraires du Palais, 1664); and the preface to Madeleine de Scudéry's *Ibrahim ou l'illustre Bassa* (Paris: de Sommaville, 1641), written by her brother Georges. The English translator of *Ibrahim* (Henry Cogan, 1652) renders Georges's "vraisemblable" regarding *L'Astrée* as "truly resembling." See Baudouin Millet, ed., *In Praise of Fiction: Prefaces to Romances and Novels, 1650–1750* (Leuven: Peeters, 2017), 36.

9. Millet, *In Praise of Fiction*, 67.

10. See Michael McKeon, *The Origins of the English Novel, 1600–1740*, 2nd ed. (Baltimore: Johns Hopkins University Press, 2002), 36–47.

11. Paul Scarron (*Le Roman Comique*, 1651) and Antoine Furetière (*Le Roman bourgeois*, 1666) re-enact Sorel's Cervantic method, the latter more effectively.

12. Charles Sorel, *The Extravagant Shepherd. The Anti-romance: or, The History of the Shepherd Lysis*, trans. John Davies (London: Thomas Heath, 1653), e2r–e2v.

13. Denis Vairasse d'Allais, *The History of the Sevarites or Sevarambi* (London: Henry Brome, 1675), A3v–A4r.

14. Marie, Comtesse d'Aulnoy, *The Ingenious and Diverting Letters of the Lady———Travels into Spain* (London: Samuel Crouch, 1691), A4r.

15. D'Aulnoy, *Ingenious and Diverting Letters of the Lady*, B1v.

16. Pierre Bayle, *The Dictionary Historical and Critical of Mr Peter Bayle* [1697], trans. P. Desmaizeaux, 2nd ed. (London: Knapton et al., 1734–1748), IV, 365–366.

17. See Arthur J. Tieje, "A Peculiar Phase of the Theory of Realism in Pre-Richardsonian Fiction," *PMLA* 28, no. 2 (1913): 213–252.

18. See Harth, *Ideology and Culture*, 171–179; also Robert Darnton, *The Literary Underground of the Old Regime* (Cambridge, MA: Harvard University Press, 1982).

19. René Rapin, *Instructions pour l'histoire* (Paris: Sébastien Mabre Cramoisy, 1677), trans. Erica Harth in *Ideology and Culture*, 145.

20. René Rapin, *Réflexions sur la poetique D'Aristote* (Paris: François Muguet, 1674), trans. Douglas Lane Patey in *Probability & Literary Form*, 81.

21. Pierre Corneille, "Of the Three Unities of Action, Time, and Place" [1660], in *The Continental Model: Selected French Critical Essays of the Seventeenth Century, in English Translation*, ed. Donald Schier and Scott Elledge, rev. ed (Ithaca, NY: Cornell University Press, 1970), 109–110 (further citations appear parenthetically in the text).

22. For two valuable studies that take distinct approaches to the subject, see Mary Poovey, *A History of the Modern Fact: Problems of Knowledge in the Sciences of Wealth and Society* (Chicago: University of Chicago Press, 1998); and Barbara J. Shapiro, *A Culture of Fact: England, 1550–1720* (Ithaca, NY: Cornell University Press, 2000).

23. See ch. 1 in this volume; also McKeon, *Origins*, pts. 1 and 3; and Nicholas D. Paige, *Before Fiction: The Ancien Régime of the Novel* (Philadelphia: University of Pennsylvania Press, 2011), IV.9.

24. Patey, *Probability & Literary Form*, 77–78, 83. English translations of d'Urfé, d'Aulnoy, Rapin, Corneille, and Du Bos that render "vraisemblance" as "probability" provide concrete evidence of this preference. In addition to texts already cited, see Rapin, *Réflexions sur la poetique D'Aristote*, A7r, a2r. Thomas Rymer translates Rapin's "vraisemblance" into "probability." René Rapin, *Reflections on Aristotle's Treatise of Poesie*, trans. Thomas Rymer (London: H. Herringman, 1674); Patey translates it back. See also Jean-Baptiste Du Bos, *Réflexions Critiques sur la Poesie et sur la Peinture. Nouvelle edition* (Paris: Pierre-Jean Mariette, 1733), sec. 30; and *Critical Reflections on Poetry, Painting and Music*, 5th ed., trans. Thomas Nugent, 3 vols. (London: John Nourse, 1748), ch. 30, vol. 1. Other evidence is not hard to find: see Millet, *In Praise of Fiction*, 53, 83, 90, 195, 247, 256, 297, 431; Ioan Williams, ed., *Novel and Romance, 1700–1800: A Documentary Record* (New York: Barnes & Noble, 1970), 34, 61, 114, 132–133, 139–140, 151, 193, 257, 302, 309, 310, 341, 393.

25. Barbara J. Shapiro, *Probability and Certainty in Seventeenth-Century England: A Study of the Relationships between Natural Science, Religion, History, Law, and Literature* (Princeton, NJ: Princeton University Press, 1983), 25–26, 32, 33, 37, 38; Patey, *Probability & Literary Form*, ch. 1; and Ian Hacking, *The Emergence of Probability* (Cambridge: Cambridge University Press, 1975), ch. 3.

26. John Locke, *An Essay concerning Human Understanding* (1689), ed. Peter H. Nidditch (Oxford: Clarendon Press, 1975), bk. 4, ch. 16, para. 6, 661.

27. Shapiro, *Probability*, 283n.158.

28. John Dryden, *Of Dramatic Poesy: An Essay* [1668], in *John Dryden. Of Dramatic Poesy and Other Critical Essays*, ed. George Watson, 2 vols. (London: Dutton, 1962), 1:26 (further citations appear parenthetically in the text).

29. Joseph Addison, *Spectator*, no. 418 (June 30, 1712), in *The Spectator*, ed. Donald F. Bond, 5 vols. (Oxford: Clarendon Press, 1965).

30. Addison, *Spectator*, nos. 411, 416, 418 (June 21, 27, 30, 1712), in Bond, *The Spectator*.

31. Addison, *Spectator*, no. 418 (June 30, 1712), in Bond, *The Spectator*.

32. Henry Fielding, *The History of the Adventures of Joseph Andrews and of His Friend Mr. Abraham Adams* [1742] and *An Apology for the Life of Mrs. Shamela Andrews* [1741], ed. Douglas Brooks-Davies and Thomas Keymer (Oxford: Oxford University Press, 1999), bk. 3, ch. 1, 162 (further citations are given parenthetically in the text).

33. I'll note in passing *Tristram Shandy* (1759–1767), in which Laurence Sterne follows Fielding's lead in applying a critique of the dramatic unities to narrative form (see vol. 2, ch. 8).

34. Williams, *Novel and Romance*, 393.

35. Michael McKeon, ed., *Theory of the Novel: A Historical Approach* (Baltimore: Johns Hopkins University Press, 2000), 607–608.

36. McKeon, *Theory of the Novel*, 608.

37. Douglas Lane Patey, "Ancients and Moderns," in *The Cambridge History of Literary Criticism*, vol. 4, *The Eighteenth Century*, ed. H. B. Nisbet and Claude Rawson (Cambridge: Cambridge University Press, 1997), 60.

38. Du Bos, *Critical Reflections on Poetry*, 1:22–23.

39. Du Bos, *Critical Reflections on Poetry*, 1: 24. For other formulations of realism in early French theory, see, e.g., Jean-François Marmontel, *Éléments de Littérature* [1787], ed. Sophie Le Ménahèze (Paris: Éditions Desjonquères, 2005), especially the entries "Drame," "Illusion," "Poète," and "Vraisemblance," 418–425, 633–638, 926–936, 1164–1179.

40. See Michael McKeon, "Watt's Rise of the Novel within the Tradition of the Rise of the Novel," *Eighteenth-Century Fiction* 12, nos. 2–3 (January–April 2000): 253–276 for this comparison, in contrast to Ian Watt, *The Rise of the Novel: Studies in Defoe, Richardson, and Fielding* (London: Chatto and Windus, 1957).

41. For a fuller argument, see Michael McKeon, "The Eighteenth-Century Challenge to Narrative Theory," in *Narrative Concepts in the Study of Eighteenth-Century Literature*, ed. Liisa Steinby and Aino Mäkikalli (Amsterdam: Amsterdam University Press, 2017), 39–77.

42. Gérard Genette, *Narrative Discourse: An Essay in Method* [1972], trans. Jane B. Lewin, foreword by Jonathan Culler (Ithaca, NY: Cornell University Press, 1980).

43. Roland Barthes, "The Reality Effect" [1968], trans. R. Carter, ed. Tzvetan Todorov, in *French Literary Theory Today: A Reader* (Cambridge: Cambridge University Press, 1982), 11, 12 (further citations appear parenthetically in the text). Genette calls these words "details" or "descriptions." Genette, *Narrative Discourse*, 165, 166.

44. Genette, *Narrative Discourse*, 165, 166, 170, 171; see McKeon, "Eighteenth-Century Challenge," 47, 48, 49.

45. Catherine Gallagher, "The Rise of Fictionality," in *The Novel*, vol. 1, *History, Geography, and Culture*, ed. Franco Moretti (Princeton, NJ: Princeton University Press, 2006), 337.

46. Catherine Gallagher, *Nobody's Story: The Vanishing Acts of Women Writers in the Marketplace, 1670–1920* (Chicago: University of Chicago Press, 1994), xvi (further citations appear parenthetically in the text).

47. Nicholas Paige supports Gallagher's thesis that before the novel, narrative was taken to refer to actually existent subjects, replacing her caution with a boldly spurious misreading of the *Poetics*. According to Paige, Aristotle stipulates as a generic rule that "tragedy deals with real people" (Paige, *Before Fiction*, 8).

48. Michael McKeon, *The Secret History of Domesticity: Public, Private, and the Division of Knowledge* (Baltimore: Johns Hopkins University Press, 2005), 746n.159 (my response to the first version of this argument in *Nobody's Story*).

49. McKeon, *Secret History of Domesticity*, 746n.159.

50. See McKeon, *Secret History of Domesticity*, chs. 1, 2, 4, and 6.

CHAPTER 3 — THE HISTORICITY OF LITERARY CONVENTIONS

1. Sigmund Freud, "Family Romances," in *Jensen's 'Gradiva' and Other Works*, vol. 9 of *The Standard Edition of the Complete Psychological Works of Sigmund Freud*, trans. and ed. James Strachey and Anna Freud (London: Hogarth Press, 1959), 237, 239.

2. This is what Otto Rank calls "the myth of the birth of the hero": *The Myth of the Birth of the Hero and Other Writings* (1914), ed. Peter Freund (New York: Vintage, 1959), 14–64 for "The Circle of Myths."

3. James Frazer, *The New Golden Bough* (1890), ed. and abr. Theodor H. Gaster (New York: Mentor, 1964), pts. 3 and 4.

4. H. J. Rose, *A Handbook of Greek Mythology* (New York: E. P. Dutton, 1959), 182–196.

5. F. W. Maitland, *The Constitutional History of England: A Course of Lectures Delivered by F. W. Maitland* (1908; rpt., Cambridge: Cambridge University Press, 1965), 37, 156–157; G. O. Sayles, *The Medieval Foundations of England* (New York: A. S. Barnes, 1961), 211.

6. F. L. Ganshof, *Feudalism*, trans. Philip Grierson, 3rd English ed. (New York: Harper Torchbooks, 1964), 139–140.

7. Peter Laslett, *The World We Have Lost Further Explored*, 3rd ed. (New York: Charles Scribner's Sons, 1984), 239–241; Jack Goody, *The Development of the Family and Marriage in Europe* (Cambridge: Cambridge University Press, 1983), 44; Lawrence Stone and Jeanne C. Fawtier Stone, *An Open Elite? England, 1540–1880* (Oxford: Clarendon Press, 1984), 397.

8. G. M. Vogt, "Gleanings for the History of a Sentiment: Generositas Virtus, Non Sanguis," *Journal of English and Germanic Philology* 24, no. 1 (1925): 102–124.

9. Michael McKeon, *The Origins of the English Novel, 1600–1740* (Baltimore: Johns Hopkins University Press, 1987; 2nd ed., 2002), 132–133, 150–159, 164–167, 189–211.

10. Daniel Defoe, *The True-Born Englishman. A Satyr* (London, 1700), 20, 22; *The Compleat English Gentleman* (writ. 1728–1729), ed. Karl D. Bülbring (London: D. Nutt, 1890), 16–17.

11. William Sprigg, *A Modest Plea for an Equal Common-Wealth against Monarchy* (London: Giles Calvert, 1659), 62–63, 68–69.

12. Edmund Bolton, *The Cities Advocate, in This Case or Question of Honor and Armes; Whether Apprentiship Extinguisheth Gentry?* (London: William Lee, 1629), pt. 4, 52; Daniel Defoe, *The Complete English Tradesman*, 2nd ed., 2 vols. (London: Charles Rivington, 1727), 1:311.

13. Thomas Deloney, *Thomas of Reading* (1600), in *Shorter Novels: Elizabethan*, ed. George Saintsbury and Philip Henderson (London: J. M. Dent, Everyman's Library, 1972), 98; Gervase Holles, *Memorials of the Holles Family, 1493–1656*, ed. A. C. Wood, Camden Society, 3rd ser., vol. 55 (London: Offices of the Society, 1937), 34–35.

14. *Charles II's Escape from Worcester: A Collection of Narratives Assembled by Samuel Pepys*, ed. William Matthews (Berkeley: University of California Press, 1966), 40, 50, 88, 94, 96, 107, 160.

15. On the episodes of the black box and the warming pan, see Michael McKeon, *The Secret History of Domesticity: Public, Private, and the Division of Knowledge* (Baltimore: Johns Hopkins University Press, 2005), 499–503, 549–557. On the preference for internal, "religious nobility" over external, genealogical nobility in the deposal and replacement of James II, see McKeon, *Origins*, 181–182.

16. "Lord of Learne," ll. 285–286, and "The Nutt browne mayd," ll. 135–137, 199–200, in *Bishop Percy's Folio Manuscript. Ballads and Romances*, ed. J. W. Hales and F. J. Furnivall, 3 vols. (London: N. Trübner, 1868), 1:193; 3:182, 184.

17. Robert Greene, *Penelope's Web* (1587), second tale ("Calamus and Cratyna"), in *Prose*, vol. 5 of *Life and Complete Works in Prose and Verse of Robert Greene*, ed. Alexander B. Grosart, 15 vols. (1881–1886; New York: Russell and Russell, 1964), 203, 204, 215, 216; Gabriel Harvey, "A Noble Mans Sute to a Cuntrie Maid," in *Letter-Book of Gabriel Harvey, 1573–1780*, ed. Edward J. L. Scott, Camden Society, n.s., 33 (London: Nichols and Sons, 1884), 144, 145.

18. T[homas] H[ooker,] *The Christians Two Chiefe Lessons viz. Selfe-Deniall, and Selfe-Tryall. As Also the Priviledge of Adoption and Triall Thereof. In Three Treatises on the Texts Following: viz. Matt. 16.24. 2 Cor. 13.5. Iohn 1.12, 13* (London: P. Stephens and C. Meredith, 1640), 288; John Bunyan, *Grace Abounding to the Chief of Sinners* (1666), ed. Roger Sharrock (Oxford: Clarendon Press, 1962), 32; Thomas Edwards, "The Holy Choice" (1625), quoted in Michael Walzer, *The Revolution of the Saints: A Study in the Origins of Radical Politics* (Cambridge, MA: Harvard University Press, 1965), 235.

19. Samuel Richardson, *Pamela; or, Virtue Rewarded* (1740), ed. Thomas Keymer and Alice Wakely (Oxford: Oxford University Press, 2001), 53 (further citations appear parenthetically in the text).

20. For Pamela's refutation of the purity of lineages, see 258. For Mr. B. on Pamela as a novel, see 231–232 (but the terms themselves are not clearly distinguished here).

21. Henry Fielding, *The History of the Adventures of Joseph Andrews, and of His Friend Mr. Abraham Adams. Written in Imitation of the Manner of Cervantes, Author of Don Quixote* (London, 1742), in *Joseph Andrews and Shamela*, ed. Douglas Brooks-Davies and Thomas Keymer (Oxford: Oxford University Press, 1999), 33, 132–133 (further citations appear parenthetically in the text).

22. See McKeon, *Secret History*, ch. 6. On the parodic uses Fielding makes of Joseph's "feminine" chastity, see McKeon, *Origins*, 398–400.

23. See *Historicizing the Enlightenment*, vol. 1, chap. 4.

24. [Nathaniel Lancaster], *The Pretty Gentleman: or, Softness of Manners Vindicated from the False Ridicule Exhibited under the Character of William Fribble, Esq.* (London: M. Cooper, 1747), 25–26.

25. Ruth Perry, *Novel Relations: The Transformation of Kinship in English Literature and Culture, 1748–1818* (Cambridge: Cambridge University Press, 2004).

26. Frances Burney, *Evelina or the History of a Young Lady's Entrance into the World* (1778), ed. Edward A. Bloom and Vivien Jones (Oxford: Oxford University Press, 2002), 51–53, 69–72, 85–87 (further citations appear parenthetically in the text).

27. For "filiation/affiliation," see Richard Braverman, *Plots and Counterplots: Sexual Politics and the Body Politic in English Literature, 1660–1730* (Cambridge: Cambridge University Press, 1993).

28. Jane Austen, *Pride and Prejudice* (1813), ed. James Kinsley, Frank W. Bradbrook, and Isobel Armstrong (Oxford: Oxford University Press, 1990), 60, 61 (further citations appear parenthetically in the text).

29. Not long after, Mr. Bennet's viewpoint is again validated by the narrator's, this time regarding Mr. Collins (48, 53).

CHAPTER 4 — THE HISTORICITY OF LITERARY GENRES

1. At this point a few words on terminology are necessary. "Eclogue" means simply "selection." Virgil called his eclogues not "pastorals" (from the Latin "herdsman" or "shepherd") but "bucolics" (from the Greek "cowherd") after his master Theocritus. "Georgic" is a Latinization of the Greek for "the facts of farming." What we call Theocritus's "idylls" are not limited to themes of rustic life and were defined by him not thematically but metrically as a subcategory of "epos," which shares its hexameters. Theocritus, *Idylls*, in *Greek Bucolic Poets*, trans. J. M. Edmonds, Loeb Classical Library, vol. 28 (Cambridge, MA: Harvard University Press, 1912).

2. Virgil, *Georgics*, in *The Works of Virgil Translated by John Dryden*, intro. by James Kinsley (Oxford: Oxford University Press, 1961). Compare the useful discrimination between "hard" and "soft" primitivism: the former conceives natural existence as meager and arduous, the latter as indulgent and beneficent. See Arthur O. Lovejoy and

George Boas, *Primitivism and Related Ideas in Antiquity* (Baltimore: Johns Hopkins University Press, 1935), 1:10–11.

3. Virgil, Eclogue 2, ll. 28–30, 56–57 (trans. Paul Alpers), in Paul Alpers, *The Singer of the Eclogues: A Study of Virgilian Pastoral* (Berkeley: University of California Press, 1979), 16–19.

4. Horace, Epode 2, ll. 1–4, 67–70, in *The Complete Works of Horace*, trans. Charles E. Passage (New York: Frederick Ungar, 1983), 99–101.

5. Frank Kermode, editor's introduction to *English Pastoral Poetry from the Beginnings to Marvell: An Anthology*, ed. Frank Kermode (New York: Norton, 1972), 14 (further citations appear parenthetically in the text).

6. Hesiod, *Works and Days and Theogony*, trans. Stanley Lombardo, intro. Robert Lambertson (Indianapolis: Hackett, 1993).

7. See, respectively, the fifth eclogue and the first idyll.

8. George Puttenham, *The Arte of English Poesie* (London, 1589), 30–31.

9. Samuel Johnson, *The Lives of the English Poets; and a Criticism on Their Works* (1779; London, 1795), 1:202.

10. Raymond Williams, *The Country and the City* (New York: Oxford University Press, 1973), 16 (further citations appear parenthetically in the text).

11. I use this term, the narrative version of "the aesthetic," to refer to the understanding arrived at over the course of the Enlightenment that the novel combines the detailed representation of common life with the self-conscious and explicit acknowledgment that this representation is artifactual, not factual. For my full discussion, see chs. 1 and 2 in the present volume.

12. Kermode's thinking about, and knowledge of, pastoral goes beyond this acute but relatively brief introduction. For a fuller sense of his sophisticated and erudite scholarship on Renaissance pastoral forms and their rootedness in both antiquity and the encounter with the New World, see Kermode's seventy-five-page introduction to *The Tempest* in *The Arden Edition of the Works of William Shakespeare* (Cambridge, MA: Harvard University Press, 1954).

13. See E. A. Wrigley, "Urban Growth and Agricultural Change: England and the Continent in the Early Modern Period," in *People, Cities, and Wealth: The Transformation of Traditional Society* (London: Blackwell, 1987), 174, 177, 189–191, and passim. For the purpose of these data, "the early modern period" ends around 1800 but has a terminus a quo that varies from 1520 to 1600. Correlations between these figures are therefore approximate.

14. Wrigley, "Urban Growth and Agricultural Change," 170, table 7.4.

15. At this point in my argument and in order to sustain its continuity I repeat several paragraphs of the account provided in vol. 1, ch. 3 of *Historicizing the Enlightenment*.

16. Jonathan Parry and Maurice Bloch, eds., *Money and the Morality of Exchange* (Cambridge: Cambridge University Press, 1989), introduction, 29.

17. Cf. Francis Bacon's usage in "Of the True Greatness of Kingdoms and Estates," no. 29 in *Essays or Counsels Civil and Moral* (1612), in *The Philosophical Works of Francis Bacon*, trans. and ed. Robert L. Ellis and James Spedding, ed. John M. Robertson (London: Routledge, 1905), 770–774.

18. Daniel Defoe, *The Compleat English Gentleman* (writ. 1728–1729), ed. Karl D. Bülbring (London: Nutt, 1890), 62–63.

19. See Robert Brenner, "The Agrarian Roots of European Capitalism," in *The Brenner Debate: Agrarian Class Structure and Economic Development in Pre-industrial Europe*, ed. T. H. Ashton and C.H.E. Philpin (Cambridge: Cambridge University Press, 1985), 291–299; and his *Merchants and Revolution: Commercial Change, Political Conflict, and London's Overseas Traders, 1550–1653* (1993; rpt., London: Verso, 2003), 647–653. My summary of Brenner's hypothesis is indebted to Ellen Meiksins Wood, *The Origin of Capitalism: A Longer View* (London: Verso, 2002).

20. Jean-Christophe Agnew, *Worlds Apart: The Market and the Theater in Anglo-American Thought, 1550–1750* (Cambridge: Cambridge University Press, 1986), 41–42 and ch. 1.

21. For a fuller discussion see *Historicizing the Enlightenment*, vol. 1, ch. 4.

22. Joseph Addison, *Spectator*, no. 69 (May 19, 1711), in *The Spectator*, ed. Donald F. Bond, 5 vols. (Oxford: Clarendon Press, 1965).

23. See Margot C. Finn, *The Character of Credit: Personal Debt in English Culture, 1740–1914* (Cambridge: Cambridge University Press, 2003).

24. Jonathan Swift, *The Examiner*, no. 13 (November 2, 1710) and no. 34 (March 29, 1711), in *The Prose Works of Jonathan Swift*, ed. Herbert Davis (Oxford: Blackwell, 1940), 3:6–7, 119.

25. Daniel Defoe, *A Review of the State of the English Nation*, 3, no. 126 (October 22, 1706); 5, no. 107 (December 2, 1708); 6, nos. 31, 32 (June 14, 16, 1709); Addison, *Spectator*, no. 3 (March 3, 1711), in Bond, *The Spectator*.

26. Karl Marx, *Manifesto of the Communist Party* (1848), https://www.marxists.org/archive/marx/works/1848/communist-manifesto/.

27. Friedrich Engels and Karl Marx, *The German Ideology* (writ. 1845–1846, pub. 1932), 2000, pt. 1, D, https://www.marxists.org/archive/marx/works/download/Marx_The_German_Ideology.pdf.

28. E. P. Thompson, "The Patricians and the Plebs," in *Customs in Common: Studies in Traditional Popular Culture* (London: Penguin, 1991), ch. 2.

29. Cf. Marx's well-known use of "parody" in *The Eighteenth Brumaire of Louis Bonaparte* (1852).

30. In some cases this evidence represents, on the level of content, the change in the genre as the direct product of material change. But in many cases, the evidence is not of a causal but of an analogous formal relationship between the emergence of capitalism and the reform of pastoral. In *Historicizing the Enlightenment*, vol. 1, ch. 3, I suggest how Marx's use of "form" as a category of analysis might adumbrate this analogy.

31. Thomas Tickell, *Guardian*, nos. 28, 30 (April 13, 15, 1713), in *The Guardian*, ed. John C. Stephens (Lexington: University Press of Kentucky, 1982).

32. Stock names for pastoral nymphs, which by the eighteenth century had become for many poets, including Swift himself in other poems, shorthand for bad poetry.

33. Richard Steele, *Tatler*, no. 9 (April 30, 1709), in *The Tatler*, ed. Donald F. Bond, 3 vols. (Oxford: Clarendon Press, 1987). The Swift scholar Irvin Ehrenpreis, discussing the generic complexity of the "Description," is in no doubt that it's both a pastoral and a reflection on pastoral. Irvin Ehrenpreis, *Swift: The Man, His Works and the Age* (London: Methuen, 1967), 2:248–249.

34. Swift was unrivaled in his skill at turning pastoral to a variety of parodic purposes. His most radical reduction of rustic folk is probably "A Pastoral Dialogue" (1732).

35. Among the best known are Lady Mary Wortley Montagu's *Six Town Eclogues* (1747).

36. John Evelyn, *Fumifugium: or The Inconveniencie of the Aer and Smoak of London Dissipated* (London, 1661).

37. John Milton, *Paradise Lost* (1667, 1674), bk. 9, ll. 425, 444–452, 455–457, in *John Milton: Complete Poems and Major Prose*, ed. Merritt Y. Hughes (New York: Odyssey Press, 1957).

38. On the imaginative virtuality of the emergent market, see also the frontispiece to this volume, which depicts these several "walks" within the courtyard of the Royal Exchange; courtyard is pictured on the cover.

39. Andrew Marvell, "The Garden" (writ. c. 1668), ll. 33–40, in *The Poems of Andrew Marvell*, ed. Nigel Smith (London: Pearson Longman, 2003); Addison, *Spectator*, no. 69 (May 19, 1711), in Bond, *The Spectator*.

40. In this respect, pastoral and georgic—or at least their abstract types—lack their usual correlativity. The eighteenth-century resurgence of georgic, and of its confident attention to the improvement of nature by art, directly reflected an Enlightenment impatience with ancient and unexamined principles. But the transformation of pastoral was just that sort of examination, a subtle experiment in comparing supposed incomparables.

41. Addison, *Spectator*, no. 131 (July 31, 1711), in Bond, *The Spectator*.

42. Walpole to Mann, October 3, 1743, in *A Selection of the Letters of Horace Walpole*, ed. W. S. Lewis, 2 vols. (New York: Harper, 1926), 1:32; James Boswell, *Boswell's London Journal, 1762–1763*, ed. Frederick A. Pottle (New York: McGraw-Hill, 1950), 96. On the commercialization of leisure, see Penelope J. Corfield, *The Impact of English Towns, 1700–1800* (Oxford: Oxford University Press, 1982), ch. 4.

43. Steele, *Tatler*, no. 143 (March 9, 1710), in Bond, *The Tatler*.

44. John Philips, *The Splendid Shilling. An Imitation of Milton* (1701; 3rd ed., London, 1719). Philips's poem received much praise for its burlesque of Milton's poetic style.

45. Brendan O Hehir, *Expans'd Hieroglyphicks: A Study of John Denham's Coopers Hill* (Berkeley: University of California Press, 1969), 1642 text, 109–134 (further citations appear parenthetically in the text).

46. *Coopers-Hill* was republished in 1668, when the balance of powers had been reversed once more with the Restoration of the Stuart line. However, the poem now appears in a collection of Denham's poetry and is a virtual reprint of the 1655 version: Brendan O Hehir, *Harmony From Discords: A life of John Denham* (Berkeley: University of California Press, 1968), 236.

47. John Dyer, "Grongar Hill," in *John Dyer: Selected Poetry and Prose*, ed. John Goodridge (Nottingham, UK: Trent Editions, 2000), ll. 1–6. Citations of Dyer's *The Fleece*, excerpted from this same edition, appear parenthetically in this chapter by page numbers.

48. E. A. Wrigley, "A Simple Model of London's Importance in Changing English Society and Economy, 1650–1750," in *People, Cities, and Wealth: The Transformation of Traditional Society* (London: Blackwell, 1987), 133.

49. On this, see Steele, *Tatler*, no. 144 (March 11, 1710), in Bond, *The Tatler*.

50. William Cowper, *The Task* (1785), bk. 1, ll. 715–719, 749, in William Cowper, *The Task and Selected Other Poems*, ed. James Sambrook (London: Longman, 1994).

51. Daniel Defoe, *A Tour Thro' the Whole Island of Great Britain, Divided into Circuits or Journies, Giving a Particular and Entertaining Account of Whatever Is Curious, and Worth Observation; in Three Volumes* (1724–1726), vol. 2, letter 5. Further quotations come from this letter.

52. Richard Steele, *Spectator*, no. 454 (August 11, 1712).

53. Thomas Legg [attribution by Eighteenth Century Collections Online], *Low-Life: or One Half of the World, Knows Not How the Other Half Live. Being a Critical Account of What Is Transacted by People of Almost All Religions, Nations, Circumstances, and Sizes of Understanding, in the Twenty-Four Hours between Saturday-Night and Monday-Morning* (London, [1755?]), v, vi (hereafter cited parenthetically in the text).

54. The logic of this schematic historical development in conceiving categorial relations—from classical distinction to Enlightenment separation to Enlightenment conflation—is a fundamental argument of the present volume; see the introduction. Gotthold Ephraim Lessing, *Laocoon: An Essay upon the Limits of Painting and Poetry* (1766), trans. Edward Allen McCormick (Baltimore: Johns Hopkins University Press, 1984), sec. 15, 16. For a fuller discussion of this Scottish Enlightenment innovation, see *Historicizing the Enlightenment*, vol. 1, intro.

55. Legg's experiment might be compared to Robert Henry's *The History of Great Britain from the First Invasion of It by the Romans under Julius Caesar. Written on a New Plan* (1771). Henry's new plan entails ten books that in ten periods cover the entire chronology in diachronic order, but each of which is internally ordered synchronically, proceeding through the same series of seven chapters that are devoted to the same topics (civil and military history, religion, laws, learning, arts, commerce, and manners). Thanks to Mark Phillips for bringing this work to my attention.

The Enlightenment experiment in conflating time and space notably features the Scottish Enlightenment coordination of diachrony and synchrony, as well as its hypothesis of stadial theory, which posits for all spatially fixed cultures a temporal development through the same series of stages (see note 54 in this chapter).

56. Alexander Pope, "A Discourse on Pastoral Poetry" (1709), in *The Poems of Alexander Pope. A One-Volume Edition of the Twickenham Text*, ed. John Butt (New Haven, CT: Yale University Press, 1963), 120; Samuel Johnson, *Rambler*, no. 37 (July 24, 1750), in *The Yale Edition of the Works of Samuel Johnson*, vol. 3, *The Rambler*, ed. W. J. Bate and Albrecht B. Strauss, 23 vols. (New Haven, CT: Yale University Press, 1969), 201, 203.

57. John Gay, *The Shepherd's Week. In Six Pastorals* (1714), in *John Gay: Poetry and Prose*, ed. Vinton A. Dearing and Charles E. Beckwith (Oxford: Clarendon Press, 1974), 1:90–92 (further citations appear parenthetically in the text).

58. *The Beauties of English Poesy. Selected by Oliver Goldsmith* (1767), in *Collected Works of Oliver Goldsmith*, ed. Arthur Friedman (Oxford: Clarendon Press, 1966), 5, 322.

59. Mary Leapor, "On Winter" (1748), in *The Works of Mary Leapor*, ed. Richard Greene and Ann Messenger (Oxford: Oxford University Press, 2003), 141–142, ll. 15, 19, 35–40; George Crabbe, "The Village" (1783), bk. 1, ll. 7–12, 15–20 in *Eighteenth-Century English Literature*, ed. Geoffrey Tillotson, Paul Fussell, and Marshall Waingrow, with the assistance of Brewster Rogerson (New York: Harcourt Brace and World, 1969), 1423 (further citations appear parenthetically in the text). Samuel Johnson, true to the indignation he shows in his words on "Lycidas," contributed lines 15–18.

60. To make this claim it's necessary to treat "The Village" as though it consists only of book 1. I haven't discussed book 2, because its divergence from the project of the first makes it of little interest in the present context.

61. Stephen Duck, "The Thresher's Labour," in *Poems on Several Subjects* (1730), rev. ed., in *Poems on Several Occasions* (London, 1736) (further citations appear parenthetically in the text).

62. See more fully *Historicizing the Enlightenment*, vol. 1, intro., ch. 3. See most recently Frank Palmeri, *State of Nature, Stages of Society: Enlightenment Conjectural History and Modern Social Discourse* (New York: Columbia University Press, 2016).

63. See E. P. Thompson's classic essay "Time, Work-Discipline and Industrial Capitalism," ch. 6 in *Customs in Common*, 352–403.

64. Mary Collier, *The Woman's Labour: An Epistle to Mr. Stephen Duck; In Answer to His Late Poem, called The Thresher's Labour* (London, 1739). Duck: "Next Day the Cocks appear in equal Rows" (202); Collier: "We . . . nimbly turn our Hay upon the Plain; . . . / Or how should Cocks in equal Rows appear?" (ll. 59, 60, 62).

65. See Ludmilla Jordanova, who argues the connection between pastoral and gender oppositions in "Natural Facts: An Historical Perspective on Science and Sexuality," ch. 2 in *Sexual Visions: Images of Gender in Science and Medicine between the Eighteenth and Twentieth Centuries* (Madison: University of Wisconsin Press, 1989), 22–23.

66. On the sexual division of labor in the early modern English countryside, see above, n.21 and *Historicizing the Enlightenment*, vol. 1, ch. 4.

67. See "Remark (M)" and "Remark (T)" in vol. 1 of Bernard Mandeville, *The Fable of the Bees* (London, 1705, 1714), ed. F. B. Kaye (Oxford: Clarendon Press, 1924); Addison, *Tatler*, no. 116 (January 5, 1710); Addison, *Spectator*, no. 69 (May 9, 1711), in Bond, *The Spectator*. On

the preoccupations of the new "woman of leisure," see "Mrs. Crackenthorpe," *Female Tatler*, nos. 9, 67 (July 25–27, December 7–9, 1709), in *The Female Tatler*, ed. Fidelis Morgan (London: J. M. Dent, 1992); Johnson, *Rambler*, nos. 128, 191 (June 8, 1751; January 14, 1752), in Bate and Strauss, *The Rambler*.

68. Cf. Daniel Defoe, *Review*, vol. 3, no. 5 (January 10, 1706); vol. 7, nos. 55, 57, 59 (August 1, 5, 10, 1710); vol. 7, no. 116 (December 21, 1710).

69. Lady Mary to Wortley, March 24, August 6, 1711; Lady Mary to Lady Bute, July 10, 1748, in *The Complete Letters of Lady Mary Wortley Montagu*, ed. Robert Halsband, 3 vols. (Oxford: Clarendon Press, 1965–1967).

70. Mary Leapor, "Complaining DAPHNE. A PASTORAL," in Greene and Messenger, *Works*, ll. 10, 19, 27, 31, 61, 66, 68, 98, 99, 102, 108.

71. James Thomson, *The Four Seasons, and Other Poems* (London: printed for J. Millan, 1735), "Winter," ll. 208, 424–429, 431–433, 436–439, 572–573, 579–582 (further citations appear parenthetically in the text). In this edition, the four books are separately paginated.

72. Oliver Goldsmith, *The Deserted Village*, in *The Poems of Thomas Gray, William Collins, and Oliver Goldsmith*, ed. Roger Lonsdale (London: Longman, 1976), "Dedication to Sir Joshua Reynolds," ll. 19–23 (further citations appear parenthetically in the text).

73. On imperialism as macro-pastoralism, see also *Historicizing the Enlightenment*, vol. 1, intro.

74. On the analogy, see in general Seymour Drescher, *Capitalism and Antislavery: British Mobilization in Comparative Perspective* (New York: Oxford University Press, 1987).

75. On the reciprocal racialization of African Americans and Irish Americans, see Noel Ignatiev, *How the Irish Became White* (New York: Routledge, 1995).

76. This opposition recapitulates the terms of a common version of east-west nationalist opposition. Below a certain latitude, however, the terms of the north-south opposition are inverted: England is to Scotland as England is to Spain.

77. William Collins, "An Ode on the Popular Superstitions of the Highlands of Scotland, Considered as the Subject of Poetry" (writ. c. 1750), in *The Poems of Gray, Collins and Goldsmith*, ed. Roger Lonsdale (London: Longman, 1969), ll. 31–32. ("His" refers to "the untutored swain," l. 30.)

78. On this see John Brewer, *The Sinews of Power: War, Money, and the English State, 1688–1783* (New York: Knopf, 1989).

79. See Anne Janowitz, *England's Ruins: Poetic Purpose and the National Landscape* (Oxford: Blackwell, 1990).

80. See the present volume's introduction, nn.33–34.

81. Samuel Johnson, *London: A Poem in Imitation of the Third Satire of Juvenal*, in vol. 6 of *Works*, ed. E. L. McAdam Jr. and George Milne. See ll. 7–10, 210–211, 257.

82. In Juvenal's third *Satire*, Greece is Rome's antagonist.

83. On stadial theory see *Historicizing the Enlightenment*, vol. 1, intro., ch. 3.

CHAPTER 5 — POLITICAL POETRY

1. Michael McKeon, *Politics and Poetry in Restoration England: The Case of Dryden's Annus Mirabilis* (Cambridge, MA: Harvard University Press, 1975), 1.

2. William Butler Yeats, "Politics" (1939), in *The Collected Poems of W. B. Yeats, Definitive Edition* (New York: Macmillan, 1956), 337.

3. Gwendolyn Brooks, "First Fight. Then Fiddle," in *Selected Poems* (New York: Harper, Row, 1963), 54. Brooks's use of enjambment in this Italian sonnet bears comparison to Milton's in the same form: "When I Consider How My Light Is Spent" (c. 1652).

4. Bertolt Brecht, "Solely Because of the Increasing Disorder" (1937), in *Bertolt Brecht: Poems, 1913–1956*, trans. Frank Jellinek (London: Methuen, 1976), 225.

5. Nikki Giovanni, "For Saundra," in *Nikki Giovanni, Black Feeling, Black Talk* (privately printed, 1968), 89–90.

6. Muriel Rukeyser, "In Our Time" (1968), in *The Collected Poems of Muriel Rukeyser* (New York: McGraw-Hill, 1982), 438.

7. Adrienne Rich, "Poetry: I," in *The Collected Poems of Adrienne Rich, 1950–2012* (New York: W. W. Norton, 2016), 624.

8. Lucille Clifton, "at last we killed the roaches," in *An Ordinary Woman* (New York: Random House, 1974), 81.

9. Imamu Amiri Baraka, "Political Poem," in LeRoi Jones, *The Dead Lecturer* (New York: Grove Press, 1964), 74.

10. LeRoi Jones, "Black Art," in Imamu Amiri Baraka, *Black Magic: Collected Poetry 1961–1967* (Indianapolis: Bobbs-Merrill, 1969), 116–117.

11. Audre Lorde, "Power," second version (1978), in *The Collected Poems of Audre Lorde* (New York: W. W. Norton, 1997), 319–320.

12. Pablo Neruda, "I'm Explaining a Few Things," trans. Nathaniel Tarn, in *Pablo Neruda, Selected Poems, a Bilingual Edition*, ed. Nathaniel Tarn (New York: Dell, 1972), 151.

13. Zbigniew Herbert, "Five Men," in *Selected Poems*, trans. Czeslaw Milosz and Peter Dale Scott (Harmondsworth: Penguin, 1968), 58–60.

14. "Anthology" here is, literally, a collection of flowers.

15. Carolyn Forché, "The Colonel," in *The Country between Us* (New York: Harper-Collins, 1981), 16.

16. Mike Gold, "Examples of Worker Correspondence," in *Social Poetry of the 1930s: A Selection*, ed. Jack Salzman and Leo Zanderer (New York: Burt Franklin, 1978), 88. Open Library: Creative Commons Public Domain.

17. See Ernst Cassirer, *The Myth of the State* (Garden City, NY: Doubleday, 1946), ch. 12; Maurizio Viroli, *From Politics to Reason of State: The Acquisition and Transformation of the Language of Politics, 1251–1600* (Cambridge: Cambridge University Press, 1992).

18. Charles I, "Answer to the Nineteen Propositions," June 18, 1642, in J. P. Kenyon, *The Stuart Constitution 1603–1688: Documents and Commentary* (Cambridge: Cambridge

University Press, 1966), 23. Jack Cade and Wat Tyler led popular revolts in the fourteenth and thirteenth centuries, respectively.

19. On this phenomenon see *Historicizing the Enlightenment*, vol. 1, intro and ch. 3.

20. On these matters see Fredrick Seaton Siebert, *Freedom of the Press in England, 1476–1776: The Rise and Decline of Government Control* (Urbana: University of Illinois Press, 1952), chs. 13–15; and Laurence Hanson, *Government and the Press, 1695–1763* (Oxford: Clarendon Press, 1936), ch. 2.

21. For a highly instructive reading of Dryden's *The State of Innocence*, an operatic adaptation of *Paradise Lost*, see Matthew C. Augustine, "How John Dryden Read His Milton: *The State of Innocence* Reconsidered," in *Texts and Readers in the Age of Marvell*, ed. Christopher D'Addario and Matthew C. Augustine (Manchester: Manchester University Press, 2018), 224–242. On Milton's own ambivalence regarding the relation of *Paradise Lost* to mock heroic and heroic poetry, see ch. 6 of the present volume.

22. John Dryden, *Absalom and Achitophel* (1681), in *The Works of John Dryden*, vol. 2, *Poems 1681–1684*, ed. H. T. Swedenberg Jr. and Vinton A. Dearing, 20 vols. (Berkeley: University of California Press, 1972), 29, ll. 795–796. For an extended reading of *Absalom and Achitophel* in this light, see Michael McKeon, "Historicizing *Absalom and Achitophel*," in *The New Eighteenth Century*, ed. Felicity Nussbaum and Laura Brown (New York: Methuen, 1987), 23–40.

23. See chs. 1 and 2 of the present volume, and *Historicizing the Enlightenment*, vol. 1, ch. 1.

24. Richard Lovelace, "To Lucasta, Going to the Warres," in *Lucasta: Epodes, Odes, Sonnets, Songs, &c. to Which Is Added Aramantha, a Pastoral* (London, 1649), 3.

25. William Sherlock, Dean of St. Paul's, *The Case of the Allegiance Due to Soveraign Powers* (1691). Cf. Edward Stillingfleet, *A Discourse concerning the Unreasonableness of a New Separation* (1689), 32: "A King *de jure* is one, who comes in by lineal Descent, as next Heir, and whose Right is Owned and Recognized by the Estates of the Realm. A King *de facto* is one, who comes in by Consent of the Nation, but not by Virtue of an immediate Hereditary Right." Both quoted in Gerald M. Straka, *Anglican Reaction to the Revolution of 1688*, State Historical Society of Wisconsin (Madison: University of Wisconsin Press, 1962), 71, 55.

26. For a searching and deeply informed study of the poems on affairs of state that doesn't find in them a significant departure from political poetry as such, see Ruth Nevo, *The Dial of Virtue: A Study of Poems on Affairs of State in the Seventeenth Century* (Princeton, NJ: Princeton University Press, 1963).

27. *Poems on Affairs of State from the Reign of K. James the First, to the Present Year* (1703), "The Preface," sig. A2v; *Poems on Affairs of State* (1697), "The Preface," sig. A4r–A5v; *Poems on Affairs of State [. . .] Part Two* (1697), "The Preface," sig. A2v. An ample, rich, and copiously annotated selection of poems on affairs of state, mostly from these miscellanies, appears in *Poems on Affairs of State: Augustan Satirical Verse, 1660-1714*, 7 vols., ed. George deF. Lord et al. (New Haven, CT: Yale University Press, 1963–1975) (hereafter cited as *POAS*).

28. On the secret history see ch. 6 of the present volume and *Historicizing the Enlightenment*, vol. 1, ch. 5. See also *The Secret History in Literature, 1660–1820*, ed. Rebecca Bullard and Rachel Carnell (Cambridge: Cambridge University Press, 2017).

29. *The Diary of Samuel Pepys*, ed. Robert Latham and William Matthews, 11 vols. (Berkeley: University of California Press, 1974), 8: 1667, 439. Pepys was clerk of the acts to the Navy Board.

30. Joseph Addison, *Spectator*, no. 567 (July 14, 1714), in *The Spectator*, 5 vols., ed. Donald F. Bond (Oxford: Clarendon Press, 1965).

31. Dryden, *The Vindication [. . .] of [. . .] the Duke of Guise* (London, 1683), 2, 7; Thomas Shadwell, *The Medal of John Bayes: A Satire against Folly and Knavery* (1682), in *Poems on Affairs of State*, vol. 3, *1682–85*, ed. Howard H. Schless (New Haven: Yale University Press, 1968), 81–95; John Dennis, *The Characters and Conduct of Sir John Edgar* (1720), in *The Critical Works of John Dennis*, vol. 2, *1711–1729*, ed. Edward Niles Hooker (Baltimore: Johns Hopkins University Press, 1943), 2nd part, letter 3, 201.

32. Andrew Marvell, "An Horatian Ode upon Cromwell's Return from Ireland" (1681), in *The Poems of Andrew Marvell*, ed. Nigel Smith (London: Longman, 2003), 273, ll. 1–4.

33. John Dryden, "To My Honour'd Kinsman, John Driden, of Chesterton in the County of Huntingdon, Esquire" (1700), in *Works of Dryden*, vol. 7, *Poems, 1697–1700*, ed. Vinton A. Dearing (2002), ll. 201–204.

34. *Some Reflections upon the Pretended Parallel in the Play Called the Duke of Guise* (1683), 25, quoted in *POAS*, 6: *1697–1704*, ed. Frank H. Ellis (1970), xxxi.

35. Samuel Garth, *The Dispensary* (1699), canto 4, ll. 21–22, in *POAS*, 6:92; Nahum Tate, "Old England" (1682), ll. 23–24, in *POAS*, 3: *1682–1685*, ed. Schless (1968), 186.

36. Henry Mildmay, *The Progress* (1688), ll. 1–10, in *POAS*, 4: *1685–1688*, ed. Galbraith M. Crump (1968), 330–331.

37. Henry Fielding, *An Apology for the Life of Mrs. Shamela Andrews* (1741), in *Joseph Andrews and Shamela*, ed. Douglas Brooks-Davies and Thomas Keymer (Oxford: Oxford World's Classics, 1999), 340; and *The Life of Mr. Jonathan Wild the Great* (1743), ed. David Nokes (Harmondsworth: Penguin, 1982), 102.

38. Sarah Malthus, *The Baboon A-la-Mode. A Satyr against the French* (1704), 1, quoted in *POAS*, 7: *1704–1714*, ed. Ellis (1975), xxviii.

39. Andrew Marvell, *The Last Instructions to a Painter* (1667), ll. 117–124, in *POAS*, 1: *1660–1678*, ed. George deForest Lord (1963), 105–106. Marvell writes in a subgenre that flourished briefly during the Restoration, the advice to a painter poem. "Cabal," derived from the mystical and esoteric Kabbala, is an acronym for the group of powerful state ministers responsible for policy during the 1660s.

40. Jonathan Swift, "Ode to the Honorable Sir William Temple" (writ. c. 1692), ll. 92–93, 97–100, in *The Poems of Jonathan Swift*, ed. Harold Williams, 2nd ed., 3 vols. (Oxford: Clarendon Press, 1958), 1, 29.

41. Jonathan Swift, *Examiner*, no. 38 (April 26, 1711), in *The Prose Works of Jonathan Swift*, ed. Herbert Davis, vol. 3, *The Examiner and Other Pieces Written in 1710–11*, 14 vols. (Oxford: Basil Blackwell, 1940), 141.

42. Fleetwood Sheppard, "A Description of a Hampton Court Life" (1689), in *POAS*, 5: *1688–1697*, ed. William J. Cameron (1971), 55.

43. See Genesis 2:23–24 (King James Version); for the Anglican marriage service, see David Cressy and Lori Anne Ferrell, eds., *Religion and Society in Early Modern England: A Sourcebook* (London: Routledge, 1996), 51–54.

44. Cf. "Hey, diddle diddle." For a brief discussion of this popular ballad meter—two lines of two beats per line alternating with one line of three beats—put to satiric use, see Harold Love, *The Culture and Commerce of Texts: Scribal Publication in Seventeenth-Century England* (1993; rpt. Amherst: University of Massachusetts Press, 1998), 232–233.

45. *OED*, s.v. "uplock": to lock up.

46. Already in 1610 James Whitelocke was able to say that "the soveraigne power is agreed to be in the king: but in the king is a two-fold power, the one in parliament, as he is assisted with the consent of the whole state; the other out of parliament, as he is sole, and singular, guided merely by his own will. . . . The power of the king in parliament is greater than his power out of parliament." *Cobbett's Complete Collection of State Trials* [. . .], ed. Thomas B. Howell (London: Hansard, 1809–1826), vol. 2, cols. 482–483, quoted in Margaret A. Judson, *The Crisis of the Constitution: An Essay in Constitutional and Political Thought in England, 1603–1645* (1949; rpt. New Brunswick, NJ: Rutgers University Press, 1988), 86–87. On the tradition of "the King in Parliament," see generally Charles H. McIlwain, *The High Court of Parliament and Its Supremacy* (New Haven, CT: Yale University Press, 1910).

47. "Jack Sprat" was said to allude to the Commons' refusal to fund Charles I's war against Spain in 1625 (denying him fat), his pursuit of hostilities financed by the dowry Henrietta Maria (eating no lean) brought him on their marriage that year, and his failed campaign at Cadiz. Charles dissolved Parliament, and the royal couple licked the platter clean. See Linda Alchin, *The Secret History of Nursery Rhymes* (New York: Nielsen, 2004), 55, www.rhymes.org.uk.

48. Andrew Marvell, "The Coronet," in *Poems of Marvell*, ed. Smith, 48–49.

49. On the doctrine of accommodation in relation to Christian poetry, see ch. 6 of the present volume.

50. The "meaning" of deviation from a metrical norm in (political) poetry doesn't possess a predictable content but is structural and dependent on context. In William Wordsworth's sonnet "The World Is Too Much with Us," the natural is signified by iambic regularity; in Gerard Manley Hopkins's sonnet "God's Grandeur," iambic regularity signifies the unnaturalness imposed by labor, trade, and civilization.

51. William Blake, *Jerusalem* (1804–1820), plate 57, l. 10; see David V. Erdman, *Prophet against Empire* (Princeton, NJ: Princeton University Press, 1954), 207. For an argument that the beginnings of this long-term process can be seen in the separation and confla-

tion of "civil" and "religious" liberty around the turn of the eighteenth century, see *Historicizing the Enlightenment*, vol. 1, ch. 2.

52. I adopt the language of historical preservation and storage from Ernst H. Kantorowicz, *The King's Two Bodies: A Study in Medieval Political Theology* (Princeton, NJ: Princeton University Press, 1957), 234–235.

53. See also *Historicizing the Enlightenment*, vol. 1, ch. 1.

54. Samuel T. Coleridge, *Biographia Literaria* (1817), ed. George Watson (London: Everyman, 1965), 2, xiv, 169.

CHAPTER 6 — *PARADISE LOST* AS PARODY

1. John Milton, *Paradise Lost: A Poem in Twelve Books*, ed. Thomas Newton, 2nd ed., 2 vols. (London, 1749), 1: bk. 2, ll. 1–6. Text references are to books and lines of this edition.

2. John Milton, *Areopagitica* (London, 1644), ed. Ernest Sirluck, *Complete Prose Works of John Milton*, vol. 2, *1643–1648*, ed. Don M. Wolfe et al. (New Haven, CT: Yale University Press, 1953–1982), 514 (hereafter cited as *CPW* by volume and page number; here, *CPW*2, 514).

3. John Milton, *Eikonoklastes: In Answer to a Book Entitled Eikon Basilike, the Portraiture of His Sacred Majesty in His Solitudes and Sufferings* (London, 1649), ed. Merritt Y. Hughes, *CPW*3: *1648–1649*, 486–487.

4. John Dryden, *Mac Flecknoe* (1682, writ. 1676), ed. V. A. Dearing, in *Poems 1681–1684*, vol. 2 of *The Works of John Dryden*, ed. H. T. Swedenberg Jr., E. N. Hooker, et al. (Berkeley: University of California Press, 1956–1989), ll. 106–107 (hereafter cited as *WJD*).

5. Alexander Pope, *The Dunciad* (1742–1743), ed. James Sutherland, in vol. 5 of *Twickenham Edition of the Poems of Alexander Pope*, ed. John Butt and others (New Haven, CT: Yale University Press, 1939–1961), bk. 2, ll. 1–5 (hereafter cited as *TE*).

6. To name only the best known of these, see John Barclay's *Argenis* (Latin 1621; English 1625, 1629); John Denham's *Coopers Hill* (1642, 1655, 1668); Abraham Cowley's *The Civil War* (1643); William Davenant's *Gondibert* (1650–1652); and Percy Herbert's *The Princess Cloria* (1661).

7. See Christopher Hill, *Milton and the English Revolution* (New York: Viking Press, 1978), ch. 29.

8. See the thoughtful investigation by Patrick J. Daly Jr. in "'Rome's Other Hope': Charles, Monmouth, and James in the Summer of 1676," *ELH* 66, no. 3 (1999): 655–676.

9. Pope, *The Dunciad*, "Ricardus Aristarchus of the Hero of the Poem," 5, pp. 255–256. However, this shouldn't be taken to support the old notion, now discredited, that Augustan or "neoclassical" literature treated the classics as a strictly normative standard against which to register the bathos of modernity: see Intro. to this volume.

10. For supporting readings, see Michael McKeon, *The Origins of the English Novel, 1600–1740* (Baltimore: Johns Hopkins University Press, 1987, 2002), chs. 11 and 12. For critical and scholarly support in this chapter, I refer the reader to my other writings because those are the texts in which more extended arguments along these particular

lines have been made. But in doing so I ask the reader to assume my grateful acknowledgment of the scores of secondary sources by which my arguments have been informed. Readers interested in a more wide-ranging account of how Enlightenment poets and critics responded to and were influenced by *Paradise Lost* will do no better than Dustin Griffin's consistently judicious *Regaining Paradise: Milton and the Eighteenth Century* (Cambridge: Cambridge University Press, 1986).

11. John Milton, "On the Morning of Christ's Nativity" (writ. 1629, pub. 1645).

12. In *Annus Mirabilis* (1667), published in the same year as the ten-volume *Paradise Lost*, Dryden makes a different use of typology to frame contemporary events; see Michael McKeon, *Politics and Poetry in Restoration England: The Case of Dryden's "Annus Mirabilis"* (Cambridge, MA: Harvard University Press, 1975), 162–175.

13. For a fuller version of the argument made in this paragraph, see Michael McKeon, "Historicizing *Absalom and Achitophel*," in *The New Eighteenth Century: Theory, Politics, English Literature*, ed. Felicity Nussbaum and Laura Brown (New York: Methuen, 1987), 23–40.

14. [John Dryden], *Absalom and Achitophel* (1681), in *WJD*, 2: ll. 130–133. Dryden also economically refutes damaging charges made by Charles's antagonists.

15. See *Paradise Lost* 6, "The Argument" and 6.470–506. For some precedents, see Claude Rawson, *Satire and Sentiment, 1660–1830* (Cambridge: Cambridge University Press, 1994), 48–54.

16. See John Milton, *Christian Doctrine*, ed. Maurice Kelley, trans. John Carey, in *CPW6: 1658–c 1660*, ch. 2. For a brief and acute account of problems with the theory and with Milton's interpretation of it, see A. D. Nuttall, *Overheard by God: Fiction and Prayer in Herbert, Milton, Dante and St John* (London: Methuen, 1980), 98–100. See also the helpful discussions of N. K. Sugimura, *Matter of Glorious Trial: Spiritual and Material Substance in Paradise Lost* (New Haven, CT: Yale University Press, 2009), ch. 6; and Joad Raymond, *Milton's Angels: The Early Modern Imagination* (Oxford: Oxford University Press, 2010), ch. 6.

17. John Milton, *Of Education. To Master Samuel Hartlib* (1644), ed. Donald C. Dorian in *CPW2*, 368–369.

18. A[ndrew] M[arvell], "On Paradise Lost," in *Paradise Lost: A Poem in Twelve Books*, 2nd ed., by John Milton (London, 1674), ll. 1–8, 12, 15–16, 33–34.

19. John Bunyan, *The Pilgrim's Progress* from *This World, to That Which Is to Come*: . . . (1678), ed. W. R. Owens (Oxford: Oxford University Press, 2003), 5, ll. 107–112.

20. Samuel Taylor Coleridge, *Coleridge's Miscellaneous Criticism*, ed. T. M. Raysor (London: Constable, 1936), 31.

21. See generally Michael McKeon, *The Secret History of Domesticity: Public, Private, and the Division of Knowledge* (Baltimore: Johns Hopkins University Press, 2005).

22. [John Milton], *A Defence of the People of England* (1651), ed. William J. Grace, trans. Donald Mackenzie, *CPW4: 1650–1655*, 326–327.

23. See Erich Auerbach, *Mimesis: The Representation of Reality in Western Literature*, trans. Willard Trask (Garden City, NY: Doubleday Anchor Books, 1957), 63; and Auerbach, *Literary Language and Its Public in Late Latin Antiquity and in the Middle Ages*, trans. Ralph Manheim, Bollingen Series 74 (New York: Pantheon, 1965), chs. 1, 2.

24. For a fuller discussion, see McKeon, *Secret History*, 33–43, 182–184. Under Roman Catholicism, a select minority found the blessing of humility in a life of ascetic renunciation; Protestantism aimed to empower all Christians to find the blessing of humility in the lowly callings of their daily lives.

25. For a fuller discussion, see McKeon, *Origins*, ch. 8.

26. See Matt. 12.50, 19.29 (King James Version).

27. The dinner scene in book 5 has made a major contribution to what appears to be a scholarly consensus that Milton is a philosophical materialist—that is, a monist. But if that is so, we might wonder why he believes that to describe angels, for example, requires an accommodation of their spiritual entity to sensible or material form. The question leads in a number of directions that are beyond the scope of this chapter. But it may be useful to distinguish between Milton's philosophical materialism, which Raphael's discourse propounds, and the theological or religious heterodoxy evident in the seemingly unpremeditated ease with which his accommodations can be undertaken. It's this latter practice whose formal dimension is centrally germane to my argument in this chapter.

28. McKeon, *Origins*, 35–39.

29. See Joel E. Spingarn, *A History of Literary Criticism in the Renaissance*, 2nd ed. (New York: Columbia University Press, 1912), 112–124; Bernard Weinberg, *A History of Literary Criticism in the Italian Renaissance* (Chicago: University of Chicago Press, 1961), 2:954–1073; Alban K. Forcione, *Cervantes, Aristotle, and the "Persiles"* (Princeton, NJ: Princeton University Press, 1970), chs. 1, 2 (at 23 on "heroic poetry"). Colin Burrow's approach to the problem of how romance stands in relation to epic begins in antiquity and culminates in an illuminating consideration of *Paradise Lost* that shares many of this chapter's broadest concerns. Colin Burrow, *Epic Romance: Homer to Milton* (Oxford: Clarendon Press, 1993).

30. [Samuel Butler], *Hudibras. The First Part. Written in the Time of the Late Wars* (1663), *Hudibras, The Second Part. By the Author of the First* (1664), ed. John Wilders (Oxford: Clarendon Press, 1967), pt. 1, canto 1, l. 708n. (p. 22); canto 2, ll. 4–8 (p. 28).

31. Cf. Marvell's famously measured expression of regret: "Whether it were a War of Religion, or of Liberty, is not worth the labour to enquire. Which-soever was at the top, the other was at the bottom; but upon considering all, I think the Cause was too good to have been fought for." Andrew Marvell, *The Rehearsal Transpros'd*, pt. 1 (1672), ed. Martin Dzelzainis, in *The Prose Works of Andrew Marvell: 1672–1673*, ed. Annabel Patterson, Martin Dzelzainis, N. H. Keeble, and Nicholas von Maltzahn, 2 vols. (New Haven, CT: Yale University Press, 2003), 1:192.

32. For a fuller reading, see McKeon, *Secret History*, 209–210, 396–398.

33. [Aphra Behn], *Love-Letters between a Nobleman and His Sister*, ed. Janet Todd (Harmondsworth, UK: Penguin, 1996) (further citations appear parenthetically in the text). For a full reading of *Love-Letters*, see McKeon, *Secret History*, ch. 11.

34. Building on recent work, Matthew Augustine has gone far in rescuing the parodic subtlety of *The State of Innocence* from the ignominy to which older criticism had consigned it: "How John Dryden Read His Milton: *The State of Innocence* Reconsidered," in *Texts and Readers in the Age of Marvell*, ed. Christopher D'Addario and Matthew C. Augustine (Manchester: Manchester University Press, 2018), 224–242.

35. Milton, *Eikonoklastes*, in *CPW*3, 421. On "effeminate," see McKeon, *Secret History*, 581.

36. The *Anecdota* was first translated into English in 1674, as *The Secret History of the Court of the Emperor Justinian*, from an earlier French translation, then reissued in 1682. On Procopius and the seventeenth-century English secret history, see McKeon, *Secret History*, ch. 10.

37. In this judgment I diverge from what appears to be the consensus; see Robert H. West, *Milton and the Angels* (Athens: University of Georgia Press, 1955), 162, 170; Stephen M. Fallon, *Milton among the Philosophers: Poetry and Materialism in Seventeenth-Century England* (Ithaca, NY: Cornell University Press, 1991), 144; and Raymond, *Milton's Angels*, 282–283, 338. But see Sugimura, "Matter of Glorious Trial," 175–176. I agree that Milton leaves no doubt about the philosophical materiality of his angels. I question whether Raphael describes them as expressing their love in the material and sensible terms of "immediate touch" that's at the heart of Adam's concern, and I take this to be important not philosophically but as a literary matter of characterization and imputed motive.

38. Milton writes at a time when the traditionally flexible distinction between male outside and female inside work in the agrarian economy was becoming a more ossified division of labor. The division Eve proposes would go against that historical tendency but at the same time accord with a modernizing movement toward greater efficiency and productivity. See *Historicizing the Enlightenment*, vol. 1, ch. 4.

39. See chs. 1 and 2 in the present volume. Fielding's epistemological breakthrough was inspired by that of Cervantes one and a half centuries earlier, and it was exemplified in English as early as *Incognita; Or, Love and Duty Reconcil'd. A Novel* (London, 1692), by Milton's contemporary William Congreve.

40. For an illuminating approach to this eighteenth-century conflict between models of marriage from a broadly anthropological perspective, see Ruth Perry, *Novel Relations: The Transformation of Kinship in English Literature and Culture, 1748–1818* (Cambridge: Cambridge University Press, 2004).

41. This should not be mistaken as an exercise in the spirit of Mikhail Bakhtin's thesis that traditional literary forms were "novelized" in the eighteenth century. That thesis amounts to a one-sided historiography of discontinuity that runs counter to my premise that historical process is a dialectic of continuity and discontinuity. See M. M. Bakhtin, "Epic and Novel: Toward a Methodology for the Study of the Novel," in *The Dialogic Imagination: Four Essays by M.M. Bakhtin*, ed. Michael Holquist, trans. Caryl

Emerson and Michael Holquist (Austin: University of Texas Press, 1981), 3–40. In fact, my epitome credits Bakhtin's notion of novelization, brilliant though it is, with a greater coherence than it actually possesses; see *Theory of the Novel*, ed. Michael McKeon (Baltimore: Johns Hopkins University Press, 2000), 317–319.

42. See Richard Steele, *Tatler*, no. 217 (August 29, 1710), in *The Tatler*, ed. Donald F. Bond, 3 vols. (Oxford: Clarendon Press, 1987). Matthew Augustine's acute reading of, as he puts it, "the loucheness of Dryden's Adam and Eve" makes me wonder if Steele's parody may have been indebted to *The State of Innocence* (Augustine, "State of Innocence Reconsidered," 234, 235). In any case, Steele's parody deserves to be reproduced:

"'Madam, If my Advice had been of any Authority with you when that strange Desire of Gadding possessed you this Morning, we had still been happy: But your cursed Vanity and Opinion of your own Conduct, which is certainly very wavering when it seeks Occasions of being proved, has ruined both your self, and me who trusted you.'

Eve had no Fan in her Hand to ruffle, or Tucker to pull down, but with a reproachful Air she answered,

'Sir, Do you impute that to my Desire of Gadding, which might have happened to your self with all your Wisdom and Gravity? The Serpent spoke so excellently, and with so good a Grace, that—Besides, What Harm had I ever done him, that he should design me any? Was I to have been always at your Side, I might as well have continued there, and been but your Rib still: But if I was so weak a Creature as you thought me, Why did you not interpose your sage Authority more absolutely? You denied me going as faintly, as you say I resisted the Serpent. Had not you been too easie, neither you or I had now transgressed.'

Adam replied, 'Why, *Eve*, hast thou the Impudence to upbraid me as the Cause of thy Transgression for my Indulgence to thee? Thus it will ever be with him who trusts too much to Woman: At the same Time that she refuses to be governed, if she suffers by her Obstinacy, she will accuse the Man that shall leave her to her self.'

Thus they in mutual Accusation spent
The fruitless Hours, but neither self condemning:
And of their vain Contest appear'd no End. (9.1187–1189)

This to the Modern will appear but a very faint Piece of Conjugal Enmity; but you are to consider, that they were but just begun to be angry, and they wanted new Words for expressing their new Passions. But her accusing him of letting her go, and telling him how good a Speaker, and how fine a Gentleman the Devil was, we must reckon, allowing for the Improvements of Time, that she gave him the same Provocation as if she had called him Cuckold. The passionate and familiar Terms with which the same Case, repeated daily for so many Thousand Years, has furnished the present Generation, were not then in Use; but the Foundation of Debate has ever been the same, a Contention about their Merit and Wisdom."

43. In the following account, italics and parenthetical citations indicate Milton's actual usages. Where a citation is absent there has been more than one use of the term or phrase.

Source Notes

CHAPTER 2 — "FROM ANCIENT MIMESIS TO MODERN REALISM: A DIACHRONIC INQUIRY"

This chapter is based on "From Mimesis to Realism: The Role of Factuality and the Real in the History of Narrative Theory and Practice," in *Narrative Factuality: A Handbook*, ed. Monika Fludernik and Marie-Laure Ryan (Berlin: DeGruyter, 2020), 487–510. Copyright © 2020 Walter de Gruyter GmbH, Berlin. Reprinted with permission of the publisher.

CHAPTER 3 — "THE HISTORICITY OF LITERARY CONVENTIONS: FAMILY ROMANCE"

This chapter is based on "The Afterlife of Family Romance," in *The Afterlives of Eighteenth-Century Fiction*, ed. Daniel Cook and Nicholas Seager (Cambridge: Cambridge University Press, 2015), 43–71. Copyright © 2015 Cambridge University Press. Reprinted with permission of the publisher.

CHAPTER 4 — "THE HISTORICITY OF LITERARY GENRES: PASTORAL POETRY"

This chapter is based on "The Pastoral Revolution," in *Refiguring Revolutions: Aesthetics and Politics from the English Revolution to the Romantic Revolution*, ed. Kevin Sharpe and Steven N. Zwicker (Berkeley: University of California Press, 1998), 267–289. Copyright © 1998 University of California Press. Reprinted with permission of the publisher.

CHAPTER 5 — "POLITICAL POETRY: COMPARATIVE HISTORICIZING, 1650–1700, 1930–1980"

This chapter is based on "Political Poetry," in *Eighteenth-Century Genre and Culture: Serious Reflections on Occasional Forms: Essays in Honor of J. Paul Hunter*, ed. Dennis Todd and Cynthia Wall (Newark: University of Delaware Press, 2001), 280–301. Copyright © 2001 Rosemont Publishing and Printing Corp. All rights reserved. Reprinted with permission.

"Politics," by W. B. Yeats, from *The Collected Works of W. B. Yeats, Volume I: The Poems, Revised*, by W. B. Yeats, edited by Richard J. Finneran. Copyright © 1940 by Georgie Yeats, renewed 1968 by Bertha Georgie Yeats, Michael Butler Yeats, and Anne Yeats. Reprinted with the permission of Scribner, a division of Simon & Schuster, Inc. All rights reserved.

Gwendolyn Brooks, "First fight. Then fiddle." Reprinted by consent of Brooks Permissions.

"Solely because of the increasing disorder," originally published in German in 1964 as "Ausschliesslich wegen der zunehmenden Unordnung," translated by Frank Jellinek. Copyright © 1964, 1976 by Bertolt-Brecht-Erben / Suhrkamp Verlag, from *Bertolt Brecht: Poems, 1913–1956*, by Bertolt Brecht, edited by John Willet and Ralph Manheim. Used by permission of Liveright Publishing Corporation.

"In Our Time," by Muriel Rukeyser, in *The Collected Poems of Muriel Rukeyser*. Copyright © 2005 by Muriel Rukeyser. Reprinted by permission of ICM Partners.

"Poetry: I," from *Collected Poems: 1950–2012*, by Adrienne Rich. Copyright © 2016 by the Adrienne Rich Literary Trust. Copyright © 1986 by Adrienne Rich. Used by permission of W. W. Norton.

Lucille Clifton, "at last we killed the roaches," from *How to Carry Water: Selected Poems*. Copyright © 1974, 1987 by Lucille Clifton. Reprinted with the permission of The Permissions Company, LLC on behalf of BOA Editions, Ltd.

"Political Poem" by Amiri Baraka. Used by permission of Chris Calhoun Agency © Estate of Amiri Baraka.

"Black Art" by Amiri Baraka. From *S.O.S. Poems 1961–2013*. Copyright © 2014 by The Estate of Amiri Baraka. Used by permission of Grove/Atlantic, Inc. Any third-party use of this material, outside of this publication, is prohibited.

"Power." Copyright © 1978 by Audre Lorde. From *The Collected Poems of Audre Lorde*, by Audre Lorde. Used by permission of W. W. Norton.

"The Colonel," from *The Country between Us*, by Carolyn Forché. Copyright © 1981 by Carolyn Forché. Used by permission of HarperCollins Publishers.

"Examples of Worker Correspondence," by Mike Gold. Used by permission of International Publishers.

CHAPTER 6 — "*PARADISE LOST* AS PARODY: PERIOD, GENRE, AND CONJECTURAL INTERPRETATION"

This chapter is based on "*Paradise Lost* in the Long Restoration, 1660–1742: The Parody of Form," in *Milton in the Long Restoration*, ed. Blair Hoxby and Ann Baynes Coiro (New York: Oxford University Press, 2016), 503–530. Reprinted with permission of the publisher.

Index

Abrams, Meyer, 6, 7–8, 9–10, 12, 14
Absalom and Achitophel (Dryden), 174–175, 177–178, 191–192
absolutism: of Charles Stuart, 10, 87; devolution of, from royalty to private property, 113–115, 136, 153; religious, 185, 186; royal, 172, 175, 178, 215–216; of Thomas Hobbes, 178
accommodation, 184, 192–194, 196–200, 201, 206, 208, 209–211
Addison, Joseph, 28–34, 49, 54–55, 71–72, 115, 119–120, 177, 180
Adorno, Theodor W., 18
aesthetics, as distinct from the aesthetic, 20
the aesthetic: 20, 60, 235n11; as continuous from the Enlightenment to Wordsworth, 9–10, 37–39; as informing emergent social sciences, 39–46; as narrative realism, 54–59, 61–76; as theory of dramatic judgment, 35–37; as theory of dramatic response, 28–35; as theory of narrative response, 46–49
African Eclogues (Chatterton), 144
Age of Sensibility, 13
The Alchemist (Jonson), 27
Allegory, 191, 193, 194, 196, 201–202, 209–210
All for Love (Dryden), 203
Ancients and Moderns, 4, 20–28, 31, 54
Anecdota (Procopius of Caesarea), 203
antiromance movement, 208–209, 212. See also family romance
The Anti-romance: or, The History of the Shepherd Lysis (Sorel), 64
anti-slavery movement, 145–146, 176–177
Antony and Cleopatra (Shakespeare), 203
"Apology for Heroick Poetry, and Poetick License" (Dryden), 203
arcana imperii, 172
aristocratic ideology, 52, 83–90
Aristotle: critique of, 21; Genette on, 74–75; on history *vs.* poetry, 62; *Poetics*, 8, 26, 66; on verisimilitude and probability, 4, 62–63
L'Astrée (d'Urfé), 63–64
Augustanism, 4, 8, 9, 10, 13, 245n9. See also neoclassicism
Austen, Jane, 18, 96–100, 101

Bacon, Francis, 21, 23, 68
Bakhtin, Mikhail, 16, 74, 248n41
Baraka, Amiri, 160–163, 171
Barthes, Roland, 18, 75–77
Bate, Walter Jackson, 4–5
Bayle, Pierre, 65
beatus ille (Horatian tag), 106, 121, 143, 152
Behn, Aphra, 47–48, 140, 201–202, 204
Bentinck, Hans Willem, 180
"Black Art" (Baraka), 160–162, 171, 184
Blake, William, 185
Bloom, Harold, 12
Botany-Bay Eclogues (Southey), 144
Brecht, Bertolt, 156–157
Brenner, Robert, 114
Brooks, Gwendolyn, 156, 175
Brown, Marshall, 13
Buckingham, George Villiers, Duke of, 27
Bull, John, 148
Bunyan, John, 89, 193–194, 195–197, 209–210
Burke, Edmund, 33–34, 39–41, 72, 174
Burney, Frances, 94–96
Butler, Samuel, 180, 187, 200–202, 212

Capitalism: allegory of, 109; analogy of wage and enslaved labor and, 145; as infrastructure, 116; Enlightenment universality and, 45, 52; explicitation and, 113, 114, 116, 117, 136; sexual division of labor and, 138–139; virtualization and, 113, 114–115, 136; quantification and, 137–138; origins in and transformation of the countryside, 110–112, 135–136, 153; *Robinson Crusoe* and, 51–52
Castle, Terry, 223n31
Charles I, 172, 182, 203, 204, 244n47
Charles II, 86–87, 146, 204
Chatterton, Thomas, 144
chronique scandaleuse, 65
civil war. See English Civil War
city eclogues, 118. See also *Eclogues*
claim to historicity, 46–49, 55–56, 65, 68–69, 72, 76–77, 209
Clifton, Lucille, 159
Coleridge, Samuel, 17, 38, 40, 74
Collins, William, 12, 144, 146–147
"The Colonel" (Forché), 169–170

253

Columbus, 65
commoners: daily life of, 115, 118, 129, 179; as pastoral objects, 37, 87, 88, 92, 211; as pastoral subjects, 138–139
common life, Enlightenment notion of, 37, 43, 44, 109–110, 130, 132, 181, 235n11
common time (musical term), 129
Communist Party of America, 170–171
Compton, Henry, 181–182
Congreve, William, 180
convention. *See* literary conventions
Coopers-Hill (Denham), 122–124, 238n46
Corneille, Pierre, 66–67, 70, 71, 75, 77, 225n20
"The Coronet" (Marvell), 183–184
courtly love, 83, 97, 104, 176, 201–203
Cowper, William, 6
Crabbe, George, 133–135
Cromwell, Oliver, 86, 123
cultural imperialism, 145, 149

D'Allais, Denis Vairasse, 65
D'Aulnoy, Comtesse, 65, 66
Davies, John (translator), 64
Defoe, Daniel, 55, 86, 113, 115, 126, 127, 180. See also *Robinson Crusoe* (Defoe)
Deloney, Thomas, 86
Denham, John, 122–124
The Deserted Village (Goldsmith), 142–143
diachrony, diachronic, 18, 21, 22, 36, 43, 61, 113, 129, 151, 211–212, 238n55. *See also* synchrony, synchronic
didacticism, 8, 9, 158, 171, 186, 222n14
Discourse concerning the Original and Progress of Satire (Dryden), 11
distinction-separation-conflation, historical schema, 1–2, 154, 186, 212, 238n54
domestication, 181–182, 194–199, 201, 209–212
Don Quixote (Cervantes), 64, 208
dramatic unities: three, 26, 63, 66–67, 70, 231n33; two, 4, 38, 46–47, 54–55, 56, 57, 63, 69, 70, 71–72, 77
The Drapier's Letters (Swift), 146
Drury Lane Theater, 45
Dryden, John, 11, 180; *Absalom and Achitophel*, 174–175, 177–178, 191–192; *All for Love*, 203; *Of Dramatic Poesy*, 11–12, 21–22, 26–27, 70; *The Duke of Guise*, 177; *The State of Innocence, and Fall of Man*, 203
Du Bos, Jean-Baptiste, 74
Duck, Stephen, 135–138
Duff, David, 11–12
The Duke of Guise (Dryden and Lee), 177
Duppa, Thomas, Usher of the Black Rod, 182
Dyer, John, 124

East India Company, 148
East-West Axis, 148–153
Eclogues (Virgil), 234n11; complementary and reciprocal relation to *Georgics*, 104–105; fourth, 107–108, 149, 151; principle of transvaluation in, 105–106, 144, 150, 151; relation of, to *Idylls* of Theocritus, 108–109; in Virgilian progression, 152. See also *Georgics* (Virgil)
Edwards, Thomas, 89
The Eighteenth Brumaire of Louis Bonaparte (Marx), 80
Elegy Written in a Country Churchyard (Gray), 143
Empiricism: as based in sense experience, 5, 20, 21; as ground of the aesthetic, 20, 31, 35; factuality and, 55; quantifiability and, 36; Locke and, 58; Milton and, 209; naïve, 46, 54, 56, 67; Swift and, 118; time of representation and, 57
English Civil War, 113, 123, 166, 171–173, 175, 178, 188, 192, 201, 214
Evelina (Burney), 94–96, 97
"Examples of Worker Correspondence" (Gold), 170–171
exchange value, 51, 78, 114, 115; as version of aesthetic value, 42–43
Exclusion Crisis (1679–1682), 173
experiment: novelistic plots as, 49–54; origins of, 22–25, 69; thought, 36, 42, 69
The Extravagant Shepherd (Sorel), 64

The Faerie Queene (Spenser), 187
The Fair Jilt (Behn), 47
family romance, 80–102
feudalism, 6, 82–83, 101, 112–116, 136, 138, 146, 195
fictionality, 61, 77–79, 226n29
Fielding, Henry, 17, 18, 56–57, 72–73, 92–93, 180, 189–190
Financial Revolution, 114–115
Finch, Anne, Countess of Winchilsea, 140
"Five Men" (Herbert), 167–169
The Fleece (Dyer), 124
Fontenelle, Bernard de, 22, 32
Forché, Carolyn, 169–170
form: of, or fetter on, production, 116–117, 152–153; genre as model for choosing, 15; mnemonic function of, under orality, 61–62; modernism on, 18–19, 61; "politics" of, 165–171; reflexivity of, 16; as definitive of "poetry," 61–62; as superstructure, 116
Foucault, Michel, 14, 15, 17
"The Four Times of the Day" (Legg), 129
Freud, Sigmund, 16–17, 80–82, 101, 223n31
Frye, Northrop, 13

Gallagher, Catherine, 77–78
"The Garden" (Marvell), 141
Gay, John, 126, 130–133
Genette, Gérard, 18, 74–75
genre, 15–19, 117, 103–153
Georgics (Virgil), 234n1; complementary and reciprocal relation to *Eclogues*, 104–105, 135, 138; in Virgilian progression, 152. See also *Eclogues* (Virgil)
Gerusalemme Liberata (Tasso), 187
Gildon, Charles, 4
Giovanni, Nikki, 157, 170, 176
Glanvill, Joseph, 52–53
"God's Grandeur" (Hopkins), 244n50
Godwin, William, 40
Gold, Mike, 170–171
golden age, 104, 107–109, 130–131, 136, 140–141, 146, 152, 154, 173
"The Golden Age" (Behn), 140
Goldsmith, Oliver, 131, 133–134, 142–143
gothic, 17, 148
Gray, Thomas, 7, 12, 13, 133, 143
Greene, Robert, 88
Grongar Hill (Dyer), 124
The Guardian (periodical), 117, 118, 131, 140
Gurr, Jens Martin, 18
gypsy topos, 91

Harvey, Gabriel, 89
Havelok the Dane, 83, 87
Haywood, Eliza, 48
Hazlitt, William, 6
Henry, Robert (historian), 238n55
Herbert, Zbigniew, 167–169
heroic poetry, 174, 199–203, 204, 208–209, 211–212, 242n21
Hesiod, 107, 113, 152
History of the Royal Society (Sprat), 25
Hobbes, Thomas, 25, 40, 49–50, 178
Hogarth, William, 129, 130
Holles, Francis, 86
Homer, 35, 107, 189
Hooke, Robert, 24, 36, 38
Hopkins, Gerard Manley, 244n50
Horace (Roman poet), 4, 8, 21, 121, 129; second epode by, 106
Horkheimer, Max, 18
Hudibras (Butler), 187, 200–201
Hume, David, 14, 35, 39, 42, 58–59
Humphry Clinker (Smollett), 149

imagination: aesthetic knowledge and, 27, 30, 31, 71; financial credit and, 44, 115; as mediating sympathy, 41–43; as parallel to the understanding, 12, 28–30, 31–32, 35–36, 37; travel narrative and, 64–65

"I'm Explaining a Few Things" (Neruda), 165–166
imitation, 61–79; as double structure, 8, 9, 18–19, 34, 62
the impartial spectator (Smith), 41–43
imperialism, 144–153; as macro-pastoralism, 144–145, 146, 149, 150, 153; cultural, 145, 149
"In Our Time" (Rukeyser), 157–158
Ireland, 146

Jamaica, 145
James, Duke of Monmouth, 87
James, Duke of York, later James II, 87, 180
Jameson, Fredric, 15
Johnson, Samuel, 5, 34–37, 44–45, 109, 130, 149–150
Jonathan Wild (Fielding), 190
Jonson, Ben, 27
Joseph Andrews (Fielding), 17, 56, 68, 72, 92, 93–94, 189–190
Juvenal (Roman poet), 4, 149

Kermode, Frank, 106, 109–110, 112, 118, 235n12
king's two bodies, doctrine of the, 113, 181–182
kinship, 81–82, 94, 95, 101, 195. See also family romance

labor discipline, 51, 90–91, 137
Leapor, Mary, 133, 140
Leavis, F. R., 17, 18
Lee, Nathaniel, 177
Legg, Thomas, 128–130
Leviathan (Hobbes), 49
libel, 65, 78, 173, 177–178, 180
liberty, positive vs. negative, 8, 16
liberty of conscience, 51
literary conventions, 7, 52, 65, 107, 150, 152. See also family romance
locational (loco-descriptive, topographical, prospect) pastorals, 121–125. See also pastorals and pastoralism
Locke, John, 14, 24, 33, 50, 58, 68–69
locus amoenus (pastoral topos), 104, 107, 119, 120, 141, 152
London, 45, 95, 118, 120, 121, 122, 125–130, 149–150
London (Johnson), 149–150
The London Spy (Ward), 125
Longinus, 33, 45
Lorde, Audre, 163–165, 168
"Lord of Learne" (ballad), 87–88
Lovelace, Richard, 175–176
Love-Letters between a Nobleman and His Sister (Behn), 47–48, 201–202, 204, 211
Lukács, György, 18, 74

Lycidas (Milton), 109
Lyrical Ballads (Wordsworth), 7, 10, 37

macro-pastoralism, 144–145, 149, 152–153. See also micro-pastoralism; pastorals and pastoralism
Margites (Homer), 189
Mann, Thomas, 155
the market, 42–45, 51, 114–115, 136, 139
Marvell, Andrew, 109, 120, 141, 183–185, 192–193, 243n39, 247n31
Marx, Karl, 80, 116
Mary II, 87, 180–181
micro-pastoralism, 141–144, 152. See also macro-pastoralism; pastorals and pastoralism
Milton, John, 119, 176, 187. See also *Paradise Lost* (Milton)
mimesis, 61–79
The Mirror and the Lamp (Abrams), 9–10
mock epic, 174, 188–192, 199, 208, 212
modernism, 3, 15, 19, 61, 158, 184, 186
Moderns. See Ancients and Moderns

nation, nationalism, 146–148
natural (new) philosophy, 21–26, 27–28, 31, 35–36, 39
Navigation Acts (1651, 1660), 145
neoclassicism, 3–5, 6, 8–9, 11–12, 26, 110, 245n9. See also Augustanism
Neruda, Pablo, 165–167
Norman Conquest, 82–83
North-South Axis, 145–148
novel: as a genre, 16; as parody, 90–100; plots of, as experimental hypotheses, 49–54; as realist, 54–60, 72–77; tradition of, 18–19

"An Ode on the Popular Superstitions of the Highlands of Scotland, Considered as the Subject of Poetry" (Collins), 146–147
Oedipus complex, 81, 101
Of Dramatic Poesy (Dryden), 11–12, 21–22, 26–27, 70
"Of the Standard of Taste" (Hume), 35
"On Winter" (Leapor), 133, 140
Oroonoko (Behn), 47

Pamela; or, Virtue Rewarded (Richardson), 48, 52–54, 55–56, 90–92, 189, 211
Paradise Lost (Milton), 119, 176; Christian accommodation and, 192–194; Christian typology and, 190–192; domestications in, 196–199; as formal parody, 187–188; as heroic poetry, 199–203; as mock epic, 188–190, 199; as secret history, 203–209

pastorals and pastoralism: 103–153
Patey, Douglas Lane, 62
patrilineage, 82–83, 84, 86–87, 180, 211
Peri Bathous, or of the Art of Sinking in Poetry (Pope), 44–46
periodization, 2–3, 107–110, 187, 221n1
persona, doctrine of, 8–9
"The Petition for an Absolute Retreat" (Finch), 140–141
Petty, William, 49–50
Philips, Ambrose, 131, 132
Philips, John (poet), 121
Philosophical Enquiry (Burke), 33–34, 39, 72
The Pilgrim's Progress (Bunyan), 193–194, 195–197, 209–210
Plato, 74–75
The Plays of William Shakespeare (Johnson), 34, 44–45, 72
Poems on Affairs of State (miscellanies), 176–183
Poetics (Aristotle), 8, 26, 66
"Poetry: I" (Rich), 158
political arithmetic, 49–50
"Political Poem" (Baraka), 160, 162–163
political poetry: 154–186
Pope, Alexander, 13, 44–46, 130, 132, 154, 180, 226n38
Popish Plot, 189, 191, 204
postcolonialism, 19
postmodernism, 15, 19
poststructuralism, 3, 15, 18, 60
"Power" (Lorde), 163–164
preromanticism, 12–13
Preromanticism (Brown), 13
Pride and Prejudice (Austen), 96–100, 101
Printing Act (1694), 173
probability, 4, 26, 27, 41, 59, 61–64, 67–75, 79. See also verisimilitude; *vraisemblance*
Procopius of Caesarea, 203
Puritanism, 89–90, 201, 202, 213, 215
Puttenham, George, 109

quantification, 23–24, 36, 39, 52, 68–69, 72, 111, 127, 136–137
Quarrel of the Ancients and the Moderns, 4, 20–23, 25–26, 28, 31, 32, 54
Quayle, Thomas, 5

racism, 52, 145. See also slavery
realism, 54–60, 61, 72–77
reflection, double, 8, 16, 17–18, 97–98
Reflections on the Revolution in France (Burke), 39
reflexivity, 16, 17–18, 30, 54–55
The Rehearsal (Buckingham), 27
religious poetry, 183–186

The Renaissance, 4, 6, 7, 20, 21, 110, 130, 132, 187, 199
Revolution: American, 13; capitalist, 111, 137; "century of," 10; change in meaning of, 6, 10; English, 10; Financial, 114–115; French, 6, 10, 39–40; Glorious, 87, 146, 176; Romantic, 9, 12, 13, 15
Rich, Adrienne, 158
Richardson, Samuel, 48, 52–54, 55, 90–92, 211
Robinson Crusoe (Defoe), 48, 50–52
roman à clef, 63–64, 66, 201, 210–212
romance: antiromance, 64; courtly love and, 83; Enlightenment critique of, 90–94; family, 80–102; medieval, 83–84; pejorative connotations of, 66; separation of, from history, 64; synthesis of, with epic, 199–203
Romanticism, 3–16, 222n13
Royal Exchange, frontispiece, 115, 119–120, 125
Royal Society of London, 5, 23–25, 27, 52–53, 69
Rukeyser, Muriel, 157–158
The rules, 4–6, 11–12, 15–16, 34
Rushton, William, 12–13
Russian formalism, 18
Rymer, Thomas, 4

Sannazaro, Jacopo, 117, 118
Saussure, Ferdinand de, 18
Savile, George, Marquess of Halifax, 10
Scotland, 146–147, 149
Scottish Enlightenment, 146, 152, 238n54
The Seasons (Thomson), 141, 150–153
Second Treatise of Government (Locke), 50
secret history, 65, 176–177, 203–212
secularization, 43, 185–186, 210
sensibility, 13, 95
Shadwell, Thomas, 177–178, 180
Shakespeare, William, 36, 45, 203
Shamela (Fielding), 189
The Shepherd's Week (Gay), 130–131, 132
Sheppard, Fleetwood, 180–181
Sherburn, George, 5, 13
Shklovsky, Viktor, 18
Siskin, Clifford, 17–18
slavery, 51–52, 145–146, 176–177, 228n59
Smith, Adam, 40–43, 44
Smollett, Tobias, 149
social sciences, 39
Sollers, Philippe, 15
"Sonnet on the Death of Mr. Richard West" (Gray), 7
Sorel, Charles, 64–65, 66, 67, 79
Southey, Robert, 5–6

Spenser, Edmund, 89
Sprat, Thomas, 23–24
"Spring" (Thomson), 151–152
stadial theory, 136, 152, 238n55
The State of Innocence, and Fall of Man (Dryden), 203
state poetry, 176–183
Steele, Richard, 118, 128, 129, 131, 180, 212, 249n42
Sterne, Laurence, 18, 57–58, 231n33
structuralism, 3, 15, 18–19, 61, 74–77
superstructure and infrastructure, 116
Swift, Jonathan, 115, 146, 179–180, 227n39, 237n34
synchrony, synchronic, 18, 20, 21–22, 36, 130, 211–212, 238n55. *See also* diachrony, diachronic

tacit *vs.* explicit knowledge, 1, 2, 8, 16, 17, 20–21, 30, 79, 114
Tate, Nahum, 178–179
Tatler, The (periodical), 118, 121, 131
The Tempest (Shakespeare), 27
Temple, William, 179–180
Theocritus, 105, 107–109, 110, 131, 132, 135, 234n1
The Theory of Moral Sentiments (Smith), 40–41, 42–43
Thomas of Reading (Deloney), 86
Thompson, E. P., 117
Thomson, James, 141–142, 151–153
"The Thresher's Labour" (Duck), 135–138
Tickell, Thomas, 117
"To Lucasta, Going to the Warres" (Lovelace), 175
A Tour Thro' the whole Island of Great Britain (Defoe), 126–127
town eclogues, 118. *See also Eclogues* (Virgil)
Treatise of Human Nature (Hume), 39
Tristram Shandy (Sterne), 18, 57–58, 231n33
Trivia: or, the Art of Walking the Streets of London (Gay), 126
A True Relation of the Apparition of One Mrs. Veal (Defoe), 48
typology, Christian, 174, 190–192, 201, 208, 212

the uncanny (Freud), 16–17, 120, 148, 153, 223n31
uneven development, 116
unities. *See* dramatic unities
universality, universalism: capitalist contrasted with Enlightenment, 45, 52, 228n59
urbanization, 95, 111, 125

urban pastorals, 118. *See also Eclogues* (Virgil)
ut pictura poesis (Horatian tag), 129

verisimilitude, 18, 61–63, 65, 66, 68, 70, 73, 75–76. *See also* probability; *vraisemblance*
"The Village" (Crabbe), 133–135
Virgil. *See Eclogues* (Virgil); *Georgics* (Virgil)
virtual witnessing, 36, 41
The Virtuoso (Shadwell), 27
voyages, imaginary, 64–65
vraisemblance, 63–68, 76, 230n24. *See also* probability; verisimilitude

Wahrman, Dror, 13–15
Ward, Ned, 125

War of the Spanish Succession (1701–1714), 145
The Wealth of Nations (Smith), 42
Weinberg, Bernard, 62–63
Wellek, René, 15, 222n13
West-Indian Eclogues (Rushton), 144
Whitelock, James, M. P., 244n46
William of Orange, later William III, 87, 180–181
Williams, Raymond, 109, 110, 113
Wordsworth, William, 6–7, 9–10, 18, 37–38, 244n50
Works and Days (Hesiod), 107
"The World Is Too Much with Us" (Wordsworth), 244n50
Wotton, William, 23

Yeats, W. B., 155–156

About the Author

MICHAEL MCKEON is a Board of Governors Distinguished Professor Emeritus at Rutgers University–New Brunswick in New Jersey. He is the author of *Politics and Poetry in Restoration England: The Case of Dryden's "Annus Mirabilis"*; *The Origins of the English Novel, 1600–1740*; *The Secret History of Domesticity: Public, Private, and the Division of Knowledge*, and scores of articles, as well as the editor of *Theory of the Novel: A Historical Approach*.